Energy Law in Venezuela

Energy Law in Venezuela

Second Edition

Henry Jiménez Guanipa

This book was originally published as a monograph in the International Encyclopaedia of Laws/Energy Law.

Founding Editor: Roger Blanpain
General Editor: Frank Hendrickx
Volume Editors: Kurt Deketelaere & Bram Delvaux

Wolters Kluwer

Published by:
Kluwer Law International B.V.
PO Box 316
2400 AH Alphen aan den Rijn
The Netherlands
E-mail: lrs-sales@wolterskluwer.com
Website: www.wolterskluwer.com/en/solutions/kluwerlawinternational

Sold and distributed by:
Wolters Kluwer Legal & Regulatory U.S.
920 Links Avenue
Landisville, PA 17538
United States of America
E-mail: customer.service@wolterskluwer.com

ISBN 978-94-035-4319-2

e-Book: ISBN 978-94-035-4329-1
web-PDF: ISBN 978-94-035-4339-0

The Author

Henry Jiménez Guanipa is a Venezuelan legal scholar. He earned his Law degree from Universidad Santa María (Caracas) and obtained a postgraduate degree in Criminal Sciences and Criminology from Universidad Católica Andrés Bello (Caracas). He later earned a Master of Laws (LLM) from the University of Heidelberg and a PhD in Law from Ruhr University Bochum, Germany.

He has taught in both master's and doctoral programmes and has participated in research projects at various academic institutions across Europe and Latin America, including: Ruhr University Bochum and the Max Planck Institute for Comparative Public Law and International Law (Germany); the Heidelberg Center for Latin America (Chile); the Pontifical Catholic University of São Paulo (Brazil); the National Autonomous University of Mexico (UNAM), the Autonomous University of Baja California (UABC), the Central University of Venezuela; Universidad del Norte, Universidad del Rosario and Universidad de La Sabana (Colombia); the Center for Legal, Economic and Political Studies (Paraguay); the Technological and Artistic University of Paraguay; the University of Salamanca and the University of Seville (Spain); among others.

He serves as a visiting researcher at the Max Planck Institute for Comparative Public Law and International Law (Heidelberg, Germany) and at the Institute for Mining and Energy Law at Ruhr University Bochum.

From 1992 to 2003, he worked in the Venezuelan oil industry, where he held various positions and responsibilities. He currently serves as a Senior Consultant specializing in regulatory energy transition and efficiency, collaborating with the law firms Wirth Rechtsanwälte (Germany) and Ollarves & Asociados (Venezuela).

In addition, he coordinates several academic programmes focused on the energy transition, climate change litigation, and sustainable development and its relationship with human rights. These initiatives are carried out in cooperation with the Heidelberg Center for Latin America of the University of Heidelberg, the University for Peace (Costa Rica), the Central University of Venezuela, the University of the North (Colombia), the Polytechnic and Artistic University of Paraguay, among many other academic institutions across the region.

He is the President of the International Network on Climate Change, Energy and Human Rights (RICEDH), an academic platform for inter-university cooperation that promotes critical analysis and knowledge production on the legal challenges of climate change and energy transition, with a strong human rights perspective.

His publications include a wide range of books and academic articles in his areas of expertise. To explore them in detail, click here.

Table of Contents

List of Abbreviations

AA	Association Agreements
AEPI	Strategic Associations for Integrated Projects *(Asociaciones Estratégicas para Proyectos Integrados)*
ALADI	Latin American Integration Association *(Asociación Latinoamericana de Integración)*
ALBA	Bolivarian Alliance for the Peoples of Our America
AM	Mining Arc (*Arco Minero*)
BCV	Central Bank of Venezuela *(Banco Central de Venezuela)*
BP	British Petroleum
CADAFE	Public Power Corporation S.A. *(Compañía Anónima de Administración y Fomento Eléctrico)*
CAGc	Agreements under the Profit-Sharing Scheme *(Convenios para la Exploración a Riesgo y Producción de Hidrocarburos bajo el Esquema de Ganancias Compartidas)*
CAMIMPEG	Anonymous Military Company of Mining, petroleum and gas *(Compañía Anónima Militar de Industrias Mineras, Petrolíferas y de Gas)*
CAN	The Andean Community of Nations *(Comunidad Andina de Naciones)*
CDB	Chinese Development Bank (Banco de Desarrollo de China)
CN	Constitution of Venezuela *(Constitución Nacional de 1961)*
CNEE	National Commission for Electric Energy *(Comisión Nacional de Energía Eléctrica)*
CORPOELEC	National Electric Corporation (*Corporación Eléctrica Nacional*)
CRBV	Constitution of the Bolivarian Republic of Venezuela *(Constitución de la República Bolivariana de Venezuela)*
CRP	Paraguana Refinery Center *(Centro de Refinación de Paraguaná)*
CSJ	Supreme Court of Justice *(Corte Suprema de Justicia)*

List of Abbreviations

CSN	South American Community of Nations *(Comunidad Sudamericana de Naciones)*
CVF	Venezuelan Development Corporation
CVP	Venezuelan Petroleum Corporation (*Corporación Venezolana del Petróleo, filial de PDVSA*)
DELTAVEN	PDVSA subsidiary
E/S	Gas Station *(Estación de Servicio)*
ECLAC	Economic Commission for Latin America and the Caribbean
ECSC	Economic Coal and Steel Community
ECT	Energy Charter Treaty
EIA	US Energy Information Administration
EP	Energy Poverty
EURATOM	European Atomic Energy Community
FAN	National Armed Force
FANB	Bolivarian National Armed Force
FONDEN	*Fondo Nacional para el Desarrollo Nacional*
FPO	Orinoco Oil Belt *(Faja Petrolífera del Orinoco)*
FTAA	Free Trade Area of the Americas
GDP	Gross Domestic Product
GNV	Natural Gas for Vehicles *(Gas Natural para Vehículos)*
HG	Gaseous Hydrocarbons *(Hidrocarburos Gaseosos)*
HPP	Hydroelectric Power Plant
ICC	International Chamber of Commerce
ICJ	International Court of Justice
ICSID	International Centre for Settlement of Investment Disputes
IEA	International Energy Agency
IMF	International Monetary Fund
INE	National Institute for Statistics (*Instituto Nacional de Estadísticas)*
IRR	Internal Rate of Return
ISR	The Income Tax in Venezuela
JFCA	Federal Board of Conciliation and Arbitration
JV	Joint Ventures *(Empresas Mixtas)*
KV	Kilo Volts
KW	Kilowatt
KWH	Kilowatt-Hour
LAC	Latin American and Caribbean
LCCGE	Law on the Coordination of the Competences of the Services of Domestic Gas and Electricity (*Ley de Coordinación de Competencias de los servicios de Gas y Electricidad*)

LEEM	Law of Migration to Joint Ventures *(Ley de Emigración a Empresas Mixtas)*
LH	Hydrocarbons Law *(Ley de Hidrocarburos)*
LISLR	Income Tax Law (*Ley de Impuesto sobre la Renta*)
LM	Mining Law (Ley de Minas)
LN	Nationalization Law *(Ley de Nacionalización)*
LNG	Liquefied Natural Gas *(Gas Natural Licuado)*
LOA	Organic Law on the Environment (*Ley Orgánica del Ambiente*)
LOAMI	Organic Law on the Opening of the Domestic Market *(Ley Orgánica de Apertura del Mercado Interno)*
LOC	Organic Law on the Communes *(Ley Orgánica de las Comunas)*
LOCC	Organic Law of Communal Councils
LOH	Organic Law on Hydrocarbons *(Ley Orgánica de Hidrocarburos)*
LOHG	Organic Law on Gaseous Hydrocarbons *(Ley Orgánica de Hidrocarburos Gaseosos)*
LOPP	Organic Law on the People's Power *(Ley Orgánica del Poder Popular)*
LOPPM	Organic Law on the Municipal Public Power (*Ley Orgánica del Poder Público Municipal*)
LOREICH	Organic Law that Reserves the Industry and Commerce of Hydrocarbons for the State (*Ley que Rerseva al Estado la Industria y el Comercio de los Hidrocarburos*)
LORMI	Organic Law for Reorganizing the Domestic Liquid Fuels Market (*Ley Orgánica para la Reorganización del Mercado Nacional de los Combustibles Líquidos*)
LORSE	Organic Law on the Reorganization of the Energy Service *(Ley Orgánica de Reorganización del Servicio Eléctrico)*
LOSE	Organic Law on the Electric Service (*Ley Orgánica del Servicio Eléctrico*)
LOSSE	Law on the Electric Power System and Service *(Ley Orgánica del Sistema y Servicio Eléctrico)*
LPG	Liquefied petroleum gas *(Gas Licuado de Petróleo)*
LPPELC	Law to Promote and Protect the Exercise of Free Competition *(Ley para la Promoción y Protección de la Libre Competencia)*
LREBSC	Organic Law Reserving Goods and Services Related to Primary Hydrocarbon Activities to the State (*Ley Orgánica que Reserva al Estado Bienes y Servicios Conexos a las Actividades Primarias de Hidrocarburos*)

List of Abbreviations

LREIGN	Law Reserving the Industry of Natural Gas to the State *(Ley que Reserva al Estado la Industria del Gas Natural)*
LRMI	Law Reserving the Exploitation of the Domestic Market for Hydrocarbons Products to the State *(Ley que Reserva al Estado la Explotación del Mercado Interno de los Productos Derivados de Hidrocarburos)*
LRP	Law on Property Subject to Reversion in Hydrocarbons Concession *(Ley de Bienes Afectos a Reversión en las Concesiones de Hidrocarburos)*
LRPPAP	Law for the Regulation of Private Participation in Primary Activities *(Ley de Regularización de la Participación Privada en las Actividades Primarias)*
LSE	Electric Service Act (*ley del Servicio Eléctrico*)
MBD	Million Barrels per Day
MBOE	One Thousand Barrels of Oil Equivalents
MCFD	Million Cubic Feet Per Day
MEM	Ministry of Energy and Mines (*Ministerio de Energía y Minas*)
MENPET	Ministry of Energy and Petroleum
MERCOSUR	Southern Common Market (*Mercado Común del Sur*)
MMbls	Million Barrels
MMBOE	Million Barrels of Oil Equivalents
MMBOED	Million Barrels of Oil Equivalents per Day
MPPEE	Ministry of Popular Power for Electric Energy
MPPP	Ministry of People's Power with Competence in Petroleum Matters
MT	Metric Ton
Mtoe	Million tonnes of oil equivalent
MVA	Mega Volt-Amperes
MW	Mega Watt
NGO	Non-governmental Organization
OAs	Operating Agreements *(Convenios Operativos)*
OCGR	Office of the Comptroller General of the Republic
OFAC	Office of Foreign Assets Control
OPEC	Organization of the Petroleum Exporting Countries
PDVSA	*Petróleos de Venezuela Sociedad Anónima*
PLC	Puerto La Cruz
RFT	Fixing Resolution for Freight Transport *(Resolución para la Fijación de Fletes de Transporte)*
RLOHG	Regulation of the Organic Law on Gaseous Hydrocarbons *(Reglamento de la Ley Orgánica de Hidrocarburos Gaseosos)*

SEN	National Power System *(Servicio Eléctrico Nacional)*
Sq km	Square Kilometre
Sq mi	Square Mile
TSJ	Supreme Tribunal of Justice *(Tribunal Supremo de Justicia)*
UNASUR	*Union of South American Nations* (*Unión Suramericana de Naciones*)
UNEP	United Nations Environment Programme
UNFCCC	United Nations Framework Convention on Climate Change
US	United States
VAT	Value Added Tax

General Introduction

Chapter 1. General Background

§1. Political System

1. The Bolivarian Republic of Venezuela – the name assigned to the Republic of Venezuela in the Constitution of 1999 – is defined therein as a decentralized, democratic, and social Federal State of Right and Justice. The national territory is divided into 23 States; 335 Municipalities; 1 Capital District, which includes the city of Caracas; 235 islands; and 71 islets and cays in the Caribbean Sea, which constitute the Federal Departments. The Venezuelan State maintains a claim on the territory known as Guayana Esequiba or *Zona en Reclamación* (area claimed).[1]

2. The Bolivarian Republic of Venezuela is governed by a presidential system, headed by a President of the Republic, who is the Chief of State and Chief of the National Executive Branch. The government of the Bolivarian Republic of Venezuela and the political entities that make up the Republic are and will always be democratic, participatory, elective, decentralized, alternative, responsible, pluralist, and with revocable terms of office. Public Power is distributed among the Municipal Power, that of the States' Power, and the National Power. The National Public Power is divided into the Legislative, Executive, Judicial, Citizen, and Electoral branches. Each of the branches of the Public Power has its own functions, but the organs charged with exercising the same shall cooperate with one another in attaining the ends of the State.[2]

3. The States are autonomous entities governed and administered by a Governor elected for a four-year term, who may be immediately re-elected for one more term only. The Legislative is exercised by the Legislative Council per State. The States shall decentralize and transfer to the Municipalities the State services and powers which the Municipalities are capable of exercising, as well as management of the associated resources, in the areas in which concurrent jurisdiction exists as between these two levels of Public Power.[3]

---

1. Constitution of the Bolivarian Republic of Venezuela, preamble, Arts 10, 11, 16 (1999).
2. *Ibid.*, preamble, Arts 2, 6, 225 (1999).
3. *Ibid.*, Arts 159 et seq. (1999).

4. The Municipalities constitute the primary political unit of the national organization, with autonomy within the limits provided for in the Constitution of the Bolivarian Republic of Venezuela (CRBV – *Constitución de la República Bolivariana de Venezuela*) and the law. Municipal autonomy includes: (1) election of their authorities; (2) management of matters within their jurisdiction; and (3) creation, collection, and investment of their income. The Municipality is to discharge its duties, including citizens, in the definition, execution, control, and evaluation of the results of its management. The Mayor is in charge of the Municipality's government and administration, and is elected for a four-year term, and may be immediately re-elected for one additional term only.[4]

5. The characteristics of the Venezuelan Constitutional State previously indicated correspond to the Constitution in force, which arose in 1999 out of a National Constituent Assembly held for that purpose. Although the new constitutional text provides for some changes to the structure and operation of the State, like the division of the Public Power into five powers, the elimination of the Senate as part of the National Legislative, the enforcement of the presidential re-election, the creation of the figure of the Vice President of the Republic, the creation of the figure of the Ombudsman, among others, such novelties did not entail a structural reform of the Constitution. In 2007, a constitutional reform to the terms of Articles 342 et seq. of the CRBV was proposed by the President of the Republic, Hugo Chávez and his party, which had the majority in the National Assembly.[5]

6. It is stated that such reform represented a transformation of the current Constitutional State, as its intention was to establish a Communal State. Hence, it had to be subject to popular consultation after the National Assembly approved the project on 2 November 2007. The referendum took place a month later, on 2 December 2007, resulting in a negative to the reform proposal, namely, people were against and rejected it. Notwithstanding the result of the referendum, the National Assembly insisted on its purpose of establishing a Socialist and Communal People's Power State, but through a set of organic laws. In fact, and in view of the majority of the votes in the Parliament favourable to the government party, the legal basis of the Communal State was finally approved through the issue of organic laws: Organic Law on the People's Power (LOPP – *Ley Orgánica del Poder Popular*), Organic Law on the Communes (LOC – *Ley Orgánica de las Comunas*), Organic Law on the Communal Economic System, Organic Law on Public and Communal Planning, and Organic Law on Social Comptrollership.[6]

7. The main objective of these laws is the organization of the 'Communal State', whose main cell is the commune, to take over the Municipality, which holds the nature of 'primary political unit of the national organization' under Article 168 of

4. *Ibid.*, Arts 168 et seq. (1999).
5. *See* detailed study, of the constitution regarding the regulation of this State Constitutional Model, in Allan R. Brewer-Carías, *La Constitución de 1999. Derecho Constitucional venezolano*, 2 vols., Editorial Jurídica Venezolana, Caracas 2004; and *La Constitución de 1999 y la Enmienda Constitucional de 2009*, Editorial Jurídica Venezolana, Caracas 2011.
6. O.G. No. 6.011, 21 Dec. 2010.

the CRBV. The objectives of the People's Power are provided for in Article 7 of the LOPP, particularly (1)(2), 'the consolidation of the *revolutionary, leading democracy, the construction of the bases of the socialist society and the promotion of values and principles of socialist ethics'*. (Emphasis added.) These principles and values challenge those provided for in the Constitution in force, which provides for otherwise in Article 2:

> Venezuela constitutes itself as a Democratic and Social State of Law and Justice, which holds as superior values of its legal order and actions those of life, liberty, justice, equality, solidarity, democracy, social responsibility and, in general, the preeminence of human rights, ethics and political pluralism. (Emphasis added.)

8. These principles are reaffirmed in Article 6 of the CRBV, which provides:

> The government of the Bolivarian Republic of Venezuela and the political organs comprising the same is and shall always be democratic, participatory, elective, decentralized, alternative, responsible and pluralist, with revocable mandates. (Emphasis added.)

9. Alternatively, the basis of the Communal State is supported by the modification of the sense of Article 5 of the Constitution in force, which provides that:

> Sovereignty resides untransferable in the people, who exercise it directly in the manner provided for in this Constitution and in the law, and indirectly, by suffrage, through the organs exercising Public Power. The organs of the State emanate from and are subject to the sovereignty of the people. (Emphasis added.)

In other words, the aim is to substitute the principle of representative democracy and the principle of the exercise of sovereignty in an indirect manner through suffrage, by a system based on the direct exercise of sovereignty.

10. This system of direct exercise of sovereignty by the people, which corresponds to the concept of Communal State, does not establish a voting system through universal, direct, and secret suffrage – as provided for by the Constitution – to elect the 'spokespersons' of the authorities of the People's Power provided for in the LOPP. For instance, the Organic Law of Communal Councils (LOCC) is the only one that provides that spokespersons are 'elected' through a 'popular-election' process, but not by the Electoral Power. Such election is made in open meetings, where suffrage is not guaranteed. However, the law referred hereto does provide that all the authorities of the People's Power 'elected by popular vote' may be revoked as from half the term of the corresponding administration, under the conditions provided for by Article 17 of the law. The use of the universal, direct, and secret vote in the Communal State system is provided for in Article 66 of the LOCC in the event a referendum is required to amend the Founding Letter of a Commune, which may be incorporated by the vote of the simple majority of the citizens of the organized communes participating in the process.

11. The LOC defines the Communal State as:

> The form of political-social organization founded on the democratic and social State subject to the rule of law and justice provided for in the Constitution of the Republic, where the power is directly exercised by the people through communal self-governments, with an economic model oriented towards social ownership and endogenous and sustainable development that allows achieving the supreme social happiness of the Venezuelan people in the socialist society.

12. The LOC also provides for the organizational system of the Communal State, which counts on the Bank of the Commune, the Communal Economy Council, the Communal Controllership Council, the Communal Gazette, a Communal Parliament, Socialism as a doctrine, and the authorities of the People's Power, including, among others, the communal councils, the communes, the communal cities, the communal federations, the communal confederations, and others that, under the LOC, may arise out of the people's initiative as provided for in the Constitution of the Republic and the law.[7]

13. On the contrary, the Communal Power lacks autonomy and depends directly on the Executive Branch. Under Article 25 of the LOPP, the Executive Branch has the authority to plan and coordinate the initiatives from the People's Power. The Executive will exercise this power jointly with the organizations and authorities of the People's Power in order to maintain coherence with national, regional, local, communal, and community strategies and policies. In fact, the Executive Branch is empowered to grant legal status to the organizations and authorities of the People's Power by their registration with the Ministry of People's Power, with jurisdiction over the matters of citizen involvement. Therefore, the decision to register or not a communal council, a commune, or a communal city is in the hands of the National Executive Branch, for which it may be relevant whether the organization wanting to be recognized is in agreement with the interests of the socialism imposed by the LOPP or not. Furthermore, the LOPP imposes on the Republic, the States, and the municipalities the obligation to transfer jurisdictions to the authorities of the People's Power in conformity with the law that will rule the jurisdiction and power transfer and decentralization process. Should this process materialize, the framework of jurisdictions corresponding to the Constitutional State, its bodies, and powers would be violated.

14. It is clear then that the communes have been created as an authority apart from the municipality, and they constitute a new power, the territory of which could be one or more municipalities. The Organic Law on the Municipal Public Power (LOPPM – *Ley Orgánica del Poder Público Municipal*) clarifies that the Communal Power is not part of the Municipal Power. That is inferred from Article 5 of the

7. Organic Law on the Communes (LOC), Arts 4 and 60.

LOPPM, which provides the legal framework of local municipalities and entities, where communes are exempted due to their special condition as local entities regulated by the laws ruling the incorporation, composition, organization, and operation thereof.

15. There are countless objections and rejections to the communal system, as it lacks legitimacy and constitutionality. However, the Constitutional Division of the Supreme Court of Justice (CSJ – *Corte Suprema de Justicia*), endorses this system and affirms that 'according to the principle of sovereignty provided for in the preamble of the Constitution, the people are authorized to exercise it both "directly" and "indirectly" through the bodies of the Public Power'. The Division also indicates that Article 62 *ejusdem* 'provides for the people's right to freely participate in public matters' and that in Article 70 of the same constitutional text, 'self-administration as a mechanism of the people's leading role in exercising their sovereignty is recognized'.[8]

16. Finally, it is conclusive to say that two contrasting models of State as to principles and values coexist in the structure of the political system in Venezuela: the Constitutional State endorsed by the Constitution of 1999 and the Communal State supported by a set of laws inferior to the Constitution.

§2. Economic Characteristics

17. The pillar of the Venezuelan economy has traditionally been the extraction and refining of oil for export and domestic use. Based on the Gross Domestic Product (GDP), it was the fourth largest economy in Latin America after Brazil, Mexico, and Argentina. Venezuela also has other mineral resources for commercial purposes, such as iron, bauxite, coal, gold, salt, phosphates and limestone, and vast water resources for energy generation.

18. Over the past two decades, Venezuela has experienced some of the most extreme economic volatility in the world, marked by cycles of rapid expansion and deep crisis. In the early twenty-first century, the country underwent a period of swift growth fuelled by high oil prices, which served as the state's primary source of income. However, since 2014, the Venezuelan economy has plunged into a severe crisis, driven by a combination of falling oil prices, economic mismanagement, and the impact of international sanctions. This combination of factors has led to hyperinflation, a sharp contraction in GDP, and a profound humanitarian emergency, characterized by the collapse of essential public services and an unprecedented wave of migration across the region.[9]

8. Supreme Court (Venez.), Case No. 10-0197 (26 Feb. 2013), available at https://vlexvenezuela.com/vid/alejandro-silva-rodriguez-425597958 (last accessed 30 Mar. 2025).
9. Economic Commission for Latin America and the Caribbean, *Annual Report 2018: The Economy of Latin America and the Caribbean* (ECLAC 2018), available at https://www.cepal.org/en/publications (last accessed 30 Mar. 2025).

19. According to the International Monetary Fund (IMF), Venezuela's GDP in 2017 was 35% lower than in 2013 – or 40% lower in per capita terms (Figure 1).[10] This represents a far steeper contraction than that experienced by the United States during the Great Depression (1929–1933), when GDP is estimated to have fallen by 28%. Venezuela's decline was slightly more severe than the downturns seen in Russia (1990–1994), Cuba (1989–1993), and Albania (1989–1993). However, it was less dramatic than the collapses experienced by other former Soviet republics during their transitions, including Georgia, Tajikistan, Azerbaijan, Armenia, and Ukraine, as well as by war-torn nations such as Liberia (1993), Libya (2011), Rwanda (1994), Iran (1981), and, more recently, South Sudan.[11]

Figure 1 Venezuela's GDP Decline, 2013–2017

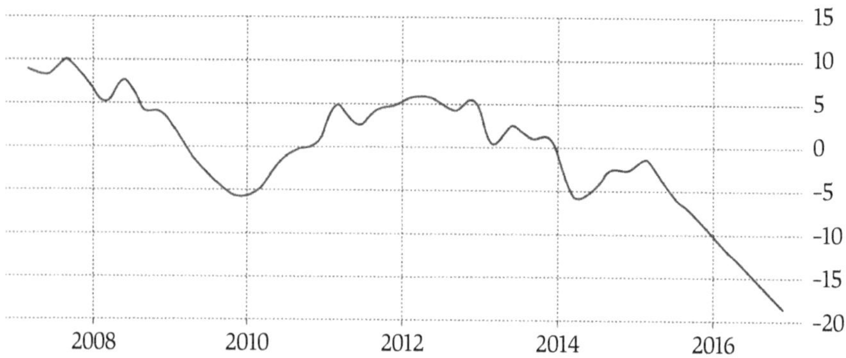

20. The negative behaviour of the Venezuelan economy has deteriorated, reaching recession levels never seen before. The latest Economic Commission for Latin America and the Caribbean (ECLAC) report on the Economic Outlook for Latin America 2018 refers to an expected recession of 8.5% for Venezuela.[12] However, the IMF forecasts an inflation rate of 1,000,000% for Venezuela by the end of 2018, comparing the situation with that of Germany in 1923 or Zimbabwe at the end of the 2000s. The Fund is also upwardly correcting the forecast of a fall in Venezuela's GDP for this year. From an estimated 15% in April this year, it is now down by 18%, the third consecutive double-digit year, 'driven by a significant decline in oil production widespread distortions at the micro level as well as broad macroeconomic disproportions'. The accumulated decrease over the last five years amounts to 48%.[13]

---

10. Michael Roberts, *The Tragedy of Venezuela*, https://weknowwhatsup.blogspot.com/2017/08/the-tragedy-of-venezuela.html (last accessed 30 Mar. 2025).
11. *Ibid.*
12. OECD, CAF & ECLAC, *Latin American Economic Outlook 2018: Rethinking Institutions for Development* (OECD Publishing 2018), available at http://dx.doi.org/10.1787/leo-2018-es (last accessed 30 Mar. 2025).
13. *Ibid.*

21. Had the IMF's forecasts been realized, the hyperinflation Venezuela was experiencing would have already been the most severe in Latin America in recent decades – surpassing Argentina in the late 1980s, where prices rose by more than 3,000% annually; Peru, which recorded inflation rates of 3,398% in 1989 and 7,482% in 1990; and Nicaragua, where prices increased by 13,110% in 1987, according to IMF data.[14] In fact, the actual economic outcome not only confirmed but also exceeded these projections. According to estimates from both the IMF and alternative sources such as the Venezuelan National Assembly, inflation in the country surpassed 1,300,000% in 2018 – far beyond the IMF's initial forecast of 1,000,000%. This episode marked Venezuela as the country with the most extreme case of hyperinflation in the region in decades, eclipsing all previous historical cases.[15]

22. IMF data paint a picture representing a major exception across the region. Colombia, which shares some 2,200 km of border with Venezuela, will grow by 2.7%, Brazil by 2.3%, Argentina by 2%, Chile by 3.4%, Bolivia by 4%, Peru by 3.7%, and Ecuador by 2.5%. The IMF's most pessimistic forecasts point to the collapse of the oil industry and its exports. In December 2017, production fell to 1.62 million barrels per day (MBD), a decline of more than 700,000 in a year, plummeting to 1980s levels. Expectations for the sector are dire and could close 2018 at nearly one million a day.[16]

23. In November 2017, the credit rating agencies, Standard & Poor's and Fitch, declared Venezuela in partial default[17] for the serious liquidity problems following a default of USD 200 million on the interest on bonds maturing in 2019 and 2024. Added to this is rampant corruption that is destroying what little remains of *Petróleos de Venezuela Sociedad Anónima* (PDVSA). Among some measures that the Government has adopted is the implementation of a monetary system centred on a virtual currency called 'the Petro', which uses oil reserves as a guarantee, but has not been successful in alleviating the basic needs of the people.

24. One of the government's additional measures was the introduction of a new currency, the Bolívar Soberano (VES), which replaced the Bolívar Fuerte (VEF) on 20 August 2018, by removing five zeros from its denomination. As a result,

---

14. Francesco Manetto, *The IMF Forecasts That Prices Will Increase in Venezuela by 1,800,000%*, El País (17 Apr. 2018), https://elpais.com/economia/2018/04/17/actualidad/1523934621_077871.html (last accessed 30 Mar. 2025).
15. International Monetary Fund (IMF), *World Economic Outlook: Growth Slowdown, Precarious Recovery* (IMF 2019).
16. International Monetary Fund (IMF), *World Economic and Financial Surveys: World Economic Outlook, April 2018* 56, https://www.ft.com/content/062f6250-9695-30fc-acb5-0478c96b3b6e (last accessed 30 Mar. 2025).
17. Edward White, *S&P Declares Venezuela in Default After Missed Payments*, Financial Times (14 Nov. 2017), https://www.ft.com/content/062f6250-9695-30fc-acb5-0478c96b3b6e (last accessed 30 Mar. 2025).

50,000,000,000 bolívares fuertes became 500 bolívares soberanos.[18] A similar decision had previously been implemented on 6 March 2007, through Decree No. 5229, which introduced the Bolívar Fuerte (VEF) as a transitional monetary unit.

25. The economic collapse also predicts that unemployment will reach one-third of the active population, which would be equivalent to the highest unemployment rate in the world, above countries such as South Africa, Sudan, Bosnia, or Greece.

26. The grants and subsidies implemented by the national government and financed with oil revenues and that had helped reduce poverty and inequality in Venezuela have reversed dramatically. According to ECLAC in Venezuela, the poverty rate increased 6.7% points between 2012 and 2013 (from 25.4% to 32.1%) and the indigence rate by 2.7% points (from 7.1% to 9.8%) in the same period.[19] According to the institution's latest report presented in 2016, the number of people living in poverty in Latin America reached 186 million, including 61 million in extreme poverty, after a decade of reduction in most countries.[20] The primary reason for this increase is the stagnation of economic growth in the region, and most particularly the increase in poverty in two major countries, Brazil and Venezuela.[21]

27. Starting in 2022, the Venezuelan economy began to show tentative signs of recovery. Inflation, which had peaked at a staggering 1,000,000% in 2018, declined significantly in the years that followed – falling to 234.1% in 2022 and further to 189.8% in 2023, according to the Central Bank of Venezuela (BCV – *Banco Central de Venezuela*). Nevertheless, the prolonged period of hyperinflation had already triggered a de facto dollarization of the economy, further eroding citizens' purchasing power and deepening the ongoing social crisis.

The Venezuelan government reported that the national economy grew by over 9% in 2024, exceeding the 5.5% growth recorded in 2023.[22] This rebound has been largely attributed to a recovery in key sectors, particularly hydrocarbons. Yet the outlook remains uncertain. On 26 February 2025, President Donald Trump announced the revocation of Chevron's licence to operate in Venezuela, effective 3 April 2025. The licence, originally granted by the Biden administration on 26 November 2022, was part of an agreement aimed at easing sanctions and promoting electoral guarantees. Trump's decision was based on the Maduro regime's failure to

18. Central Bank of Venezuela, *Bolívar Soberano*, http://www.bcv.org.ve/billetes-y-monedas/bolivar-soberano (last accessed 30 Mar. 2025).
19. Economic Commission for Latin America and the Caribbean (ECLAC), *Social Panorama of Latin America, 2014* 17, U.N. Doc. LC/G.2635-P (2014).
20. ECLAC, *Panorama Social de América Latina 2017* 88, https://repositorio.cepal.org/bitstream/handle/11362/42716/7/S1800002_es.pdf (last accessed 30 Mar. 2025).
21. *Ibid.*, at 90.
22. Reuters, *Venezuela Economy Grew Over 9% in 2024, President Says*, Reuters (1 Jan. 2025), https://www.reuters.com/world/americas/venezuela-economy-grew-over-9-2024-president-says-2025-01-01/ (last accessed 31 Mar. 2025).

implement electoral reforms and address issues related to the repatriation of Venezuelan migrants. The cancellation of this licence – which had temporarily authorized limited oil operations – could severely hinder Venezuela's ability to export crude oil and attract foreign investment, potentially undermining the country's economic prospects in the years ahead.

§3. Geography and Population

28. The Bolivarian Republic of Venezuela is a country located in Northern South America. It has a continental and insular area of 916,445 square kilometres (sq km) (353,841 square miles (sq mi)), a land area of 915,175 sq km (353,351 sq mi), and an insular area of 1,270 sq km (490.35 sq mi).[23] Venezuela borders on the territorial waters of the Dominican Republic, the Netherlands, Puerto Rico, Virgin Islands, Martinique, Guadalupe, Trinidad and Tobago, and Dominica to the North; the Federative Republic of Brazil and the Republic of Colombia to the South; the Atlantic Ocean and Guyana to the East; and the Republic of Colombia to the West (Figure 2).[24] It has a coastline of approximately 2,718 km long.[25]

29. Of all Venezuela's border regions, its eastern boundary with Guyana remains the most contested, due to a longstanding territorial dispute over the Essequibo region, which spans approximately 160,000 square kilometres. The roots of this claim trace back to the 1899 Paris Arbitral Award, which granted the territory to what was then the British colony of Guiana, under United Kingdom administration. Venezuela has consistently rejected the ruling, asserting that the arbitration process was flawed and unduly influenced by political pressures.[26] Following Guyana's independence in 1966, the Geneva Agreement was signed by Venezuela, the United Kingdom, and Guyana to establish a framework for peacefully resolving the dispute. Yet decades of diplomatic negotiations have failed to produce a conclusive settlement, prolonging tensions between the two nations. Recent developments have further heightened these tensions – particularly the discovery of substantial oil reserves in the disputed area. In response, Guyana has granted exploration and production concessions to international companies, a move Venezuela considers a direct violation of the Geneva Agreement, as it disregards the unresolved legal status of the territory.[27]

---

23. Latin American and Caribbean Economic System (SELA), *Venezuela*, https://www.sela.org/en/member-states/venezuela/ (last accessed 31 Mar. 2025).
24. Instituto Geográfico de Venezuela Simón Bolívar, *Histórico de Mapas*, https://igvsb.gob.ve/adminigvsb/pdf/pdf_1658170367.pdf (last accessed 9 Jun. 2025).
25. Fundación Empresas Polar, *Las Costas*, https://igvsb.gob.ve/adminigvsb/pdf/pdf_1658170367.pdf http://bibliofep.fundacionempresaspolar.org/media/16814/geo_u1_l26_costa_costa_linea-costera.pdf (last accessed 31 Mar. 2025).
26. International Court of Justice, *Request for the Indication of Provisional Measures in the Case Concerning the Arbitral Award of 3 October 1899 (Guyana v. Venezuela)*, https://www.icj-cij.org/case/171 (last accessed 31 Mar. 2025).
27. Rafael Ramírez, *La Disputa entre Venezuela y Guyana por el Esequibo*, Política Exterior (14 Mar. 2024), https://www.politicaexterior.com/la-disputa-entre-venezuela-y-guyana-por-el-esequibo/ (last accessed 31 Mar. 2025).

30. In 2018, Guyana brought the case before the International Court of Justice (ICJ), seeking a judgment that would affirm the validity of the 1899 Arbitral Award. Venezuela, however, has contested the ICJ's jurisdiction, arguing that the Geneva Agreement requires bilateral negotiations as the sole legitimate mechanism for resolving the dispute.[28]

31. The ongoing dispute over the Essequibo constitutes a multifaceted geopolitical challenge, with significant economic, strategic, and diplomatic implications. Its resolution will likely hinge on both parties' willingness to engage in sustained and constructive dialogue, within the bounds of international law, in order to promote long-term regional stability.

28. Stephany Hernández Mahecha, *Análisis prospectivo del conflicto territorial entre Guyana y Venezuela, Bie3: Boletín IEEE* (Instituto Español de Estudios Estratégicos), ISSN-e 2530-125X, No. 16, 2019, at 1023-1052.

Figure 2 República Bolivariana de Venezuela

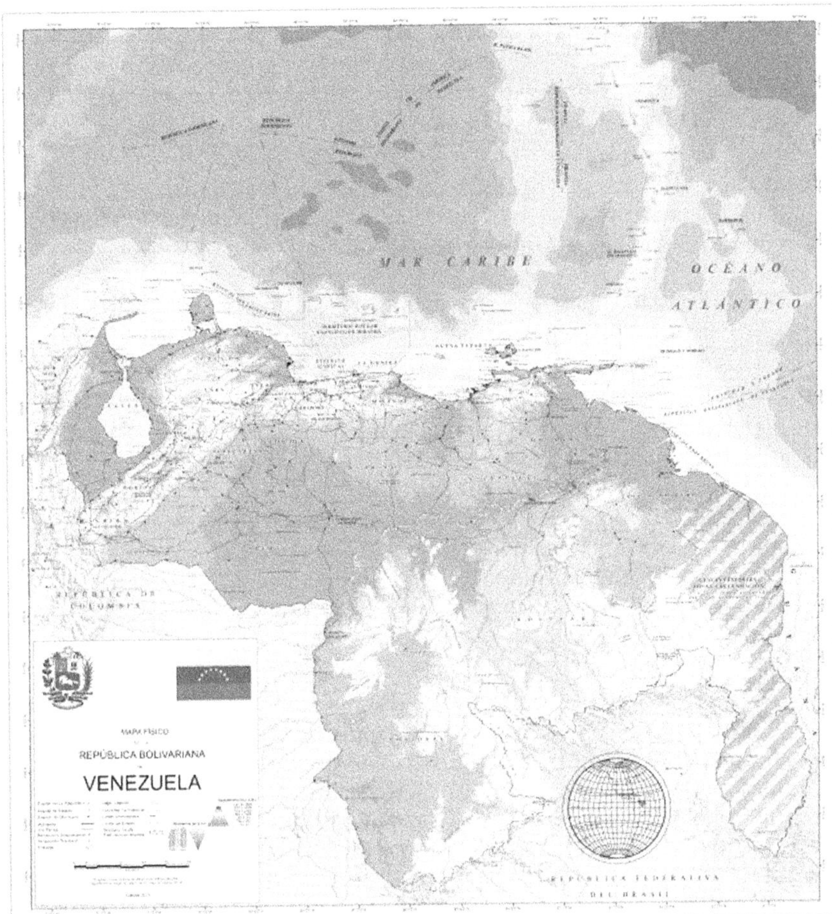

32. Geographically, Venezuela stands out due to its special condition of Amazonian, Andean, Atlantic, Caribbean, and Plain country, with a climate diversity ranging from permanent snow in the Andes to desert or semi-desert areas in the State of Falcon, a wide range of habitats, including coral reefs, savannas, tepuyes, mountain chains, flooded savannas, moorlands, moriche swamps, and many others. This variety of habitats allows Venezuela to have warm and steady temperatures all year long, ranging between 15°C and 35°C (59–95°F), depending on the area, with an average temperature of 26°C (78.8°F). It only has two defined seasons: winter or rainy season (May–December) and summer or dry season (December–April).[29]

33. Venezuela also has some natural wonders like Pico Bolívar in the State of Mérida, the highest point of the country at 50,000 m, home of the highest and the second largest cable car in the world, 12.5 km (7.8 mi) long, reaching an altitude of 4,765 m (15,633 ft); the Salto Angel (Angel Falls) in Canaima, State of Bolívar, is the world's highest waterfall, which is 979 m (3,212 ft) high; in the State of Zulia, the Maracaibo Lake, the largest in South America; and the Orinoco River, the third largest in South America. The geography and climate of Venezuela place the country among the ten countries with the biggest biodiversity on the planet.[30]

34. The geographical and economic features have been determinant in the concentration of the population in the coastal mountain system, characterized by the valleys and foothills of the Coastal and Andean mountains. This region, consisting of coastal States, part of the Andean States and the States in the north-central part of the country, corresponds to approximately 20% of the national territory, where 80% of the total population is concentrated.

35. Since 2017, Venezuela has experienced a major demographic shift, largely fuelled by mass migration resulting from prolonged economic and social instability. According to World Bank estimates, the country's population decreased from approximately 30.6 million in 2015 to around 28.3 million in 2022, reflecting the exodus of millions of Venezuelans in pursuit of improved living standards.[31]

36. The last official national census was conducted in 2011, while the 15th National Population and Housing Census began in 2023 but has not yet released its results (National Institute for Statistics (INE – *Instituto Nacional de Estadísticas)*, 2023; XV Censo.gob.ve, 2024). According to data from the 2011 census, the Indigenous population was estimated at 724,592 individuals, accounting for 2.8% of the total population. Their distribution was primarily concentrated in the states of Zulia (443,669), Amazonas (76,148), Bolívar (54,691), Delta Amacuro (41,535), Anzoátegui (33,959), Sucre (22,219), Monagas (17,939), Apure (11,572), and other regions (23,939) (INE, 2011). However, due to the absence of more recent official data, it remains difficult to assess how migration may have affected both the size and geographic distribution of these communities.

---

29. República Bolivariana de Venezuela, Ministerio del Ambiente y de los Recursos Naturales, Programa de las Naciones Unidas para el Desarrollo & Fondo Mundial para el Medio Ambiente, *Primera Comunicación Nacional sobre Cambio Climático* (2005), available at https://unfccc.int/documents/145102 (last accessed 31 Mar. 2025).
30. Richard A. Haggerty, ed., *Venezuela: A Country Study* 44 (U.S. Government Printing Office 1990), available at https://countrystudies.us/venezuela/8.htm (last accessed 31 Mar. 2025).
31. World Bank, World Development Indicators: Population, Total – Venezuela (Bolivarian Republic of), Data retrieved from World Bank DataBank, https://databank.worldbank.org/source/world-development-indicators (accessed 20 Apr. 2025).

As of the 2011 census, Zulia was the most populous state in the country, with 3,704,404 inhabitants, while Amazonas had the smallest population, totalling 146,480 residents.[32]

37. Figure 3 displays a comparative population pyramid showing the age and sex structure of Venezuela in 2000 and 2024. The horizontal axis indicates the percentage of the total population, with males represented on the left and females on the right. The comparison reveals a clear demographic shift: the pyramid for 2000 exhibits a classic expansive shape with a broad base, indicative of high birth rates, while the 2024 pyramid shows a narrowing base and a more columnar shape, reflecting declining fertility and population aging. The proportion of older adults has increased visibly, particularly in the 60+ age groups. As of 2023, the estimated sex ratio was approximately 102.4 females for every 100 males, suggesting a slight predominance of women. This gender imbalance becomes more evident in the upper age brackets, consistent with the trend of higher female life expectancy.[33]

Figure 3 Population Pyramid of Venezuela (Bolivarian Republic of), Years 2000 and 2024

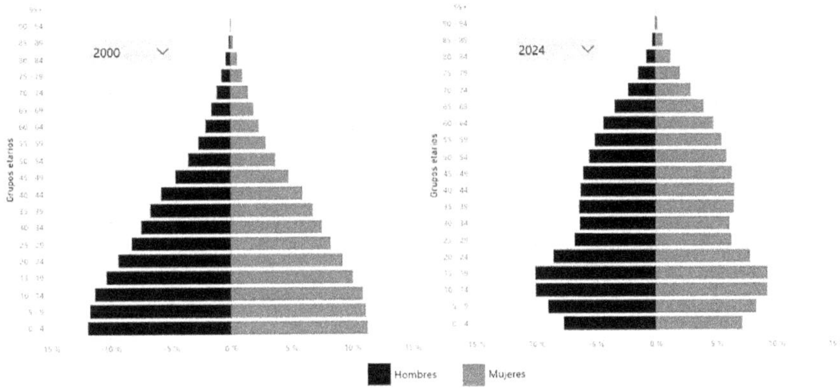

38. Children and adolescents (ages 0–14) currently account for 27.4% of the total population, down from 32.1% in previous years, indicating a demographic shift toward population ageing. Meanwhile, the proportion of individuals over the age of 65 has increased to 10.4%, with an ageing index of 37.9 older adults for every 100

32. República Bolivariana de Venezuela, Ministerio del Poder Popular de Planificación, Instituto Nacional de Estadística, *XIV Censo Nacional de Población y Vivienda* 13 (December 2014), available at https://ine.gob.ve/wp-content/uploads/2024/09/Censo-Nacional-2011.pdf (last accessed 10 Jun. 2025).
33. Organización Panamericana de la Salud, *Perfil de Salud del País: Venezuela*, https://hia.paho.org/es/perfiles-de-pais/venezuela (last accessed 31 Mar. 2025).

individuals under the age of 15.[34] This trend suggests a demographic transition that could significantly impact labour market dynamics, dependency ratios, and social policy in the decades ahead.

39. Additionally, mass migration has significantly reshaped the country's population structure, especially within the core working-age group (ages 25–45), many of whom have emigrated in recent years. The full extent of these demographic shifts will become clearer once the results of the 15th National Population and Housing Census are officially released.[35]

40. The decline in oil prices and production since 2014 has plunged Venezuela into a deep economic crisis, marked by widespread shortages of food, water, and medicine, hyperinflation, rising unemployment, and escalating violence. In addition, the country faces a collapse of public services, with frequent power outages, limited access to potable water, and a deteriorating public transportation system.[36]

41. The crisis has been further exacerbated by chronic shortages of gasoline and domestic cooking gas, affecting both rural and urban areas. Despite possessing the world's largest proven oil reserves, Venezuela has seen a drastic decline in fuel production and refining capacity, resulting in severe gasoline shortages and long queues at service stations. Many households have been forced to adopt rudimentary cooking methods, such as using firewood, even in urban settings. The lack of investment in refineries, depletion of skilled technical personnel, and pervasive corruption have all contributed to the worsening situation. Additionally, international sanctions have restricted the country's ability to import essential refining inputs, further compounding the energy crisis.[37]

42. As a result, more than 7.7 million Venezuelans have migrated since 2014, constituting one of the largest displacement crises globally.[38] The principal destinations for this mass migration have been South America, the United States, and Europe.

43. In *Colombia*, the Venezuelan migrant population remains at *2.8 million*, while in *Peru*, it has grown from *27,000 in 2016 to over 1.6 million in 2024*.[39] In the United States, official deportations resumed in October 2023, and in March

34. *Ibid.*
35. Instituto Nacional de Estadística (INE), *XV Censo Nacional de Población y Vivienda 2023* (INE 2023), available at https://xvcenso.gob.ve (last accessed 31 Mar. 2025).
36. Human Rights Watch, *World Report 2024: Venezuela*, https://www.hrw.org/world-report/2024/country-chapters/venezuela (last accessed 31 Mar. 2025).
37. Alonso Moleiro, *La Isla de Margarita se Queda a Oscuras Durante 20 Horas al Día*, El País (25 Nov. 2024), https://elpais.com/america/2024-11-25/la-isla-de-margarita-se-queda-a-oscuras-durante-20-horas-al-dia.html (last accessed 31 Mar. 2025).
38. Inter-Agency Coordination Platform for Refugees and Migrants from Venezuela (R4V), *Refugees and Migrants from Venezuela*, available at https://www.r4v.info/en/refugeeandmigrants (last accessed 31 Mar. 2025).
39. United Nations High Commissioner for Refugees (UNHCR), *Venezuela Situation*, available at https://www.unhcr.org/emergencies/venezuela-situation (last accessed 31 Mar. 2025).

2025, the Trump administration launched the CBP Home app to facilitate 'self-deportation' for undocumented immigrants.[40]

44. In Spain, the Venezuelan population increased from 518,918 in 2023 to 599,769 in 2024. Approximately 44,000 new migrants arrived during the first half of the year, representing a 7% growth.[41] This migration crisis poses considerable challenges for host countries and highlights the urgent need for structural solutions that address the root causes of Venezuelan migration, such as economic collapse, declining public services, fuel shortages, and precarious living conditions.

45. Regarding the origin of the Venezuelan people, there is general consensus that Venezuelans descend from Indigenous Venezuelan Amerindians, European immigrants, and Africans – the latter two dating back to the colonial era. Historically, these groups have contributed at different levels to the anthropological and cultural composition of Venezuela. The subsequent massive European immigration in the twentieth century has continued moulding the main aspects of the life and culture of what the current Venezuelan is and represents.

46. Nevertheless, based on data from the 2011 census, it was determined that 49.9% of the population affirmed to be brown, while 42.2% identified themselves as white, 3.5% affirmed to be black or Afro-descendant, and 2.7% affirmed to be part of a native group. The remaining 1.7% did not answer or answered 'other'.

---

40. U.S. Department of Homeland Security (DHS), *United States to Resume Removals of Venezuelans Who Do Not Have a Legal Basis to Remain in the United States to Venezuela*, available at https://www.dhs.gov/archive/news/2023/10/05/united-states-resume-removals-venezuelans-who-do-not-have-legal-basis-remain-united (last accessed 31 Mar. 2025).
41. Instituto Nacional de Estadística (INE), *Población Residente por Fecha, Sexo, Grupo de Edad y País de Nacimiento*, available at https://www.ine.es/jaxiT3/Tabla.htm?L=1&t=9675 (last accessed 31 Mar. 2025).

Chapter 2. Basic Principles of Energy Law

§1. Evolution

47. Energy law seems to require even more academic impetus in order to achieve its strategic position in the areas, fields, and activities it regulates. Perhaps its amplitude, extension, and, why not, the complexity of its object are the reflection of this noticeable lag. However, there is no reason to justify it. Since the sixteenth century, first metallic and then non-metallic mines, as of the eighteenth century, which included coal, bitumen, tar, and oil, had a very important regulatory component that evolved, achieving the current legal advances of fossil energy sources, particularly in oil, coal, and natural gas.

48. Other energies, called clean, renewable, environmentally friendly, or low-carbon, have had a more recent legal development after the Second World War when their exploitation spread throughout Europe, the US, and other nations: among them, nuclear energy, natural gas, hydroelectricity and wind, solar, and other renewable energies.[42] The latter represent regulatory challenges for all nations of the world in the face of challenges arising from commitments to combat environmental damage and the effects on climate change caused by carbon-intensive emissions and other polluting substances.

49. The Energy Law in Venezuela must take into consideration the previous existence, since the late nineteenth century and during the twentieth century, of a generic mining law that governed the early mining and hydrocarbon activities of the period and that today represents essential components of a conceptualization of the Energy Law. As a matter of fact, this conjoint regulatory view of both activities (mines and hydrocarbons) has remained ever since the first Mining Code of 1854 and its regulations, and during the successive Mining Laws (LMs – *Ley de Minas*) and Codes of 1885, 1887, 1891, 1893, 1904, 1905, 1910, and 1915 until de enactment of the LM of 1920, which set forth that 'the exploitation of hydrocarbons, carbons and the rest of the mineral fuels would be governed by special law'.

50. This sets clear-cut limits in Venezuela between mining regulations, on the one hand, and the hydrocarbons regulations, on the other hand, as well as the emergence of their corresponding definitions. In this sense, for Gonzalez Berti, the mining law is understood as 'the organic array of principles of public law that govern the activity of the State and the individuals, by reason of the economic use of mineral wealth';[43] and for Ramirez Uscátegui, within the framework of hydrocarbons, the Petroleum Law has been defined as 'the whole of juridical regulations that rule the organized activity that has the objective of preliminary research, surveying, extraction, transportation, refining or transformation and distribution of liquid and

---

42. Raphael J. Heffron & Kim Talus, *The Development of Energy Law in the 21st Century: A Paradigm Shift?*, 9 J. World Energy L. & Bus. 191 (2016).

43. Luis González Berti, *Compendio de Derecho Minero Venezolano*, vol. II, 77 (Universidad de Los Andes 1970) (Venezuela).

gaseous mineral hydrocarbons'. He also adds that there are some who understand that the Petroleum Law should be restructured as a branch within the broadest concept of the Energy Law, characterized as a technological law that includes other branches such as the Right to Electricity and the Right to Nuclear Energy as well. This last concept was developed in Mexico by Francoz Rigalt, who holds that:

> It deals with the creation of juridical rules and principles applicable to physical and chemical nuclear phenomena, as well as to the human activities jointly developed with them. It is a special branch of the juridical science that takes into consideration the causes that originate such phenomena and activities, while producing legal effects, as well as the social relationships inter se, both public and private and national and international.[44]

51. At the international level, Energy Law has been, is, and will continue to be of strategic importance. At European and global level, treaties of the stature of the Economic Coal and Steel Community (ECSC) 1951; the *European Atomic Energy Community* (EURATOM) 1957; the agreements promoted by the United Nations (UN) since the Stockholm Declaration on the Human Environment in 1972; the Kyoto Protocol to the United Nations Framework Convention on Climate Change (UNFCCC) of 11 December 1977; the Vienna Convention for the Protection of the Ozone Layer of 22 March 1985; the Montreal Protocol on Substances that Deplete the Ozone Layer of 16 September 1987; the Aarhus Convention on Access to Information, Public Participation in Decision-making and Access to Justice in Environmental Matters of 25 June 1988; the Energy Charter Treaty (ECT) 1991; the UNFCCC of 9 May 1992; the Convention on Environmental Impact Assessment in a Transboundary Context of 25 February 1991; and most recently the Paris Agreement 2016 on Climate Change, among others, represent genuine energy treaties, with rules and commitments that demonstrate the importance of Energy Law.

52. In other countries, Germany, for example, the fundamental regulations of the Energy Law, seen in a restrictive sense, are contained in the Law of the Energy Market, in addition to their respective regulations, and are exclusively applicable to the market of electricity and gas, which are understood as network energies. In other energy markets that are not considered network energies, such as coal and petroleum, not only specific regulations are applied but also some general regulations are contained in civil law, commercial law and free competition rules. Nevertheless, in the broadest sense, the German doctrine also groups as rules of the Energy Law those related to the protection of the environment, the legal framework for renewable energies and nuclear energy. Hence, some agree that the Energy Law is not a systematic field of rules, but rather a varied whole of disciplines, not only of a legal nature but also of a technical, economic, and political character that must be harmonized with the European Union (EU) Law and be taken into consideration by the Member States.

---

44. Antonio Francoz Rigalt, *Los Principios y las Instituciones Relativas al Derecho de la Energía Nuclear: La Política Nuclear* 16 (UNAM 1988) (México).

53. For Ramón Martin Mateo, the traditional Energy Law is the result of the accumulation of a series of juridical techniques with dissimilar origins applied to regulate the relationships between suppliers and users adequately adapted to the postulates of equity and respect of the collective interests. As a characterization of the Energy Law, we may add that it is marked by a series of elements and legal concepts that are present in a great number of legal systems, such as the following: the character of public property of the energy resources, the system of concessions, authorizations, licences, and expropriations; and the notion of public benefit, the general and strategic interest of public services or national convenience, and the quite traditional concept of legal reserve. These characteristic elements are increasingly associated with measures that evolve towards environmental protection, conditioning and restricting the actions that tend to produce damage as a result of the exploitation of natural resources.[45]

§2. Fundamental Principles

54. By reason of the close relationship that the Energy Law has with the Administrative Law, derived from the nature of the activities it regulates and where the State plays a predominant role not only as a regulator but also as a participant, the principles of the latter may be adopted by the Energy Law as basic principles, without representing a limitation for incorporating other principles that govern in other branches of Law.

55. Among the principles of Administrative Law that allow the application of the Energy Law to regulate the relationships between the State and individuals, we may find the following:

1. the principle of legality, which is based particularly on the constitutional supremacy;
2. the principles relative to the organization of the State, to the vertical distribution of the Public Power;
3. the principles of the organic separation (horizontal) of the Public Power and the inter-organic nature of the Public Administration;
4. the principles relative to the inter-functional nature of State acts and administrative acts; and
5. the principle of control of the Public Administration and the administrative responsibility.

56. Other constitutional and legal principles within the sphere of the Competition Law and the Economic Sciences add to the set of practices and criteria of the Energy Law, such as the following:

---

45. Kyoto Protocol to the United Nations Framework Convention on Climate Change, available at http://unfccc.int/resource/docs/convkp/kpeng.pdf (accessed 7 Nov. 2013).

1. The promotion and protection of the exercise of free competition and efficiency.
2. The prohibition of monopolistic and oligopolistic conduct and practices and other means that may hinder, restrict, distort, or limit the enjoyment of economic freedom.

57. Within the field of the national and international Environmental Law, the Energy Law also incorporates some fundamental principles that allow it to have a wide juridical base inspired in international treaties and agreements, such as the Rio Declaration and other documents of the UN, where there is reference to 'the integral and interdependent nature of the Earth'; or to the control of its use; or that 'the States must cooperate to preserve, protect, and re-establish the health and integrity of the ecosystem of the Earth'. Based on such fundamental principles, the Energy Law incorporates the following principles:

1. Sustainability
2. Globalization
3. Solidarity
4. Prevention
5. Interdisciplinarity
6. Contaminator-payer
7. Rational management of the environment
8. Environmental laws
9. Quality of life
10. International cooperation on environmental matters.

§3. CONCEPTUALIZATION

58. In the Venezuelan case, the Energy Law has not been considered an ordered system of legal rules. On the contrary, the dispersal, and in many cases the intricacy, of its contents has given rise to interpretations completely opposed in the doctrine, as well as in the jurisprudence. Under a restrictive perspective, the definition would not go beyond those sectors that, within the energy field, hold a preponderant position; such is the case of liquid and gaseous hydrocarbons and the electrical sector. Other branches, Nuclear Energy and Renewable Energies, for instance, which have not been completely developed as yet, would be included later.

59. Therefore, stepping towards a current definition of Energy Law also means considering the complex network of relationships that it has with other disciplines. In our case, its bonds are close to the commercial, labour, administrative, tax, fiscal, and criminal laws, environmental law and the competition law, among others. Additionally, Energy Law is related to the economy and public policies and even to International Law, as well as to the one derived from the processes of regional and subregional integration that take place both in Europe and Latin America. To this effect, the idea is to systematize such set of provisions that have been scattered for years in different laws, regulations, decrees, and resolutions, so that there is coherence between their aims and purposes. Furthermore, Energy Law is oriented towards the regulation of activities that seek the satisfaction of the needs of general interest, the use of natural resources for energy generation, and the search for new technologies to better use and transform such resources so that they achieve their aim for providing social and economic welfare in tune with the environment.

60. Consequently, the proposal is the conceptualization of the Energy Law as the set of legal rules that govern the activities of research, exploration, generation, exploitation, refining, transformation, storage, transmission, distribution, and commercialization (national and international) of energy, whether derived from primary or secondary, renewable or alternative and non-renewable sources, and liquid or gaseous fossil hydrocarbons, whose main goal is to guarantee energy supply to meet collective needs, socio-economic welfare, wealth generation through the use of technologies oriented towards the protection and conservation of the climate, nature, and the environment in general, and making easier their accessibility to those who require it under the best possible conditions. According to this perspective, it is necessary to achieve a balance of interests among those who invest in order to make energy availability possible, whether public, private, or mixed entities; among those who need energy to meet their needs; and among nature, which all in all makes raw materials available to man for them to transform and use it. Accordingly, this branch of law must try to achieve a greater systematization in the face of the varied and complex applicable legal system in the search, if not for an Energy Law code, at least for a greater and better interrelation of the legal rules that comprise it.

§4. Towards a Contemporary Conception of Energy Law

61. In the current global context, Energy Law can no longer be limited to regulating the supply, access, and transformation of energy sources. It must now encompass new dimensions of legal analysis, particularly those related to the climate crisis, the protection of human rights, and the reinforcement of democratic governance. Energy production and consumption are not neutral phenomena; they are embedded within political, economic, and social structures that both shape and are shaped by power dynamics and demands for environmental justice (Heffron & Talus, 2021; Savaresi, 2019).[46]

62. Consequently, a modern and forward-thinking conception of Energy Law must incorporate principles of environmental, intergenerational, and social equity. It should align with the commitments established in international frameworks such as the Paris Agreement (2015), the United Nations 2030 Agenda for Sustainable Development (2015), and the Escazú Agreement (2018), which link environmental

46. Raphael J. Heffron & Kim Talus, *Energy Law: An Introduction* (2d ed. Springer 2021). Savaresi, Annalisa, *Climate Change and Human Rights: Fragmentation, Interplay and Institutional Linkages*, in *Research Handbook on Human Rights and the Environment* 121 (Anna Grear & Louis J. Kotzé eds., Edward Elgar Publ'g 2019).

protection with the rights to access information, public participation, and access to justice in environmental matters (Viñuales, 2022).[47]

63. Legal scholarship has identified various systems for regulating property rights over hydrocarbons, based on the historical foundations of mining ownership. From a comparative perspective, three main categories can be distinguished: the accession system, the res nullius system – further divided into the occupancy and regalian subcategories – and the domanial system. In the Venezuelan context, this classification has been useful in understanding the progressive assertion of the State as the original owner of natural resources, particularly since the twentieth century, when the oil industry transitioned from foreign private concessions to a structure increasingly controlled by public authority. In Latin American contexts such as Venezuela, where fossil fuels have historically dominated the economy, the development of Energy Law must support a legally grounded energy transition with a strong focus on human rights. Such a transition should ensure that energy policies and investments uphold the right to a healthy environment (American Convention on Human Rights, Article 11), the rights of Indigenous Peoples (ILO Convention 169), and the principles of transparency, participation, and accountability in energy governance (Wewerinke-Singh, 2021).[48]

64. Therefore, Energy Law must be conceptualized not only as a regulatory framework for the energy sector but also as a legal instrument for sustainability, resilience, and democratic transformation – aimed at ensuring energy justice and the equitable distribution of resources for both present and future generations. This requires advancing towards a more coherent integration with Environmental Law, International Human Rights Law, and Climate Law, as highlighted by contemporary legal scholarship advocating for intersectional and integrated legal approaches in the context of the global energy transition.

---

47. Jorge E. Viñuales (ed.), *The Rio Declaration on Environment and Development: A Commentary* (Oxford Univ. Press 2022).
48. Margaretha Wewerinke-Singh, *State Responsibility, Climate Change and Human Rights under International Law* (Hart Publ'g 2021).

Chapter 3. Historical Background of the Energy Law

65. The evolution of the Venezuelan legal framework governing mining and hydrocarbons culminated in the constitutional recognition of public state ownership over these resources, as established in the 1999 Constitution, Article 12 of which declares their inalienable and non-transferable nature. This historical principle of sovereignty over subsoil resources must now be reinterpreted in light of contemporary challenges, particularly within the context of the energy transition. The notion of energy sovereignty – traditionally linked in the twentieth century to the defence of national interests against foreign capital and the appropriation of oil rents – must be reimagined in the twenty-first century through a renewed legal perspective. This new vision should encompass the decarbonization of the energy matrix, the integration of renewable energy sources, democratic participation in energy decision-making, and equitable access to energy as both a human right and a pillar of collective well-being and environmental justice.

66. This historical trajectory has solidified a model of public ownership over energy resources in Venezuela, which now faces significant new challenges. The energy transition, international climate commitments, and the right to a healthy environment call for a critical reassessment of the historical and constitutional foundations that have guided energy regulation in the country, with a view to aligning them with principles of sustainability, intergenerational justice, and meaningful social participation in energy governance.

67. The dominion over subsoil and its associated wealth has historically been a central issue in the development of legal systems related to energy. In the Americas, two major institutional traditions coexist: private ownership of subsoil resources, characteristic of the U.S. model, and state ownership, predominant in Latin America – each inherited from British and Iberian legal traditions, respectively. In the Venezuelan context, legal regimes concerning the ownership, management, and exploitation of mining and hydrocarbon resources have evolved in close connection with the country's major political, economic, and social transformations.

Analysing this evolution provides deeper insight into current tensions between energy sovereignty, rentier dynamics, and the ecological transition.

68. Legal scholarship has identified various systems for regulating property rights over hydrocarbons, based on the historical foundations of mining ownership. From a comparative perspective, three main categories can be distinguished: the accession system, the res nullius system – further divided into the occupancy and regalian subcategories – and the domanial system. In the Venezuelan context, this classification has been useful in understanding the progressive assertion of the State as the original owner of natural resources, particularly since the twentieth century, when the oil industry transitioned from foreign private concessions to a structure increasingly controlled by public authority.

§1. PROPERTY RIGHTS SYSTEM

I. Accession System

69. In the so-called accession system, the ownership of the soil comprises both the surface and the subsoil. The subsoil is considered accessory to the soil; that is to say, the 'accessory does not lead but follows its principal' maxim prevails. The legal grounds for the accession system came into existence, according to the experts in mining law, from the '*qui dominus soli, dominus est coeli et inferos*' maxim – for whoever owns the soil, it is theirs up to Heaven and down to Hell. Historical records date back to the concept of ownership of property from the ancient Roman law, which qualifies this system as civilist, since it is based on the individual interest of the owner.

70. An example of the accession system may be found in Colonial times. In the Colonial law, monarchs' rights prevailed over the rights of the owners. Ownership of property was governed by the principle contained in the Bull of Pope Alexander VI, dated 4 May 1493,[49] which granted the Kings of Castile and León, as well as their heirs, 'authority and jurisdiction over all the islands and terra firma discovered and yet to be discovered towards the West and as from the Azores islands with free, plain and absolute power'.[50] This allocation of land appropriation was noticeable in times even earlier than the colonization of America and is described in numerous legal instruments, such as the following: the Old Fuero of Castile of 1128, the Ordinances of Alcalá of 1384, the Ordinance of Bribiesca of 1387, and the Ordinance of Valladolid of 1559, among others. Thus, conquering was merely a method through which the appropriation of the lands allocated to the Kings by said Bull materialized. Not a single person could have the right to land without a permanent title to property issued by the monarchs.

71. The ownership of all mines by the Crown was then the common denominator. During such period, the regulatory framework of Spain encompassed at first only the metallic mines. Non-metallic mines, such as asphalt, bitumen, and the rest of the fuels, had not been reserved for the Crown patrimony. However, due to the accession system, such property was incorporated as assets of the owner of the soil; that is to say, non-metallic mines were under the de dominion of the Crown as well.

72. The objections and criticism to the accession system emerged even in the National French Constituent Assembly of 1791[51] and began, thus, to decay and was later abandoned by most of the countries, though it continues to prevail, with its dissimilarities, in the US and England.

49. Luis González Berti, *Compendio de Derecho Minero venezolano*, vol. 1, 53 (Universidad de Los Andes, Mérida, 1960).
50. F. Javier Zenteno Barrios, *La Regulación de los Hidrocarburos en México*, in: *Regulación del Sector Energético*, 75–78 (Universidad Autónoma de México 1997).
51. About the historical evolution of this system, *see*, Juan V. C. Molina, *Tratado teórico y práctico del derecho minero colombiano* 21 (Bogotá, 1952).

II. *Res Nullius* System

73. This system starts out from the assumption that mines do not belong to anyone. Hence, the State, as the guarantor of public wealth and representative of the public interest, is responsible for granting the concessions once the mines are discovered. The property right to mines does not exist prior to the granting of the concessions; they only represent things that become assets after the concession. According to the postulates of this theory, the concession of a mine is an 'investitive' rather than a directive fact of the property.[52] Among the various unfavourable remarks to this system, the contradiction implied in it stands out first, since it affirms that mines are *res nullius* while upholding that the State grants ownership of the mines to individuals. In the *res nullius* system, two viewpoints have been identified: the occupancy system and the regalian system, which are explained hereafter.

A. Occupancy System

74. This system originates from de premise that the ownership of the soil and that of the subsoil are different, so the dominium of mines is attributed to whoever discovers the field and occupies and effectively works such field. The individual right arises then by means of occupancy, in agreement with the State. Given that undiscovered mines are regarded as common things, property rights are assigned to whoever discovers them.[53] Nonetheless, this theory has been considered unacceptable within the organization of the State because of the complex problems it brings about.[54]

B. Regalian *System*

75. This system is defined from the notion that mines are *res nullius*. However, the State, when exercising on them a privilege that for its royal origin is called 'regalia', distributes or grants mines; namely, the State creates the individual right in favour of one person, watches over the compliance of the limits established by the own State on the concessions, and imposes taxes, burdens, and participations. The focal point of this system lies then in the power the State has to regulate the destination of subsoil ownership, granting the privilege to exploit it to those who can offer better performance.

76. Hence, payment conditions of the licence granted for the exploitation of a mine, which was nothing more than royalties owed to the 'owner' (the Spanish Crown), gave rise to the so-called regalian system. This system basically prevailed as of the Ordinances of Aranjuez of 1783, also known as the Ordinances of New

52. Edouard Dalloz, *'De la propriété des mines et de son organization legale' en France et en Belgique*, vol. I, 28 (Paris, 1862).
53. Carlos Puyuelo, *Derecho minero*, 10 (Madrid, 1954).
54. Guillermo García Montufar, *Apuntes de Derecho Minero Común*, 37 (Lima, 1989).

Spain, enacted in Mexico by King Charles III[55] and in force in Venezuela by Royal Resolution on 27 April 1784. This system established that, for the exploitation of a mine – whatever its nature and whether metallic or not – a miner or farmer needed to obtain a licence from the King in exchange for royalties. However, though the ordinances had provided for the granting of ownership on mining concessions, such concessions were not separated from the Royal Patrimony. In such a way, said ordinance set forth that:

> Without separating them from my Royal Patrimony, I shall grant ownership and possession of them to my vassals, so that they may sell, exchange, lease, donate, bequeath such concessions, or in any other way transfer the right they have to such concessions under the same terms they are owned by my vassals and to the persons that may acquire them.[56]

77. As a result, the Crown granted a mine, establishing a particular ownership of such mine in favour of a third party, without abandoning its original dominium, and, if the individual owner did not comply with the pre-established conditions, the mine could be recovered and granted to another petitioner.

78. The authority of the Crown for granting mining concessions came to an end with the enactment of the Decree on the Preservation and Ownership of Mines declared by the Liberator Simón Bolívar in Quito, Ecuador, on 24 October 1829, against any attack and against the easiness to make confusing or lose such ownership. Such decree transferred to the Republic all the rights that, up to such date, were exercised by the Spanish Crown and made the Republic the new grantor of the ownership and possession to those who made a petition. Pursuant to this decree, the regalian system remained in force before such decree came into effect, and it imposed the grantor, in accordance with Article 2 *ejusdem*, the obligation to satisfy the tariffs set, as well as the payment of PHP 30 to the treasury of the corresponding province, for the rights derived from the title to property of every metal and gemstone mine granted.

79. Note that the decree enacted by the Liberator, more than acknowledging that the Republic is the owner of the mines (which in fact it is), tends to protect miners to whom the Republic has transferred property rights. We can even assert that the decree reveals characteristics that steer it more towards a private property system than a public property system. This may be drawn from the Third Whereas Clause *ejusdem*, which sets forth that 'mine ownership must be guaranteed against any attack and against the easiness to make confusing and lose such ownership', making reference to certain disputes and disagreements that had taken place among some miners (Second Whereas Clause of the Decree). Likewise, it points out 'the expediency to promote the scientific knowledge of mining and mechanics, for

55. Vanesa Ramos Boassi, *El Dominio del Estado sobre las Minas en la Legislación Chilena*, 3 (Universidad Central de Chile, 1998).
56. Eduardo Martiré, *Historia del derecho minero argentino*, 59 (Buenos Aires, 1997).

instance the spreading of the spirit for association and entrepreneurship, so that mining reaches the high level of perfection needed for the development of the State' (Fourth Whereas Clause *ejusdem*). In these postulates, the Liberator's thinking has a clear tendency towards the promotion and protection of private ownership of property, giving special value to the benefit that the State may obtain from the exploitation of such property by third parties.

80. Nevertheless, Article 1 of said Decree clearly acknowledges that property rights to mines, whatever their type, are vested in the Republic in accordance with the law, and hence the government has the right to grant ownership and possession to those who so request it.

C. Domanial System

81. The first Hydrocarbons Law (LH – *Ley de Hidrocarburos*) of 1920, where mining and petroleum activities are separated, sets apart the power of the State to exploit hydrocarbons directly or assign their exploitation to another agent that could comply with the legal requirements, without expressly setting forth public property of hydrocarbons in favour of the State. Between 1920 and 1938, a clear development towards the domanial system is observed, except for the aforementioned LH that established a mixed system (regalian and domanial).

82. Over this period, seven LHs were passed, and each represented an advance in the rentier position of the State. As petroleum exploitation increased, and the interest of the State and individuals along with it, Venezuelan legislation undertook important steps that changed the passive role of the State with regard to the hydrocarbons exploitation activity. This way, the State was no longer a mere grantor of concessions and opened ways to a more direct participation in the considerable benefits of the business, which was not necessarily the immediate consequence but rather an achievement in the long run.

83. In the so-called domanial system, mining ownership is distinguished from surface ownership, and the State makes use of the mines as its property, basically in view of public interest. The essential characteristic of the domanial system is that the State owns the patrimonial property of the mines, explicitly, the right to use, enjoy, and dispose within the limits set forth by law, which was applied in the same way for the hydrocarbons area. This premise has been widely embraced in contemporary compared legislation. The domanial system on the ownership of mines and hydrocarbons was reaffirmed in Venezuela and has been in force ever since.[57]

---

57. César Balestrini C., *La industria petrolera en América Latina*, 42–50 (Caracas, 1971).

§2. System Adopted in Venezuela

84. Article 12 of the CRBV assigns the Republic 'property rights to mining and hydrocarbon fields, whatever their nature, that exist in the national territory, beneath the territorial seabed, in the exclusive zone and the continental shelf, as public property and, therefore, inalienable and imprescriptible'. In this fashion, the Republic is given the exclusivity for exploitation and management and, thus, is able to grant concessions for a fixed term, guaranteeing at all times the existence of compensation or repayment appropriate for the public interest (Article 113).

85. Ever since the enactment of the Liberator's Decree of 1829, property rights to the mines and the subsoil have passed from the Republic to the State, from the State to the Nation, and from the Nation again to the Republic. The first acknowledgement in favour of the Republic was represented by said Decree by the Liberator. Afterwards, on 4 January 1855, the Regulations of the laws contained in the Mining Code stipulated that property rights to mines were vested originally in the State – not in the Nation as established by the French law of 1791, or in the Republic as set forth by the Decree of 1829. In the Constitution of 1961, reference was made indirectly to the Nation as the holder of property rights to mines, including hydrocarbons. As a matter of fact, Article 103 of said Constitution read:

> Lands acquired for the exploration or exploitation of mining concessions, including the hydrocarbons and the rest of the fuel minerals, shall become absolute ownership of the Nation, without any compensation whatsoever, once the respective concession period ends for whatever reason.

86. Likewise, Article 150 of the aforementioned Magna Carta made reference to the term Nation in relation to the authorization required by the Executive Branch for transferring the ownership of Nation-owned real property.

87. The assignment of property rights to energy resources to the Republic, the State, or the Nation does not seem to have major legal consequences. However, it is appropriate to analyse the differences existing among the three terms for explaining the model adopted by the CRBV of 1999 and determine, under our interpretative approach, possible errors in the Constitution in force.

I. Conceptualization of the Republic, State and Nation

88. Republic, from Latin *res publica* (*res* = 'thing' and *publica* = 'common', belonging to 'all'), is a term whose meaning has created ambiguities throughout time, and it has been even used vaguely and inappropriately as a substitute for the word State or, traditionally, as a synonym, for instance, when used as 'Constitution of the Republic' or the 'Republic of Ecuador'.[58] From a historical perspective, it has been claimed that the Republic has a rather abstract meaning linked to the political

58. Schultze Dieter Nohlen, *Rainer-Olaf: Lexikon der Politikwissenschaft*, vol. 2, 817 (Munich, 2002).

power[59] and that it is a legacy the Romans left us as a model structured in an organic form by means of the law.[60] The Republic is defined as the antithesis of the Monarchy, especially in the context of the deep changes promoted by the French Revolution. The Republic is characterized by the division of the powers of the State within the framework of an elective, representative, alternative, and responsible political system. In the theory of the State, the Republic is positioned as a form of government.[61]

89. The State may be defined as a technical form of organization for the political relations of cooperation of the people or nation, or as a sociopolitical conglomerate legally established, based on a territory, subject to an authority that is exercised through its own bodies and whose sovereignty is recognized by other States. Georg Jellinek defines the State from the legal point of view as 'the corporation formed by a country endowed with an original power and based on a certain territory'.[62] Authors then identify the people, the territory, the political power, and sovereignty as the constituent elements of the State, although there are three elements that have been traditionally considered essential to or that give existence to the State: Human Beings or the People, the Territory, and the Power. These elements must concur for the State to exist. If at least one is missing, there is no State.

90. The word 'Nation', from the Latin *natio*, means birth, though its reach has nothing to do with a natural or biological reality but rather with an ethical-social scope. This term is historically linked to the Western-European framework and became politically active in times of the 'French Revolution'. Even in the French Constitution of 1791, the term Nation was used instead of Republic, which further received from such text the title of sovereignty. According to the most classical definition, the Nation is a human community that shares the same ethnic origin, is endowed with a cultural, religious, linguistic, and customary unit, and holds a common historical heritage and a common national purpose. Generally, the terms Nation and State have been confused, when in fact they are different. As stated by some authors, such confusion represents a mistake, and they even distinguish the concepts of sociological Nation (human beings who belong to a nation where the ethnic group is indispensable) from nationality (which is granted by a State on the grounds of *ius sanguinis* or *ius soli*).

91. In many texts, both terms, State and Nation, are interchanged in the same paragraph, and we can hardly discriminate the reasons the author had for choosing sometimes State or other times Nation. The Nation is the human and historical foundation *ab inmemorabli*. It is the subject of the constituent power, the group of individuals who epitomize sovereignty and exercise their political rights (first, the *ius*

59. Aurora Arnáiz Amigo, *El Estado y sus fundamentos institucionales*, 36 (México, 1995).
60. Patricio Colombo Murúa, *Curso de Derecho Político*, 108 (Buenos Aires, 2000).
61. Arturo Pellet Lastra, *Teoría del Estado*, 113–127 (Buenos Aires, 1999).
62. Georg Jellinek, *Teoría General del Estado* (Buenos Aires, 1970). A critical analysis of his thought in Möllers, Christoph: Skizzen zur aktualität Georg Jellinek, in Keller, Christian (Ed.), Victor Ehrenberg und Georg Jellinek, 155 (Frankfurt am Main, 2005).

sufragii). Authors who defend the conceptual pre-eminence of the idea of the Nation over that of the State fall in this line of reasoning.[63]

A. *The Notion of Republic in the Decree on the Mines of 1829*

92. Once these terminological clarifications have been made, it is possible to come closer to the historical sense that the use of the notion of Republic had by the Liberator in the Decree of 1829, in which property rights to mines were assigned to the Republic and not to the Nation or the State. Without any doubt, as in the French Revolution – which had bathed the entire American continent with its euphoria and political scope – the war for independence that unchained Venezuela from the Spanish dominium also had the immediate effect of substituting one form of government for another, namely, the Crown for the Republic. The Liberator himself offers us in a series of documents the possibility of drawing conclusions on the meaning of the terms Nation, Republic, and State. For instance, in the Organic Decree published on 27 August 1828, in Bogotá, making reference to the Republic, he stated: 'After a detailed and sound deliberation, I have decided to take charge, as I do from this moment on, of the Supreme Power of the Republic, which I shall exercise with the names of Liberator-President, granted to me by the laws and the public suffrage.' With regard to the Nation, he pointed out: 'The national vote has been unanimously casted in all the Provinces, the certificates of which have already arrived in this capital city and comprise the great majority of the Nation.' (Emphasis added.) With reference to the State, he stated:

> That the people in this situation, using the essential rights always reserved for them to free themselves from the ravages of anarchy and to provide in any possible manner for their preservation and future prosperity, has commissioned me the Supreme Magistracy to consolidate the union of the State (emphasis added), restore internal peace and make the reforms that may be deemed necessary.

93. The attempt to make valid the Decree of 1829, which transferred property rights to mines from the Spanish Crown to the Republic of Venezuela, implies the acceptance of the political connotation that such event had and the political meaning that the Republic had as a form of government contrary to the Monarchy. Even from the words of the Liberator, transcribed hereinabove, which express what Nation, State, and Republic meant to him, it is unavoidable to conclude that the first two concepts had a distinct dimension that incorporated factors such as the human, that is, the people, the territory, the power, and the sovereignty. These elements

63. Eustaquio Galán y Gutiérrez, *Los conceptos de Estado y Nación como categorías de la ciencia política y del derecho internacional*, 35 (Reus, Madrid, 1952). The Asturian professor cites numerous and varied list of authors, including Platon, Aristotle, Alfonso X the Wise and Thomas Aquinas, Suarez Hobbes, Rousseau, Kant, Weber, Meinecke, Schmitt, and Kelsen. But mostly to Mancini, who is the author of reference to support his thesis.

became essential for the changes that the constitutional frameworks of the sovereign States would undergo in the future, especially when they had to decide on the term to be used for assigning the ownership of public property and the type of legal system to be adopted for the purpose of regulating mining and hydrocarbons concessions, so that individuals could continue participating in the exploitation of such resources.

B. The Nation as Holder of the Property Rights

94. In the case of Venezuela, the tendency of the assignment of property rights to natural resources developed towards the Nation. It was established in the Regulations of the LM of 1855, the Constitution of 1961, the LH of 1943, Law on Property Subject to Reversion in Hydrocarbons Concession (*Ley de Bienes Afectos a Reversión en las Concesiones de Hidrocarburos)* (LRP) of 1971, and the Nationalization Law (*Ley de Nacionalización*) (LN) of 1975.

95. The LH of 1943, considered the most important law passed regarding hydrocarbons, makes reference in at least sixteen articles to the property rights to petroleum vested in the Nation indirectly or directly. Particularly, Article 50 *ejusdem* stands out, and we may find expressions such as the followings:

> In the event that the Federal Executive Branch decides to receive in kind the tax referred to in Ordinal 1 of Article 41, the following rules shall be followed: No. 1, letter a) the petroleum volume corresponding to the Nation shall be delivered, entirely or partially. … Letter b) the petroleum volume owned by the Nation and originated from exploitation. The Federal Executive Branch may demand the immediate delivery of part or the whole of the petroleum stored that is owned by the Nation. Letter c) If the Federal Executive Branch does not make use of the petroleum owned by the Nation once the storage term is due, the obligation by the licensee to keep it stored ceases, understanding, in fact, that the Nation sells it to the licensee at a price that shall be fixed at such time, in accordance with the rules set forth in the second paragraph of this article.

96. This same criterion on the dominion of the Nation as the holder of the property rights associated with hydrocarbons may be found in Article 9 of the LRP as follows:

> Property referred to in articles 90, 13, and 15 of this Law and declassified from the public service of the concessions shall become the absolute ownership of the Nation, free from encumbrances and burdens, without any compensation whatsoever.

97. The LN set a similar criterion in Article 15:

> The value of property allocated to the concessions that, according to the Ministry of Mines and Hydrocarbons, are under the conditions referred to in articles 90, 13 and 15 of the Law on Property Subject to Reversion in Hydrocarbon Concessions and on which resolutions ordering licensees to deliver such concessions to the Nation has not been decreed yet.

98. Article 21 of the same law pointed out:

> The Executive Branch, through the Ministry of Public Works, shall determine the geographical areas where the companies created pursuant to Article 6 will perform their activities and assign or transfer to said companies the property received by the State, in accordance with this Law and the Law on Property Subject to Reversion in Hydrocarbon Concessions, including real property owned by the State.

99. The Civil Code contains precise references about this aspect. Let us notice some provisions taken from Chapter III on 'Property in Relation to the Person to whom it belongs.' Article 538: 'Property belongs to the Nation, the States, the Municipalities, public premises and the rest of the artificial persons, and to individuals.' Article 539: 'Property owned by the Nation, the States and the Municipalities are either public property or patrimonial property.' Article 540: 'Public Property is intended for public use or private use of the Nation, the States, and the Municipalities.'

II. Erroneous Attribution of Property Rights to the Republic

100. The Constitution of 1999 and the Organic Laws on Gaseous Hydrocarbons and on Hydrocarbons of 1999 and 2001, respectively, set apart from this tradition when establishing that mining and hydrocarbon fields are public property and *belong to the Republic* (emphasis added), in contradiction with Article 113 of the same constitutional text, whose second paragraph reads as follows:

> When dealing with the exploitation of natural resources owned by the Nation or the rendering of services of a public nature, with or without exclusivity, the State may grant concessions at a fixed term, guaranteeing at all times the existence of compensations or repayments appropriate for the public interest.

101. Here, it may be inferred that Members of the Constituent Assembly fell into a contradiction that may be gathered from the writing of Articles 12 and 113 of the Magna Carta in force. The first of such articles assigns property rights to mining and hydrocarbons to the Republic; the second article recognizes that, as a natural resource, they belong to the Nation. Second, they fell into error, for they should have been coherent with the tradition, as well as with the criterion adopted in Article 113, quoted above, and assigned property rights to mining and hydrocarbons resources to the Nation, which is the human and historical element capable of inheriting not only the glories and sacrifices of its ancestors but also the corporeal property that legitimately corresponds to the Nation. This line of reasoning is supported by the constitutional tendency in Ibero-America, which does not regard the Republic as the holder of such rights, although it leans more towards the State than the Nation. In this sense, we find that the Constitutions of Bolivia (Articles 136–139), Brazil (Article 20), Chile (Article 19, No. 24), Colombia (Article 332), Cuba (Article 15), Ecuador (Article 247), Spain (Article 132), Paraguay (Article 112), and Dominican Republic (Article 103) opt for the State as the owner of the property rights to the natural resources of the soil and subsoil, while the Constitutions of Mexico and Peru choose the Nation.

102. The prevailing grounds of the legislators when erroneously writing Article 12 of the Constitution are ratified in the preliminary recitals of the Organic Law on Hydrocarbons (*Ley Orgánica de Hidrocarburos*) (LOH) of 2001, which points out the following when making reference to this issue:

> The project reiterates the principle of the property rights of the Republic on the hydrocarbon fields. This reiteration is both a homage to our Liberator, who so established it as a visionary in Quito on October 24, 1829, and an economic and political requirement. Indeed, for the first time, our fundamental law expressly grants property rights to mining and hydrocarbon fields existing in the country to the Republic.

103. Somehow, this is true. For the first time, a provision in the Constitution and the LOH grants the Republic property rights that, as we have explained, correspond to the Nation. In our opinion, the homage to the Liberator should have been instead the recognition of his heroic determination, in the Decree of 1829, to transfer the rights exercised by the Spanish Crown on the mines to the Republic. From there on, as we have noted, the concept of the Republic is associated more with a form of government rather than with an institution to which the characteristics or roles related to the State or the Nation may be assigned, depending on the notion or tradition that has been adopted. In the case of Venezuela, as previously explained, the Republic as the holder of the property rights to natural resources was the path chosen. Since 1999, this tradition has not been modified altogether due to the observations made with regard to the error and contradiction that, in our opinion, exist in Article 12 of the Constitution. Nevertheless, and from the sociological viewpoint, we share the idea that since property rights to public property, natural resources and, undoubtedly, energy resources are vested in the Nation, it is, however, through the State that citizens are compelled to express themselves, since the State is the entity that has legal personality and definitely represents such organized collectivity, as a corporation comprised by a people, endowed with original power and settled in a given territory.

104. Beyond the traditional debate over the ownership of energy resources – whether they belong to the State, the Republic, or the Nation – the recent evolution of international human rights law and comparative constitutional law has fostered a more nuanced understanding of the concept of 'state or national ownership' of natural resources. The jurisprudence of the Inter-American Court of Human Rights has been instrumental in recognizing the collective property rights of Indigenous Peoples over their ancestral territories – rights that extend beyond formal land titles – and in affirming their right to meaningful participation in decisions affecting their lands and resources (Sawhoyamaxa v. Paraguay, 2006; Saramaka v. Suriname, 2007; Xákmok Kásek v. Paraguay, 2010).[64] This approach, also upheld by national and international courts – such as in the landmark case of the Maya People of Belize (Caribbean Court of Justice, 2015) – is particularly relevant in the context of the energy transition. A significant portion of the planet's biodiversity (over 80%) and many of the critical minerals essential for this transition are located within Indigenous territories. Contemporary Energy Law must therefore integrate this legal recognition of collective Indigenous ownership as a cornerstone for ensuring a just, environmentally sustainable, and rights-respecting transition (Anaya, 2004; Barelli, 2012; Shelton, 2022).[65]

105. In this context, caution must be exercised with regard to potential state-driven tendencies to extend debates over the ownership of traditional energy resources toward more interventionist forms of control over renewable energy sources, such as solar and wind power.Spain's experience with the so-called sun tax, introduced in 2015 through Royal Decree 900/2015, serves as a cautionary example: this measure imposed a levy on photovoltaic self-consumption, discouraging distributed generation and provoking widespread legal and social opposition. The regulation was ultimately repealed in 2018 by Royal Decree-Law 15/2018, which acknowledged that such measures unjustifiably restricted the right to produce and consume clean energy (Spanish Ministry for Ecological Transition, 2018). Far from enhancing energy sovereignty or serving the public interest, these types of interventions risk eroding public trust, delaying the energy transition, and undermining the environmental commitments made by the state.Therefore, Energy Law must ensure that regulatory frameworks promote and uphold public participation, energy decentralization, and environmental equity, while avoiding the replication of extractivist practices applied to resources which – although renewable – are not exempt from social and territorial impacts (Viñuales, 2022; Savaresi, 2023).[66]

---

64. Inter-American Court of Human Rights, *Sawhoyamaxa Indigenous Community v. Paraguay*, Judgment of 29 Mar. 2006; Inter-American Court of Human Rights, *Saramaka People v. Suriname*, Judgment of 28 November 2007; Inter-American Court of Human Rights, *Xákmok Kásek Indigenous Community v. Paraguay*, Judgment of 24 Aug. 2010.
65. James Anaya,*Indigenous Peoples in International Law*, 2nd ed., Oxford University Press, Oxford, 2004.; Mauro Barelli, 'The Role of Soft Law in the International Legal System: The Case of the United Nations Declaration on the Rights of Indigenous Peoples', *Human Rights Law Review*, vol. 12, no. 1, 2012, pp. 1–29; Dinah Shelton, *Advanced Introduction to International Environmental Law*, Edward Elgar Publishing, Cheltenham, 2022.
66. Jorge E Viñuales, *The Rio Declaration on Environment and Development: A Commentary*, Oxford University Press, Oxford, 2022.

    Annalisa Savaresi, 'The Rise of Rights-Based Climate Litigation', *Journal of Human Rights and the Environment*, vol. 14, no. 1, 2023, pp. 1–22.

106. In fact, the Spanish government has faced more than fifty international arbitration claims due to retroactive changes to renewable energy incentives, including those related to the so-called sun tax. Several of these cases have been brought before the International Centre for Settlement of Investment Disputes (ICSID) and other arbitral tribunals, resulting in substantial damages awarded to investors. For instance, in Eiser Infrastructure Limited and Energia Solar Luxembourg v. Spain,[67] the ICSID tribunal ordered Spain to pay over EUR 128 million in compensation. Similarly, in NextEra Energy v. Spain, the state was ordered to pay EUR 290 million. According to Bloomberg (2024),[68] cumulative awards from these and other cases have exceeded EUR 1 billion, representing a significant burden on public finances and a cautionary lesson on the legal and economic consequences of inconsistent energy policies. Some of these decisions are also under review by EU courts (European Commission, 2017).[69]

§3. Regulation in Latin America

107. The alternation in property systems on the soil and subsoil resources has not been a predominant feature in Latin America, but rather the embracing of one or the other, as we have already seen. Nonetheless, in countries such as Mexico and Brazil, the story is different, and we can see the concurrence of the domanial and accession systems until the definite adoption in favour of the State or the Nation of the absolute ownership of the soil and subsoil resources.

108. With regard to the Mexican case, after the success of the war for Independence, the territorial property of colonial patrimony was transferred to the new Mexican Nation, including the dominium of the subsoil wealth, as recorded in paragraph 12 of the Treaty of Córdoba signed by Agustín de Iturbide y Juan O'Donojú on 24 August 1821, and in the Peace Treaty between Mexico and Spain, signed on 22 December 1836.[70]

109. This system remained until the enactment of the Mining Code of the US of Mexico of 1884, which marked the beginning of the accession system. Article 10 of this Code established:

> The owner of the soil is also the exclusive owner of the substances lying in the subsoil, and, therefore, and without the need for registering a claim or having

---

67. ICSID, *Eiser Infrastructure Limited and Energia Solar Luxembourg S.à r.l. v. Kingdom of Spain*, ICSID Case No. ARB/13/36, Award of 4 May 2017.
68. Bloomberg, 'Spain Hit with Over €1 Billion in Damages from Renewable Energy Arbitration Cases,' Bloomberg Green, February 2024. Available at: https://www.bloomberg.com/green.
69. European Commission, 'State Aid: Commission Approves Support for Renewable Electricity in Spain,' Press Release IP/17/1099, April 2017.
70. Manuel Bartlett Díaz, *La disputa por el petróleo en México: Breve historia de los hidrocarburos*, en: Jaime Cárdenas Gracia (ed.), *En defensa del petróleo*, 12 (UNAM, Instituto de Investigaciones Jurídicas, México 2009), disponible en: http://biblio.juridicas.unam.mx/libros/libro.htm?l=2729 (último acceso: 31 Mar. 2025).

> special adjudication, such owner may exploit and benefit from: ... IV. Salts that exist on the surface soil, pure and salty waters, above or underneath the surface soil, petroleum and gaseous springs or thermal and medicinal waters.[71]

110. In the Law of 6 July 1887, President Porfirio Díaz made the system even more flexible, releasing mines and petroleum from federal, local, and municipal contributions, except for the Revenue Stamp Tax. However, the LM of 23 November 1909 set forth in Article 2 that the owner of the soil has the exclusive property right to fuel mineral fields or reservoirs of all kinds and varieties.

111. The development of this legal framework, which intended, as of 1884, to promote foreign investment in the context of the novel oil industry, began concentrating a huge wealth in the hands of a few, especially during the so-called Porfiriato (period of the leadership of Porfirio Díaz), to the detriment of fair distribution for the benefit of the great majority of the Mexicans. This way, the granting of concessions for petroleum exploitation contributed to the surfacing of the armed movement that arose in 1910.

112. This revolutionary process developed on the grounds of the Guadalupe Plan of 12 December 1914, which tended towards the review of the laws pertaining to petroleum and the rest of the natural resources of the country for destroying the monopolies created by the former regime and preventing the formation of other monopolies in the future; the Decree of 7 January 1915, which ordered the ceasing of petroleum exploitation in the Republic; the Agreement of President Venustiano Carranza of 19 March 1915, with a broad view about the petroleum issue, wealth that he always believed should belong to the nation; and lastly, it materializes in the writing of Article 27 of the Political Constitution of 1917, which seeks to claim in favour of the Nation the exclusive right on the exploitation of the natural resources and the monopoly of its wealth, whether in the soil or subsoil. Thus, the fourth paragraph of Article 27 of the Constitution provides for the separation of the ownership of the soil from that of the subsoil and hands back to the Nation the dominium of the latter. Petroleum is then subject to the same system of the mines; the Nation is vested with the inalienable and imprescriptible dominium of the hydrocarbons; and the system of absolute privileges with respect to the fields is abolished.

113. In the case of Brazil, the Regalian System during the Colonial period ruled until the Constitution of 1891, which established in Article 72 the accession system, through which the owner of the soil was also the owner of the subsoil. This system was, however, attenuated in Article 72,[72] constitutional paragraph 17, which established:

---

71. Alicia Mayer (Coord.), *México en tres momentos, 1810-1910-2010: hacia la conmemoración del bicentenario de la Independencia y del centenario de la Revolución Mexicana: retos y perspectivas, Universidad Autónoma de México Volumen* 1, 181 (México 2007).
72. Lucas Abreu Barroso, *Propriedade dos recursos minerais e propriedade do solo e do subsolo no ordenamento jurídico brasileiro*, in *A Lei Agrária Nova*, vol. 2, pp. 299–309 (Juruá Editora 2006).

> O direito de propriedade mantém-se em toda a sua plenitude, salva a desapropriação por necessidade ou utilidade pública, mediante indenização prévia. As minas pertencem aos proprietários do solo, salvas as limitações que forem estabelecidas por lei a bem da exploração deste ramo de indústria.

114. Later on, the Constitutions of 1934 (118), 1937 (143) and 1946 (152), 1967 (161), and the Constitutional Amendment No. 1 of 1969 eliminated the accession system and separated the ownership of the soil from that of the subsoil: '*As minas e demais riquezas do subsolo, bem como as quedas d'água, constituem propriedade distinta da do solo para o efeito de exploração ou aproveitamento industrial.*' This criterion is adopted by the Constitution of 1967 and the Constitutional Amendment No. 1 of 1969, with the following wording: '*Jazidas, minas e demais recursos minerais e os potenciais de energia hidráulica constituem propriedade distinta da do solo para o efeito de exploração ou aproveitamento industrial.*'

115. The Supreme Federal Court of 1997 ratified the separation of the ownership of the soil from that of the subsoil, stating that:

> O sistema de direito constitucional positivo vigente no Brasil-fiel à tradição republicana iniciada com a Constituição de 1934 – instituiu verdadeira separação jurídica entre a propriedade do solo e a propriedade mineral (que incide sobre as jazidas, em lavra ou não, e demais recursos minerais existentes no imóvel).

116. The Constitution of 1988 incorporated, in Article 20, as the property of the Union: 5. the natural resources of the continental shelf and the exclusive economic zone; 6. the territorial waters; 8. the potential hydraulic energy; 9. the mineral resources, including those of the subsoil. In Article 176, the distinction is written down more accurately:

> The fields, whether in the process of mining or not, the rest of the mineral resources and the potential hydraulic energy constitute property different from that of the soil, for the purpose of exploitation or use, and belong to the Union, guaranteeing the licensee the property rights to the product derived from mining … 2. The participation of the owner of the soil in the results of the mining is guaranteed, in the form and value provided by the law.

117. The current regulatory framework of Brazil makes very clear the definite abandonment of the accession system as of 1934 and the concentration in favour of the State not only of the ownership of the resources of the soil and the subsoil but also of the power to regulate the exploitation of such resources under its authority at all times. Hence, the Constitution of 1988 ratified that the following represented a monopoly of the Union: '*I – a pesquisa e a lavra das jazidas de petróleo e gás natural e outros hidrocarbonetos fluidos.*'

Chapter 4. Role of Government Institutions in the Shaping and Administration of Energy Law and Policy: Competence Regime

§1. Constitutional Regime

118. The CRBV confers the National Public Power, in Article 156, ordinals 12th and 16th, exclusive competence on the regime and general administration of hydrocarbons, as well as on the creation, organization, collection, administration, and control of income taxes derived from their exploitation and commercialization. Likewise, Ordinal 29th of the same Article 156 grants the National Public Power the competence to establish 'the general regime for public services, specially, electricity, potable water, and gas', in which case it is a concurrent competence, since Article 164, Ordinal 8th, of the same CRBV, establishes that States have under their competences the 'creation, governance and organization of State public services', along with Article 178, Ordinal 6th, which sets forth that municipalities 'are competent to supply and manage potable water, electricity and domestic gas services … '. However and according to Article 156, Ordinal 32nd, of the Constitution, the National Power has the authority to legislate on the matters under its competences. Therefore, the scope of the competence on energy matters within the CRBV must be precisely clarified.

119. From the Constitution, it is inferred that legislative competences are classified as exclusive and concurrent. In effect, Article 156 of the Constitution of 1999 contains the catalogue of exclusive competences of the National Power that we have mentioned *infra*. Concurrent legislative competences, however, are not contained in a catalogue, as it is the case of other federal models, such as the German. According to Article 165 of the Venezuelan Constitution, the National Public Power is competent to legislate on the 'fundamental laws', while States shall lay down the 'development laws' on the respective matters, respecting the principles established in said law, namely: interdependence, coordination, cooperation, joint responsibility, and subsidiarity. This concept of 'fundamental and development laws' has its source of inspiration from the 'framework laws' of the Spanish constitutional model. For clearly stating the scope of the competence regime on energy matters, some previous considerations must be made.

120. First, what must we understand by concurrent competence? Second, why does the matter on the rendering of energy services, such as gas and electricity, represent one of the so-called concurrent competences?

121. With regard to the definition of 'concurrent competence', it refers to the competence where two competent entities exercise the same State function on the same regulation area, but the competence is distributed within the function of the State. This means that the Republic has the competence for the fundamental legislation, and the States, the competence for the juridical development. In Spain, for instance, where this distinction derives from, the State has the exclusive competence on the base of the mining and energy regime, while the Autonomous Communities have undertaken regulatory development and execution competences in the areas not attributed to the State. This way, the idea is to cause the State to establish a uniform regulation valid throughout the national territory, while competences may be exercised at the regional level in a differentiated manner, paying attention to particular interests.

122. By virtue of the joint interpretation of the constitutional rules set forth in Article 156, Ordinal 29th, Article 164, Ordinal 8th, and Article 178, Ordinal 6th, of the CRBV, it may be asserted that gas and electricity, as public services, represent a matter of concurrent competence, which now appears expressly indicated in Article 56 of the Organic Law for the Municipal Public Power of 2010. Conversely, the use of the expression 'general regime' in Article 156, Ordinal 29th, must be understood as an allusion to the competence of the National Power to pass the basic law. Nonetheless, just as it has happened with the Spanish system, in Venezuela, the hydrocarbon legislation not only contains the 'basis' but also sets out in 'detail' the regulation of the sector, leaving no space for the exercise of State or municipal competences. The Regulations of the Organic Law on Gaseous Hydrocarbons (*Ley Orgánica de Hidrocarburos Gaseosos*) (LOHG) of 1999, for instance, has the same detailed nature and the States have no margin for the legislation of a regulatory development on this matter. This means that, in practice, the National Power exercises, in a dominant manner, the regulation of the Energy sector.

123. With regard to the guarantee of the municipal autonomy for the rendering of public energy services, several contemporary constitutions, including the Venezuelan Constitution in Article 178, set forth that it is a matter of the local community, as it was already established by the Organic Law on the Municipal Regime of 1989 and ratified by the new LOPPM of 2010 in Article 56, understanding that such competence is concurrent with the National Power, as it was adjudged by the Supreme Tribunal of Justice *(Tribunal Supremo de Justicia)* (TSJ) in its judgment of November 2001, where it clarifies the concept of 'aspects of local life'. It is appropriate to mark off that the doctrine holds that, even when Article 178 of the CRBV contains a long enumeration of matters attributed to the municipalities, such competences are by no means exclusive to them. The Political Administrative Division of the TSJ has held so when it considered that:

> The competence of the municipalities is residual; all matters that are not under the competence of the national power, in the strict sense, shall be under the competence of the municipalities. So, if the matters related to local life are not reserved to the national power, they shall be under the competence of municipalities.

§2. MUNICIPAL REGIME

124. Article 56, Letter f, of the LOPPM of 2010, acknowledges the competence of the services of domestic gas, electricity, and public lighting in favour of the municipalities. Based on this mandate, the municipalities have the authority, according to Article 69 of the same special law, to choose the management system they may deem convenient for the government and administration of their competences. Therefore, for the rendering of public services, the municipalities may manage them on their own; or through the entities that, according to their hierarchy, depend on them; or by means of functional or service decentralization systems; or through the creation of municipal corporations or mixed companies. They may also enter into contracts with individuals for the management of such services. Additionally, they may (Article 46) enter into agreements with other territorial public entities for the creation of other types of intergovernmental associations in the public interest with regard to matters under their competence. Equally, the LOPPM sets forth in Article 273 the possibility that citizens organize themselves to cooperate in the exercise of the control, surveillance, supervision, and assessment of the municipal public management. This rule represents a novelty that allows the participation of the community for a more efficient operation of the public services, whether they come from public, private, or mixed companies.

125. The LOPPM maintains the authority in favour of the municipalities for the regulation of all matters related to the concessions for the rendering of public services. Thus, Article 73 *ejusdem* sets forth that the rendering of municipal public services may be subject to concessions only by means of public bidding processes involving private individuals and under certain minimal conditions which, for such purposes, the own law expressly indicates. Such conditions are related basically to price, duration, guarantees, supervision, intervention, revocation, and transfer, with due regard to other conditions that may be negotiated by the parties for the benefit of general interest. Indeed, the Organic Law on the Promotion of Private Investment, under the Concession Regime, establishes in Article 5 that the States and municipalities may apply the provisions contained in said law to grant concessions for public works and services under their competence. In such a case, the municipality or State shall be in charge of creating or deciding the agency or entity responsible for the granting, as well as for the organization and management of the bidding and granting procedures of the contracts and the supervision, surveillance, and control of their execution.

126. Therefore, within the framework of the autonomy held by the municipalities, they are enabled to convene that municipal public services be also rendered by private individuals through concessions granted by means of public bidding. In consequence, the LOPPM allows different people to cooperate with the municipal administration in the management of municipal public services through concessions.

127. Although municipal autonomy is acknowledged and is also part of an institutionalized tradition, its scope has been greatly debated, both in the doctrine and the jurisprudence.[73] An evidence of this is represented by the appeal for the declaration of nullity based on its unconstitutionality filed against the last paragraph of Article 36 of the derogated Organic Law for the Municipal Regime, where the appellants alleged that the concepts of municipal autonomy and competences had been harmed by the challenged rule, especially with regard to the competence of the municipality to set electricity rates. The TSJ pointed out in its decision that the specifications in Articles 25 and 29 of the Constitution of 1961, invoked by the appellants as being violated, are kept, in their essence, in Article 168 of the Constitution of 1999, which sets forth the following:

> The municipalities represent the prime political unit of the national organization and have legal personality and autonomy within the limits of this Constitution and the law. Such municipal autonomy comprises the following: the election of their authorities, the management of the matters under their competences, and the creation, collection and investment of their revenues.

128. Consequently, the TSJ recognizes that:

> The municipal autonomy is a concept of strict positive law; therefore, it cannot go beyond what specifically emanates from the constitutional provisions or, in other words, it is not a free government within the State, but rather a Power regulated by the Constituent Members and the Legislative Branch.

129. Take due note that Article 169 of the Magna Carta, in its heading, sets forth the following:

> The organization of the Municipalities and the rest of the local entities shall be governed by this Constitution, the regulations established by the national organic laws for the purpose of developing the constitutional principles, and by the legal provisions that, in accordance with the latter, are laid down by the states.

130. In this sense and according to the TSJ, it must be interpreted that the Constitution of 1999 guarantees the municipalities a 'conditioned' freedom for the management of the matters within their competences – regarding gas and electricity services – whose limits are imposed by the Constituent Members and national and State legislation. In another decision, this time adjudged by the Sixth Superior Court in Contentious Tax Matters of Caracas declared the following:

> With regard to the regulatory autonomy of the Municipality, such autonomy is not plenary; it has its limitations, which shall be those established by the regulations having constitutional and legal rank. Therefore, their tax authority has to conform to such constitutional and legal limitation.

73. Enrique Sánchez Falcón, *Estado Comunal y Estado Federal en Venezuela: ¿Son Ambas Formas de Estado Constitucionalmente Reconciliables? Cuadernos de la Fundación Manuel García-Pelayo* No. 18, *Cuestiones Políticas*, Caracas, 2017.

§3. Communal State Regime

131. The attempt to substitute the Constitutional State for a Communal State, contrary to the Constitution of 1999,[74] may put at risk the efficient rendering of gas and electricity services attributed to the competence of the municipalities and now redirected to have the People's Power levels providing such services.

132. In 2001, it was necessary to pass the Law on the Coordination of the Competences of the Services of Domestic Gas and Electricity (*Ley de Coordinación de Competencias de los servicios de Gas y Electricidad*) (LCCGE), in view of the array of competences and entities involved in the process for the opening and promotion of gas as a fuel for the industrial, commercial, and residential sectors. In its Preamble and Article 1, the need for setting rules that may allow for the harmonic coexistence of the various levels of government with competence in the service for the distribution of gas and electricity is highlighted for avoiding legal confusion and uncertainty between the different parties involved in this activity, given that this is a shared-competence regime.

133. The appearance of a new level, far from attaining the harmonization that the LCCGE intended, may cause greater inconveniences, bureaucracy, and probably a general decline in the system for the rendering of gas and electricity services. There is no doubt that we are moving towards a model that is at odds with the Constitution, the LOHG, and the LOPPM of 2005, which was reformed in 2010.

134. The new role that the municipalities have in the Law on the Electric Power System and Service (Ley *Orgánica del Sistema y Servicio Eléctrico*) (LOSSE) of 2010 is marginal compared to the role they had in the derogated Organic Law on the Electric Service (*Ley Orgánica del Servicio Eléctrico*) (LOSE) of 2001. In the latter, according to Article 42, the municipalities had the competence to do the following:

1. Promote the rendering of the electric power service.
2. Guarantee an adequate public lighting service in their jurisdiction, *directly or indirectly* (emphasis added).
3. Supervise the quality of the service.
4. Promote community participation in the supervision of the service.
5. Promote user organization.
6. Look out for the existence of an adequate complaint service.
7. See to the compliance with the sanctions applied by the National Commission of the Electric Power.
8. Propose measures for the improvement of the service.
9. Coordinate the expansion plans of the service of electric power companies with municipal plans for urban development.

74. Allan R. Brewer-Carías, *Dismantling Democracy: The Chávez Authoritarian Experiment*, Cambridge University Press, 2010.

10. Submit recommendations and observations to local electric power companies related to expansion plans and service quality improvement.

135. In the LOSSE in force, the municipalities have a secondary role. According to Article 32, their function shall be the following:

1. Support the supervision of the quality of the electric power service.
2. Participate in the planning for the rendering of the electric power service.
3. Foster user organization, as well as guide the organizations of the People's Power in the supervision of the quality of the electric power service.
4. Cooperate with the service operator and provider, as well as with the *organizations of the People's Power* (emphasis added), for the improvement of the electric power service in their jurisdiction.
5. See to the adequate and timely service for the electric power user.
6. Develop and execute training programmes for the users and organizations of the People's Power on the rational and efficient use of the electric power.
7. Pass and implement municipal regulations for the rational and efficient use of electric power.

136. In accordance with Articles 6 and 59 of the LOC, the communes shall exercise the administration and the management of competences and the rendering of services that, according to the decentralization process, are transferred to them, evidencing that the Communal State implicitly aims at replacing the Municipal Power, undertaking their competences: a new Power without autonomy and contingent upon the Executive Branch.[75]

75. *See supra* Part I, Ch. 1, §1. Political System, at 6–12; *Acceso a la Justicia, Democracia Participativa Amenazada por las Comunas* (17 Aug. 2022).

Chapter 5. Sources of Energy Law

137. The origin, creation, and production of juridical rules are understood as the Sources of Law. The source of the Energy Law, as every source in general of the Law, corresponds to a procedure, a methodology, which establishes a hierarchical order of priority, of competence, that defines a field of regulation for complying with the public and common interest, as the purposes of the State. In the Energy Law, as in other branches of Law, the following sources are identified according to priority: the Constitution and International Treaties, the Law, the Decree-Law, the Regulations, the Ordinances, Jurisprudence, Custom, Doctrine, and the General Principles of Law.

§1. Energy Law at the Apex of the Constitution

138. In the Venezuelan Law, the CRBV provides in Article 7 that 'The Constitution is the supreme law and the foundation of the juridical system.' Nevertheless, it is clearly accepted by the own CRBV, the Jurisprudence, and the doctrine that such governing rule is shared with the international treaties. Article 23 of the CRBV establishes the following:

> The treaties, pacts, and conventions pertaining to human rights and signed and ratified by Venezuela have constitutional rank and prevail over the internal legislation, insofar as they contain rules concerning the enjoyment and exercise of such rights that may be more favorable than those set forth by this Constitution and in the laws of the Republic and shall be applied immediately and directly by the courts and the rest of the agencies of the Public Power.

139. When we relate such rule to the purview of the protection of human rights, we find an unequivocal bond with other fundamental rights, such as the right to development. As a matter of fact, the Declaration on the Right to Development provides in Article 1.1. the following:

> The human right to development also implies the full realization of the right of the peoples to self-determination, which includes, subject to the relevant provisions of both International Covenants on Human Rights, the exercise of their inalienable right to full sovereignty over all their natural wealth and resources.

140. Article 22 of the CRBV, however, provides the following:

> The recitation of rights and guarantees contained in this Constitution and international instruments on human rights shall not be understood as the denial of others that, being inherent to the person, are not expressly mentioned in such recitation.

141. Conversely, it is important to highlight that the protection of the environment and the guarantee of its exercise as an individual and collective Human Right are interrelated with the exercise of economic freedom, which, as they are not absolute, have within their limits the protection of the environment and the need to guarantee the satisfaction of human needs of present and future generations. It is here where the connection between the protection of Human Rights and the Energy Law becomes unavoidable, insofar as their activities make possible the satisfaction of imperious needs, such as health, education, and so many others that, without the availability of energy, would not be possible to perform. Additionally, the activities for the production of energy are linked to the environment, inasmuch as they may put at risk the possibility of enjoying an environment fit for life and pollution-free as an inviolable right.

§2. Treaties and International Agreements

142. Given that Venezuela is one of the main oil-exporting countries of the world and has the greatest reserves of hydrocarbons in the planet, it seems logical that the treaties and international agreements signed by the country and where the energy and, very particularly, oil are involved represent a fundamental part of the sources of the Energy Law, derived from the International Energy Law, which is part of the Public International Law.

143. Considering the guidelines of the Public International Law, we may say that its sources apply to the International Energy Law and, in this sense, in accordance with the Statute of the International Court of Justice in Article 38, such sources would be the following:

a. International conventions, whether general or particular, establishing rules expressly recognized by the contesting States.
b. International custom, as evidence of a general practice accepted as law.
c. The general principles of law recognized by civilized nations.
d. Subject to the provisions of Article 59, judicial decisions and the teachings of the most highly qualified publicists of the various nations, as subsidiary means for the determination of rules of law.

144. It is important to point out that, in the Energy International Law, there is a predominance of the agreements among States and companies, which do not qualify as subjects of the Public International Law because they refer mainly to private contracts. Nonetheless, there are international organizations in the energy sector or agreements among countries for the supply of energy or raw material, such as oil, which would have the category of treaties or international agreements indeed. Such is the case of the Organization of the Petroleum Exporting Countries (OPEC), the Treaty on the Non-Proliferation of Nuclear Weapons; or Resolution 1803 (XVII) of the General Assembly, dated 14 December 1962, named 'Permanent Sovereignty over Natural Resources', which has been an inspiration for the regulatory frameworks of many countries that have natural wealth, hydrocarbons, and mines; or the Protocol Concerning Cooperation in Combating Oil Spills in the Wider Caribbean Region, signed in Cartagena in March 1983.

§3. LEGISLATION CONCERNING ELECTRICITY

145. As the primary source, the CRBV sets forth that, in the electricity sector, the National Public Power is the authority that exercises the competence (Article 156 No. 29), which shall be concurrent with the Municipal Power (Article 178 No. 6). Likewise, it provides the reserve of the waters as State property (Article 304). The Organic LOSSE, dated 12 January 2011, ranks as the secondary source. The Law on the Rational and Efficient Use of Energy, dated 17 February 2012, is placed in a third category. In the fourth category, there is the Organic Regulations of the Ministry, dated 21 March 2011, which determines the organic and functional structure of the Ministry of the People's Power for the Electric Power Energy and the competences corresponding to the departments that comprise it; the Technical Regulations for the Labelling of Energy Efficiency of Air Conditioners, dated 4 June 2013; and in a fifth category, there is Resolution 73, regarding Lighted Signs, which regulates and promotes the rational and efficient use of electric power energy in advertisement systems; Resolution 74, which promotes the efficient use of electric power energy throughout the national territory and, particularly, encourages the reduction of excessive monthly consumption of residential users; Resolution 75, which promotes the improvement of the power factor of industrial, commercial, and official users with loads higher or equal to 200 kVA, to reduce the voltage drop and increase availability of power in the electric network; Resolution 76 on Big-Users, which promotes the reduction of monthly energy consumption; and Resolution 77, which establishes the actions aimed at reducing electric power energy in the public sector.

§4. LEGISLATION CONCERNING PETROL

146. Regarding coal, the CRBV, as the primary source of the Energy Law, establishes the guidelines of the model for the exploitation of natural resources owned by the Nation, which include hydrocarbons, such as oil and gas (Article 113, First Paragraph). In Article 156, No. 16, the CRBV sets forth the competence of the National Public Power on the system and administration of hydrocarbons by the State and, in Article 302, the reserve and control of the State over the oil activity.

147. With regard to the scope of the control and reserve of hydrocarbons by the State, by mandate of the CRBV, such competence extends (Article 303) to the entirety of the shares of Petróleos de Venezuela, S.A.

148. The organic laws are placed at a second level: the LOH of 2001, and its modification of 2006; the Organic Law Reserving the State the Assets and Services of the Primary Activities of the Hydrocarbons of May 2009; and the Organic Law on the Reorganization of the Internal Market of Liquid Fuels of September 2008.

149. At a third level, there are the Decrees on the Migration to Mixed Companies of the Association Agreements (AA) of the Orinoco Oil Belt (*Faja Petrolífera del Orinoco*) (FPO), the Agreements under the Profit-Sharing Scheme (CAGc –

Convenios para la Exploración a Riesgo y Producción de Hidrocarburos bajo el Esquema de Ganancias Compartidas), and the Decree Reserving the Exportation or Importation of Hydrocarbon By-Products to State-Run Companies of April 2002.

150. At a fourth level, there are the Regulations of the LOH; and, at a fifth level, Resolution No. 335 on Border Trade of Hydrocarbons of January 2004; Resolution No. 236 on Export Fuels of October 1995; Resolution on the Sale of Fuel Stability Expendio of December 2004; Resolution on the Fixing of Freight Transport; and Resolutions 168 and 212 for the Determination of New Geographic Areas of PDVSA Petróleo, S.A. of June 2004 and August 2004, respectively.

§5. Legislation Concerning Gas

151. Regarding gaseous hydrocarbons, the same provisions and criteria established by the CRBV are applied for oil, which were indicated in the previous item.

152. As a secondary source, there is the LOHG of 1999. At a third level, there is the Regulation of the Law on Gaseous Hydrocarbons of June 2000. At a fourth level, we find the Resolution through which the collection of the facts pertaining to Administrative Files for cases of Infraction of the LOH is delegated to National Institute of Gas (Ente Nacional del Gas) (ENAGAS), August 2002; Resolution No. 216 on the Fixing of the Tax Value of Associated Natural Gas of March 2003; Resolution on the Fixing of the Prices for Methane Gas at the Dispatch Centres; Resolution for the Fixing of Transport and Distribution Prices of Methane Gas; Resolution No. 165 for the Fixing of Liquefied petroleum gas (LPG – *Gas Licuado de Petróleo*) Prices of June 1997; and Resolution No. 197 on Natural Gas for Vehicles (GNV – *Gas Natural para Vehículos*) of July 2004.

§6. Legislation Concerning Coal

153. As a primary source of the coal legislation, the CRBV highlights Article 156, No. 16, which assigns the National Public Power the competence on the system and administration of the mines, where the Venezuelan Law includes coal. As a secondary source, there is the LM enacted in September 1999, and at a lower level, there is the General Regulation of the LM of March 2001.

§7. Legislation Concerning Environment

154. The CRBV contains as a primary source a special regulation in Chapter IX regarding the Environmental Rights, which are developed in the Organic Environmental Law of December 2007 as a secondary source. At a third level, there are the Law on Forests and Forest Management of May 2008, and the Environmental Criminal Law of May 2012; and, at a fourth level, there is the Internal Regulation of the Ministry for the Environment and Natural Resources of September 2004 and the Organic Regulation of the Ministry for the Environment and Natural Resources of September 2003.

155. As emphasized on multiple occasions throughout this book – particularly in relation to the growing contemporary relevance of Energy Law – its sources have also undergone a process of expansion and transformation. This evolution is driven, among other factors, by the influence of international environmental law, normative frameworks on climate change, and the emergence of human rights standards with direct implications for energy governance. Beyond traditional sources such as constitutions, statutes, and international treaties, Energy Law increasingly incorporates soft law instruments (including declarations, guidelines, and principles), judicial decisions issued by regional and international courts, and multilateral mechanisms such as the Paris Agreement and the Escazú Agreement.Although many of these instruments are not legally binding in the strict sense, they shape normative expectations and influence national jurisprudence and policymaking processes. Moreover, principles such as energy justice, environmental democracy, and intergenerational equity are progressively recognized as normative frameworks that complement classical legal sources and enhance the legitimacy, coherence, and adaptability of the energy legal system in the twenty-first century (*See*, for instance: Heffron, 2021; Wewerinke-Singh, 2021; Viñuales, 2022).[76]

76. Raphael J. Heffron, *Energy Law: An Introduction*, 2nd ed. (Springer 2021); Margaretha Wewerinke-Singh, *State Responsibility, Climate Change and Human Rights under International Law* (Hart Publishing 2021); Jorge E. Viñuales,(ed.), *The Rio Declaration on Environment and Development: A Commentary* (Oxford University Press 2022).

Chapter 6. Global Energy Security: Role of Venezuela

156. Energy security is, and will continue to be, a leading priority for all governments. It is one of the major challenges the world will face in the coming generation. The definition of Energy Security for exporting countries means the security of demand, while for importing countries, this definition refers to supply security. Energy security has definitely emerged as a central foreign-policy concern for all nations. Since World War II, economic growth around the world has been fuelled largely by abundant supplies of hydrocarbons, that is, by petroleum and natural gas. The US, Europe, and Japan together have needed more oil than they can produce on their own. The developing world has plenty of oil, but little development of its national markets for use. Therefore, industrialized countries have tapped into economic resources of poor countries, perpetuating the equation: oil-exporting countries = poor countries or developing countries; consumer countries = rich or developed countries.

157. This mutual dependency is now unravelling and a new order is taking shape. It turns the tables on America, its allies, and other big energy consumers. Major exporting nations have concluded that they have more leverage than ever over consuming countries. Two forces are behind this change. The accelerating industrialization of the billion-people economies of China and India leads us to assume that global energy demand is likely to keep growing rapidly for years to come. And just as important, the world's top crude-producing countries are keeping a tighter grip on their spigots. In addition, Petro-States from Iran to Ecuador are flexing their muscles, brandishing fossil fuel supplies as a weapon in diplomatic disputes or tearing up contracts with foreign companies.

158. However, it is necessary to emphasize that 90% of the world's untapped conventional oil reserves is in the hands of governments or State-owned oil companies, far more than was the case several decades ago. Venezuela is considered vital in this matter because it possesses large reserves of conventional and non-conventional oil and gas. The government of Venezuela says that Venezuela's estimated 78 billion barrels together with an estimated 238 billion barrels of tar oil in the Orinoco Heavy Oil Belt make them 'the largest petroleum reserves in the world'. Venezuela also possesses the continent's largest gas reserves, with an estimated 5,563 billion m^3.

159. Nevertheless, Venezuela cannot be considered a safe supplier. A radical change in its petroleum policy from 1999 onwards, an internal political crisis, and a new scheme of international relations have combined to generate doubts on this issue. For example, in April 2006, Venezuela seized two oil fields from European oil companies, Total S.A. and ENI S.p.A, and officials in Iran and Venezuela have warned that they can disrupt oil supplies if threatened by the US.

160. In recent years, the deterioration of Venezuela's oil sector and its strained relationship with the United States have further diminished its role as a strategic energy supplier. Historically, Venezuela accounted for over 8% of US oil imports, with nearly 45% of its crude exports directed to the US, totalling approximately 934,000 barrels per day (MBD). However, due to political tensions, declining production capacity, and changing market strategies, Venezuela's exports to the US have fallen dramatically.

161. By October 2023, Venezuela had dropped to 9th place among US crude suppliers, with average shipments of 145,000 barrels per day, representing just 1.3% of total US oil imports. The situation worsened in March 2025 with the revocation of Chevron's operating licence in Venezuela –a decision made by the Trump administration in response to the Maduro government's failure to hold free elections. This measure is expected to further destabilize Venezuela's already weakened oil sector and exacerbate the country's broader economic crisis.[77]

162. Just as it happened during World War II, Venezuela played a pivotal role in the international petroleum market when, after severing ties with Germany, Italy, and Japan in 1941, it supplied the Allies, while Hitler's army suffered from fuel shortages (McBeth, 1983; Rivas, 2005).[78] It has been said that the war would never have been won without Venezuelan oil, although the country never received the recognition it deserved.[79]

163. Within this context, Venezuela implemented strategic reforms to strengthen its control over hydrocarbons, requiring foreign companies to refine a portion of crude oil domestically and nationalizing key assets such as the British railway and Isla de Patos. These measures marked the inception of a sovereign oil policy, later consolidated by the nationalization of the industry in 1975 and the rise of Petróleos de Venezuela S.A. (PDVSA) as a prominent actor in the international market (Mommer, 2002).[80]

164. Although Venezuela once held a pivotal role in the global petroleum market – as it did during World War II – its current position is increasingly unstable and diminished. Rather than consolidating its former leadership, decades of mismanagement, corruption, underinvestment, and the impact of international sanctions have severely weakened the country's oil sector, resulting in a dramatic decline in production and widespread economic hardship (Monaldi, 2018; Penfold, 2021).[81]

165. By the 1990s, PDVSA had established itself as one of the world's most influential oil companies, with recognized expertise in exploration, production, refining, and marketing. Its strategy focused on expanding its presence in the US

77. The Financial Times, *Washington's Pressure on Maduro's Government Intensifies After Chevron License Revocation* (2025), available at https://www.ft.com (last accessed 31 Mar. 2025).
78. Brian S. McBeth, *Juan Vicente Gómez and the Oil Companies in Venezuela, 1908–1935*, Cambridge University Press, 1983.
79. Juan Pablo Pérez Alfonso, *El petróleo en la vida venezolana*, Caracas: Ediciones del Ministerio de Energía y Minas, 1974.
80. Bernard Mommer, *Global Oil and the Nation State*, Oxford University Press, 2002.
81. Francisco Monaldi, *The Collapse of the Venezuelan Oil Industry: The Role of Mismanagement and Geopolitics*, Harvard Kennedy School Working Paper Series.

and European markets, ensuring sustained export flows and consolidating its internationalization model through the full or partial acquisition of refineries and distribution systems abroad.

166. Over the past two decades, however, Venezuela's oil industry has collapsed due to mismanagement, corruption, lack of investment, and international sanctions. Once a global production leader, the country's output fell from over 3 million barrels per day in 1998 to fewer than 700,000 in 2024, severely affecting its economy.

167. In contrast to its stabilizing role during World War II, Venezuela now faces an internal energy crisis marked by fuel shortages, dependence on imports, and deteriorating infrastructure. The collapse of the oil sector has triggered a fiscal and social crisis, limiting the state's ability to fund social programmes and exacerbating poverty.

168. Venezuela's energy policy has undergone a profound transformation, resulting in the loss of its former influence in the global oil market. Once a key player in international crude supply, the country's declining production and persistent mismanagement have rendered it increasingly marginal within the global energy landscape. In the past, Venezuela accounted for nearly 9% of US crude imports, exporting up to 830,000 barrels per day (MBD) in 2015. However, the collapse of its oil industry, combined with the rise of the US energy sector, has drastically reduced its relevance as a supplier (EIA (US Energy Information Administration), 2024).[82]

169. The United States is now the world's leading producer of oil and natural gas, surpassing 13 million barrels per day in 2023. Thanks to the fracking revolution, the country has not only reduced its dependence on foreign imports but has also become a net exporter of hydrocarbons (International Energy Agency (IEA), 2024). Within this new global context, Venezuela's energy crisis and the decline of its crude exports no longer pose a threat to US energy security or global market stability.

170. Sanctions imposed by Washington have further deepened Venezuela's oil sector crisis by restricting its export capacity and limiting access to technology and financial resources. Oil production remains below 700,000 barrels per day – a stark contrast to the over 3 million barrels per day the country produced in the late 1990s. As a result, Venezuela has become increasingly reliant on agreements with China and India, as well as opaque crude trading mechanisms involving intermediaries.[83]

171. Despite efforts to diversify its export markets, Venezuela's oil infrastructure continues to deteriorate, with refineries operating at less than 20% of their

82. International Energy Agency (IEA), *World Energy Outlook 2024*, Paris: IEA, 2024, available at https://www.iea.org/reports/world-energy-outlook-2024 (accessed 31 Mar. 2025).
83. Steve Ellner, 'Venezuela's Crisis and Its Impact on the Global Oil Market,' *Latin American Perspectives*, vol. 47, no. 6 (2020): 45–62.

capacity and chronic fuel shortages persisting in the domestic market. The loss of export revenues has further exacerbated the country's economic and social crisis, accelerating mass migration flows in recent years.[84]

172. Unlike in previous decades, Venezuela has lost its ability to influence global oil prices or pressure Washington through energy embargo threats. Its current production levels are negligible on the global scale, and its domestic crisis no longer affects market stability.

173. The rise of the United States as an energy superpower has fundamentally reshaped the geopolitical landscape of the Western Hemisphere. While in the past, a Venezuelan oil embargo might have posed a national security concern for Washington, the current reality is that Venezuela depends far more on the US as an export market than the US depends on Venezuelan crude.

174. In this context, Venezuela's energy policy faces a structural dilemma: without foreign investment or deep structural reforms, its oil industry will continue to decline, with devastating consequences for the national economy. In the short term, the government has sought to maintain strategic alliances with China and Russia; however, limited confidence in Venezuela's production capacity has constrained the scope of such agreements.

175. Despite ongoing political tensions between Caracas and Washington, the potential restoration of energy relations with the United States may represent Venezuela's only viable path to reviving part of its oil sector. Nonetheless, without meaningful internal reforms, the prospects for genuine recovery remain highly uncertain.

176. Venezuela's energy security has been fundamentally reversed, evolving into both internal and external insecurity. Once a key supplier to global markets, the country now faces a severe domestic energy crisis as a result of decades of misguided policies, chronic underinvestment, and operational collapse. Its oil production is negligible at the international level, and it can no longer meet its own domestic fuel demand. Refineries are operating at less than 20% of their capacity, leading to critical shortages of gasoline and household gas. Venezuela, once central to energy geopolitics, now plays a marginal role, with its crisis no longer posing any threat to global energy stability.

177. Since the decline in oil prices in 2014 and the deepening crisis of Petróleos de Venezuela S.A. (PDVSA), crude oil production has fallen to levels not seen since the 1940s. Once among the world's most influential oil companies, PDVSA now

84. Francisco Monaldi, *The Collapse of the Venezuelan Oil Industry: The Role of Mismanagement and Geopolitics*, Harvard Kennedy School Working Paper Series (2018).

suffers from deteriorating infrastructure, systemic corruption, and a significant loss of technical expertise – factors that have prevented any meaningful recovery (Monaldi, 2018).[85]

178. Crude oil export dynamics have also shifted. Although China and India remain key buyers, sanctions and a lack of investment have significantly constrained Venezuela's export volumes (Ellner, 2020; Sullivan & Beittel, 2023). By 2024, India's imports of Venezuelan crude had dropped below 300,000 barrels per day, while China has diversified its supply sources, increasingly favouring more stable providers from the Middle East and Russia.

179. Venezuela's decline as an energy power illustrates the fragility of resource-dependent economies in a shifting geopolitical landscape. As the global energy order is reshaped by technological innovation, climate imperatives, and emerging producers, Venezuela's recovery depends not only on market conditions but also on the country's capacity to implement structural reforms, regain institutional credibility, and reposition itself within a rapidly evolving energy transition.

85. Francisco Monaldi, *The Collapse of the Venezuelan Oil Industry: The Role of Above-Ground Risks Limiting FDI* (Baker Inst. for Pub. Policy 2020),available at https://www.bakerinstitute.org/research/collapse-venezuelan-oil-industry-role-above-ground-risks-limiting-fdi (last accessed 31 Mar. 2025).

Chapter 7. The Venezuelan Energy Law and Regional Integration

§1. CONSTITUTIONAL DEVELOPMENT

I. Under the 1961 Constitution

180. The successful development of the ECSC and the European Economic Community as of 1951 and 1957, as well as the institutionalization of a new international order to regulate the economy and the international trade through the Bretton Woods Agreements, and the creation of the General Agreement on Tariffs and Trade, influenced as determining factors for building the first integrationist projects in Latin America in the early 1960s. This event marks a great difference with Europe, which delineated a route sheet to avoid a new war and guarantee a long-lasting peace.

181. In this international context, the Venezuelan Constitution of 1961 arose after the fall of the last military dictatorship in 1958. The preamble of the Constitution offers a framework favourable for promoting integration from the perspective of a cooperative, not self-centred State closely linked with:

> The rest of the nations and, especially, with the sister Republics of the continent, the goals of the international community, based on mutual respect of sovereignties, self-determination of the peoples, universal guarantee of individual and social rights of the human person, and rejection to war, conquest and economic pre-eminence as an instrument of international politics.

182. This integrationist calling is ratified in Article 108, in the sense that 'The Republic shall favour Latin American economic integration', for which 'the coordination of resources and efforts shall be provided to foster economic development and increase common welfare and security'.

II. Under the 1999 Constitution

183. Later transformation of the concept of sovereignty, present to a great extent in the text of the preamble of the Constitution of 1961, was defined in the increasing globalization process and interaction among the international, supranational, and constitutional law. Thanks to this, the opening to a deeper integration is a fact that has permeated the legal systems of all the countries of the region.

184. With the arrival of democracy in the subcontinent, as of the 1980s, the idea of integration gained a new momentum through the inclusion of opening clauses, which do not exclude mentioning the principles of sovereignty, non-intervention, and equality of the States.

185. A key turn towards the transformation of the sovereign State to the opened State originates from the creation of supranational entities. The model of import substitution or closed model, which protected the national industry by imposing high tariffs on products coming from abroad, was left behind.

186. In this regional context, the Venezuelan Constitution of 1999 includes new guidelines for integration, which match the new South American reality with regard to the notion of an opened State. As a matter of fact, this is expressed in the preamble in the sense that:

> It promotes peaceful cooperation among nations and furthers and strengthens Latin American integration in accordance with the principle of non intervention and national self-determination of the people, the universal and indivisible guarantee of human rights, the democratization of imitational society, nuclear disarmament, ecological balance and environmental resources as the common and inalienable heritage of humanity.

187. Later on, in Article 153, it reaffirms that:

> The Republic shall promote and encourage Latin American and Caribbean integration, in the interest of advancing toward the creation of a community of nations, defending the region's economic, social, cultural, political and environmental interests. The Republic shall have the power to sign international treaties that implement and coordinate efforts to promote the common development of our nations and ensure the welfare of their peoples and the collective security of their inhabitants. To these ends, the Republic may transfer to supranational organizations, through treaties, the exercise of the necessary authorities to carry out these integration processes. In its integration and union policies with Latin America and the Caribbean, the Republic shall give privileged status to relations with Bier American countries, striving to make this a common policy throughout our Latin America. Provisions adopted within the framework of integration agreements shall be regarded as an integral part of the legal order in force and shall be applicable directly and with priority over internal legislation.

188. In Article 153 mentioned above, it promotes a paradigm shift regarding a new approach to sovereignty, legal pluralism, and acknowledgement of the competence of jurisdictional entities in the sphere of human rights and integration. As a consequence, the Constitution is no longer the single supreme regulation. Instead, it shares the space at the pinnacle of the regulatory pyramid with other provisions, as it allows the direct and preferential application in the internal legislation of the regulations that may be adopted in the framework of the integration agreements. Some authors, Flávia Piovesan, among others, turn to the trapezium figure to explain this phenomenon of a pyramid with a flat top, where the sovereign and constitutional self-contained State gives way to an opened State which guarantees human rights and is prone to integration.

189. Under such orientation, and for the first time in a special law in the field of energy, the promotion of integration is included as a fundamental goal. Actually, it is appraised in the Organic Law of the Electric Power System and Service of 2010 as one of the governing principles for the rendering of the electric service under the name of geopolitical integration. Later on, Article 11 of the same law sets forth that, for strategic and national convenience and observing the principles of integration and energy complementarity, the Venezuelan State shall promote international agreements aiming at increasing, among others, the international exchange of electricity, integration of the electric systems of the region, technology transfer, global optimization of resources, and harmonization of the regulatory and institutional frameworks. Likewise, Articles 17 and 26 of the Law grant the Ministry of the People's Power with competence on electric power matters the responsibility to prepare the energy integration policy and assess and approve the international exchange of electricity according to the integration policy and the principles of solidarity, mutual assistance, and complementarity, as well as to coordinate the use of international interconnections.

§2. Energy Integration in South America

190. Next, the energy integration projects in which Venezuela has participated and still participates will be discussed, as well as the new proposals for integration and cooperation that have polarized the Venezuelan society, between those for and against it. This fact is also perceived at the regional level, where the countries are grouped whether in the traditional blocks, such as the Andean Community of Nations (CAN – *Comunidad Andina de Naciones*) and Southern Common Market (*Mercado Común del Sur*) (MERCOSUR), or the Bolivarian Alliance for the Peoples of Our America (ALBA), promoted from Venezuela where only one group participates attracted by political and ideological similarities, or in the most recent block, Union of South American Nations (UNASUR – *Unión Suramericana de Naciones*), where all the countries of South America are grouped around energy matters and others. Particularly in the cases of ALBA and UNASUR, the presence of Venezuela's geopolitics, framed in the integration processes, trying to imbue them with its content, will be shown. The legal base of the Venezuelan proposal is in Article 153 of the Constitution, mentioned before, and in an anti-imperialist and nationalist view inspired by the thinking of Simón Bolívar for building the 'patria grande' (the 'great nation'). The idea of a Twenty-First Century Socialism has been included in the geopolitical approach since 2005 as the ideological basis for the Venezuelan regional integration policy.[86]

I. The Andean Community of Nations

191. On 26 May 1969, the Cartagena Agreement was signed. Through such agreement, Colombia, Ecuador, Peru, Bolivia, and Chile created the Andean Pact. Venezuela joined the group on 13 February 1973, and Chile withdrew on 30 October 1976. The Andean Pact was replaced by the Andean Community, whose text, in

86. *See supra* Part II, Ch. 1, §2.

the chapter related to physical integration, regards energy as one of the areas in which the Member Countries are supposed to develop joint action plans to achieve a better use of space, with a view to stimulating the subregional economic integration process. Although the CAN presents the most advanced legal and institutional transnational framework among the regional integration models in South America, political and economic instabilities, in particular the lost decade of the eighties and the debt crisis, are identified as factors that brought integration to a long halt. Only after the new century began, this integration project developed a self-contained regulatory framework in energy.

192. In this context, in February 2002, Decision 536 was issued about 'the General Framework for interconnecting subregional electric systems and intra-community exchanges of electric power', which has made electric power exchanges easier, especially between Colombia and Ecuador. The Cartagena Agreement is invoked as the source of reference since it precisely stipulates physical integration among members of the Andean Community as the mechanism to achieve the organization's goals. Decision 536 promotes a market that ensures fair competition, with prices and rates reflecting efficient economic costs and, thus, avoiding discriminatory practices and abuses of dominant position.

193. In January 2004, the CAN stipulated the bases of the Andean Energy Alliance (AEA), designed into five thematic axes:

1. Development of integrated power markets (electricity and gas) through physical networks and harmonized regulatory frameworks.
2. Insertion of hydrocarbons into international markets, in a strategic context of energy security.
3. Promotion of Andean countries' business development in 'energy clusters'.
4. Framework for energy service negotiation and classification at the World Trade Organization and other international entities.
5. Development of a renewable energy agenda and its connection with the environment agenda and the Integrated Social Development Plan.

194. Following Venezuela's withdrawal from the Andean Community (CAN) in 2006 – triggered by its opposition to the Andean countries' negotiations with the United States under the Andean Free Trade Agreement – Andean energy integration experienced a significant setback.

195. As of 2024–2025, the Andean Community has continued to advance its energy initiatives without Venezuela, strengthening cooperation among its four remaining Member States: Colombia, Ecuador, Peru, and Bolivia.

196. The most recent advancements in energy integration include the expansion of electricity interconnections between Colombia, Ecuador, and Peru, as well as agreements for natural gas exports among Andean countries. Throughout this process, Venezuela has remained entirely absent, playing no active role in subregional energy policymaking.

197. Despite being one of the regions with the greatest potential in natural resources, the Andean Community has historically underutilized its energy capacity. In recent years, however, the organization has sought to promote a renewed energy integration agenda focused on renewable energy, energy efficiency, and carbon markets, with the goal of modernizing its strategies and addressing the global energy transition and climate crisis.

II. Southern Common Market

198. The Southern Common Market (MERCOSUR) was established on 26 March 1991, through the signing of the Treaty of Asunción by Argentina, Brazil, Paraguay, and Uruguay. Its primary objective is to achieve economic and commercial integration by establishing a common market that enables the free movement of goods, services, and productive factors among Member States. Over the years, MERCOSUR has expanded its scope by incorporating associate members and advancing initiatives across various sectors, including energy.

199. In the initial phase of MERCOSUR, at the beginning of the 1990s, the theme of integration through physical infrastructure was not incorporated in the bloc's agenda. Neither the Treaty of Asunción nor the Protocol of Ouro Preto created provisions which made allusion to energy, despite being one of the most important issues for the business dynamics of the region. It is by means of Presidential Summits that the development of physical integration projects as a strategic way to consolidate regional integration is urged, involving at first just MERCOSUR members and their partners and later within a broader project considering South America as a whole. Concretely speaking, such integration includes the promotion of commercial exchange, transport, communications and energy, tending to achieve a greater social cohesion and inclusion and coping with the asymmetries that occur in the region.

200. Among the legal instruments that MERCOSUR has developed to promote energy integration are the Guidelines on Energy Policies in MERCOSUR 57/93, Decision 10/98, Memorandum of Understanding on Electric Exchanges and Electric Integration in MERCOSUR, CMC Decision number 49/07 named 'Mercosur Action Plan for Cooperation in Biofuels', Letter of Intent for energy integration between Bolivia and Brazil, which resulted in the construction of the Bolivia-Brazil Gas Pipeline, and the Framework Agreement on Regional Energy Complementarity (2005), which aims to promote integration among the member countries of MERCOSUR and associated States, promoted by Latin American Integration Association (ALADI – *Asociación Latinoamericana de Integración*).

201. These instruments providing for energy integration are in most cases general guidelines that do not follow a plan to be implemented in a stated period of time and are not ruled by an implementation timetable or schedule. Under MERCOSUR's scheme of regional energy integration, one cannot observe a medium to long-term plan to favour the development of regulatory frameworks for both the construction of physical infrastructure and the regulation of markets. The inevitable consequence is a slow evolution, leveraging bilateral exchanges (even some prior to the creation of the bloc), but not an integrated energy policy.

202. Venezuela formally joined MERCOSUR on 31 July 2012, following a membership process that began in 2006. Its accession was facilitated by Paraguay's temporary suspension from the bloc, which enabled Argentina, Brazil, and Uruguay to approve the entry without unanimous consent. This decision was highly controversial and sparked criticism from legal scholars and political actors, who argued that it violated MERCOSUR's foundational legal framework, which requires consensus for the admission of new members (Briceño Ruiz, 2013).[87] Despite warnings, the founding members proceeded with Venezuela's incorporation, marking a departure from the bloc's traditional decision-making norms.

203. However, Venezuela's membership was suspended on 2 December 2016, due to its failure to comply with the commitments outlined in its accession protocol, including economic, commercial, and democratic obligations. Subsequently, on 5 August 2017, the founding Member States invoked the democratic clause of the Ushuaia Protocol, indefinitely suspending Venezuela as a result of the breakdown of democratic order in the country. Since then, Venezuela has remained entirely inactive in MERCOSUR's integration processes, including its energy agenda.

204. In terms of energy integration, Venezuela's participation in MERCOSUR produced no significant progress. During its brief period as a full member, it failed to establish structural energy agreements with other Member States or to advance projects for interconnection or energy complementarity. This was largely due to its domestic crisis, inconsistent energy policies, and the progressive deterioration of its productive capacity in the oil and electricity sectors.

205. Since Venezuela's suspension, MERCOSUR has continued to advance its energy agenda without its participation, focusing on bilateral agreements and cooperative projects among its active Member States. However, the bloc still faces significant challenges in consolidating a fully integrated energy market and remains, for the most part, a space for policy coordination with limited structural progress.

§3. Projects Promoted by Venezuela

I. Bolivarian Alliance for the Peoples of Our America

206. The alternative project ALBA was first announced in December 2001 by President Hugo Chávez during the 3rd Summit of Heads of State and Government of the Association of Caribbean States, held on Margarita Island, Venezuela. At that time, Chávez presented ALBA as a countermodel to the Free Trade Area of the

87. J. Briceño Ruiz, 'MERCOSUR: crisis institucional y desafíos para la integración' (2013) 101 Revista CIDOB d'Afers Internacionals 137–160.

Americas (FTAA), which had been proposed by the United States in 1994. There, Chávez stated: 'We want a model that truly integrates us. [We do not need] a model that disintegrates us, that integrates some at the expense of the disintegration of others. From Venezuela, we propose to the Caribbean and Latin America that we [should] think [...][about] another alternative [...]. Integration is vital for us. Either we come together, or we sink. Let's choose our alternatives.'

207. The ALBA was first announced in December 2001 by President Hugo Chávez during the 3rd Summit of Heads of State and Government of the Association of Caribbean States, held on Margarita Island, Venezuela. At that time, Chávez presented ALBA as an alternative model to the FTAA, which had been proposed by the United States in 1994. (OAS 2001a; OAS 2001b).[88]

208. By 2004, Venezuela's vision of regional integration had shifted substantially. During the Special Summit of the Americas in Monterrey (2004), the Venezuelan delegation rejected what it described as 'unfair cooperation' and promoted an alternative integration model focused on social equity and reducing regional disparities. In this context, Cuba became ALBA's first strategic partner, laying the foundation for a model based on energy and services exchange.

209. In December 2004, during the 1st Cuba-Venezuela Presidential Summit, ALBA transitioned from a unilateral proposal to a bilateral cooperation agreement between Havana and Caracas (ALBA Declaration, 2004). Its operational structure was built upon the Cuba-Venezuela Strategic Alliance, which had originated under the Caracas Energy Agreement of 2000. Under this framework, Venezuela provided subsidized oil to Cuba in exchange for medical and educational services.[89]

210. Since its inception, ALBA has lacked a strong institutional structure. Unlike other regional mechanisms such as MERCOSUR or the Andean Community (CAN), ALBA has suffered from a constitutional deficit and an absence of clear decision-making procedures. While the Presidential Council functions as its main governing body, the alliance lacks transparent mechanisms for agenda-setting, compliance monitoring, and dispute resolution. Moreover, the concentration of power in the executive branches of Member States (e.g., Bolivia, Ecuador, Nicaragua) has hindered the development of supranational institutions.

211. Over the past decade, ALBA has experienced a marked decline in influence. Although initially presented as an alternative model of integration, its viability has diminished due to Venezuela's deepening economic crisis and the structural unsustainability of its cooperation model.

---

88. Organization of American States (OAS), *Declaration of Quebec City, 2001a.* Available at: http://www.summit-americas.org/Documents%20for%20Quebec%20City%20Summit/Quebec/plan-e.pdf (last accessed 10 Mar. 2025); OAS (2001b).
89. Fritz Thomas, *ALBA contra ALCA: La Alternativa Bolivariana para las Américas: una nueva vía para la integración regional en Latinoamérica.* Centro de Investigación y Documentación Chile–Latinoamérica (FDCL), Berlín, 2007, pp. 10–12. Available at: https://thomas-fritz.org/file_download/32/ALBA-contra-ALCA-Thomas-Fritz-ES.pdf (last accessed 31 Mar. 2025).

212. Since 2014, the drop in oil prices and the intensification of Venezuela's internal crisis have significantly impaired its capacity to finance ALBA and to provide subsidized oil to its allies. This particularly affected Petrocaribe, which at its peak included eighteen Caribbean nations. Since 2019, however, most of these countries have sought alternative energy suppliers, reducing their dependency on Venezuelan oil.

213. Despite efforts to maintain regional cooperation, Venezuela's fiscal and operational weakness has rendered ALBA ineffective as a regional integration mechanism. The alliance continues to rely on governments that are ideologically aligned with Venezuela and has failed to incorporate strategic regional actors such as Brazil, Argentina, Chile, Peru, or Colombia.

214. As of 2024, ALBA remains formally active but has seen its influence significantly diminished, with no major economic or energy initiatives currently underway. Its impact has been severely constrained by Venezuela's structural crisis and the absence of a viable, long-term model for energy cooperation.

II. Union of South American Nations

215. On 16 April 2007, both the Political Negotiations of the Heads of State and Presidents of the South American Community of Nations (CSN – *Comunidad Sudamericana de Naciones*) and the First South America Energy Summit took place in Venezuela. In this meeting, Argentina, Bolivia, Brazil, Chile, Colombia, Ecuador, Guyana, Paraguay, Peru, Suriname, Uruguay, and Venezuela decided to accept Venezuela's proposal to rename the CSN by the UNASUR for the South America's integration process.

216. In the final statement, the countries ratified as main objectives the energy integration for the integral and sustainable use of the resources of the region, in a spirit of solidarity and the development of an infrastructure for the interconnection of the region, an effort attributed to Venezuela, and decided to create the South American Energy Council as an integral part of UNASUR. These were the first steps to create UNASUR in practice, but it was officially founded on 23 May 2008, at the Third Summit of Heads of State held in Brasilia, Brazil.

217. Venezuela was adding achievements to its integration purposes provided for in Article 153 of the Constitution. Those achievements, though, were far from Chávez's expectations or wishes. To Venezuela, Unasur is understood as 'a strategic regional leverage to build a plural-polar world', and ALBA as the 'hard core' of the integration of Latin America and the Caribbean. That is why Chávez had the goal to amend Article 153 in the referendum of 2007 to grant ALBA constitutional status, thus giving more depth and scope to his integration concept, which was more South-oriented.

218. The integration of South America proposed by Venezuela – at least when President Chavez was the head of the Government – is more oriented towards a defensive alliance, in terms of ideology, politics, and security, far-off from the substance of existing integration agreements based on economic and commercial dynamics. Hence, Unasur has not been able to become what Venezuela wanted but has been kept more as an instrument of regional governance than as a classic integration bloc. Its acts have made a difference in major political processes in the region, as the political crisis of 30 September 2010 in Ecuador, the application of the Democratic Charter to Paraguay for the removal of the President of that country from office in a summary proceeding in June 2012, or the support to Venezuela's President elected in 2013, in an election process challenged by the country's opposition. In the energy field, the Energy Council has just approved the Guidelines for the South American Energy Strategy and the Action Plan for Regional Energy Integration, as well as the Structure of the South American Energy Treaty. Hence, Unasur shows little achievements as to integration and could hardly become a project resembling the ALBA, as it does not depend on a leader and shares different approaches and interests among member countries.

219. In recent years, however, UNASUR has undergone a marked decline in political relevance and institutional functionality. The withdrawal of several key Member States – including Argentina, Brazil, Chile, Colombia, Paraguay, and Peru – between 2018 and 2019, largely due to ideological divergences, significantly undermined the organization. As a result, UNASUR has lost much of its political legitimacy and operational capacity, substantially limiting its role as a regional actor.

220. Since 2019, UNASUR-led activities have come to a near standstill. Despite its ambitious founding vision for regional cooperation and integration, the organization remains effectively inactive as of 2024, with no ongoing initiatives – standing in stark contrast to its original objectives.

Part I. Regulatory Framework Concerning Electricity

Chapter 1. General Introduction

221. The beginning of the use of electric power in Venezuela dates back to 24 October 1888, when Maracaibo became the first city with power for street lighting thanks to the Maracaibo Electric Light Company. A year later, the service arrived in Valencia, due to the initiative of American Miguel F. Dooley, who installed a plant fuelled by firewood and coal. In 1897, after many attempts, electricity arrived in Caracas. Later that year, on 8 August, the President of the Republic, General Joaquín Crespo, opened the first hydroelectric plant of Venezuela, in a place known as 'El Encantado', State of Miranda. That innovative hydroelectric plant, conceived by Venezuelan engineer Ricardo Zuloaga, was the basis for founding the electric utility of Caracas Compañía Anónima Electricidad de Caracas (Elcar) in 1895, to meet the electricity service needs of the capital city of the Republic. Then the electricity service spread all over the country through small electric utilities.

222. The development at large scale of big Hydroelectric Power Plants (HPPs) in the Basin of the Caroní River began in the mid-1950s to meet the requirements of a fast-growing country as a result of the development of the oil industry. In fact, El Guri HPP became the largest worldwide at that time. In parallel to the hydroelectric development in the late 1960s, there was improvement in the national interconnection of the transmission networks at 765 kV, 400 kV, and 230 kV among the companies that were operating and supplying electricity service in different States of the country. The mid-1970s was the beginning of development of thermoelectric plants, including, among others, the Centro Thermoelectric Plant and Tacoa Thermoelectric Plant – the largest electric power generation complex of the Central-Northern-Coastal Region.

223. In the late 1990s, the electric power system of Venezuela already had eighteen electric utilities, eleven of which were State utilities that produced 90% of the power and served 69% of the consumers. The leading power generation utility was EDELCA, the hydroelectric company of the Caroní, the production of which represented over 70% of the total national power generation, while the other 30% was produced by Public Power Corporation S.A. (CADAFE – *Compañía Anónima de Administración y Fomento Eléctrico*), Elecar, and Enelven with their thermo-power plants. The leading supply company was CADAFE, which provided electricity service to 90% of the national territory and nearly 50% of the subscribers, followed by La Electricidad de Caracas (Elecar) with 30% of the subscribers located in the metropolitan area of the capital city, and so on with the rest of the utilities, including, among others: ENELBAR (State of Lara), Enelven-Enelco (State of Zulia), Seneca (State of Nueva Esparta), Calife (Puerto Cabello), Eleval (part of the city of Valencia), Elebol (Ciudad Bolivar), and Caley (State of Yaracuay).

224. Since 2007, the State took over total control of the electricity sector by creating the National Electric Corporation (CORPOELEC – Corporación Eléctrica Nacional), whereby the State merged and absorbed all public and private utilities of the electric sector and its activities, from electric power generation, transmission, and supply to commercialization thereof.

§1. Regulatory Framework until 2001

225. The electric service sector is constantly changing. Most of the countries have introduced modifications in their regulatory frameworks, transforming the traditional scheme of this market from vertically integrated undertakings (public and private) to individual and separate companies, under a private scheme, looking for free competition and towards increasing economic efficiency and social welfare. The above has caused to consider electric power as an ordinary consumption good which is subject to being transported, traded, and consumed in a market of its own and governed by competition rules.

226. Technological developments have played an important role in the changes and reforms introduced in the electric sector. This has allowed the incorporation of new companies in the market and a more flexible role of the State, standing out more as a regulating agent than an entrepreneur. Venezuela has not been unaware of the debate or the reforms of the electric sector. As a matter of fact, in 1989, a process of opening, privatization, and progressive introduction of competition in the electric market began and ended with the approval in 2001 of the LOSE. Nonetheless, and by reason of the political changes initiated in 1999, the principles and goals of said law were never applied and, in turn, a process all the way around began instead. Such process materialized through the approval of the LOSSE of 2010. This law reserves the generation, transmission, distribution, and commercialization of activities of the electric power service to the State and introduces a socialist management model. Given the magnitude and impact of these regulatory changes, we will discuss in this chapter the analysis of such regulatory instruments for establishing their differences and possible effects on the current crisis of the Venezuelan electric system.

227. The first Law of Electric Service in Venezuela was enacted in 1999. The following laws existed previously: the Law of Electric Transmission Lines Easement, in 1928; Decree No. 368, Rules for Determining Electric Service Fees as of 27 July 1989; Decree No. 2.383, providing for the Rules for the Electric Service of

18 June 1992; Decree No. 2.384, providing for the creation of the Foundation for the Development of the Electric Service (FUNDELEC) of 18 June 1992; and Decree No. 1.558, Rules for the Regulations of the Electric Service Sector in 1996.

228. However, it should be noted that this was not the case in Venezuela only, since other countries, such as Spain, also lacked legislation according to the electric service needs. In this sense, it is worth quoting Gaspar Arino Ortiz, who said that:

> it was inconceivable that, at that time, the legal framework of this sector – the major investment sector in Spain during the 1960s and 1970s and a crucial utility for the Spanish industry and economy – was the Decree for Electric Service Verifications, dated 12 March 1954.

This author further says that 'the Electric Service Regulation in Spain has always been incomplete and imprecise to solve punctual issues and, until 1994, there was no regulation for governing this activity in a systematic manner'.

229. The purpose of the Law of Electric Transmission Lines Easement of 1928 was to regulate electric facilities and power distribution networks built on third-party premises, whereby the land owner was bound to allow the installation of electric transmission lines, whether by air or underground. The easements were subject to said regulation, which provided for the authorization to install poles for electric lines and any necessary fittings and, likewise, the right-of-way for the supervision and maintenance of said lines.

230. Oil activity played a central role in driving the growth and development of Venezuela's electric power sector during the second half of the twentieth century. Between 1969 and 1978, for example, total electricity production nearly tripled, increasing from 9,135 GWh in 1969 to 15,241 GWh in 1974, and reaching 22,880 GWh by 1978. This expansion was accompanied by a steady rise in installed capacity – both thermal and hydroelectric – as well as in per capita consumption, which grew from 915 kWh/person in 1969 to 1,726 kWh/person in 1978.[90]

231. This fast increase has been driven mainly by the private sector; therefore, the Venezuelan Development Corporation (CVF) was created in 1947, and its main objective was to promote the development of an integral electric service system for electric power generation, transmission, and distribution in Venezuela. Thus, this Corporation became an important shareholder in several companies in view of the companies' default in regard to the loans granted by the CVF. In 1958, the first State-owned company of Venezuela, CADAFE, was created for the administration and operation management of fifteen State-owned electricity companies throughout the Venezuelan territory.

90. Rodolfo Tellería Villapol, *Historia del Desarrollo del Servicio Eléctrico en Venezuela, 1880–1998*, CODELECTRA (2000), pp. 212–213, available at: https://codelectra.org/wp-content/uploads/2021/04/Rodolfo_Telleria_Villapol_Libro.pdf (last accessed 10 Jun. 2025).

232. The Decree on the Rules for Determining Electric Power Service Fees of 1989 defines the electric power service as a public service and, consequently, justifies the need for the promotion of the guidelines, procedures, and legal regulations by the State to determine the method for setting the fees of the electric power service. The decree also established the importance of having a safe, continuous, and efficient electric power as a determining factor for the development of the country, recognizing the need for efficiently promoting investments of the public and private sectors.

233. In 1992, Decree No. 2383[91] on the Regulations for the Development of the Electric Power Service promotes a regulatory framework where it acknowledges the participation of the public and private sectors, although it reaffirms that the supply of electricity is a public service. It proposes for the first time the separation of the regulating and entrepreneurial roles of the State and a price system based on economic criteria that reflects the costs of the service and tends towards the correction of the distortions of the rates and eases private investment in the sector. However, it promotes the progressive opening of the sector to free competition, guaranteeing the access of energy offerers to the national transmission system.

234. In 1996, Decree 1.558,[92] repealing Decree 2.383, ratifies that the rendering of the electric power service is a national public service but fosters a model oriented towards the opening of the private sector, even through the privatization of State-owned companies. It undertakes as a principle the subsidiary role of the State in the rendering of the electric power service, whenever there is no interest by the private sector. It encourages free competition in the expansion of the generation activity and suggests the separation of the generation, transmission, and distribution activities as business units. With regard to access to electric power transmission and distribution networks, it proposes free access by third parties, without discrimination, by means of the corresponding use payment.

235. In 1999, Decree-Law on the Electric Power Service[93] was passed to cover the need for a legal framework appropriate for continuing with the changes introduced in the early 1990s of the past century. Among the noteworthy aspects of this new legal instrument, it is important to highlight the following: the promotion of free competition, legal separation of the activities of the companies of the sector, free access to the networks, ratification of the declaration of the public service nature of the generation, management, transmission, distribution, and commercialization activities, and the setting of two market levels: the Electric Power Wholesale market and the regulated-fee Market. As a guiding principle, the law promotes the formation of national capital by encouraging the participation of Venezuelan

91. *Decreto No. 2.383, por el cual se dictan las Normas sobre el Desarrollo del Servicio Eléctrico,* Gaceta Oficial No. 35.012 (21 Jul. 1992).
92. *Decreto No. 1.558, que deroga el Decreto No. 2.383 y establece el marco regulatorio del sector eléctrico,* Gaceta Oficial No. 36.085 (13 Nov. 1996).
93. *Decreto con Rango y Fuerza de Ley del Servicio Eléctrico,* Gaceta Oficial No. 36.791 (21 Sep. 1999).

individuals. It also grants the State a monopoly over hydroelectric generation activities in the Caroní, Paragua, and Caura river basins—regions that hold the country's largest freshwater reserves.

236. The National Electric Power Commission was established as an entity under the Executive Branch, responsible for regulating, supervising, and controlling the national electricity service. Additionally, the National Electricity System Operations Center was created as the core operational body of the system. Access to electricity sector activities is regulated through administrative authorizations, except for transmission and distribution, which are subject to concession arrangements.

237. This Law did not achieve its goals because of the political transition initiated in 1999. Indeed, the coming into force of a new Constitution approved on 15 December 1999 made necessary the adjustment of the said legal instrument to the new constitutional framework. Therefore, the Permanent Commission for Energy and Mines of the National Assembly began a review of said Decree-Law that ended with the approval of the Organic Law on the Electric Power Service of 2001.[94]

§2. Legal Framework for the Liberalization of 2001

238. The LOSE of 2001 does not represent any drastic changes in the manner the electric service sector has been working until this law was enacted. The main changes are focused on the delay of the lapse stated for the electric service companies – which nowadays are working in an integral manner – to perform the juridical separation of the power generation, transmission, and distribution activities, and on the due date for making effective the electric service wholesale market.

239. In view of the importance of this law, now repealed, we believe that it is necessary to offer an analysis of the most relevant aspects to have a better understanding of the evolution and development of the current legal framework of the electric power sector in Venezuela.

I. General Objectives

240. Specifically, the general objectives of the LOSE are as follows:

1. Strengthening the National Government as the regulatory entity by means of creating a Regulatory Entity with a relative autonomy and independence.
2. Separation of legal and management activities.
3. Free access to the power distribution system.
4. Creation of the electricity wholesale market.
5. Promotion for the participation of private investment with free competition.

94. *Ley Orgánica del Servicio Eléctrico,* Gaceta Oficial No. 5.568 (Extra.) (31 Dec. 2001).

6. Guaranteeing the services quality by regulating the activities classified as natural monopolies.

241. This reform process unquestionably requires at least some partial agreement for its successful application. The participation of all sectors involved is required, including the State-owned Electric Service Companies, which have the control of 82% of the electricity's consumption in the country and supply electric service to 68% of all subscribers; private electric service companies, workers, and users; and the National Government as the Regulatory Entity for electric service.

II. Free Competition in the Electricity Market

242. One of the objectives intended by the LOSE is the promotion of free competition regarding the activities inherent to electric service. However, the fact of having a law with mixed regulations for the market opening and other regulations restricting the same may be a hindrance for said purpose.

243. The LOSE, in Article 3, has stated that the Government shall promote the competition of those electric service activities as it may correspond. The scope of said provision has been restrained to the extent that other activities included in the electric service are subject to regulation. Although the LOSE does not specifically refer to which activities are included, it becomes clear that it would be referring to those activities which by their own characteristics are defined as 'natural monopolies', such as the case of the power transmission and distribution activities.

244. The law has been categorical by asserting that power generation and trading (buy-sale of power and electricity) are activities opened to free competition, prior authorization of the National Committee of Electricity, and in agreement with the LOSE and other regulatory instruments on this matter.

245. Article 3, as first mentioned, following the same path, promotes in this law the concept of freedom when, in the third statement, it emphasizes that the National Government will promote private participation in the activities of electric service; and there is no distinction among the electric service activities that, according to Article 1 of the LOSE, are for the generation, transmission, and management of the State-owned Electric Service System and those for distribution and trading of power and electricity. In this sense, the lawmaker intends to be in agreement with the constitutional principles set in Articles 113 and 299 of the CRBV, which refer to the prohibition of monopolies (Article 113) and the social-economic regime of the Republic (Article 299).

246. It is worth mentioning that the sole paragraph of Article 113 of the Constitution provides that, when developing national natural resources or rendering public services, whether exclusively or not (as in the case of electricity), the Government may grant concessions for a fixed term, thus guaranteeing existence of considerations and offsets appropriate to the public interest at all times. The above paragraph must be deemed more as an exception, as a possibility to grant concessions, than as a rule per se, given that, in some way, it strays from the main spirit of the regulation – the prohibition of any type of monopolies or abuse of the dominant position that an individual, a group of individuals, or a company or group of companies acquires or had acquired in a specific market of goods or services, irrespective of the determining cause of such dominant position (Article 113 of the CRBV). The ill-named 'natural monopolies' would be included in this category. By definition, they provide a basis for the development of concession and exclusivity-granting policies and do nothing but hold the market liberalization process, as they conflict with the basic principles of free competition.

247. According to natural-monopoly theory, competition cannot persist in the electric utility industry. But the theory is contradicted by the fact that competition has actually persisted for decades in dozens of US cities. Economist Walter J. Primeaux[95] has studied electric utility competition for more than twenty years and concluded in Direct Electric Utility Competition: The Natural-Monopoly Myth, among other things, that:

1. Direct rivalry between two competing firms has existed for very long periods of time – for over eighty years in some cities.
2. The rival electric utilities compete vigorously through prices and services.
3. Customers have gained substantial benefits from the competition, compared to cities where there are electric utility monopolies (exclusivity).
4. Contrary to natural-monopoly theory, costs are actually lower where there are two firms operating.
5. Any consumer satisfaction problems caused by dual power lines are considered by consumers to be less significant than the benefits from competition.

248. The arguments to justify the regulation of electricity transmission and distribution are now nonsense, especially if these allow maintaining the criterion that they constitute natural monopolies, which they are insofar as the legislator closes the roads to competition. What really matters and becomes necessary is the setting of clear rules for network access to be guaranteed – the only efficient means to achieve the so sought-after free competition in transmission and distribution thereof, and naturally, the collapse of the myth of the natural monopoly.

III. Legal Reserve for the State

249. The sole paragraph of Article 3 of the LOSE reserves to the Government the use or direct development of the domain of the hydroelectric generation activity in the basins of Caroni, Paragua, and Caura. Such use supposes exclusion of other uses by third parties that may be incompatible with the purposes of the reserve. The main objective of the reserve statement is its exclusive nature, as it prevails over

95. Walter J. Primeaux, *Direct Electric Utility Competition: The Natural Monopoly Myth*. New York: Praeger, 1986.

any and all prior authorizations or concessions incompatible with the reserve, hence, preventing, in general, the granting to third parties of new developments in the reserved area. In other words, if a private individual decides to exercise its right of economic freedom in hydroelectric power generation matters, such individual cannot consider the basins of Caroni, Caura, or Paragua, but any other basin, the flow of which is suitable for power generation, since development thereof has been reserved for the Venezuelan government. However, the paragraph becomes the exception to Article 24 of the LOSE, which allows the electric power generation activity to be carried out under a free-competition system, so that only the Government – through companies of its exclusive ownership – may carry out the hydroelectric generation activity in the above-mentioned rivers.

IV. Electric Service as a Public Service

250. Based on the approach of the European doctrine, it is necessary to state that liberalizing a sector of the economy aimed at creating a free-competition market, which maintains all its processes under the protection and control of the Government, defining them as a utility (Article 4 LOSE), and where the Government acts as regulatory entity and as party concerned, as well as due to its business-owner nature, is contradictory.

251. Some Venezuelan authors are of the opinion that the content of Article 4 of the LOSE does not allow deducing that the economic freedom has been removed from this market. The Political Administrative Division of the CSJ, on its part, deems that declaring an activity as utility does not entail reserve thereof to the Government. The Superintendence for the Promotion and Protection of Free Competition has taken the same direction by affirming that the activities of the electricity sector as utility do not result in inapplicability of the regulations on free competition or proscription of economic freedom.

252. However, under Article 3 of the Law to Promote and Protect the Exercise of Free Competition *(Ley para la Promoción y Protección de la Libre Competencia)* (LPPELC), the conditions for true competition to exist are incompatible with the electricity market provided for in the LOSE, given that the operators should have the possibility, that is, 'the freedom' to enter or leave the market, and that those operating in the market, including the Government, do not have the possibility to impose conditions to the exchange relationships. With the Venezuelan government having a double role as operator and regulatory entity, it is logical to suppose that it will try, or at least will tend to impose its conditions, especially if the activities of the economic process – from power generation to power marketing – have been raised to the category of utility. The electricity market may then be categorized as a regulated market, not a free-competition market.

253. Nobody questions the strategic nature and the relevance of the electric service in our society. Its price is a critical factor for most of the economy. The technological development of the electric utility industry and the need to stock up raw material determine the evolution of other industry sectors. It is already accepted, though, and there is conviction that, to guarantee power supply and the quality and accessible price thereof, the Government's intervention is required not more than as provided for by the technical regulation.

254. A good example is the Electric Service Act (LSE – *ley del Servicio Eléctrico*) in force in Spain, which excludes the traditional concept of utility from its regulations and replaces it with the express guarantee of supplying electric service to all consumers that require it within the national territory. It would have made more sense to maintain at least the approach of the LOHG, with respect to the non-inclusion of the activities intended to be left open to free competition, such as power generation and marketing, as a utility. That would have been a lot simpler since the electricity sector in Venezuela has never been under reserve by the Government under the terms of a monopoly. The legislator has even been able to choose to impose charges or obligations for utility, that is, a universal service that must be guaranteed as a mission or duty of public interest, and which the operators of the sector are bound to comply with. That would imply that certain activities deemed to be difficult to open to free competition, as power transmission and distribution, do not need to be categorized as utility.

255. The LSE of Spain provides in its statement of reasons that the power transmission and distribution activities are liberalized by generalizing network access to third parties and the exclusive use thereof will not be guaranteed in terms of ownership. Hence, it affirms that the concept of utility has lost validity and is not an overstatement, inasmuch as its inclusion in the law is more a prejudice than a way to guarantee a service that has had a significant participation of the private sector throughout history.

V. Access to Networks

256. One of the main difficulties to be solved by a regulation that intends to implement a free-competition policy, particularly in network economies or industries, is the access conditions to such networks, mainly because there is a company with a dominant position in the sale market of the final good, in addition to controlling the supply factor of an essential input for its potential competitors. The problem reaches its peak when the supply of the final product requires access to the existing network infrastructures for distribution and marketing thereof.

257. Based on the experience accumulated in the development of the powerful domestic market in Europe, it becomes crucial to reduce the risk that dominant positions and abusive behaviours may arise, particularly among the owners of the power transmission and distribution lines. In this respect, transparent, non-discriminatory fees must be guaranteed to facilitate free network access, thus ensuring protection of users' rights.

258. Consequently, free access to the transmission and distribution network has become the condition required to establish a competitive regulatory framework; otherwise, the competition would be hampered, as no free energy transactions among the operators intervening in electric service activities may be developed.

259. Aware of such regulatory need, the Venezuelan legislator has established that the transportation capacity of power transmission and distribution networks must be available for those carrying out electric service activities, unless there are technical reasons preventing it. The legislator attributed to the National Commission of Electric Power the obligation to guarantee third parties free access to power transmission and distribution systems; to the companies, the duty to allow such access, under risk of being penalized; and to the National Commission of Electric Power, the task of issuing regulations to guarantee free network access.

260. However, we have noticed that Article 17 of the regulation of the LOSE offers a different perspective by providing that the agents wanting to connect to the transmission network will have the burden to prove such feasibility. First, they must request the technical qualification of the Commission, after having heard the opinion of the Centre, and second, they must prove that the facilities subject to the requirement meet the standards inherent to this type of constructions. Based on the experience from other liberalization processes, the owner of the network usually tries to hamper access to his competitor through different resources and obstacles; but, if that requesting access also has to face additional burden, the result may be the strengthening of the dominant positions of the owners of power transmission and distribution networks to the detriment of the competition.

261. Another essential element to regulate access to power transmission and distribution networks is the establishment of a methodology to set the amounts payable by third parties. To date, there are three ways to reach agreements: the negotiated method adopted by the LOHG in Article 10, the sole-purchaser method, and the regulated method through the setting of rates by the regulatory entity empowered for such purposes. In this regard, it is inferred from Article 17 of the LOSE that the method adopted is the method of setting fees, which will correspond to the Executive Branch through the Ministry of Energy and Mines (MEM – *Ministerio de Energía y Minas*) and the Ministry of Production and Commerce with objective, transparent, and non-discriminatory criteria.

262. The methodology selected must consider a series of basic principles that guarantee the necessary balance among the operators in the electric service. Article 79 of the LOSE provides that the rate schedule must be established under the criteria of economic efficiency, rational use of energy, financial adequacy, neutrality, stability in time, simplicity, and transparency. This rule does, in turn, link together with Article 88 of the regulation that expands the criteria to set fees for the use of transmission and distribution networks as follows: minimum reasonable service cost for users, bearing in mind that reasonable differences may exist in the cost of different services (provision method, geographic location of user, distribution area patterns, level of demand as to quality of the supply, adoption of loss-reduction programmes); economic approach for the location of power generation and power loads in order to prevent network overload; and promoting the companies efficiency. In short, it is about the transmission and distribution means in efficient operating conditions that a reasonable profitability comparable with activities of similar risk may be obtained.

VI. Separation of Legal and Accounting Activities

263. In order to reach real competition in the electricity sector and prevent dominant positions in regulated activities, it is necessary to separate legal and accounting matters in liberalized and regulated electricity activities.

264. The main reason to separate activities is to facilitate and promote free competition in the liberalized segments, especially if all the operators acting in these market trenches do not manage in turn network. Otherwise, the vertically integrated undertaking can apply cross-subsidies, so that it counteracts the losses incurred in other activities with the gains from activities developed in a non-competitive framework, by applying predatory pricing to hamper the survival of rival companies. Consequently, if the vertical disintegration does not take place, the regulatory entity must make sure that the company in charge of non-liberalized activities gives the same treatment to its competitors with respect to the treatment given to its own company.

265. The legal separation does not constitute on its own an efficient defence against the different forms of anticompetitive behaviour. It allows for more transparent assets and costs and facilitates the control of profitability and management of operations in the network field. The accounting separation allows for more transparency in financial flows only, hence the need to combine and apply both systems. It is important, however, to distinguish between such legal separation and ownership unbundling. Legal separation does not imply a change of ownership of assets, while the ownership unbundling, in addition to such inherent obligation, entails legal separation and prohibition to organize holdings or a parent company.

266. In this sense, the criteria establish that, in order to ensure effective and non-discriminatory network access, it is appropriate to operate the power distribution and transportation networks through legally separated entities where vertically integrated undertakings are accepted. It is also appropriate that the power transportation and distribution network operators have effective decision-making rights with respect to assets necessary to maintain, operate, and develop networks when the assets concerned are owned and operated by vertically integrated undertakings. Hence, a non-discriminatory decision-making process should be ensured through organizational measures regarding the independence of the decision-makers in charge.

267. Article 6 of the LOSE provides for the vertical segregation of activities and the legal separation between regulated and free activities, so that they cannot be jointly carried out by the same company, but through shareholding in another company, provided that they are different companies, as established in Article 123 of the regulation of the LOSE, as to the organization of a parent company owning such companies. In this case, the holding can exercise shareholding duties only in the electricity sector, thus guaranteeing complete operational, administrative, and financial autonomy of its electric utilities.

268. Conversely, the same Article 6 ejusdem allows electric utilities to use transmission or distribution facilities for non-electrical purposes, for which they are required to have a separate accounting only to facilitate the application of assets, liabilities, income, costs, and expenses in connection with the new use. Thus, the electric utilities with no need to create new legal companies (legal separation) may venture into other mercantile activities, as telecommunications, for instance, without having to make new investments. It remains to be seen how this authorization by the LOSE may affect the service quality provided to the domestic electricity market and even the effective control that the regulatory entities of both activities must exercise to prevent abuse of dominant positions in the natural market of electric utilities and the new activities to be developed.

269. It cannot be inferred from the Law that there is a strong will to achieve the legal separation and the accounting separation at the same time. Article 108 of the LOSE was drafted under that approach, as it offers the companies the prerogative of making an accounting separation while not making the legal separation in order to facilitate the application of assets, liabilities, income, costs, and expenses of each company. In addition, this agrees with the recent suggestions from both the public and the private sectors. Since the Vice Minister of Energy recognizes the delay by the Government in the electricity sector due to the repeated deferred application of the Law, he deems it necessary to decide on a legal separation, but not an accounting separation of the companies. In addition, he said that 'the Law was intended for a sector that largely differs from the current sector.' He indicated that the text provides for the creation of a wholesale market on a 'sufficient agents' basis and argued that this resort 'is nonsense', considering that 86% of the electrical installed capacity is managed by the State. Hence, 'There is no room for competition among State-owned companies. The gathering of forces is required to improve the quality of the service provided.'

Chapter 2. Production

§1. Sources of Electricity Generation

270. The electricity system in Venezuela has been historically characterized by the predominance of hydroelectricity in power generation, mainly due to the abundance of water resources in the country. This fact promoted the development of power generation plants to make the most of the amazing flow of the Caroní River and its slope and rocky and compact riverbed, which provide support to large structures. In fact, four hydroelectric power stations have been built across the river.

271. Over time, however, the expansion of electricity generation capacity has increasingly relied on the exploitation of Venezuela's fossil fuel resources – primarily fuel oil and natural gas – rather than the development of clean and sustainable energy alternatives. Wind power, for instance, has experienced only marginal progress. As illustrated in Table 1, between 2006 and 2013, thermal generation capacity nearly doubled, while hydroelectric capacity also increased, bringing both sources to roughly equivalent levels of installed capacity by 2013. Nevertheless, this expansion did not translate into improved system reliability: although hydropower remained prominent on paper, its actual output and availability declined sharply during this period.

272. By 2020, official data indicated a total installed capacity of 36,000 MW: 17,000 MW from hydroelectric sources and 19,000 MW from thermal sources. By 2024, however, the situation had deteriorated significantly. While installed capacity remains formally unchanged, operational capacity has collapsed. Only about 8,000 MW of hydroelectric power and 2,000 MW of thermal power are currently available – amounting to approximately 10,000 MW of effective capacity. This falls short of the current national demand of around 11,500 MW, resulting in a persistent structural energy deficit. It is also worth noting that Venezuela's peak historical demand reached 18,600 MW in 2013. A particularly telling indicator of the system's collapse is the near-total disappearance of electricity consumption by the Guayana Basic Industries, whose demand has fallen from approximately 3,000 MW to nearly zero in recent years.

Table 1 Installed Generation Capacity[96]

Year	*Thermal Capacity (MW)*	*Hydroelectric Capacity (MW)*	*Total Installed Capacity (MW)*	*Remarks*
2006	7,619	7,978	15,597	Hydropower was still predominant in the energy matrix.
2013	14,806	14,700	29,506	Thermal capacity equalled hydro; total installed capacity nearly doubled since 2006, but hydro output fell sharply.
2020	19,000 (installed)	17,000 (installed)	36,000	Officially installed capacity; not reflective of operational availability.
2024	2,000 (available)	8,000 (available)	10,000 (effective capacity)	Only 28% of total capacity is functional; current demand (~11,500 MW) exceeds supply.

§2. Power Generation Infrastructure

273. As previously mentioned, electricity generation in Venezuela has historically been predominantly hydroelectric. Until 2010, more than 60% of the country's electricity was generated from this source, due to the abundance of water resources and a hydroelectric expansion policy focused primarily in the southeastern region. However, this dominance has been progressively undermined by operational deterioration, lack of maintenance, and the suspension of key projects such as the Manuel Piar Hydroelectric Plant (Tocoma).

274. The Venezuelan hydroelectric complex is concentrated in the lower Caroní River basin, in the state of Bolívar, and has historically constituted the backbone of the National Power System (Sistema Eléctrico Nacional, SEN). It comprises the following plants: (1) The Simón Bolívar Hydroelectric Plant (Guri), with an installed capacity of approximately 10,200 MW, is one of the largest in the world. However,

96. *Ministerio del Poder Popular para la Energía Eléctrica, Memoria y Cuenta 2012, Tomo I, Caracas,* 2013, pp. 393–409, available at: https://transparenciave.org/wp-content/uploads/2016/07/Memoria_y_Cuenta_2012_Tomo_I.pdf (accessed 12 Jun. 2025).

only fourteen of its twenty turbines are currently operational, significantly limiting its effective availability (Electricista en Turmero, 2023). (2) The Francisco de Miranda Hydroelectric Plant (Caruachi), with an installed capacity of 2,160 MW, has been in operation since 2003. (3) The Manuel Piar Hydroelectric Plant (Tocoma), projected to contribute 2,160 MW to the SEN, began construction in 2002 and, following multiple delays and corruption allegations, remains non-operational as of 2025 (Transparencia Venezuela, 2021).

275. When fully operational, these plants generate fuel savings equivalent to approximately 550,000 barrels of oil per day, according to CORPOELEC estimates. Outside the Caroní River axis, other hydroelectric plants are located in the Andes and the Llanos regions: (1) In the state of Barinas, the José Antonio Páez Hydroelectric Plant (120 MW) and the Juan A. Rodríguez Domínguez Plant (40 MW) stand out. (2) In the states of Táchira and Mérida lies the Uribante-Caparo Hydroelectric Complex, officially named Leonardo Ruiz Pineda, comprising the San Agatón, La Colorada, and La Vueltosa (Fabricio Ojeda) plants. Although its installed capacity exceeds 1,000 MW, its effective availability has been severely affected by technical problems and lack of sustained investment (GRZ, 2023).

276. Venezuela also possesses a widely distributed thermal generation park, with major plants such as Planta Centro (2,000 MW, Carabobo), the Tacoa Complex (1,700 MW, Vargas), Ramón Laguna (660 MW, Zulia), and Josefa Camejo (450 MW, Falcón), among others. However, various investigations and specialized press reports agree that nearly 90% of installed thermal capacity is currently out of service due to prolonged breakdowns, shortages of spare parts, and lack of maintenance (El Pitazo, 2024).

277. Following the declaration of an electrical emergency in 2009, and within the framework of international cooperation agreements – particularly with Cuba – approximately twenty-six distributed generation plants were installed in various regions of the country. These units, connected to local distribution networks, were intended to contribute around 3% of total national generation. However, their effective contribution has been marginal, with many rendered inoperative due to fuel shortages or structural failures (Grupo Ricardo Zuloaga, 2012).

278. As for non-conventional renewable energies, development has been incipient. Despite Venezuela's significant solar and wind potential, progress has been limited. The National Electric System Plan envisions the integration of 613 MW of renewable sources by 2033 – a figure that remains modest in light of the current energy gap (Mordor Intelligence, 2024).

Table 2 Selected Thermoelectric Plants in Venezuela (Installed Capacity)

Plant	*Year*	*Capacity (MW)*	*Location*
Planta Centro	1980	2,000	Carabobo
Tacoa Complex	1980	1,700	Vargas
Ramón Laguna	1940	660	Zulia
Zulia I–IV	2003–2010	1,520	Zulia
Josefa Camejo	2009	450	Falcón
Argimiro Gabaldón	2009	40	Lara
Ezequiel Zamora	2013	150	Guárico
Alberto Lovera	2009	300	Anzoátegui
Nueva Esparta	2009	200	Nueva Esparta
Cabrutica	2013	300	Anzoátegui
Cumaná	2010	450	Sucre
Luisa Cáceres de Arismendi	2011	30	Nueva Esparta
Las Hernández	2010	15	Nueva Esparta

Source: CORPOELEC, compiled from historical records and public reports.

Note: Most of these facilities are currently out of service or operating below capacity.
Note: The data reflect information available as of April 2025. Installed capacity figures do not necessarily match available or operational capacity, and this analysis emphasizes the distinction between both.

279. Following the declaration of an electrical emergency in 2009, and within the framework of international cooperation agreements – particularly with Cuba – approximately twenty-six distributed generation plants were installed across various regions of the country. These units, which were connected to local distribution networks, were expected to contribute around 3% of the country's total electricity generation. However, their actual contribution has been minimal, as many have become non-operational due to fuel shortages or structural deficiencies (Grupo Ricardo Zuloaga, 2012).

280. Additionally, due to the prolonged energy crisis, many businesses, commercial establishments, and even households have resorted to installing private thermoelectric generators. According to a quarterly survey conducted by the Venezuelan Confederation of Industries (Conindustria), by the end of 2023, approximately 80.5% of businesses were using gasoline or diesel-powered generators, while another 9% relied on natural gas generators as alternative sources to cope with frequent blackouts. Although these solutions temporarily mitigate power shortages, they also result in higher fossil fuel consumption and increased carbon emissions, thereby exacerbating environmental degradation.

281. It is also important to highlight the difficulty in accessing updated official information regarding Venezuela's energy sector. The Ministry of Popular Power for Electric Energy (MPPEE), traditionally in charge of publishing official data, has not released comprehensive reports in recent years. This lack of transparency significantly limits access to reliable information. As a result, assessments of the country's electricity sector often rely on independent research, international media, and non-governmental organizations (NGOs), all of which have consistently reported the severity and recurrence of power outages nationwide.

§3. Investments to Increase Thermal Generation: A Questionable Decision

282. The process of increasing the installed capacity for electricity generation, particularly thermal generation through plants for distributed generation, has been questioned by experts, academics, and former company technicians that made up the national electricity sector, due to the huge investments that do not correspond to the quality and availability of the service.

283. A study prepared by the Ricardo Zuluaga Group identifies two historic moments (Figure 4)[97] in the process of constructing the national electricity system: The first covers forty-eight years, from 1950 to 1998. During this period, total accumulated public and private investment was USD 48.254 billion, to install 19,696 MW, which meant that the estimated investment per MW was close to USD 2.45 million.

97. Grupo Zuloaga, *La crisis del Sistema Eléctrico*, https://app.box.com/s/w186rim89v81upqnhmd1 (accessed 2 Apr. 2025).

Figure 4 Cumulative Investment in Venezuela's National Electricity System (1950–1998)

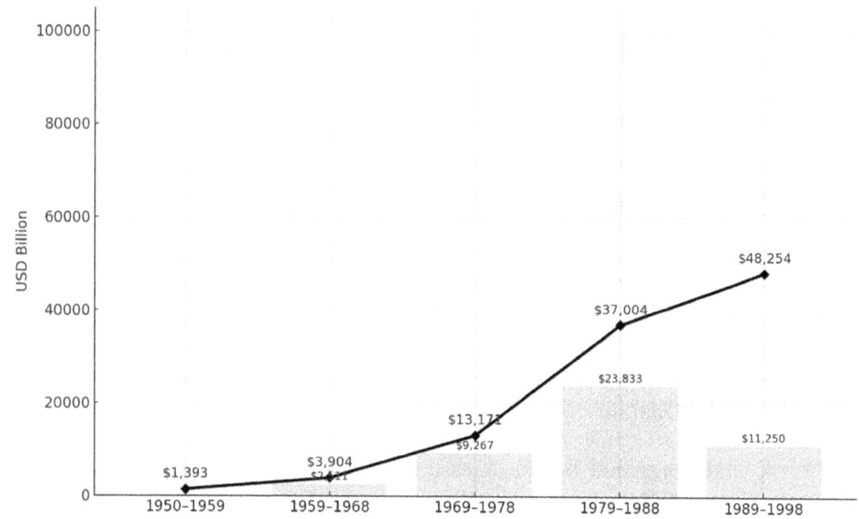

284. The second extends fourteen years, during the times of the 'Bolivarian Revolution', from 1999 to 2012 (Figure 5).[98] During these years, an 'ocean' of more than USD 94 billion was allocated to the electricity sector to install 13,335 MW, with an average cost per MW of just over 7.0 million dollars, tripling the price of the MW benchmark for the first period.

98. *Ibid.*

Figure 5 Cumulative Annual Investment in Venezuela's Electricity Sector (1999–2012)

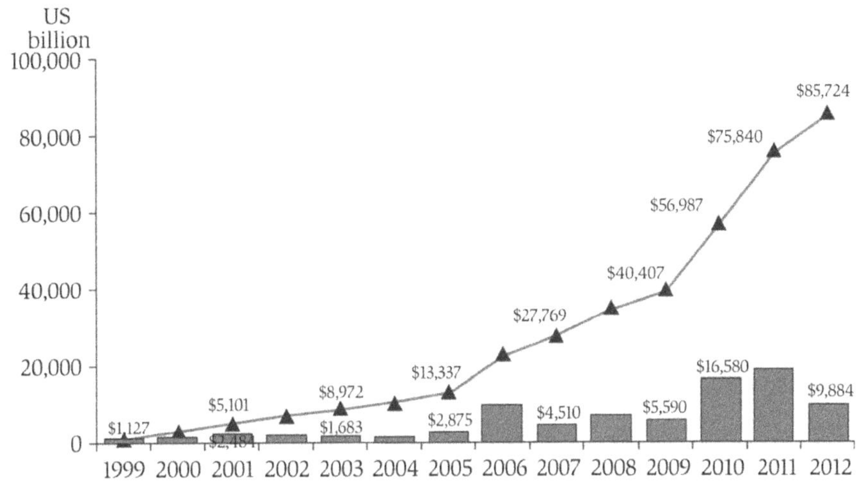

285. Given the magnitude of the aforementioned investments, questions arise about the causes of the crisis in the electric system. This aspect will be approached from the point of view of the legal reforms introduced in the electricity sector, with the purpose of understanding the process of involution of the SEN, which occurred over the past twenty years in Venezuela.

286. Experts agree that a comprehensive reform of the legal framework is essential to attract both national and international private capital and to diversify energy sources toward renewables such as solar and wind. According to Rodríguez (2025),[99] the state monopoly held by Corpoelec – established in 2007 – has not yielded positive results. Therefore, the regulatory framework must be restructured to open the market to new players willing to invest in renewable energy, including solar farms, concentrated solar power, and wind parks. Furthermore, current subsidies limit the revenue required to maintain and modernize the electricity infrastructure, making it urgent to adjust electricity tariffs – especially in the industrial and commercial sectors – in order to ensure sustainable income (Rodríguez, 2025). Without these legal and structural reforms, Venezuela risks perpetuating an unsustainable model that directly hinders its economic and social development.

---

99. J.C. Rodríguez, , *Observatorio Venezolano de Servicios Públicos: Crisis del sistema eléctrico.* Caracas: OVSP, 2025.

Chapter 3. Exploitation

§1. Legal Framework for the Nationalization from 2007

287. The political and economic reforms implemented since 1999 affected in a determinant manner the electric power sector in Venezuela. The legal framework that had supported and allowed the sector to develop with the participation of public and private companies in a free-competition environment would take an unexpected, radical turn in the opposite direction.

288. The economic model promoted by the government, defined as 'socialist', deprioritized the private sector, relegating it to a marginal role (Rodríguez, 2025). Under this model, the State is positioned as the sole driver of social transformation, while private initiative is confined to a narrow range of permitted activities. This approach led to the reservation of strategic sectors – such as oil, telecommunications, and electricity – under exclusive State control.

289. The transformation of the electricity sector followed three main steps: (1) nationalization of private companies that were participating in the generation, transmission, distribution, and commercialization activities; (2) centralization of all the processes under the direction of the MPPEE and a single national governing company: the CORPOELEC; and (3) redesign of the Electric System and Service through the introduction of the following paradigms and criteria: (1) Universal access to the electric service. (2) Reserve and Control of the State. (3) Socialist Management Model. These three steps have been under development with the enactment of the Organic Law on the Reorganization of the Electric Sector of 2007 and the Organic Law for the Electric System and Service of 2010, whose fundamental principles will be developed in this chapter.

§2. Nationalization: Privatization to Nationalization

290. The experience of nationalizing private property or activities to be exercised exclusively by the State in the electric sector is not a new phenomenon in Venezuela. In fact, in 1974, as a consequence of the 'oil crisis' that spectacularly increased crude oil prices, the first great wave of nationalizations began and extended over the Oil and Steel Industries, and some measures of this same nature were taken in the Electric Industry. In effect, the government of Carlos Andrés Pérez at the time, by means of Decree No. 62, established that new direct foreign investments would not be allowed in the generation, transmission, distribution, and selling of electricity. Furthermore, it established that the existing companies had to offer for sale at least 80% of their shares to be acquired by national investors. This decision was confirmed by Decree 2.031, dated 3 February 1977 (Article 1). Although in this case it was not a direct reserve to the State, but rather to national companies and investors, it represented indeed a strong limitation on the participation of the private sector.

291. As a consequence of this regulation, close to 30% of the private operating capacity for generation went into the hands of the public sector. In distribution, the participation of the private sector went from 45% in 1970 to 28% in 1980. Maracaibo, the second city of the country, was transferred to the public sector, just to mention some examples. Refer to Table 3.[100]

Table 3 Public and Private Sector Participation: Generation and Distribution of Electricity, 1970–1980

Table 3-A Generation of Electricity: Public and Private Participation (1970–1980)

Year	*Total Generation (GWh)*	*State*	*Private*	*% Private*
1970	10,441	5,991	4,450	44%
1975	16,674	11,558	5,116	31%
1980	29,070	25,529	4,544	16%

Table 3-B Distribution of Electricity: Public and Private Participation (1970–1980)

Year	*Total Distribution (GWh)*	*State*	*Private*	*% Private*
1970	8,447	4,684	3,764	45%
1975	13,822	7,899	5,924	43%
1980	21,780	15,682	6,098	28%

292. It is important to point out that the aforementioned Decree referred to foreign companies, in accordance with the policy imposed in the framework of the Cartagena Agreement, through which the Andean countries restricted the entry of foreign capital in the area. Consequently, private companies organized with national capital, such as Eleval, Calife, and Elecar, were not affected by the nationalization policies.

293. A new scenario came into sight as of 1999 in a context of low oil prices, which were around USD 20 per barrel. A new model characterized by deregulation and economic opening, rationalization, and privatization of public companies was proposed. In the electric sector, the reforms that were fostered had little success, although a legal framework for this purpose was approved and framed within the Law on Privatizations of March 1992 and the progressive opening of the sector to free competition.

100. Rodolfo Tellería Villapol, *Historia del Desarrollo del Servicio Eléctrico en Venezuela,* 1880–1998, CODELECTRA (2000), pp. 212–213, available at: https://codelectra.org/wp-content/uploads/2021/04/Rodolfo_Telleria_Villapol_Libro.pdf (last accessed 10 Jun. 2025).

294. The economic situation, worsened by a severe political crisis since 1989, hindered the advancement of the measures adopted to transform the electric sector. Some events took place, such as the so-called Caracazo (1989), a popular unrest against the package of adjusting measures imposed by President Carlos Andrés Pérez; a military coup (1992) led by Hugo Chávez; the dismissal of the President of the Republic by the National Congress on the grounds of corruption (1993); and the election, by the National Congress, of a new President of the Republic (1993), who governed with the National Congress against his government. Actually, the only company privatized was Seneca, in the State of Nueva Esparta, which represented less than 2% of the total subscribers of the country.

295. A second nationalization wave took place in Venezuela as of 2007, coinciding with the largest stage of high oil prices in the entire history of the Oil Industry. This event, without any doubt, gave greater decision-making power. In this stage, which lasted from 2007 to 2010, far-reaching decisions were made. In the electric sector, the State acquired all the shares of the private companies, which represented 10% of the transmission and distribution networks of the country and close to 20% of the generation capacity.[101]

§3. Centralization of the Electricity National System

296. The concentration by the State of all the companies of the electric sector via the approval by the President of the Republic of the Decree-Law for the Organic Law on the Reorganization of the Energy Service (LORSE – *Ley Orgánica de Reorganización del Servicio Eléctrico*) of 2007 laid the grounds for the process of State centralization and control of the entire electric industry in Venezuela (Rodríguez, 2025; Caracas Chronicles, 2019).[102] In order to achieve such goal, the LORSE created a single company, CORPOELEC, S.A., attached to the Ministry of the People's Power for Energy and Petroleum, which is responsible for 'carrying out the activities of generation, transmission, distribution, and commercialization of electric power and energy' (Article 2). The entirety of the capital of CORPOELEC is subscribed by the Bolivarian Republic of Venezuela, through the Ministry of the People's Power for Energy and Petroleum (Article 3).

297. Conversely, the LORSE decreed the immediate merge of CORPOELEC with all the public companies of the public sector, such as ENELVEN, ENAGEN, CADAFE, CVG, EDELCA, ENELCO, and ENELBAR (Article 6), and all private companies, subsidiaries or affiliates that, at the moment, were in the process of acquisition by the Venezuelan State. To this effect, 'they must transfer all their assets and liabilities to the latter', which 'shall be the Universal successor of the rights and obligations of the former' (Article 7).

---

101. *See* Ch. 1. General Background.
102. J.C. Rodríguez, *Observatorio Venezolano de Servicios Públicos: Crisis del Sistema Eléctrico*, Caracas: OVSP, 2025.

298. Moreover, the LORSE, in Article 12, intends to empty the municipal and State powers of their competence for the rendering of the electric power service, by establishing 'that its regulation and rendering exceed the municipal and state level'. Such action against the municipalities broadens in the same article when it establishes that the activities of generation, transmission, distribution, and selling of electric power and energy shall not be subject to the payment of State and municipal taxes, given that such matter is, by class and nature, under the competence of the National Power.

299. Undoubtedly, this element constitutes a fallback without precedents that is framed to substitute the Constitutional State for a Communal State, in contradiction with the Constitution of 1999 in force. This way, it not only consolidates a system of management of the centralized electric service but it also builds an unconstitutional organization and a 'socialist' regime that fail to recognize the functioning of the Constitutional State foreseen in the Constitution of 1999 to be replaced by a Communal State outside the institutional framework that emanates from the representative democracy.[103]

§4. The Socialist Management Model

300. As already explained, until now in Venezuela, a legal architecture has been built to substitute the de facto Constitutional State for a Socialist, Centralized State designated as a Socialist State for the People's Power, or Communal State dependent on the National Power. In this context and aiming at consolidating such purpose, in June 2010, the LOSSE was approved, taking an additional step towards the advances introduced in the LORSE of 2007, which centralized the National Electric Service. In this sense, we will discuss below the most relevant aspects of this law, which represents a paradigmatic proposal in its style, where the view of universal access, the electric service as public service under the reserve and control of the State, and the socialist management model stand out.

I. Universal Access

301. Universal access or service may be defined as the right that every person has to the supply of electricity in a continuous manner and at reasonable prices. Article 6 of the LOSSE acknowledges universal access to the electric service, which shall be guaranteed by the State to all persons who have the duty to make a rational and efficient use of the same.

103. *See* Ch. 1. General Introduction, Ch. 1 §1. Political System, and Ch. 4 §3 Communal State Regime.

302. According to the data obtained from the World Bank, Venezuela is ranked, along with Chile, among the countries with the highest level of access to the electric service (95.5%), above the Latin American average (73.7%). Nevertheless, universal access represents one stage of the electric service system, measured not only by the infrastructure installed but also by the true and material possibility of having electricity available as a sine qua non to affirm that it effectively exists. This is important when evaluating the quality of the service. In Venezuela, the existence of a severe crisis in the supply of electricity is well known. We may infer from the LOSSE that users are responsible to a great degree when it imposes in Article 6 that they have the duty to make a rational and efficient use of the service, taking for granted that the service is in fact available. This is not negative per se. However, it may just be the opposite case; in other words, that the service may not be available or that the rendering of the same is neither efficient nor continuous. It is here where the LOSSE does not establish a regulation for the protection of the user before what may be a non-compliance by the provider to the safe access to the universal service.

303. Article 26 of the LOSSE authorizes the Ministry of the People's Power with competence on the matter to guarantee the protection of the rights and interests of the users and meet electricity demand. In Article 27, the law grants competence to the governing entity to lay down the rules to regulate the relationship between the operator and provider of the service and the users, in order to give timely and adequate answer to users' complaints and solve other conflicts submitted for its consideration, in accordance with such Law, its Regulations, and the rest of the applicable rules.

304. Therefore, we are facing a system that leaves users unprotected before a governing entity that undertakes all the functions. On the one hand, such governing entity generates, transmits, distributes, and commercializes electricity, and on the other hand, it acts as the governing entity, regulating and defending users' rights. This, without any doubt, is a contradiction and a fallback before the advances achieved by the LOSE of 2001. In effect, that law created the National Commission for Electric Energy (CNEE – *Comisión Nacional de Energía Eléctrica)* as a decentralized entity which, although attached to the Ministry with competence in the matter, had its own and independent patrimonial property, with functional, administrative, and financial autonomy to exercise its competences. Nonetheless, what matters most is that its principles were oriented towards the protecting the rights and interests of the users; promoting the efficiency, reliability, and safety of the supply of electricity; supervisinging that the entire electricity demand is met; and, in short, guaranteeing compliance with the rights and obligations of the agents of the electric service.

305. In the Comparative Law, the EU has developed a regulation for the protection of the rights of users that is mandatory for the providers of the electric service. For instance, it establishes the right to sign a contract specifying the following: services rendered, level of quality proposed, type of maintenance service proposed; how to obtain updated information of the applicable fees and maintenance expenses;

term of the contract, conditions for renewing and terminating the services, cancellation of the contract without costs; compensation and reimbursement agreements applicable if the levels of quality contracted are not met, including erroneous and delayed billing; and a method for bringing an action for conflict settlement, information on the rights of the consumers, including information related to the complaint process, and all such information delivered clearly through invoices or the Internet sites of the electricity companies. This regulation in the law of the EU is part of the commitment that State Members have undertaken to guarantee that all clients enjoy the right to a universal service in their territory, that is to say, the right to the supply of electricity with a given quality and at reasonable prices, easily and clearly comparable, transparent, and non-discriminatory.

II. Reserve (Monopoly) on the Electricity Sector

306. The debate on whether the State must reserve or not the dominion and control of the rendering of the electric service has remained linked to the debate on its classification as a strategic public service of national interest. The doctrine of French Administrative Law offers an eclectic conceptualization where the public and private sectors share these activities, defining them as 'those of relevant general interest that may be met directly by the State or private individuals under the control of the public power' (Brown, 1998).[104] Under this conception, the State keeps a leading role in the control of the efficient rendering of the service, although it may assign its competences to entities or private individuals. This doctrine was adopted by the Venezuelan legal system and included in the Constitution of 1999, Article 113, as public services reserved to the State, exclusive but not excluding, assignable or grantable to individuals.

307. Nevertheless, the enactment of the LOSSE in 2010 has caused a significant change in the objective of the Constituent Members of 1999, with the aim of preventing the private sector from participating in said activities, not because the electric service is a public service, which still is, but rather because the LORSE has determined so in Article 8, declaring the exclusive reserve to the State of the activities of Generation, Transmission, Distribution, and User Service (former commercialization), as well as the activity of Electric System Dispatch.

308. This regulation is openly in opposition to the spirit of the Constitution of 1999, the doctrine and the legal tradition in Venezuela, where both the public and private sectors have shared, and even competed for, the rendering of the electric service. The dominion and control of the State is part of the design of a new management system called the socialist management model.

104. Brown, Lionel Neville, John Bell & Jean-Michel Galabert. *French Administrative Law*. Oxford University Press, 1998.

III. Socialist Management Model

309. Pursuant to Article 9 of the LOSSE, the socialist management model must be governed by the National Economic and Social Development Plan, which represents a transition programme towards socialism and the radicalization of the protagonist participatory democracy. In this model, according to the LOSSE, all the activities of the National Electric System must be oriented towards meeting the needs for electricity supply to the entire population and guaranteeing the leading and co-responsible participation of the workers of the operator and provider of the service and the users, as well as the organizations of the People's Power. The State is responsible for guaranteeing that the rendering of the electric service is performed under the criteria enumerated in Article 9 of the LOSSE (Figure 6). To assess the novelty or originality of the socialist model, we will compare the criteria set forth in the LOSSE with the principles established in the 2001 LOSE, highlighting the similarities and differences between the two frameworks.

Figure 6 Comparison of Service Provision Principles in the 2001 LOSE and the Socialist LOSSE Framework

Criteria LOSSE 2010, Article 9	Principles LOSE 2001 (derogated), Article 2
Equality	Economic balance
Continuity	Reliability
Flexibility	Efficiency
Integrality	Quality
Impartiality	Equity
Transparency	Solidarity
Participation	Non-discrimination
Reliability	Transparency
Efficiency	Lowest cost possible
Co-responsibility	Rational use
Solidarity	*Efficient use of resources*
Equity	*Preservation of environment*
Economic and financial sustainability	*Protection of the users*

310. We have underlined some criteria in the first column which do not appear in the LOSE of 2001 and that may mark a substantial difference between both models. The continuity criterion, although it is not in the second column, was considered by the legislator of 2001, in Article 14, and is associated with the security of the supply. Likewise, we underlined, in the second column, the efficient use of the resources, which the legislator of 2010 indicates in Article 55 as the optimal use of the resources for the benefit of the users.

311. With regard to the preservation of the environment in the second column, the legislator of 2010 establishes it in Article 27 as a competence of the governing entity of the system, which must protect against the contamination of the environment in the activities of the National Electric System.

312. In connection with the protection of users in the second column, such criterion is regulated by both legal instruments in a very similar manner, making a distinction related to the management model. While in the LOSE, the competent ministry had the authority to provide timely and adequate responses to users' complaints and resolve other conflicts submitted for its consideration, in the LOSSE, this competence is attributed to an independent entity, as was the case with the CNEE.Similarly, while in the LOSSE, the administration of the sanctions and fines correspond to the same entity, divided between the service operator and provider as the first instance and the Ministry of the People's Power with competence on the electric energy matter as the second instance, in the LOSE, the competence was attributed to the CNEE, before which it was possible to file an action for reconsideration, exhausting the administrative via, and its actions were appealable before the jurisdictional entities, without the need to previously exercise the aforementioned action. The current model, by concentrating all the powers in the same entity, leaves users with no space and is subject to the will of a single governing entity of the system.

313. With reference to the criteria of flexibility, integrality, participation, and co-responsibility, it is important to highlight that the first two are not developed in the LOSSE, and the other two criteria are aligned with the objectives of the National Economic and Social Development Plan, which seeks to establish a socialist management model, not only for the electric service but also for the political regime in general. Specifically, participation is regulated in Articles 36, 37, and 38, and it refers to the active incorporation of the organizations of the People's Power (communal councils, energy technical roundtables, cooperatives, higher education institutions, research centres, workers of the service operator and provider, among others) in activities related to the electric service. These entities, once they are trained, will give support to the Ministry of the People's Power with competence on the matter regarding the supervision of the quality of the electric service and cooperation for the training, education, and participation in programmes for the rational and efficient use of the electric energy. Likewise, they will be required by the service operator and provider for the readings and consumption of electricity and for the execution of projects to adapt, expand, and improve low-voltage networks.

314. With respect to co-responsibility, aside from representing one of the criteria considered essential for the socialist management of the electric service stipulated in Article 9, it also appears as part of the governing principles for the rendering of the electric service indicated in Article 9, both of the LOSSE. Social co-responsibility is related to the scope of planning and authorizes the Ministry of the People's Power with competence on the matter to request, pursuant to Article 19 of the LOSSE, information from the workers of the service operator and provider, users, municipalities, organizations of the People's Power, and the rest of the people involved in the national electric sector and any other entity it may deem necessary for the purpose of formulating the National Electric System Development Plan. In short, both criteria are in line with the project for building a Communal State, as it has been discussed in Chapters 1 and 2 of this work.

Chapter 4. Transmission

315. Venezuela has a transmission system that interconnects the HPP of the region of Guayana, State of Bolivar, with the consumption centres located both in the region and in the rest of the country. Transmission and supply are carried out through a system that operates at 765 kV, 400 kV, and 230 kV. The system extends to four points located in the States of Apure and Táchira to exchange electric power with Colombia and to one point to interconnect with Brazil through the States of Bolívar and Roraima, as shown below.

316. In accordance with the report of the Electric Power Ministry 2012 referred hereto, most of the power losses were mainly due to faults of the transmission, distribution, and marketing systems, and the losses due to problems caused by illegal electricity connections by residential and commercial users are in second place. The reasons that could explain the weaknesses in the transmission systems may be inferred from the Annual Report. The maintenance and operation plan for 2012 was fulfilled to 56.65% only. As to increasing the availability of the existing systems, the plan was fulfilled to 20.95%. The official information indicates that CORPOELEC incorporated only five new lines and substations, ranging between 400 kV and 765 kV. The plans for lower voltage lines were not fulfilled since only one out of twenty-five projects was carried out.

317. Most of the current transmission lines of Venezuela were built in the 1970s. They had a useful life expectancy of twenty-five to thirty years; hence, they must be replaced.[105] However, such lines transport much more electricity than when they were built, thus generating bottlenecks and service interruptions. As evidenced in Table 4,[106] the expansion of the transmission system came to a halt and has practically remained unchanged over the last fourteen years. The 230 kv lines have increased, but not in tune with the demand (less than 2,000 km/1,242.7 mi). This situation is particularly serious and has undoubtedly contributed, in one way or the other, to the electrical crisis currently experienced in Venezuela. Figure 7 shows the transmission system's scope in a very general way.[107]

105. Diana Colorado, *Diagnóstico del Estado Actual del Sistema de Transmisión Eléctrico en Venezuela*, 26, available at: http://repositoriodigital.uma.edu.ve:8080/jspui/bitstream/123456789/581/1/TEG_EPG4_2010.pdf (accessed 13 Nov. 2025).

106. Nelson Hernández, '*Venezuela: Situación Actual de la Interrelación Sector Hidrocarburos y Sector Eléctrico*,' *La Pluma Candente*, 17 Oct. 2018, available at: https://plumacandente.blogspot.com/2018/10/venezuela-situacion-actual-de-la.html (last accessed 3 Apr. 2025).

107. *Comisión Nacional de Electricidad de Venezuela, Informe sobre el Estado del Sistema de Transmisión Eléctrica en Venezuela,* 2024, p. 45.

Table 4 Electricity Transmission Network (km)

230 kv	*400 kv*	*765 kv*			
1998	2012	1998	2012	1998	2012
5,840	7,563	2,949	3,606	2,083	2,236

Figure 7 National Transmission Grid Map of Venezuela

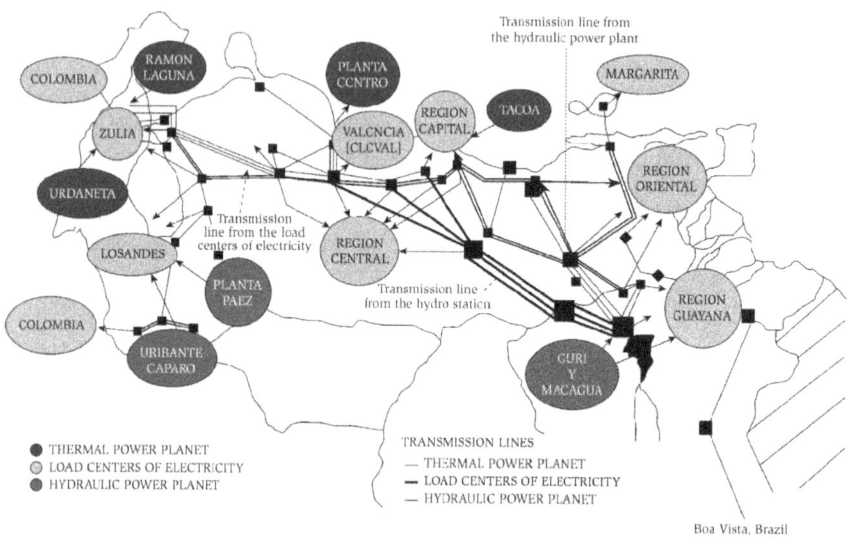

318. In the international sphere, Venezuela's electrical interconnections with Colombia and Brazil have played a significant role in the country's transmission system, albeit with markedly different outcomes in recent years. The transmission lines connecting the states of Apure and Táchira with the Colombian grid have operated intermittently, not so much due to technical limitations but primarily due to operational instability on the Venezuelan side – characterized by low effective generation, poor maintenance, and financial constraints. In 2019, electricity cooperation between the two countries was suspended following diplomatic tensions and increased tariffs. Conversely, the interconnection with Brazil's Roraima state, via Venezuela's Bolívar state, had long been crucial for securing electricity supply to isolated Brazilian regions. However, in the same year, Brazil suspended electricity imports due to frequent outages in Venezuela and the declining reliability of its power system. In 2023, Brazil partially resumed electricity imports for Roraima, citing significant cost savings from replacing diesel generation with hydroelectric power from the Simón Bolívar (Guri) plant (Últimas Noticias, 2025).[108]

319. Concurrently, Venezuela's domestic transmission system continues to face deep structural challenges. Most high-voltage transmission lines, built in the 1970s and 1980s, have long exceeded their intended service life. This obsolescence, compounded by chronic maintenance neglect, has led to frequent service disruptions and electricity losses exceeding 35%. These losses stem from both technical and non-technical factors, including widespread electricity theft and illegal connections. A key symptom of systemic failure is the shutdown of the San Gerónimo B substation in Guárico state. This facility, the country's main transmission hub, channels electricity from the Simón Bolívar (Guri) dam to Caracas and nearly 80% of the country via 765 kV lines. As of early 2019, the substation was out of operation, abandoned, and lacking qualified staff, making it technically impossible to stabilize the national grid (Kurmanaev, 2019).[109] While CORPOELEC claims an installed capacity above 34 GW, actual effective generation is far lower – mainly due to over-reliance on Guri, adverse climate conditions, and widespread inefficiencies. The severity of the crisis was evident in the blackouts throughout 2024, including a nationwide outage in August that affected Caracas and almost the entire country. These structural deficiencies continue to seriously undermine the stability and quality of electricity supply across Venezuela (El Nacional, 2024).[110]

108. Últimas Noticias, *Brasil Retoma Importación de Energía de Venezuela Tras Seis Años de Suspensión* (March 2025), available at: https://www.infobae.com/espana/agencias/2025/02/18/brasil-retoma-la-importacion-de-energia-de-venezuela-tras-seis-anos-de-suspension/ (last accessed 10 Jun. 2025).

109. A. Kurmanaev, *Estación clave para recuperar el sistema eléctrico de Venezuela está apagada*, Tal-Cual Digital, 11 Mar. 2019, available at: https://talcualdigital.com/estacion-clave-para-recuperar-el-sistema-electrico-de-venezuela-esta-apagada/ (last accessed 2 Apr. 2025).

110. El Nacional, '*Caracas y otras entidades reportaron fuerte bajón eléctrico: el segundo en 24 horas*,' *El Nacional*, 6 Sep. 2024, available at: https://www.elnacional.com/venezuela/caracas-y-otros-estados-sintieron-fuerte-bajon-electrico-segundo-en-24-horas/ (last accessed 2 Apr. 2025).

Chapter 5. Distribution

320. The distribution of electric power is aimed at giving users access to the electricity system. This is the final stage of the complex process of producing electricity in power generation plants, transmitting it, and allowing customers, whether public or private, industrial or residential, to enjoy it through low-voltage lines, transformers, electrical substations, meters, among other equipment. Management and marketing are included in this closing stage of the power system cycle.

321. In Venezuela, the process to distribute electric power generated and transmitted by CORPOELEC is carried out through 572 substations with a transformation capacity of 9,200 MVA and an 88,000 km long distribution network, which is as obsolete as the transmission system, since it has been used for over twenty-five years. In addition, since they have not been replaced, they continue working beyond their useful capacity, thus producing recurring faults in power supply.

322. The electric power marketing is going through an unprecedented crisis as well, considering that prices have been frozen since 2002 at 2.1 Cents/kWh, over the average 10 Cents/kWh in Latin America. However, there are fewer possibilities to recover the investments, bearing in mind that CORPOELEC has established as 'Cash Recovery Index' a value of 50%, while this international factor is at 80% and 90%. Another factor that worsens the situation of the SEN is related to utility billing. For instance, 2012 was the year when Venezuela generated more electricity, but it was also the year with the highest proportion of unbilled electricity. Based on the information in the 2012 Annual Report of the Electric Power Ministry, CORPOELEC failed to bill 33.35% of the gross electricity generated. Upon reviewing the record of the last five years, it is evident that unbilled power is on a progressive rise. In 2007, 22.9% was not billed, but in 2012, the unbilled power increased to 33.35%. Additionally, the official figures indicate that, in 2011, CORPOELEC billed 86,717 GW/h, while in 2012, only 85,045 GW/h were billed. In other words, though more electricity is generated, the earnings are lower.[111]

323. In recent years, Venezuela's electricity distribution sector has experienced notable policy shifts, particularly with the partial reinstatement of user billing. After years of frozen tariffs and widespread subsidies, CORPOELEC launched the Borrón y Cuenta Nueva ('Clean Slate') programme in late 2022, starting in Zulia State. The initiative aimed to update user records and gradually reintroduce billing across several regions, including the Capital, Central, Llanos, Eastern, and Guayana zones (Aporrea, 2025).[112] By February 2024, official residential electricity rates ranged from 46.20 to 156 bolivares – equivalent to approximately USD 1.80 to USD 6, depending on the exchange rate. Reports from early 2025 noted steep bill increases – some exceeding 300% – and the introduction of a USD 20 reconnection fee for unpaid accounts.

---

111. *Ibid.*
112. Aporrea, *Venezuela's Electricity Distribution Reform* (2025), available at: https://www.aporrea.org/ (last accessed 2 Apr. 2025).

324. Despite these developments, electricity tariffs in Venezuela remain significantly below the Latin American average of USD 0.10 per kWh (CAF, 2019).[113] The partial return to billing represents a substantial policy shift in the management of public utilities. However, the country's severely deteriorated infrastructure and persistent systemic inefficiencies continue to undermine both the reliability of electricity supply and the financial sustainability of the sector. Frequent blackouts in regions such as Mérida and Zulia underscore the ongoing structural deficiencies of the national electricity grid.

113. CAF, *Electricity Tariffs in Latin America*, CAF Report, 2019.

Chapter 6. Consumption

§1. Difference Between Supply and Demand

325. The difference between electricity supply and electricity demand in Venezuela has increased in recent years. The main cause hampering the electric power demand from being met is the high level of non-available electric power, especially in thermo-power plants, which reaches 40%.

326. Figure 8 shows the increase in installed capacity from 1998 to 2018, almost doubling from 19.8 GW to 36.6 GW. But at the same time, it is observed that the maximum demand met only reaches 14.0 GW, with a rationing of 2.5 GW, converted into a deficit. The operating reserve, which was used to make up for system failures, disappeared in 2006, while demand fell considerably from 2015 onwards due to the worsening of the country's economic crisis, characterized in the electricity sector by recurrent power cuts.

Figure 8 Installed Capacity vs. Demand and Deficit in Venezuela's Power System (1998–2018)

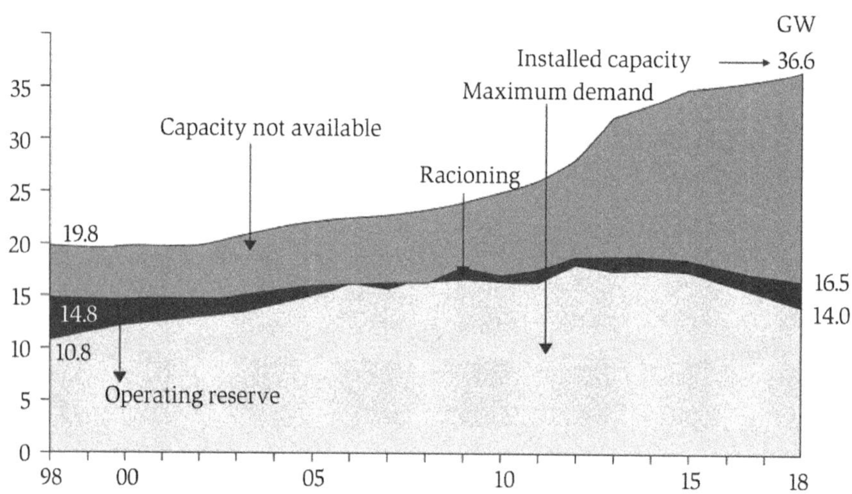

§2. Crisis on Consumption and Demand: Measures

327. As it may be recalled, the power emergency or crisis in Venezuela, caused by an unbalance between electric power generation and demand, as previously explained, intensified in 2009 and has extended to 2015 and 2016. The authorities in charge determined as the immediate cause of the crisis the extended drought that affected the dam of the Simón Bolívar HPP as a result of the climatic phenomenon known as El Niño, developing since July 2009. In order to address the crisis, the

National Government issued the electrical emergency Decree No. 7228, published in Official Gazette No. 39363 of 8 February 2010, for a sixty-day period subject to extension. At the same time, the National Government implemented an electricity rationing programme nationwide, saved for the capital city of Caracas, which was officially suspended in June 2010 due to the recovery of the dams. However, the interior of the country is still experiencing power outages due to faults in other parts of the system. Hence, the government was forced to declare the 'electrical emergency' again by Decree No. 09, published in Official Gazette No. 40151 of 21 June 2013, for a ninety-day period. When this period elapsed, the government issued a new decree on 4 October 2013, published in Official Gazette No. 40153, which provides for the intervention of CORPOELEC for a six-month period. Based on the foregoing, it seems that the electrical emergency is still in place.

328. Another element that noticeably affects users refers to the factor of service restoration that measures the response capacity after a fault or interruption. For instance, in 1998, the average time to restore the service was sixty minutes, while, in 2012, the service was restored in an average time of 988 minutes, that is, over half a day.

329. The state of crisis in the electricity system is clearly shaking the Venezuelan society and hitting its economy. This was also documented by the IMF in its October 2013 report on growth forecasts, which affirmed that 'growth in other commodity-exporting countries is generally expected to remain strong, except in Venezuela, where energy shortages and exchange controls are curtailing economic activity'.

330. The permanent emergency in which the national electrical system finds itself has radically changed the standards and lifestyle of Venezuelans. The immediate effect of this grave situation is the violation of fundamental human rights, such as access to a dignified life, the right to health, the right to food, and the right to education, among others. In the same manner, the exclusion and deprivation of universal access to energy have pushed millions of Venezuelans to live in subhuman conditions, which has given rise to the concept of energy poverty (EP) with its unique characteristics relative to the Venezuelan case.

331. In this scenario, the EP concept applies to the variable limitation or restriction of access to energy services, due to the disabling, dismantling, destruction, and ruin of the National Electricity Service attributable to its managers. The size of the EP in Venezuela is measured by comparing the state of the ES in 1998, a period in which it had an installed capacity of 19,696 MW, an energy production of 14,787 MW, a population of 23.24 million inhabitants and a maximum demand of 10,854 MW, compared to an installed capacity of 36,600 MW in 2018, a production of 14,000 MW, a current demand of more than 16,000 MW, and a population of over 31 million inhabitants.

332. The result of this equation shows a negative balance of energy supply. Therefore, while in 1998, the SEN produced 3,418 kWh/year per inhabitant and generated a per capita consumption of 2,563 kWh/year, twenty years later, these amounts are equivalent to a loss of about 50%, which means that in absolute terms, the Venezuelan per capita consumption would be close to 1000 kWh/year, which would mean that Venezuela would no longer be compared with Chile or Argentina, but rather with Cuba, Ecuador, or Peru.

333. The electricity crisis in Venezuela continues to have a profound impact on society, significantly lowering living standards and deepening EP. According to recent surveys by the Observatorio Venezolano de Servicios Públicos (OVSP),[114] power outages have shifted from weekly to daily events, affecting more than half of the population, with interruptions typically lasting between two and six hours (OVSP, 2023). Official data from the MPPEE remains largely outdated, as comprehensive reports have not been released since 2015, making accurate assessment and transparency difficult (MPPEE, n.d.).[115] As a result, independent analyses and media reports have become the primary sources documenting the ongoing severity and frequency of outages throughout Venezuela (Comité de Afectados por los Apagones, 2023).[116]

114. Observatorio Venezolano de Servicios Públicos, *Informe sobre el Servicio Eléctrico en Venezuela* (2023), available at: https://www.elimpulso.com/2023/11/23/ovsp-767-de-los-venezolanos-percibio-negativamente-la-calidad-del-servicio-electrico-23nov/ (last accessed 12 Mar. 2025).
115. Ministerio del Poder Popular para la Energía Eléctrica, *Memorias y Cuentas del Ministerio del Poder Popular para la Energía Eléctrica* (n.d.), available at: http://mppee.gob.ve/?page_id=702 (last accessed 12 Mar. 2025).
116. Comité de Afectados por los Apagones, *Reporte Nacional sobre Fallas Eléctricas 2023*, available at: https://mundour.com/2023/05/07/comite-de-afectados-por-apagones-contabilizo-casi-7-000-fallas-electricas-solo-en-abril/ (last accessed 12 Mar. 2025).

Chapter 7. Energy Efficiency Policy and Challenges in Venezuela's Electricity Sector

334. Energy efficiency has become a critical component of modern energy policies worldwide, especially in countries facing structural challenges in their electricity sectors. In Venezuela, the need to optimize the energy system led to the enactment of the Law on the Rational and Efficient Use of Energy in 2011, a major milestone in the country's energy policy. This legislation seeks to promote energy efficiency across all levels – from production to final consumption – by encouraging greater awareness of the importance of using energy resources responsibly.[117] The law establishes a comprehensive framework that includes educational programmes and certification mechanisms, aimed at optimizing energy consumption and reducing environmental impact.

335. A fundamental component of the law is the introduction of energy efficiency certification, aimed at encouraging improvements in equipment and buildings. This mechanism seeks not only to reduce energy waste but also to foster technological innovation within the sector. Additionally, the legislation has spurred initiatives in the field of alternative energy, such as the installation of photovoltaic systems to strengthen the telecommunications infrastructure of the national electricity sector.

336. However, the effective implementation of the law has faced significant challenges. The centralization of the electricity sector under the CORPOELEC since 2007 has hindered the successful application of efficiency measures. Similarly, Venezuela's ongoing electricity crisis has revealed deep-rooted structural issues, such as the lack of investment in maintenance and the obsolescence of infrastructure – both of which have severely undermined efforts to achieve more efficient energy use.[118]

337. Despite establishing a framework for the development of alternative energy sources, the law has failed to significantly diversify Venezuela's energy matrix. The country continues to rely primarily on hydroelectric and thermoelectric generation, with limited progress in adopting clean and sustainable technologies. The lack of comprehensive legislation to promote the large-scale development of renewable energy sources – such as solar and wind power – has prevented these technologies from becoming viable alternatives within the Venezuelan electricity system.[119]

---

117. Asamblea Nacional de la República Bolivariana de Venezuela, *Ley de Uso Racional y Eficiente de la Energía*, Gaceta Oficial No. 39.823, 19 Dec. 2011, available at: https://www.ariae.org/sites/default/files/2017-03/LEY-USO-RACIONAL-EFICIENTE-ENERGIA-2011.pdf (last accessed 12 Mar. 2025).
118. Diego Bautista Urbaneja, *La política venezolana desde 1958 hasta nuestros días* (Centro Gumilla 2013).
119. José Luis Hernández, *Panorama de las energías renovables en Venezuela*, 59(2) Revista Geográfica Venezolana 398 (2018).

338. Although the Law on the Rational and Efficient Use of Energy represents an important step toward improving energy efficiency in Venezuela, its impact has been limited due to the absence of a comprehensive energy policy and the structural challenges of the electricity sector. Achieving meaningful transformation will require Venezuela to diversify its energy matrix and adopt policies that promote investment in sustainable energy sources – supported by a robust regulatory framework and effective implementation.

Part II. Regulatory Framework Concerning Petrol

Chapter 1. General Introduction

§1. The Beginning of Oil Exploitation: The First Steps

339. In 1864, the federal political regime of the Nation was restored and, hence, the provinces became Autonomous Entities. Some of them passed their own mine codes and began granting rights to individuals for the exploration and exploitation of hydrocarbons. In 1865, the State of Zulia granted the first concession to Mr Camilo Ferrand. The following year, the State of Nueva Andalucía granted a concession for twenty-five years to Manuel Olavarría for an area that today comprises the entire territory of the States of Sucre and Monagas. And, in 1878, the State of Táchira granted Manuel Antonio Pulido exploitation rights over a 100 ha area for a term of fifty years.[120] This Venezuelan entrepreneur organized Petrolia del Táchira, taking the credit for being the first company that produced petroleum in Venezuela. The first oil well exploited was named Eureka-1, followed by others that, with undersized volumes, fed a small refinery that processed fifteen barrels of oil per day and even came to export kerosene to Colombia. Petrolia ceased its activities on 8 April 1934, after more than fifty years of work. Unfortunately, this company, Venezuelan and pioneer of the oil exploitation in the country, could not pave the way that may have written a new history about this industry, which had already begun to rise as the most powerful on the planet in the mid-twentieth century. The reasons for the failure of Petrolia del Táchira have been attributed to the small-scale prospecting of the territory granted, later corroborated by a similar failure of Shell, in addition to the lack of capital, organization, and technology required by the oil industry.[121]

§2. Transnational Oil Companies in Venezuela

340. The granting of concessions continued under the dictatorship of Juan Vicente Gómez. The main beneficiaries were the dictator's friends and family

120. Toyin Falola & Ann Genova, *The Politics of the Global Oil Industry: An Introduction*, 232 (Stanford University 2005).
121. Vallenilla Luis, *Petroleo venezolano, auge, declinación y porvenir*, 29–59 (Caracas 1975).

members,[122] who later transferred such concessions to the main foreign companies, essentially to the Caribbean Petroleum Company, a subsidiary of the Royal Dutch Group, in exchange for umpteen sums of money. By 1912, over 30 million ha had been negotiated.[123]

341. On 31 July 1914, the Caribbean Petroleum Company began the exploitation of the Zumaque well, located in the eastern part of Maracaibo Lake, which became, as of that date, the first commercial oil well in Venezuela, exposing the great oil basin of Maracaibo Lake. Following Vallenilla, the year 1917 may be set as the starting point of the Venezuelan oil industry, first because uninterrupted official information about oil production became available as of that year, and second because the vertical structuring of the oil industry was accomplished, from exploration, exploitation, transportation, exportation, and refining to internal marketing. The same year, the first commercial refinery (San Lorenzo) and the first oil pipeline, between the refinery and the Mene Grande fields, located at Maracaibo Lake, began to operate. Both facilities were owned by the Caribbean Petroleum Company.

342. American companies began to arrive in Venezuela as of 1919, after World War I ended. In 1921, the Standard Oil Company de Venezuela, a subsidiary of the Standard Oil Company of New Jersey, was established in the country and began its direct operations in the Maracaibo Lake basin and, later on, in the eastern part of the Republic, an area that commercially developed as of 1926. The Lago Petroleum Corporation, established in Venezuela on 19 June 1923, was the first American company that exported oil from Venezuela. By 1932, eleven companies were at the exploitation stage and were owned by three powerful international groups. The Royal Dutch Group owned the Caribbean Petroleum Company, Venezuelan Oil Concessions, Colon Development Company Limited, British Controlled Oilfields, North Venezuelan, and Central Area Exploitation Company Limited. The Standard Group owned the Standard Oil Company de Venezuela (which later became the Creole Petroleum Corporation), Lago Petroleum Company, and Orinoco Oil Company. The Gulf Group held the Venezuelan Gulf Oil Company. These groups remained until the nationalization of 1975. The truth is that the development of the Venezuelan oil industry, with its pros and cons, has always been linked to foreign companies.[124]

§3. Institutionalization and Development: Key Factors

343. The death of Dictator Juan Vicente Gómez on 17 December 1935 opened the door to important political changes and allowed the draining of the renovating ideas of the Generation of 1928 with direct effects on the national oil industry. A

122. McBeth, *Brian Juan Vicente Gomez and the Oil Companies inVenezuela, 1908–1935*, 37–39 (Cambridge U. Press 1983).
123. Vallenilla Luis, *Petroleo venezolano*, 41–43.
124. *Ibid.*, 43.

still controversial stage in the oil history of Venezuela was about to come to an end. Perhaps, Anglo-Dutch companies never anticipated that this event would change the conditions that, for over eighteen years, they had enjoyed under the direct protection of the dead dictator-president. This and other unexpected events of a national and international nature that occurred between 1935 and 1945 changed in a decisive manner the destiny of the oil industry in Venezuela. In this chapter, we intend to make a brief reference to three factors that directly had an effect on the course of the National Petroleum Industry: the role played by the working and the political classes, the expropriation of the Oil Industry in Mexico, and World War II.

I. Role of the Workers

344. Before labour and political actions, as well as significant legal reforms as of 1936, took place, the living conditions of the Venezuelan people were deplorable. Particularly, oil workers were practically 'oil hired hands' enslaved by the oil companies in connivance with the government.

345. The approval of the Labour Law of 1936 was projected to a great extent in an attempt to revert the lousy labour conditions to which some 12,000 people who worked in the oil sector were subject, with low wages and, in general, totally helpless.

346. The political environment created after General Eleazar López Contreras – successor of General Juan Vicente Gómez – took office immediately reflected on the labour field. The new legal framework allowed workers to build the first labour unions, through which they defied the huge power of the Multinational Companies. In fact, on 11 December 1936, workers from Cabimas and Lagunillas came out on strike until 22 January 1937.[125] Their main demands were related to the recognition of the Unions as legitimate representatives of the employees and workers, the establishment of a minimum wage, equal treatment among Venezuelans and foreigners, medical and hospital assistance for professional diseases, and other improvements, such as transportation, potable water, and restroom hygiene. The answer of the oil companies, as expected, was a total rejection of their demands and came back with multiple abuses and stalking. The government, far from defending the workers, which could also be expected, decreed the return of the strikers to work, and the companies merely granted a salary increase way below their demands. Although this victory may be assessed as pyrrhic from the standpoint of economic and social achievements, its consequences were not. The valiance and freehandedness shown by the working class, who did not hesitate to challenge the power of the large oil companies, hold the memory of this transcendental event as an epic that shored up

125. A. Robert, *Rómulo Betancourt and the Transformation of Venezuela,* 111 (Transaction Books 1982).

unexpected changes. A decade later, in 1946, the perseverance in their fight gave oil workers their first collective bargaining agreement and a decisive prominence they would never leave behind.[126]

II. Expropriation of the Mexican Oil Industry

347. A similar situation would appear in Mexico a year later, with more promising results for the working class and the country and very detrimental results for the oil companies. Their stubbornness and prepotency faced an organized working class who appealed to a strike as a natural means and also to arbitral instances allowed by the Labour Law in force. After a bungled attempt through the stoppage of the activities, the organized workers turned to the Federal Board of Conciliation and Arbitration (JFCA) to seek evaluation of their fair demands, as well as the financial conditions of the companies. On 18 December 1937, the JFCA decreed by means of an Arbitration Award that the companies had the capacity to accede to the demands of the oil workers' unions.

348. As a sign of rejection, the companies turned to the CSJ to demand the annulment of said Arbitration Award, which was ratified by the Highest Court of the Republic on 1 March 1938. The reaction of the oil companies was one of contempt with regard to the mandate of the CSJ, to which the oil workers replied with a decisive strike.[127] In view of this situation, the national government confronted the companies, announcing the decision to expropriate them. It is worth remembering the statement of Mexican President Lázaro Cárdenas:

> The attitude adopted by the oil companies refusing to comply with the mandate of the National Justice that, through the Supreme Court, ordered them to pay their workers the amount of the economic demand that the own companies took to court due to inconformity with the resolutions of the Labor Courts, imposes on the Executive Branch of the Union the duty to seek for an effectual means in our legislation that may definitely avoid, for the present and the future, the nullity of justice decisions or the ambition of softening such decisions by the sole will of the parties or one of them by means of a simple declaration of insolvency, as it is intended in this case.[128]

349. This situation had a determining impact on Venezuela. On the one hand, it became a warning for foreign companies about the consequences they had to take if they continued rejecting the legitimate aspirations of the workers[129] and, on the

126. *See*, Henry Jiménez Guanipa, *La Gobernanza de los Hidrocarburos en Venezuela. Aciertos, desaciertos y desafíos*, pp. 146–147, in Tablante, Carlos and Jiménez Henry, *Petróleo: Bendición o Maldición. 100 años del Zumaque* 1. Editorial La Hoja del Norte, Caracas, 2014.
127. Maurer Noel, *The Empire Struck Back: The Mexican Oil Expropriation of 1938 Reconsidered,* 71 J. Eco. Hist. 603–660 (2011).
128. Oil Expropriation Act, President Lázaro Cárdenas, 18 Mar. 1938.
129. Singh Kelvin, *Oil Politics inVenezuelaDuring the López Contreras Administration (1936–1941),* 21 J. Latin Am. Stud. 89–104 (1989).

other hand, it cleared the way so that Venezuela, along with the US, could take up the absolute leadership of the oil industry in the Western Hemisphere.

III. World War II

350. The need for supplying the international oil market during World War II was a key element that Venezuela knew how to take advantage of to reach a negotiated agreement for the political and social crisis. In fact, it is acknowledged that the State Department forced oil companies to accept the demands of the working class and the emerging political class, as well as the national government. This may be explained by the concern the US and its European allies had about having the expropriation process that began in Mexico spread to Bolivia and Venezuela, endangering the supply of crude oil to the international market.

351. The approval of the LH of 1938, which included the possibility that the State could directly take up the management of the IPN and the demands for increasing oil revenues materialized in the Income Tax Law (LISLR – *Ley de Impuesto sobre la Renta*) of 1942, joined to kindle the already rarefied political environment as an irrefutable evidence of the changes the country was experiencing. The sum of all these elements forced an agreement and paved the way for the approval of the LH of 1943, regarded as the best well-structured and advanced legal instrument the country has had in oil matters. Although Venezuela did not reach everything it was entitled to by law, it managed to overcome the utterly poor and humiliating situation, to say the least. Under the hands of the succeeding regime of the sell-out dictatorship, the oil exploration, exploitation, manufacturing, and transportation activities were declared of public utility. Royalties for 16 2/3%, as in the US, and the obligation to refine 10% of the oil production in the Venezuelan territory were established, all of which started a large-scale industrialization process. Nevertheless, the most important legal contribution of this law is represented by the construction, for the first time, of a uniform legal framework that would be equally applied to all oil concessions, putting an end to the perverse and ancient regime that practically gave to each concession separately particular rights to the detriment of the economic interests of the country. However, oil companies achieved a truly substantial agreement upon obtaining concession renewal for a period of forty years, until 1983, which guaranteed them stability in the long run.[130]

§4. Stabilization and Development of the Oil Industry

352. The effects of this agreement were soon felt in the country. The distribution of oil revenues had passed from 95% in favour of the companies before the

130. Ramón Rivas, *Venezuela, petróleo y la segunda Guerra Mundial (1939–1945): un ejemplo histórico para las nuevas generaciones*, 215 (*Revista Económica* no. 10, Universidad de los Andes 1995).

reformed law of 1943 to 50%. Employment recovered (Figure 9),[131] reaching some 50,000 jobs in 1949, to later stabilized around 40,000. Labour conditions substantially improved as well. Oil production increased in ten years from 500,000 b/d to over 2 million b/d, as may be seen in Figure 10.[132]

Figure 9 Employment Growth in Venezuela's Oil Sector after the 1943 Hydrocarbons Law Reform

131. *See*, Espinaza Vendrell, *El marco fiscal petrolero venezolano: evolución y propuestas 'Regímenes fiscales en economías petroleras', 271.* (Revista Banco Central de Venezuela, Segundo Encuentro Internacional de Economía 1999).
132. *Ibid.*, 272.

Figure 10 Crude Oil Production Increase in Venezuela (1943–1958)

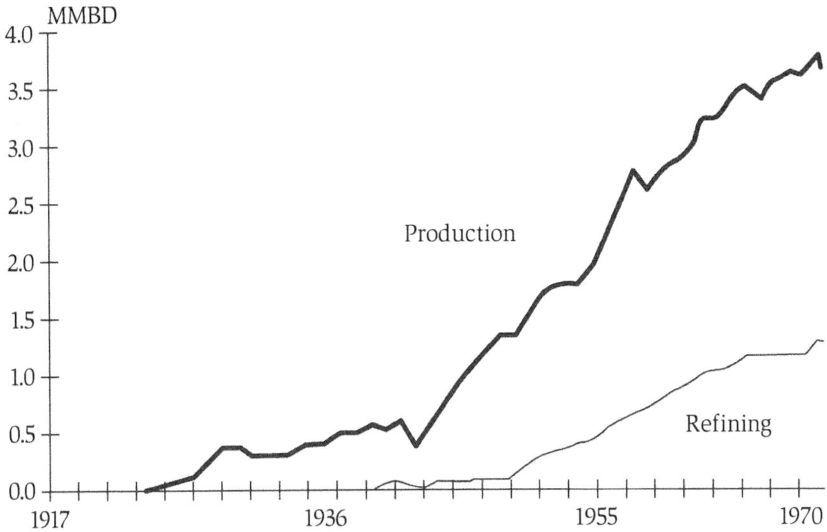

353. Even though the Law of 1943 did not expressly establish that benefits would be distributed in equal parts between the companies and the State, this objective was implicit in its content. Nonetheless, and for making this concrete, the LISR was reformed in 12 December 1948, including an extra tax called 'additional tax', which later led to the well-known fifty-fifty tax, defined as a fiscal action according to which the benefits of the oil industry would be distributed equally between the State and the licensees.[133]

354. Political instability continued until the collapse of the last military dictatorship in 1958, which, incidentally, had renewed the concessions of the multinational companies, taking a step contrary to the spirit created in the 1940s. The establishment of a democracy allowed taking up again the debate on oil revenues and the possibility of achieving better benefits than the 50% agreed in the reform of 1948, adding the possibility of competing in the business through a new national company as set forth by the LH of 1936.

355. These aspirations were satisfied to a great extent by the electoral victory of a sector of the political class that had promoted the improvement of oil revenues from its beginning and, particularly, through the reform of the LISR of 1948. It is important to point out that the governance agreement reached in 1943 significantly retook its spirit and purpose in this new stage when Dr Pérez Alfonso took over the guidance of the national oil policy. This way, the State reoriented its strategic view on the control of the oil and gas industry, setting the benefits at a ratio of 40% for

133. Daniel Yergin, *The Prize: the Epic Quest for Oil, Money, and Power*, 79 (Simon & Schuster 1991).

the licensees and 60% for the State, through the implementation of a policy aimed at not granting new concessions. Multinational companies significantly reduced their investments in the sector as a response and promoted a negative matrix about the future of the main industry of the country, which was reflected in the estimate reduction of oil reserves.

§5. Progressive Nationalization (1961–1975)

356. The strengthening of a new and eminently rentier vision about the management of the hydrocarbons industry had fallen into such a dimension since 1958[134] that it practically made unsurprising the nationalization of the oil industry as a whole. In fact, this intention acquired constitutional rank in 1961 (Article 97) and was ratified in the reform of the LH of 1967. The OPEC itself, which had been foster in Venezuela, backed its members on this purpose, seeking a counterbalance in the international market controlled by the big multinational companies known as the '7 sisters'. So, the process of direct control of the IPN has those elements as context, it develops gradually by sectors, and props on the high oil revenues as of the mid-1970s. In this chapter, we will analyse the three nationalizing processes of the hydrocarbon industry: reserve on Natural Gas, reserve on domestic hydrocarbon market, and complete nationalization of the Hydrocarbons Industry.

I. State Control over the Natural Gas Industry

357. On 12 August 1971, Venezuela passed the first gas law called the Law Reserving the Industry of Natural Gas to the State (*Ley que Reserva al Estado la Industria del Gas Natural*) (LREIGN). Pursuant to this law, the State, through the State-run company Corporación Venezolana del Petróleo, began to exercise directly the exploitation of natural gas, participating in the entire business chain (exploration, exploitation, industrialization, and commercialization). The decision was based on the fact that its use had been limited to the reinjection in oil wells, as domestic and industrial fuel, and as raw material for the manufacturing of some petrochemical products, without a true large-scale development programme that would allow obtaining greater benefits as a result of the large proved reserves, the increasing world demand, as well as the availability of adequate technology for its liquefaction and transportation.

358. In the framework of the LREIGN (Article 3), the beneficiaries of the hydrocarbon concessions were forced to give the State, at the time, measure and conditions established by the National Executive Branch, the gas produced in their operations, having the State the authority to take up (Article 8) directly the operations of collection, compression, and treatment of the licensees' plants, upon acknowledging the corresponding compensation for an amount equivalent to the

134. Mejía Alarcón, Pedro Esteban, *La industria del petróleo en Venezuela*, 114 (Caracas, 1972).

not-depreciable portion of the cost of the facilities. This LREIGN smooths the way for the establishment of the monopoly of the State on the hydrocarbons industry.

II. State Control over the Domestic Market

359. The Venezuelan Petroleum Corporation (CVP – *Corporación Venezolana del Petróleo, filial de PDVSA*) played a singular role in the domestic market. The enactment of Presidential Decree No. 187 of 1964 marked the beginning of the participation of the State in the activities of the domestic market for hydrocarbon products. This rule compelled licensees the assignment of market share in favour of CVP, until reaching a share between one-third and two-thirds, in accordance with the estimates proposed in the National Development Plans. Trade margins fluctuated in a range of VEB 1 billion, a substantial amount for the time, taking into account the global dimension of the Venezuelan economy and an exchange rate of VEB 4.30 per dollar. Therefore, the following question came up: Why should we leave such a profitable business in foreign hands when Venezuela could take it up? As expected, the companies were reluctant to comply with the said decree, defying the authority of the Ministry of Mines and Hydrocarbons, which was trying to exercise a greater control over this market.[135]

360. In 1973, thus, the direct intervention was decided by means of the enactment of the LRMI. This Law set forth, in favour of the State and for national interest reasons, the reserve of the exploitation of the domestic market of the products derived from hydrocarbons.

361. The participation of the private sector in the domestic market regarding storage, transportation, distribution, and retail business activities of products derived from hydrocarbons, defined for the public interest and national convenience, was subject to the signing of commercial agreements between the interested parties and the CVP and to the granting of the corresponding permit by the MEM. The law granted preferential rights to those natural or artificial persons who were exercising the activities referred to in the law to continue exercising such activities, as long as they complied with the conditions that would be established by the Venezuelan Oil Corporation.

III. Nationalization of the Hydrocarbons Industry

362. The nationalization of the hydrocarbons industry was the result of a wide, intense, and plural debate, where the different political forces and, in a fruitful manner, a group of reputed Venezuelan experts representing all ideological currents were part of the Presidential Commission for Oil Reversion created by President Pérez in March 1974. After arduous debates in the National Congress, in August

135. Luis E. Lander, *Globalización y mercado interno de los hidrocarburos en Venezuela* (Universidad Central de Venezuela, Nos 2–3, Caracas 1998).

1975, the LN was passed and was declared to become effective on 1 January 1976, in a symbolic act held at the site of the Zumaque well discovered in 1914.

363. Congress debate focused on whether the nationalization should reserve the hydrocarbons industry and commercialization, totally and absolutely, to the State, or if it should leave open the possibility of allowing the private sector to participate in the activities reserved. This discussion was transferred and solved through the approval of Article 5 of the LN, which finally left open the possibility of the State to enter into operating and AA with private entities, prior authorization of both Chambers in joint session. The nationalization of the hydrocarbons industry in Venezuela, in addition to the unquestionable legality it had, endorsed by Article 97 of the national Constitution of 1961, was the result of a broad national agreement where all the major political forces accepted it, and even the own licensees acceded, leaving behind the prepotency that once characterize them.

364. Despite the wide consensus that supported this historic decision, a minority sector is still convinced that this proposal twisted the true nationalization proposed by the Presidential Commission for Petroleum Reversion, comprised of all the sectors of society, from political parties to universities. According to this hypothesis, the Law Reserving the Industry and Commerce of the Hydrocarbons to the State, prepared by said Commission and submitted to the President of the Republic on 23 December 1974, would have allowed a nationalization that would truly be for the Venezuelan people, that would create and secure the decision autonomy and whose essence, purpose, and true reason for a genuine nationalization were modified, as confirmed by recent history.

365. The evaluation of the nationalization of the hydrocarbons industry in Venezuela began to irreconcilably space out two views on the petroleum policy. While one sector deemed that the compensations to licensees were the key to achieve an agreement and secure a painless transfer of activities for the country, another sector assessed this action as erroneous, since the amounts paid[136] (BS. 4,300,000,000)[137] exceeded the benefits that could have been reached if the operations had continued until 1983, date set for the petroleum reversion by reason of the expiration of the licences granted in 1943 and Articles 90, 13, and 15 of the Law on Property Subject to Reversion in Hydrocarbon Concessions.

366. However, it has been a practically undisputable and accepted fact that licensees had overlooked key aspects of the industry and had stopped investing for

136. José Honorio Martínez, 'La política petrolera del gobierno Chávez o la redefinición del Estado ante la globalización neoliberal', *Historia Actual Online*, vol. 24, invierno 2011, pp. 7–15, available at: https://dialnet.unirioja.es/descarga/articulo/3670847.pdf (last accessed 2 Apr. 2025).

137. Ramirez Rafael, *De la privatización a la nacionalización de la industria petrolera en Venezuela*, Rocio Ramirez y Los Calculos Financieros: De la privatización a la nacionalización de la industria petrolera en Venezuela(accessed 5 Sep. 2013); Alí Rodríguez Araque, *El proceso de privatización petrolera en Venezuela*, Fondo Editorial Darío Ramírez (2014), https://www.rafaelramirez.net/wp-content/uploads/2022/12/Privatizacion-Petrolera_Ali-Rodroguez_Fondo-Editorial-Dario-Ramirez.pdf (last visited 2 Apr. 2025).

several years in the face of the immediacy of the end of the concession system. As a result of this situation, it was necessary to push forward the nationalization, taking advantage of the increase in oil prices, which made the Venezuelan State a rich and powerful entrepreneur. Due to this circumstance, the State became the owner of the petroleum, iron and steel, gas, and petrochemical industries, the generation of hydroelectricity and thermoelectricity, and many other economic activities, and the government became the greatest employer of the country.

367. With regard to the topic of compensation payments, the President of the Republic pointed out the difficulties of the negotiations, particularly the decision adopted by Venezuela about paying exclusively the book value of the assets not depreciated as compensation, and he upheld that these negotiations were carried out:

> Not out of fear, and at no time sacrificing the national interest, but rather because we wanted to reveal the example that it was possible, within the system of representative democracy, respecting the legitimate interests that were represented in the petroleum industry, to perform the nationalization without arriving at a confrontation.[138]

368. Hence, it was not a confiscation, but rather the exercise of the right of a sovereign State to recover the management of a resource of its own, compensating those who had been doing so by means of agreements with the State.

369. The dilemma facing the country was to determine which course of action best served the national interest. There is no doubt that foreign companies had obtained exorbitant profits from the exploitation of Venezuelan oil – many of them since the early twentieth century. One option could have been to deny compensation, as established in the Law on Property Subject to Reversion in Hydrocarbon Concessions, and to accept the presence of companies unable to produce a single drop of oil due to the chronic lack of maintenance and investment that had plagued the industry, especially in light of the imminent shutdown of operations in 1983. Alternatively, the government could proceed with the takeover of the facilities through a negotiated nationalization, acknowledging the value of the infrastructure through fair compensation. We support the decision made by the government at that time.IV. Nationalization Process Assessment

370. The risk undertaken to bring forward the nationalization was favoured by the high oil prices. The decision to wait until 1983 to avoid compensating the licensees would have faced a low-price scenario and an economic crisis that would have undoubtedly held up the investments to keep the production that had been declining in a constant manner. It is worth mentioning that OPEC responded by cutting production in an effort to float prices, without success. This action, far from working, brought about just the opposite, to the point of having a production decrease from 32 MMBD to 16 MMBD and, in the case of Venezuela, from 3.7

138. Brewer Carias Allan, *Aspectos organizativos de la industria petrolera nacionalizada*, in Archivo de Derecho Público y Ciencias de la Administración, UCV Vol. III (Caracas 1981), 407–492.

MMBD to 1.7 MMBD. Figure 11 *illustrates this dynamic, showing the parallel evolution of international crude oil prices and Venezuela's average daily production between 1970 and 1998. Notably, despite the price surge during the second oil shock (1979–1981), Venezuela's output fell sharply—a reflection of both domestic constraints and OPEC restrictions. The figure also highlights two key historical moments: the nationalization of the oil industry in 1976, and the oil reversion in 1983. From the early 1990s onward, production recovered steadily, consistent with sectoral liberalization policies.* At all events, the consensus had been reached to undertake the nationalization under the terms already explained. During the national debate, this was confirmed, and all the political forces participated and made clear their respective points of views. Nonetheless, it was approved by a considerable majority that adopted the system proposed by the National Executive Branch. This way, the existence of an agreement that made possible the governance of the IPN was confirmed; however, the source of what would grow to be later reforms, intense debates and two viewpoints that even today seem unfortunately irreconcilable were planted in its contents to the detriment of the Nation.

Figure 11 Oil Production Collapse: OPEC and Venezuela (1979–1985)

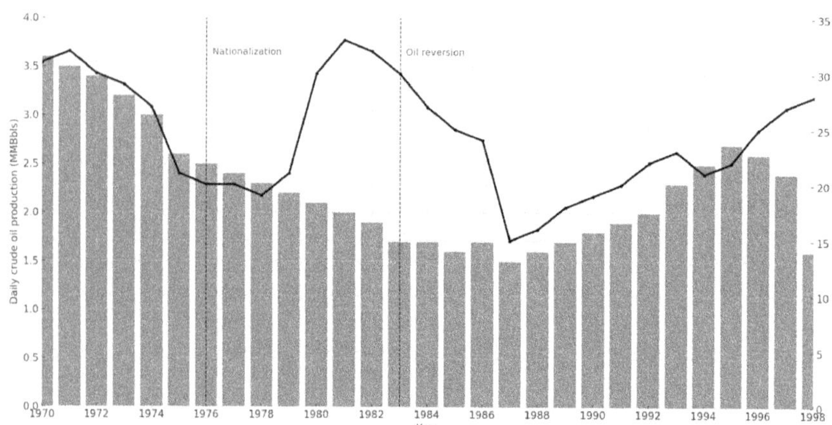

Source: OPEC.

§6. Progressive Oil Opening: (1989–1999)

371. The oil boom that had eased the nationalization of the hydrocarbons industry as a whole had come to an end in the mid-1980s. This fact, along with the high debt levered by high oil prices, would have very negative effects on the national economy, precisely because adequate measures to face an adverse circumstance of price drop were not adopted. In this chapter, we will explain how this circumstance favoured a change in the petroleum policy, passing from the predominant rentier viewpoint observed until now to an opening strategy that would favour a productivist viewpoint. Additionally, the differences existing among the petroleum policies implemented in Venezuela will be shown to establish if they have been the result of national agreements and their effects on the management and governance of the IPN.

I. Justification

372. The orientation of the oil policy during the first few years after the nationalization did not change with regard to its rentier orientation, supported by OPEC. Note that, before the production-level cutting between 1970 and 1980, prices increased. However, this relation was reverted between 1980 and 1985. As a matter of fact, the production-level cutting policy did not work this time; on the contrary, prices plummeted, as may be seen in chart No. 7.

373. During the 1980s, high prices decreased demand and generated a larger production by the non-OPEC member countries. This event made the organization lose capacity to defend oil prices, which inexorably led it to a collapse and, with it, its own rentier capitalist model in the international market. In fact, in 1986, Venezuela, along with the rest of the OPEC member countries, abandoned the volume-cutting policy to defend the sales price per barrel and steadily increased oil production, which went from 1.7 to 3.3 MBD between 1985 and 1997.

374. In contrast, the dilemma on whether to persist in pushing the oil industry to obtain greater fiscal revenues now that the State was the owner and manager or take advantage of such condition to reduce tax and fiscal pressure in order to make it grow was present. Changing the equation was the position opted for: the State would allow reasonable revenues to the IPN, giving up a good share of the oil revenues so that PDVSA could make the investments needed for its reactivation. This way, the transition from an orientation oil policy towards a productivist orientation policy was sealed as of the end of the 1980s. One of the first actions undertaken was the reform of the LISLR of 1991, which reduced from 67.7% to 34% the income tax for extra-heavy crude oil and free gas projects. This was done because of the drastic oil price plummeting without recovery scenarios. With this measure, financial analyses would be alluring for private investments, as in fact they were.

375. The strategy for tax and fiscal reform continued with the Law on the Gradual Elimination of Export Fiscal Values of 1993 to undertake the oil production expansion plan. About the Export Fiscal Value (VFE), Gustavo Coronel has expressed the following: 'Once the industry was nationalized and the state-run company was the only company exporting, what was the role of the Fiscal Value of Exports? Was the State going to steal from itself?' The obvious consequence was that direct taxes, which include income tax and the VFE, would drop steadily as of 1993. Nonetheless, such income reduction was compensated by the increase in crude oil volumes produced, which represented an additional income of more than USD 5.6 billion. Conversely, revenues from PDVSA in 1996 allowed declaring dividends for over USD 2 billion, which contributed to the cutback of fiscal revenues due to the elimination of the VFE. Failure to do so would not have allowed production volume to increase, without which the potential VEF collection would not have been possible either.

376. Then again, the State implemented a tax reform through the introduction of the value added tax (VAT), which reached 4.7% of the GDP in 1997, representing 46.5% of non-oil revenues. Therefore, the oil expansion plan was financed to a great extent by the fiscal effort of the non-oil economy to fill the gap that the new oil policy would leave behind. One of the main efforts that the State had to make through PDVSA was to try and allure private investment, a measure that may be assessed as successful because today over 30% of the total oil production in Venezuela comes from projects developed with foreign investments under the productivist-oriented oil opening policy.

II. Instruments and Mechanisms

377. The oil opening policy was, besides an economic strategy, part of a process that was built progressively, without being an isolated or exclusive event of Venezuela. As a matter of fact, Brazil initiated a similar, and even more aggressive, process, privatizing part of Petrobras as of the constitutional reform of 1996. Europe also engaged in a structural reform through the approval of the directives of 1996 and 1998, which liberalized the electricity and natural gas markets.

378. Its implementation had plenty of hurdles, basically because of the lack of consensus to adopt its fundamental basis and an adequate legal framework. Actually, the judicial option, as well as the involvement of the Executive Branch, was appealed to through some stratagems in order to create the legal conditions that would allow the participation and private investment in certain activities, which were not possible via the legal framework in force.

379. Upstream, the first step towards the opening policy may be found in the decision of the CSJ of April 1991, in which, at the request of Lagoven, the incompatibility of the provision set forth in the first paragraph of Article 2 of the LREIGN is decreed, so that the Executive Branch could exploit natural gas through an entity different from CVP. Such decision made an ineffective part of the articles of said LREIGN, paving the way to private participation in all the stages of the gas industry. According to the analysis of the Highest Court, Articles 5 and 6 of the LN allow the National Executive Branch, by reason of the integral reserve of the hydrocarbons, to exploit these resources not only directly but also through State-run entities, without any authorization or formality whatsoever, as required by said Article 2 of the LREIGN.

380. A second step was achieved by invoking Article 5 of the LN in order to approve Operating Agreements (OAs – *Convenios Operativos*) (1991, 1992, and

1997), strategic associations for the development of extra-heavy crude oil of the Orinoco Belt (1993 and 1997), and risk service agreements (1996).

381. Downstream, a decisive step was taken in 1994 for the liberalization of the lubricant market after the approval and publication of Resolution 537 by the National Executive Branch in 1994. Through such resolution, PDVSA's affiliate companies were authorized to enter into supply agreements for base oils with foreign industrializing companies located in the country that made use of such base oils as raw material or supplies in the manufacturing of all types of finished lube products for the national market, as well as the export market. Three years later and based on Articles 2, 7, 9, and 10 of the LRMI, the National Executive Branch decreed Resolution 438 in 1997 to allow other companies and brands to participate in the distribution and selling of fuels in the national market.

382. Such resolution was subject to multiple critiques, given that it was liberalizing the national fuels market under the legal framework of the LRMI, still in force, as it was argued for the entire process of the opening policy. The legality of such resolution was objected to, until 2 September 1998, when the Organic Law on the Opening of the Domestic Market (LOAMI – *Ley Orgánica de Apertura del Mercado Interno*) was passed for setting forth the rules of the opening process initiated with Resolution 438.

383. Without any doubt, Decree 2.532, enacted by the President of the Republic on 28 May 1998, was a decisive impulse for the opening of the natural gas market. This decree established that the activities related to the industrialization of methane and ethane gases, as well as the transportation, storage, distribution, and commercialization of these products in the national territory, could be exercised by the private sector. This way, there was an effort to broaden the offer of gas for the domestic market, regulating the methods for private participation in these activities and allowing the preparation of a gasification programme in the main cities of the country.

384. This set of actions intended to propel the oil opening policy in the hydrocarbons market in Venezuela faced resistance from some sectors associated to the academic, political, and legal fields, who turned to the CSJ (today the TSJ) to request its nullity on the grounds of unconstitutionality of the first, second, fourth, sixth, tenth, seventeenth, and twenty-first clauses of Article 2 of the Agreement of the Congress of the Republic approved on 4 July 1995, which authorized the formalization of risk services of new areas and hydrocarbons production agreements under the scheme of profit-sharing, allowing the participation of private capital in the oil exploration and exploitation process. This unprecedented action gave rise to the so-called case of the Oil Opening Policy, which extended for over three years and ended in 1999 with the decree of DISMISSAL by the defunct CSJ.

385. It is worth mentioning that such a significant and transcendent decision coincided with the also noteworthy process of political change after the election of

President Chávez in 1998. As a matter of fact and on account of the political relationship of the impugners with the elected president and his movement, they became directly or indirectly the administrators of the energy policy of the country by taking up key positions in the new government. Undoubtedly, the development of these events marked, on the one hand, the confrontation of two visions clearly differentiated on the approach of the oil policy – one, eminently rentier, and the other, eminently productivist – and, on the other hand, the beginning of the rupture of a fragile national agreement reached in 1999, through which a new Constitution and the LOHG and, in 2001, the Organic LOH, and the Organic Law on the Electric Power Service were passed. Such laws were oriented towards the promotion of the participation of the private sector in the development of the energy sector in Venezuela.

III. Trial and Arguments Against the Oil Opening

386. Given the importance of the judicial process against the so-called oil opening policy,[139] we will expound next an analysis of the key elements of the legal line of reasoning of the parties during the trial, certain that it will allow a greater understanding of the complex legal, economic, and political situation that has affected, and most probably will continue affecting, the development of the hydrocarbons industry in Venezuela.

387. This action was filed on 14 December 1995, through a brief containing the action for annulment due to unconstitutionality of the first, second, fourth, sixth, tenth, seventeenth, and twenty-first clauses of Article 2 of the Agreement of the Congress of the Republic of Venezuela approved on 4 July 1995, authorizing the execution of risk services of new areas and profit-sharing AA. A similar action, this time a petition for annulment due to illegality of the first, second, tenth, and twenty-first clauses of Article 2 of the same agreement of the Congress of the Republic, was filed on 23 January 1996, before the Political Administrative Division, which declined jurisdiction by writ of 27 February 1996. Subsequently, on 2 July 1996, the CSJ agreed to the consolidation of both causes.

A. Assignment of General Rights

388. The plaintiffs claimed the annulment due to the illegality of the first clause of the agreement, as it violated the first paragraph of Article 5 of the LN and Article 1.141 of the Civil Code. The Clause referred to provides that:

> The National Government, through the Ministry of Energy and Mines (MEM), in exercise of its legal powers, shall determine the geographical areas described in Appendix ‘B’ in favor of a PDVSA subsidiary to carry out activities related

139. TSJ 812-829 (17 Sep. 1999) in: *El Caso de la Apertura Petrolera*, https://allanbrewercarias.com/wp-content/uploads/2007/09/57.-I-2-22.-APERTURA-PETROLERA.-DOCUMENTOS-DEL-JUICIO.pdf (accessed 3 Apr. 2025).

to the exploration and exploitation of hydrocarbon reservoirs, with transportation through special lines, storage, and trade of the production from the areas, and with the works required for the management thereof, the foregoing in conformity with the LN.

389. According to the appellants, the first clause, as approved, was intended to grant general rights to carry out the broadest range of activities – including the exploration, exploitation, transportation, storage, and commercialization of hydrocarbons (i.e., medium, light, heavy, and extra-heavy crude oil, as well as associated or non-associated natural gas) – within unspecified geographic areas. Although the agreement published in Official Gazette No. 35,754 of 17 July 1995 refers to an 'Appendix B', said annex is not included in the text of the agreement itself. In the view of the plaintiffs, this provision conflicts with the first paragraph of Article 5 of the LN, which permits the performance of such activities only 'in special cases'. This expression, they argue, is overly broad, vague, and indeterminateHowever, the appellants argued that the general nature of the agreements signed would conflict with Article 1.141 of the Civil Code, which provides for the definition of the object as a basic requirement to execute contracts, which in this case is undetermined and undeterminable, as the areas where the authorized activities would be carried out are not published and determined; hence, the definition of the object of the agreements is not possible.

390. The CSJ rejected the plaintiffs' petition based on Article 21 of the LN, under which the National Government, through the MEM, may determine the geographical areas where the contracting companies should carry out their activities. Therefore, the Supreme Court stated:

> It is inferred from both articles (5 and 21 of the LN) that, in an attempt to optimize the exploitation of such resources, the legislator made the reserve regime more flexible, thus authorizing the State to carry out such activities through its entities 'to improve the discharge of its duties', and even to enter into association agreements with private entities.

391. As to the argument that the areas where the authorized activities would be carried out were not published and determined, the Supreme Court clearly stated:

> There was proof that 'Appendix B', referred to in the first clause of Article 2 of the agreement challenged, is included in a certified copy and indicates the location of the geographical areas to be subject to the Association Agreements.

Additionally, the Supreme Court stated that:

> A copy of Official Gazette 35.881 of January 17, 1996, produced in due course by the appellants, which evidences the publication of Resolution 002 of January 16, 1996, issued by the MEM, whereby that Office, in compliance with article 21 of the LN, determines the geographical areas where the activities will be carried out, is duly recorded.

392. Regarding this matter, the Supreme Court clarified that the contested clause does not conflict with Article 5 of the LN above-mentioned, as the areas on which the AA referred to in the agreement of the Congress of 4 July 1995 would be entered into were sufficiently determined. Additionally, the ruling held that the AA did meet the 'special cases' condition as required under Article 5 of the aforementioned Law, as they were based on the promotion of the oil industry planning policies that aimed at the expansion through private capital and expansion of broader markets critical to the Venezuelan economy.

B. Violation of the Principles of Specificity and Lex Superior

393. The plaintiffs requested annulment due to unconstitutionality and illegality of the Second Clause on the bidding processes that 'The Subsidiary' will carry out to select the private investment companies with which it will enter into AA for carrying out the activities described in the First Condition, pursuant to Article 5 of the LN.

394. The appellants claimed that the constitutional principles of specificity and lex superior provided for in Article 163 of the Constitution of Venezuela (CN – Constitución Nacional de) of 1961 for laws issued in matters regulated by organic laws were violated, since the Organic Law of the Central Government has such category by mandate of Article 193 of the CN, and that pursuant to the jurisdiction provided for in Article 136(10) of the CN, the Venezuelan Republic is in charge of the hydrocarbon system and management. The appellants specifically stated that:

> It is a legislative jurisdiction that refers to the Organic Law of the Central Government, in the specified articles, the hierarchy of which must be construed as provided for in such article 163, as it is an Organic Law, so that the political management in hydrocarbon matters corresponds to the Ministry of Energy and Mines as direct entity of the President of the Republic.

395. They held that, notwithstanding the Congress Agreement, which is legally binding, the intention was for the 'Appointed Subsidiary' to be in charge of the management of the hydrocarbons policy, as well as of the actions derived from such management, as inferred from the Second Clause claimed.

396. Finally, they stated that any contract, agreement, or association entered into with private entities without the direct intervention of the MEM is void ab initio as it openly conflicts with Articles 163, 193, and 136(10) of the CN and Article 35(1)(5) of the Organic Law of the Central Government in force at that date. In this regard, the CSJ stated:

> Basically, it is important to refer to two provisions – Article 5 and Article 21 of the LN – in order to resolve the claims of the plaintiffs. Article 5 provides that the activities referred to in article 1 of the Law, that is, exploration and exploitation of reservoirs and domestic and foreign trade of those substances,

shall be carried out by the State, directly through the National Government or through its entities, being able to enter into operating agreements necessary for the best discharge of its duties.

397. However, the law also provides that:

> In special cases, and when convenient for the public interest, the National Government or the aforementioned entities may, in the exercise of any of the above activities, enter into association agreements with private entities with a share that guarantees control by the State for a established term, prior authorization of the Chambers in joint session, under the conditions they establish, after being duly informed by the National Government about all the relevant circumstances.

398. The CSJ affirmed:

> The thorough analysis of this provision inevitably leads to conclude that the oil subsidiaries, 'State-owned companies', are indeed authorized to enter into such associations with private entities with everything this involves, that is, including the selection of companies that guarantee 'the best performance', as provided by the law, of the activities they are entrusted with. This does not mean, as the appellants claim, that the National Government is being excluded from this activity or that its scope of powers is being invaded; on the contrary, the provision itself includes an example on how, in spite of delegating, the planning and management over the exploitation of hydrocarbon resources is still present; hence, it is inferred from the law that such agreements must be preceded by the information provided by the National Government of all relevant circumstances, which evidences a clear inherence in all the aspects related to the execution of the Agreements.

399. The CSJ concludes that there is no conflict between the second clause contested and the constitutional and legal regulations mentioned; hence, the Court declared the petition of the plaintiffs inadmissible.

C. The Government's Loss of Control over the Agreements

400. The appellants pleaded as grounds of illegality due to the unconstitutionality of the fourth clause regarding the appointment of a Control Committee:

> No company or corporation, like PDVSA or any of its subsidiaries, may exercise the duty of controlling the activities provided for in the First Clause of the agreement here partially challenged, let alone a Control Committee with the participation of private parties, completely unaware of the State's defined duties, as it is intended by the Fourth Clause of Article 2 of the agreement of the Congress of the Republic of July 4, 1995.

401. The plaintiffs insisted that the LN eliminated the concession system. Therefore:

> There are still two legal precepts in full force, namely, assignment and association, the Government maintaining the strict control at all times, as provided for in the case of associations by article 5 of the Organic Law Reserving to the State the Industry and Trade of Hydrocarbons, and, in agreement therewith, article 35(5) of the Organic Law of the Central Government.

402. Therefore, they infer that:

> there are no provisions in our current law on hydrocarbons that grant legal authority to PDVSA or its subsidiaries to have control over such activities. Let alone the Congress of the Republic can authorize a control with participation of private parties.

403. This clause is once again contested due to violation of the principles of specificity and *lex superior* provided for in Articles 136, 190, 193, and 163 of the CN.

404. In order to issue a ruling, the Supreme Court considered that Article 5 of the Organic Law Reserving to the State the Industry and Trade of Hydrocarbons provides that the State shall carry out the activities reserved to itself in Article 1, that is, all hydrocarbon-related activities 'whether directly or through its entities'. Likewise, it provides for the possibility of entering into AA with private entities 'with a share that guarantees control by the State'.

405. The text evidences, first, that PDVSA subsidiaries may have control over the decisions in AA since the law grants this power to the State, which may exercise it whether directly or through its entities, as exactly provided for. Second, in view of the appellants' claims, it must be clarified whether the State loses that control when exercised through the subsidiaries, which are 'State-owned' entities, for allowing, with the creation of the Control Committee, the intervention of private entities.

406. In this regard, upon reviewing the content of the Fourth Clause that provides for the creation of a Control Committee, it is observed that such committee must be set up by an equal number of members appointed by investors and by PDVSA subsidiary, but shall be chaired by a member appointed by the latter. It is also required that the members appointed by the subsidiary be present and agree for the deliberations and decisions to be valid, and the President has the casting vote to resolve a tie. The Supreme Court stated:

> Such provisions guarantee that the control to be exercised by the State, directly or through its entities (the subsidiaries), is present in every Association agreed upon. The foregoing without impairing the administrative control the State

must continue having through the corresponding entities, but on the contrary, it guarantees its deciding presence in the Association thus constituted.

407. Therefore, the conditions that determine the existence of a Control Committee reveal the strict control intended through hydrocarbon-related policies and in making the crucial decisions of the Association that affect such policies. Hence, a Control Committee jointly constituted by representatives of the subsidiary and the investor, chaired by a representative of the subsidiary with a casting vote to resolve ties, definitely guarantee the State's presence in the destiny of these Associations, even though it has a share of up to 35% of the capital stock. The foregoing also reveals that it is not possible to infer that the existence of the Control Committee impairs the jurisdiction of the State as to hydrocarbon control because the internal control of that Committee bolsters the external control of the State, which remains unaffected before that body.

D. One-Sided Clause Against the Investor

408. Another ground of illegality claimed by the appellants referred to an alleged disadvantage position against the investor, that is, the so-called one-sided clause. The appellants declared:

> Under the agreement of the Congress, the investor is liable for all potential losses arising out of the exploration stage, as it establishes the investor's commitment to carry out exploration activities in the area at the investor's risk based on an 'Exploration Plan', which, when fulfilled, the continuance of the exploration effort shall be approved by the Control Committee.

409. In the opinion of the appellants, such clause was invalid based on the provisions in Article 1.664 of the Civil Code; thus, should there be a decree of annulment of such clause at any time, the investors think they could require Venezuela to assume part of the losses arising out of their exploration works.

410. As to the appellants' petition, the Supreme Court pointed out:

> The Sixth Clause of the agreement issued by the Congress of the Republic laid the principles to be observed by Strategic Association Agreements, which – as established – contain, per se, the notion of public service, since these agreements are considered like those of a more definite administrative condition. Therefore, by establishing the provisions therein as a condition to enter into these agreements, the Congress of the Republic is maintaining and protecting the general interest included in said agreements, establishing that the risk involved in the exploration of hydrocarbons corresponds to the investor only, thus giving meaning and purpose to the 'extraordinary clause' required by this type of agreements, without which the protection of the collective interest – an obligation and not a choice of the Public Administration – would be insubstantial.

411. By virtue of the foregoing, the Supreme Court concluded:

> The Sixth Clause may not be classified as 'One-sided', hence, it does not violate the content of Article 1664 of the Civil Code – as claimed by the appellants – as this concept does not apply to the field of administrative agreement, where unbalance and disproportion between the interests of the parties, is not only permitted but also essential, provided that the collective interest is protected, as it is the case at hand.

412. Additionally, as PDVSA's defence alleged, since the appellants are not part to the Agreement, arguments lack the standing required to claim annulment of such clause, given that since it is an annulment on relative grounds, if any, only those with the condition of associates could file a legal action against PDVSA, and not third parties. Moreover, there is no actual interest by the appellants that may authenticate their petition to annul such clause, as it is based on hypothetical facts, like the 'possibility of the Republic of Venezuela being subject to claims by investors with losses in the exploration stage'.

E. Violation of the Legal Reserve in Tax Matters

413. The alleged violation of the legal reserve in tax matters claimed by the appellants refers to a tax exemption that would try to be supported by Article 7 of the LN and does not apply to new companies arising out of the AA, which according to the plaintiffs is contrary to Articles 162, 177, and 224 of the CN, as it violates the principle of legal reserve provided for in Article 224 that reserves the granting of 'exemptions' to the law.

414. In this regard, the appellants said:

> The Tenth Clause of the agreement is an evident and flagrant violation of the legal reserve, as it provides that 'The execution and enforcement of the Agreement shall be subject to the system provided for in the Organic Law Reserving to the State the Industry and Trade of Hydrocarbons given that the object thereof is limited to the performance of the activities reserved to the State only, pursuant to article 1 of such Law.' Accordingly, since such activities are regulated by the National Power, they shall not be subject to the payment of municipal or state taxes.

415. In addition, appellants stated that only the acts ratified by the chambers as legislative bodies (Article 162 of the CN) are to be understood as law. In turn, Article 177 ejusdem provides that 'laws are superseded by other laws only'. The appellants then stated that the tenth clause 'violates' Articles 29, 31(3), 224, 162, and 177 of the CN, including the legal reserve provided for in Article 40(20) of the Organic Tax Code, under which 'Only the law is to regulate the following matters subject to the general rules of this Code: 2. Grant tax exemptions and tax credits … ' According to the appellants, 'The Tenth Clause contested flagrantly violates the legal mandate as it provides for a tax exemption through an agreement that fails to meet the formal law requirements required by Article 162 of the CN.'

416. In this regard, the Supreme Court decreed:

> It is inevitable to conclude that the entire regulation on that matter, which naturally includes fiscal treatment thereof, must be included in a national Law, and therefore, it must be issued by the Congress within the limitations provided for in article 162 et. seq. of the Constitution. Overall, it is not possible that the municipalities extend their tax jurisdiction to activities that correspond to income matters exclusive of the National Power. On the contrary, upon defining the limits which this political unit – the Municipality – should be subject to, the constitutional text specifies the income matters of national jurisdiction.

417. Thus, the Supreme Court added:

> It is not that the tenth clause, claimed to be unconstitutional, provides for an exemption from municipal tax payment obligations for associated companies in the respective agreements, but it simply establishes the criteria on fiscal matters jurisdiction previously analyzed in the constitutional law, defining income-related jurisdictions corresponding to the national power only, and which, as seen, do not concern to the local system of rules; otherwise, – it is emphasized – it would imply an invasion by the Municipality to income-related jurisdictions reserved to the National Power. The plaintiffs confuse a matter pertaining to the allocation and organization of jurisdictions among territorial entities with that of misuse of positions, in this case, establishing an exemption, which on principle means a minimum jurisdiction on the matter by the Municipality, which is none, as established.

418. In the Supreme Court's opinion, the provisions of the Organic Tax Code, specifically Article 4(2) and Article 40(20), were not violated, since the tenth clause contested does not provide for an exemption from municipal tax payment obligations.

F. Violation of the Jurisdictional Sovereignty

419. The appellants also claimed the alleged unconstitutionality of the Seventeenth Clause of Article 2 of the agreement, which provides that:

> The controversies in matters that do not fall under the jurisdiction of the Control Committee and that cannot be settled through agreement between the parties shall be resolved through arbitration under the rules of proceeding of the International Chamber of Commerce in force upon signing the Agreement. In this regard, the appellants say that this provision 'flagrantly contradicts Article 127 of the CN, which reads: "In public interest contracts, if not admissible due to the nature thereof, a clause providing that the doubts and controversies that

may arise from such agreements and that could not be settled by any off-court's agreements of the parties involved shall be submitted to the jurisdiction of the Courts of the Republic and be subject to the laws thereof, without any further claims even outside the national territory, and deemed as included even if not expressly stated therein".'

420. The appellants defend the argument that the sole exception provided for by the aforementioned article refers to agreements entered into by and between two sovereign States or by and between one sovereign State and the entities of Public International Law; therefore, the wording of the subject article is sufficiently clear and categorical. In fact, they said: 'The subject matter is about association agreements, which entail an undeniable public interest.'

421. As to the arguments of the plaintiffs, the Supreme Court was categorical when expressing its disagreement with the statement of the appellants, 'since the wording of the referred article does not allow, neither semantically nor conceptually, making such distinction'. From the wording of Article 127 of the CN, 'it is evident that the authors of the Constitution did not specify that the exception therein referred to contracts entered into by and between two sovereign States or by and between one sovereign State and the entities of the Public International Law'.

422. As to the arbitration clause authorized under the Agreement and contested by the appellants, it is worth mentioning that the same Seventeenth Clause of Article 2 provides: 'The Agreement shall be governed and construed under the laws of the Republic of Venezuela.' And it also provides that the matters under the jurisdiction of the Control Committee shall not be subject to arbitration. And only this Control Committee (whose largest participation corresponds to representatives of the subsidiary) shall know the fundamental decisions of national interest in connection with the enforcement of the Agreement, which allows deducting that the matters that the Arbitration Board might know would not be fundamental to the national interest; therefore, as included in the case provided for in the Constitution, the Supreme Court decides to declare the argument of unconstitutionality inadmissible for this case.

G. Illegality in Applying the Royalty System

423. The appellants claimed the illegality of the twenty-first clause of Article 2 of the agreement as it contradicts the provision in the Sole Paragraph of Article 41 of the LH, which provides for the possibility that the oil royalty, called exploitation tax, could be reduced by the National Government from commencement of the exploitation activities if the subject reservoir is not deemed commercially viable.

424. In this regard, the appellants say that the above-mentioned article indeed refers to:

A potential and logical increase of the production costs due to the exhaustion of reservoir exploitation processes. This means that due to reservoir exhaustion, the production cost rocketed to a level that the exploitation is no longer commercially viable. In such case, and by way of exemption, the Government may establish percentages below 16 2/3%. In turn, in direct violation of article 41 ejusdem, the Agreement provides for the possibility of a royalty reduction from commencement of the reservoir exploitation activities if the reservoir is not deemed commercially viable.

425. Such interpretation by the plaintiffs in this trial arises from the fact that Article 41 of the LH aims to 'extend the financial exploitation of certain concessions', which would always imply for this type of incentive to be applicable that the reservoir is already being exploited and not, as provided by the clause contested, a benefit that may be agreed from commencement of exploitation activities.

426. The Supreme Court dismissed the above approach on the grounds of the actual meaning of the article in question. What matters in order to agree on the reduction of exploitation taxes is to extend the financial exploitation of the resource, that is, to allow extending the financial benefit generated by the activity to make the most of it. The foregoing statement necessarily implies that the operation must be financially viable in order to justify the investment required for such exploitation.

427. Accordingly, the viability of the project does not necessarily need the project to be in progress, as it is perfectly possible, particularly with the modern technology available for such purposes, to determine the approximate costs entailed. However, as provided for in such article, the adjustment made by the National Government may be reviewed and re-established to its original amount if it is determined that the causes generating the reduction have been modified. The Supreme Court concluded that the twenty-first clause of the Agreement in any way contradicts Article 41 of the LOH.

§7. Assessment of the Oil Opening

428. The opening of the hydrocarbons sector to private participation guaranteed capital flow, technology, and market opportunities for the Venezuelan crude oil. It caused a change of paradigm in the petroleum-society relationship, moving from the rentier State model to one with an increasing participation of the private sector, generating thousands of jobs. However, it produced a transformation without precedents of the national oil company, PDVSA, which became an efficient and competitive corporation, feasible in a competition environment and prepared to face the challenges of the time yet to come.

429. However, one of the most extraordinary achievements of the oil opening was, without any doubt, the possibility of developing the FPO, the largest hydrocarbon reservoir on the planet. The FPO remained unknown, at least with regard to its enormous potential, until the early 1980s not only because its exploitation was neither feasible nor profitable but also because there was no refinery in the world capable of receiving and processing the thousands of barrels of bitumen, heavy and extra-heavy crude oil zealously guarded for years.

430. Thus, the exploration and production projects developed in the FPO, including the technology and commercialization of Orimulsion and the offshore projects related to non-associated natural gas, not only increased the gas and oil reserves but also allowed maintaining a practically unlimited potential of production and a virtually secured place in the international markets. Likewise, the OAs opened up lost opportunities for old fields that were simply declining towards their lowest economic limit.

Chapter 2. Production

§1. Official Government Reports

431. In its latest report, published in 2016, PDVSA acknowledged a decline in production of approximately 292 kb/d, along with a 248 kb/d reduction in total refining capacity and a 236 kb/d decrease in exports. Unlike in previous years, this production decline affected all geographical areas, including the FPO, which had shown consistent growth for several consecutive years.[140]

432. Since then, *it has not been possible to access new official reports from PDVSA or the relevant ministry*. However, various organizations and institutions with access to this data continue to publish annual reports. Based on this information, it has been possible to *reconstruct the evolution of production, refining capacity, reserves, and other key indicators*, which are presented below.

§2. Reports from International Agencies

433. The following data is derived from the OPEC and other secondary sources, including the EIA, the IEA, the British Petroleum (BP) Statistical Review of World Energy, and Bloomberg. Reports from these specialized agencies substantiate that Venezuela's oil production has exhibited a persistent decline over the past two decades, with the reduction becoming especially pronounced in the last ten years.

434. According to the EIA, Venezuela's crude oil production declined from over 3 million barrels per day (mb/d) in 1999 to its lowest point in 2020, reaching merely 360,000 barrels per day (b/d). This precipitous decline is attributed to a variety of factors: (1) International sanctions: Since 2017, the United States has imposed financial sanctions on PDVSA, restricting the company's ability to acquire new debt or refinance existing obligations, which significantly impacted its operational capacity. (2) Deterioration of PDVSA: Lack of investment, maintenance, and inefficient management led to a substantial decrease in the state-owned company's productive capacity. (3) Exodus of professionals: The mass migration of qualified personnel weakened the technical capacity of the oil sector, affecting its efficiency and productivity. (4) Shortage of diluents: The lack of essential diluents needed to process extra-heavy crude limited oil production. (5) *Energy crisis*: Blackouts in 2019, particularly in the western part of the country, disrupted production, adversely affecting the oil industry. In 2015, Venezuela's crude oil production amounted to 2.6 million barrels per day (mb/d). However, by 2019, production had declined to 877,000 barrels per day (b/d), marking a loss of over 1 million barrels per day in just four years. This downward trend intensified in 2020, when production reached

140. *See*, ECOANLITICA, *Informe semanal*, No. 32, August 2017. http://www.pdvsa.com/images/pdf/Inversionistas/INFORMEDEGESTION2016.pdf (accessed 10 Jun. 2025).

its lowest point since 1973. Figure 12 illustrates Venezuela's historical oil production from 1918 to the present, incorporating key events that have influenced fluctuations in oil production.

Figure 12 Historical Oil Production in Venezuela (1918–Present)

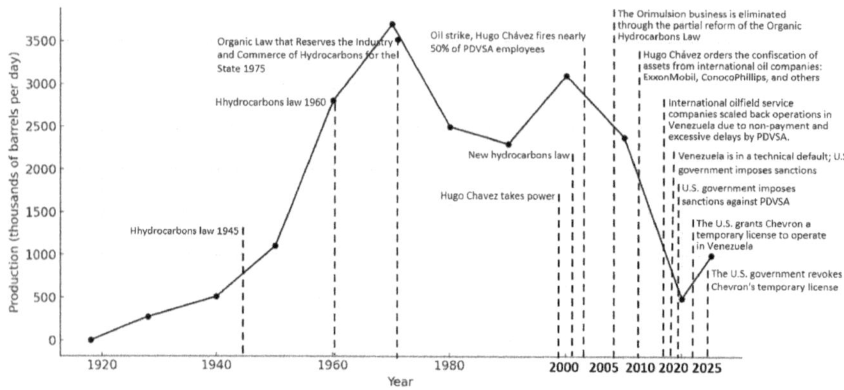

435. Venezuela's crude oil proved reserves by the end of 2024 were at 302,81 billion barrels, considered the biggest in the world (Figure 13).[141] Table 5 shows these reserves classified by basin and as developed and undeveloped.

Figure 13 Venezuela's Crude Oil Proved Reserves by Basin (End of 2024)

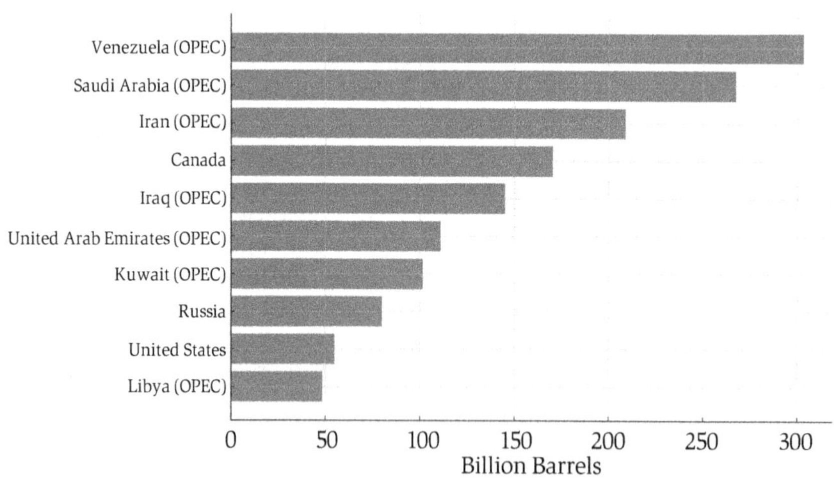

141. U.S. Energy Information Administration, *Country Analysis Brief: Venezuela*, 8 Feb. 2024, available at: https://www.eia.gov/international/content/analysis/countries_long/Venezuela/pdf/venezuela_2024.pdf (last accessed 3 Apr. 2025).

Table 5 Venezuela Oil Reserves (Billion Barrels)

Basin	*Proved*	*Proved/Developed*	*Production*
Maracaibo-Falcon	20,045	5,159	597
Barinas-Apure	1,093	195	27
Western (including FPO)	280,769	7,590	1,839
Carupano	343	–	–
Total	302,250	12,944	2,463

436. Particularly remarkable is the FPO, located south of the States of Guarico, Anzoategui, and Monagas, with an area of 55,314 sq km (21,357 sq mi) and a current exploitation area of 11,593 sq km (4476.1 sq mi). The main hydrocarbon reservoir on the planet is located in this region, integrated into the Western Basin. It contains 258,809 MMBls of crude oil, 3,935 MMBls of which correspond to heavy crude oil and 254,874 MMBls to extra-heavy crude oil. Other estimates on the amount of oil in the FPO have been made for more than seven decades.

437. In 1935, the exploitation of the FPO began with the drilling of the first wildcat well named 'Canoa 1'. In 1965, geologists Hugo Velarde and José Antonio Galavís estimated the reserves in the FPO at 700,000 million barrels, calculating a recovery of 5%–10%. Renowned Venezuelan geologist Aníbal Martínez affirmed in his book La Faja del Orinoco (The Orinoco Belt) that the original oil in the belt amounts to 913 billion barrels, 65.5% of which corresponds to extra-heavy crude oil and 34.5% to bitumen. The US Geological Survey established that the average estimate of oil recoverable resources of the Orinoco Belt amounts to 513 million barrels of crude oil.

438. In view of the realization of the vast hydrocarbon reserves in the FPO, the MEM created in 1974 the FPO Directorate, and, in the late 1980s, PDVSA started an exploitation programme that materialized with the approval by the Congress of the Republic of several agreements and associations to be developed in the blocks formerly called Petrozuata, Sincor, Hamaca, and Cerro Negro, which were renamed within the framework of the 'Magna Reserva' project as Boyacá, Junín, Ayacucho, and Carabobo, and segmented at the same time in twenty-eight blocks of approximately 500 sq km (193.05 sq mi) each. The magnitude of the FPO is evident in Figure 14.

Figure 14 Orinoco Oil Belt Project Blocks

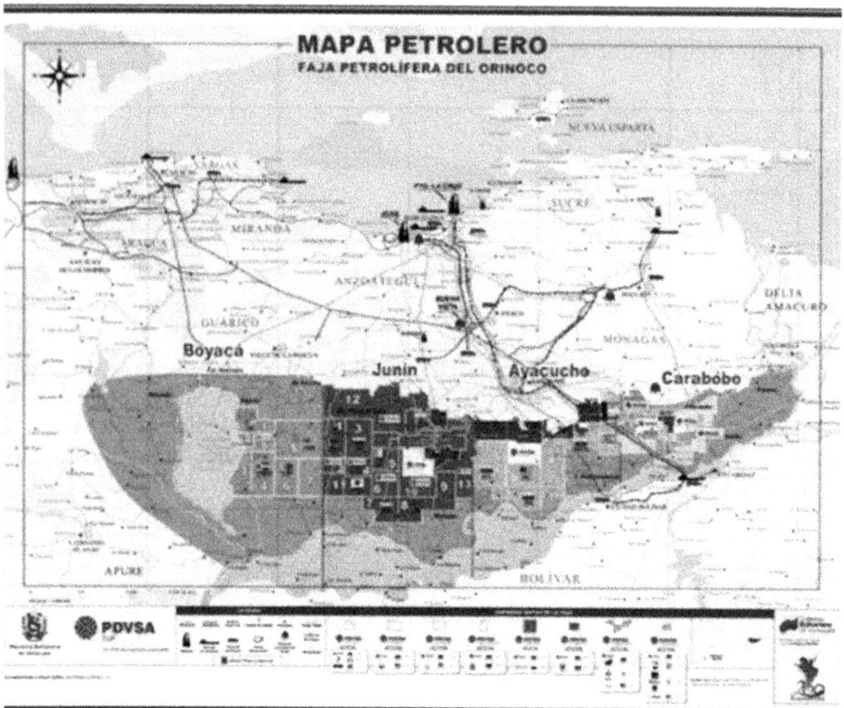

Source: PDVSA.

439. In 2005, the Magna Reserva Project was initiated, through which Venezuela obtained certification for the FPO, consolidating the country as possessing the largest proven hydrocarbon reserves in the world. The certification, updated in 2016, reaffirmed Venezuela's position at the top of the list of the ten most oil-rich countries globally.[142]

§3. New Conception of the National Oil Industry

440. Since 1999, the first actions taken by the current government were aimed to transform the structure, vision, and values that were the foundations of Petróleos de Venezuela back in 1975, as it was convinced that they would not be compatible with the goals and purposes the company would have to assume in the future under the new economic, social, and political model that was brewing.

142. BP, Statistical Review of World Energy June 2018.

441. The National Oil Industry and PDVSA arose from the idea developed in the Report submitted by the Oil Reversion Presidential Commission of 1974, which was projected in a Decentralized Administration of State nature, and subject to State guidelines contained in the Nation's Plans.

442. What can also be inferred from this Report is the will to keep the oil industry apart from the bureaucratic policies and practices in force for public agencies. In this regard, the State companies engaged in the oil activity needed to have administrative autonomy, financial self-sufficiency, and ability to renew their management. However, they were organized as State legal entities but as limited companies governed by private law. This criterion was included in the decree of the creation of PDVSA, whereby it was organized as a Limited Company of private law, regulated by the LN, under a private and a public law system. A good example of this special system is Article 8 of the LN, which provided that the executives, administrators, employees, and workers of State-owned companies would not be considered public officers or employees. This regulation was deliberately excluded from the 2001 LOH. Hence, PDVSA workers and, in general, those working in companies where the State is the majority partner, did not lose only a jurisdiction protecting employment stability but also a mechanism that prevented position assignment abuse and political manipulation. In fact, the subsidiaries and the large workforce of the IPN were exempted from the political dynamics, subject to its own rules, regulations, and employment contracts only, merit-based, as a method that rewarded effort and devotion to promote within the organization. Thus, from the decree of the 2001 LOH, the new administration opened the doors to the politicization evident today in the IPN, hence distorting public employee status, as if it were not worthy of respect.

443. Accordingly, the thesis that the PDVSA existing from 1976 to 2002 was incompatible with the new management style of the national oil industry was confirmed. However, changing the legal framework only did not guarantee institutional control and control over the workers. A dramatic change was necessary; hence, the 2003 crisis, considered the break point, the collision of two approaches, the big oil industry crisis, only paralleled to the events of 1936. The result was an unprecedented civil strike and the layoff of around 20,000 workers. The President of the Republic claimed these events and assumed to be the intellectual author thereof in order to have final political control of PDVSA's entire structure. Certainly, this provocation and the subsequent layoff of specialized workmanship, though it meant a political triumph for President Chavez, also gave rise to a new crisis, an operational crisis, due to the lack of qualified staff. Accidents have rocketed to record levels in the last hundred years. Industrial accidents with tragic consequences occur on a daily basis, to a higher or lower degree. Based on PDVSA's records until 2002, less than two accidents per million man-hours of exposure occurred in the refineries per year, and only 0.5–0.2 were fatal. In the current PDVSA, based on the 2010 Report, an average of 9.40 accidents and 5.97 deaths per million man-hours of exposure are reported. Since 2003 to date, 300 large-scale accidents have occurred, where 70 workers were killed and 2,805 were injured. These figures do not include the most recent cases, like the explosion in the Amuay refinery on 25 August 2012, resulting in 55 people killed and 156 injured.

444. In 2017, PDVSA could be regarded as an administrative extension of the central government, with a workforce exceeding 140,000 employees. This represented an increase of over 150% compared to historical levels, which ranged between 40,000 and 50,000 employees and contractors. However, according to statements made by the company's president, Pedro Tellechea, in 2024, the workforce had been reduced to approximately 90,000 employees.[143]

445. The new vision of both the company and the national oil policy assigns PDVSA responsibilities and duties that have no relation to its core activities or activities related thereto. Some responsibilities include import and sale of food, housing, building, and agricultural activities. However, PDVSA makes substantial contributions to the different Social Missions implemented by the national Government and to Social Projects developed with the Independence 200 Fund, Simón Bolívar Comprehensive Reconstruction Fund, PDVSA's Social Development Fund, Petrobonos Fund, Asphalt Fund, and Fund of Socially-Owned Companies, in addition to the contributions to the National Development Fund, the Fund for Economic and Social Development of Venezuela, and the Chinese Fund. According to the 2011 management report, these contributions amounted to USD 39,604 million by 2011 and USD 123,696 million since 2001.

446. The adverse effects of assigning the oil industry other non-oil-related activities, even forcibly and openly participating in political activities, are the main cause of the current dangerous operating situation of the company. The fact that the Minister of Energy and Oil is at the same time the president of the company is clear evidence that the roles exercised by each institution in the past no longer exist. MENPET should control, supervise, and request accounts of PDVSA's activities. If the financial reports and the statements of operations are submitted to the same authority issuing them, what error could the minister find? What could he suggest? How does that affect the company's transparency and the management of resources from oil sales?

447. According to Transparency International's 2017 report, Venezuela was ranked as the most corrupt country in Latin America and placed among the eleven most corrupt countries globally, only ahead of North Korea, Equatorial Guinea, Guinea-Bissau, Libya, Sudan, Yemen, Afghanistan, Syria, South Sudan, and Somalia. Uruguay and Chile were ranked as the most transparent countries in the region. This perception has persisted in subsequent years, and in 2024, particularly serious cases were reported. In April of that year, former Minister of Petroleum Tareck El

143. Infobae, '*Trabajadores denunciaron que decenas de empleados fueron obligados a renunciar a PDVSA por no apoyar al régimen de Maduro*,' 21 Aug. 2024, available at: https://www.infobae.com/venezuela/2024/08/21/trabajadores-denunciaron-que-decenas-de-empleados-fueron-obligados-a-renunciar-a-pdvsa-por-no-apoyar-al-regimen-de-maduro/ (last accessed 3 Apr. 2025).

Aissami was arrested in connection with the alleged disappearance of over 20 billion U.S. dollars in oil revenues (Infobae, 2024).[144] Later, in October, PDVSA's then-president Pedro Tellechea was detained for allegedly providing strategic information to companies linked to foreign intelligence services (Huffington Post España, 2024).[145]

448. The perception of corruption shown in Transparency International's 2017 report, which has been consistently observed in previous reports, was investigated by the opposition-controlled Venezuelan Parliament. A detailed report presented by the Permanent Commission for Comptrollership (Case No. 1648), led by Congressman Freddy Guevara in November 2016, shows at least ten corruption cases amounting to a gigantic amount of more than 11 billion dollars extracted from PDVSA through different schemes. It is important to point out that the study is largely based on the reports of the Office of the Comptroller General of the Republic (OCGR), published between 2006 and 2013.

449. Given that this institution has not been characterized precisely by its impartiality in the face of the innumerable corruption cases registered in the Chavez and Maduro governments, it is plausible to think that the list of cases analysed by the Parliament scarcely represents a fraction of the total number of cases, which has led to bankruptcy, not only in the company but also to the whole country, mired in a humanitarian crisis, in the face of the extraordinary wealth displayed by the regime's hierarchs.

450. Beyond the events documented between 1999 and 2017, the situation at PDVSA has continued to deteriorate. The reduction of its workforce to approximately 90,000 employees in 2024 has not been accompanied by any substantial transformation in management or operational recovery. On the contrary, technical reports and media investigations indicate that oil production remains significantly below installed capacity, while accidents, brain drain, and infrastructure decay persist. The company also faces a severe loss of institutional legitimacy, exacerbated by corruption scandals and a lack of transparency. In this context, the recovery of PDVSA cannot be understood merely as a technical or economic challenge, but as a structural one – requiring comprehensive reform in governance, accountability, and reconnection with its legal mandate and public function.

---

144. Al Jazeera, *Venezuela's Ex-Oil Minister Arrested for Alleged Ties to U.S.*, 21 Apr. 2024, available at: https://www.aljazeera.com/news/2024/10/21/venezuelas-ex-oil-minister-arrested-for-alleged-ties-to-us (last accessed 3 Apr. 2025).

145. Huffington Post España, *Venezuela Detiene al Exministro de Petróleo Pedro Tellechea por Delitos Contra la Nación*, October 2024, available at: https://www.huffingtonpost.es/global/venezuela-detiene-exministro-petroleo-pedro-tellechea-delitos-nacionbr.html (last accessed 3 Apr. 2025).

§4. Oil Production to Unconventional New Business

I. Chinese Fund

451. The 'Chinese Fund' is a Bi-national Collaboration fund aimed at financing projects in Venezuela and made up of contributions from the Chinese Development Bank (CDB) and *Fondo Nacional para el Desarrollo Nacional* (FONDEN). The funds are managed through Bandes (Economic and Social Development Bank). The First Heavy Fund (Fondo Pesado) was signed in November 2007 and expired in November 2010. The Second Heavy Fund was signed in February 2009 and expired in February 2012. The Large-Volume Fund was signed in September 2010 and expired in September 2020, as indicated on the website of PDVSA. The loans agreed are itemized in Table 6.[146]

Table 6 China's Loans to Venezuela

Year	*Borrower*	*Lender*	*Amount (MM USD)*	*Purpose*
2008	Bandes–PDVSA	CDB	4,000	Infrastructure development and social programs
2009	Bandes–PDVSA	CDB	4,000	Infrastructure
2009	CVG	CDB	1,000	Mining project
2010	PDVSA	CDB and BES	1,500	Financial structure
2010	PDVSA–Bandes	CDB	20,000	Infrastructure
2011	PDVSA	CDB	4,000	Infrastructure
2011	PDVSA	CDB	4,000	Housing construction
2013	PDVSA	CDB	5,000	Social development
2015	Bandes	CDB	5,000	Rollover of Tranche B of the China–Venezuela Joint Fund
2017	Bandes	CDB	5,000	Tranche C of the China–Venezuela Joint Fund
			53,500	

146. Fabiana Culshaw, *El Fondo Chino Auxilia al Gobierno Venezolano en la Crisis Económica*, available at: http://virtual.iesa.edu.ve/servicios/wordpress/wp-content/uploads/2016/04/2014-abr-jun-culshaw.pdf (last accessed 3 Apr. 2025).

452. This mechanism to obtain cash was implemented prior to the decree of the Approving Law of the Agreement between the Government of the Bolivarian Republic of Venezuela and the Government of the People's Republic of China, concerning the Financing Fund of 18 September 2008. Conversely, this agreement provides for a particular line of credit endorsed by agreements for the supply of oil (goods of the Republic), not extracted from the subsoil for future delivery. Therefore, one may wonder how this mechanism could have been implemented without an appropriate legal framework and in gross violation of Article 93 of the Organic Law of the Financial Administration of the Public Sector, which provides that 'Public credit operations may not be contracted through guarantees or encumbrances on state or municipal assets.' The Government has not answered this question, and neither the Office of the Comptroller General nor the General Prosecutor's Office has started an investigation despite the claims filed by State Representative Miguel Ángel Rodríguez.

453. The doubts are focused on establishing the price agreed to repay the dollars and yuans lent by China. The Minister of Planning and Finance, Jorge Giordani, assures that part of the debt from the Chinese Fund was repaid at the market price of USD 100.41, hence, contradicting the President of PDVSA, Rafael Ramírez, who in a report submitted to Chávez indicated that Chinese Funds 1 and 2 were calculated based on the oil barrel valued at USD 40. This means that USD 60 per barrel would be somewhere floating – over USD 3,000 million referred to by Minister Giordani. Anyway, if Giordani is telling the truth and Rafael Ramírez otherwise, the Chinese Fund has given over USD 22,000 million to the National Executive Branch, while PDVSA has sent to China 346.3 million oil barrels in four years, which is equal to 240.4 MBD and over USD 30,000 million.

454. As explained by the Minister and President of PDVSA, that figure currently amounts to 640,000 barrels of crude oil and by-products per day, 273,000 barrels of which are used to repay the loans from the Chinese Fund. Based on another analysis presented by Parsifal D'Sola Alvarado, China would be keeping USD 70 per barrel as payment of the debt, and PDVSA receives for its oil the difference between USD 70 and the market price of the barrel only. The foregoing only generates more doubts, though: At what price is PDVSA offsetting the oil barrels it must give to China? It is unlikely to be at market price, unless Venezuela assumes the high transportation costs, since China may acquire oil at a better price from the Middle East, which is just 6,000 km (3.728 mi) away, rather than acquiring it from Venezuela, which is more than 16,000 km (9,941 mi) apart.

455. In addition, what happens with the payment of royalties and taxes for the oil 'export'? Do the amounts of money negotiated go to PDVSA's cash because the barrels are produced by the State-owned company? How to justify that Venezuela and PDVSA need to be as indebted if the current oil prices are at the highest ever in the longest period of history? How and who manages the Chinese Fund, and to which entity are the corresponding accounts rendered?

456. It is evident that this type of unprecedented businesses in the oil history of Venezuela, characterized by the lack of control and transparency, facilitates the acts of corruption that have been reported by State Representatives of the National Assembly since 2011 and have scandalized the country throughout 2013; and no response has been given regarding this atypical method to receive money in exchange of oil in the future.

457. In recent years, the use of the Chinese Fund has significantly declined. Economic monitoring reports and official statements indicate that, since 2020, China has restricted new lines of financing due to Venezuela's payment defaults, contractual breaches, and overall financial instability. By the end of 2023, no new operations were reported under this mechanism, suggesting its exhaustion as a strategic source of funding. According to the LAC Network for Democracy and Transparencia Venezuela, no new disbursements have been issued since 2017, despite repeated efforts by the Venezuelan government to secure additional loans (Transparencia Venezuela, 2020).[147] This situation reflects a broader deterioration in the bilateral energy relationship and raises serious concerns about the long-term viability of debt models tied to natural resources without clear, transparent, and verifiable accountability mechanisms (Bloomberg, 2023; Reuters, 2024).[148]

II. Petrocaribe

458. The Venezuelan government has set in motion a series of businesses that compromise and cast doubts on their commercial purposes and seems to give more importance to the ideological relation with political purposes. Some lack legal, ethical grounds and offer totally unfavourable terms and conditions. That is the case of the Petrocaribe Energy Cooperation Agreement, which establishes that PDVSA shall provide oil and products to State oil companies of the signatory countries, under certain terms and conditions that are, from our point of view, extremely unfavourable for the country.

459. In the case at hand, Venezuela, through PDVSA, sells to eighteen countries an estimate of 332,000 barrels per day (BD) of oil and refined products, which are paid by the beneficiary countries as follows:

147. Transparencia Venezuela, *The China Deals: A Project by Transparencia Venezuela and the Latin American and Caribbean Network for Democracy*, October 2020, available at: https://transparenciave.org/wp-content/uploads/2020/10/The-China-Deals-Transparencia-Venezuela-oct-2020.pdf (last accessed 3 Apr. 2025).

148. Bloomberg, *LatAm Sees Return of Chinese Bank Lending After Covid Pause*, 24 Mar. 2023, available at: https://www.bloomberg.com/news/articles/2023-03-24/latam-sees-return-of-chinese-bank-lending-after-covid-pause (last accessed 3 Apr. 2025); Reuters, *China's CNPC Pulls Back on Venezuela Investments Amid Debt Tensions*, 27 Aug. 2024, available at: https://www.reuters.com/business/energy/china-cnpcs-global-oil-gas-investment-2024-08-27/ (last accessed 3 Apr. 2025).

1. The total bill is divided into two parts, which shall depend on the price of the oil barrel. Each part of the bill may have a financing ranging between 5% and 50%.
2. The first part is to be paid within ninety days (three months).
3. The second part is to be paid within twenty-five years at 1%, with a two-year grace period.

460. These terms and conditions are described in the Fourth Title of the agreement, on financing mechanisms and payments itemized in Table 7.

Table 7 Oil Price and Financing Percentage

Barrel Price	*Financing %*
>=USD 15 per barrel	5
>=USD 20 per barrel	10
>=USD 22 per barrel	15
>=USD 24 per barrel	20
>=USD 30 per barrel	25
>=USD 40 per barrel	30
>=USD 50 per barrel	40
>=USD 100 per barrel	50

461. As may be observed, the barrel price determines the terms and conditions of the agreement. Under the current circumstances, with a barrel over USD 30, financing is at 25%, two-year grace, twenty-five-year term, and a 1% interest. In addition, the agreement establishes that Venezuela shall accept goods and services as part of the deferred payment for which it would offer preferential prices, including, among others, sugar, bananas, or other goods or services that may be determined, and whose amount is indeed undetermined. Then, how, and under which criteria is the amount in cash payable for the deferred debt established, and who establishes it? Will it be 10%, 20%, or 40%?

462. Let us see a specific example of a credit to deferred payment in Table 8:[149] In 2011, Nicaragua received 27 MBD, representing the amount of USD 2.7 million per day. Half corresponds to the payment deferred for twenty-five years, at 1%, that is, the amount of USD 1.3 million per day and a total of USD 468 million per year.

149. PDVSA, *Informe de Gestión Anual 2011*, p. 170, available at: http://www.pdvsa.com/images/pdf/RELACION%20CON%20INVERSIONISTAS/Informes%20Anuales/informe%20de%20gestion/2011/Informe%20de%20Gestion%20Anual%202011.PDF (last accessed 3 Apr. 2025).

Table 8 Products Received by Venezuela as Payment of the Oil Bill

Country	*Product*	*Unit*	*Amount Received*		*Variation 2010 Versus 2011*	*% Variation 2010 Versus 2011*
2010	*2011*					
Guyana	White rice	MT	18,900	46,700	27,800	147
	Paddy rice		67,391	121,209	53,818	80
Nicaragua	Oil	MT	16,657	15,280	(1,377)	(8)
	Sugar	MT	20,000	42,440	22,440	112
	Coffee	MT	17,385	28,822	11,437	66
	Beans	MT	13,540	9,760	(3,780)	(28)
	Meat	MT	27,998	33,677	5,678	20
	Milk	MT	23,091	15,024	(8,067)	(35)
	Palm oil				15,630	New
	Stabilak	MT			0.5	New
	Beans seeds	MT			25	New
	Steers	Unit	16,669	13,778	3,109	29
	Plants	Unit		19,397	19,397	New
	Heifers	Unit	2,087	2,631	544	26
Dominican Republic	Liquid sugar	MT	2,294	5,275	2,781	112
	Beans	MT	800	1,795	995	124
	Pasta	MT	1,389	8,278	6,890	496
El Salvador	Coffee	MT	1,832		(1,832)	(100)
Total		MT	**211,477**	**343,916**	**132,439**	**63**
	Unit	**12,756**	**35,806**	**23,050**	**181**	

463. According to the table above, Nicaragua decided to pay its account with young bulls, heifers, and pants. This last item seems to be expressed in units, though its value is not clear, let alone the total in US dollars, and there is no specification on whether they are jeans or other types of pants. This trade agreement precept of the current government undoubtedly makes, on the one hand, the follow-up and control of those operations difficult, and, on the other, adversely affects the national production, which, instead of having incentives, they are rather applied to other countries' economy. So, where are those heifers and pants? Who distributes them, to whom, and based on which criteria? Those are goods that belong to the Venezuelan people and are being traded by really irresponsible and unscrupulous people. This modality actually facilitates the setup of corruption networks not only in Venezuela but also in the beneficiary countries. If these figures are projected to the total oil barrels traded under the current modality, it would evidence that the country is facing a critically alarming situation.

464. As previously said, Petrocaribe 'trades' around 332 MBD with eighteen countries – USD 10 million per day; in other words, USD 3,600 million per year (2016). And of that amount, 25% (USD 900 million) practically turns into uncollectible receivables or disappears through this dishonest trade mechanism.

465. In recent years, the Petrocaribe mechanism has remained largely paralyzed. The sharp decline in PDVSA's production capacity, combined with corruption scandals and international sanctions, resulted in the suspension of most shipments. However, since 2022, Venezuela has expressed its intention to revive the agreement. In November of that year, Saint Vincent and the Grenadines became the first country to resume imports under the Petrocaribe scheme. Throughout 2023 and 2024, negotiations have continued with other Caribbean Member States to re-establish supply arrangements, although the volumes remain limited and contingent upon political and diplomatic conditions.

§5. Refining Sector

I. Private Participation

466. According to the LOH (Article 10), refining activities including distillation, purification, and transformation of natural hydrocarbons may be performed by the State and private individuals, jointly or separately (Article 50). The facilities and existing works, and their annexes and modifications, owned by the State or the companies exclusively owned by the State that are committed to the refining of natural hydrocarbons in the country and the main transportation of products and gas are reserved for the State under the terms set forth by this Law.

II. Objectives

467. The promotion of private participation (Article 51) has the following purpose:

1. Promote the largest and deepest transformation of refined hydrocarbons.
2. Promote the investments in projects generating substances to support the development of the national industrial sector.
3. Make sure that the hydrocarbon processing refineries and plants under the control of the State guarantee with top priority, with regard to the alternative of

exportation, timely supply for the subsequent processing of the basic substances in the amounts and with the quality and price schemes and commercial conditions that may allow the development of competitive companies in the international markets.

4. Develop industrial parks around the refineries and in areas where the supply of hydrocarbons or their by-products may be eased.
5. Endorse the creation and participation of financial entities in the industrialization of hydrocarbons in the country.
6. Have companies performing activities for the industrialization of hydrocarbons in the country promote, in turn, the industrialization of the input material they produce downstream.
7. Foster the formation of national capital and link such capital to a greater added value of the input material processed, generating more competitive products in the international market (Article 52).

III. Permits

468. Private companies involved in the activities of industrialization of refined hydrocarbons in the country must obtain a permit that shall be granted by the Ministry of Energy and Oil, prior to compliance with the following requirements (Article 53):

1. Identification of companies and their representatives.
2. Indication of the supply source of the raw material.
3. Definition of the Project, pointing out the destination of the products.
4. Inscribe in the register that shall be kept by the Ministry of Energy and Oil (Article 54) for such purpose.

IV. Existing Infrastructure

469. Venezuela, through PDVSA, has a global refining capacity of 2,806 MBD distributed in fourteen refineries: five in Venezuela, five in the US, three in the Caribbean, and one in Europe.

470. In the US, CITGO, PDVSA's largest subsidiary abroad, refines oil and sells fuel, lubricants, and petrochemical products. CITGO has an estimated 14,000 gas stations (E/S – *Estación de Servicio*), approximately fifty-five storage and distribution terminals.

471. In Europe, the crude oil and by-products refining activities are carried out through the subsidiary, PDV Europe B.V., with a 50% stake in Nynas AB, a company that operates in Sweden and the United Kingdom. PDVSA refines crude and markets and transports bitumen, lubricants, and other refined products through Nynas.

472. In the Caribbean, PDVSA operates three refineries in Curacao, Jamaica, and the Dominican Republic, as indicated in Table 9.[150]

Table 9 Global Refining Complex of PDVSA

Name	*Location*	*Capacity MBD*	*Participation of PDVSA*
CRP	Falcon, Venezuela	940	100%
Bajo Grande	Zulia, Venezuela	16	100%
San Roque	Zulia, Venezuela	5	100%
PLC	Anzoategui, Venezuela	192	100%
EPL	Carabobo, Venezuela	140	100%
Isla	Curacao	335	Rented
Kingston	Jamaica	35	49%
Refidomsa PDV	Dominican Republic	34	49%
Lake Charles	Golfo de México, US	425	100%
Corpus Christi	Golfo de México, US	157	100%
Lemont	Illinois, US	167	100%
Chalmette	Louisiana, US	184	50%
Merey Sweeny	Texas, US	168	50%
Nynas AB	Sweden, Europe	8	50%
Total Refining Capacity		**2,806**	

473. It is important to point out that until 2002, PDVSA's refining complex abroad included nineteen refineries (including the Curacao Island refinery under lease). However, upon instructions from the Chavez government, PDVSA proceeded to sell five of its refineries in the US: Paulsboro, Savannah, Lyondell, Chalmette, and Saint Croix, as well as its interest in four refineries in Germany: Gelsenkirchen, Schwedt, Neustadt, Karlsruhe, and one in Belgium: Antwerp, and

150. PDVSA, *Refinación*, pp. 26–29, available at: http://www.pdvsa.com/images/pdf/cuadernos/Refinacion.pdf (last accessed 3 Apr. 2025).

subsequently acquired stakes in those of Jamaica, the Dominican Republic, and Cuba, taking into account the fact that in 2017 it has lost, 49% of the shares it held in the latter country due to non-payment of its interest as a shareholder. Following these refinery sales and purchases, PDVSA and its foreign partners' refining capacity was reduced from 3,270,000 b/d to 1,513,000 b/d, of which 749,000 b/d are still exclusive to PDVSA, maintaining a refining capacity of 764,000 b/d together with its partners.

474. In terms of national potential, it should be noted that the Paraguana Refining Centre (CRP – *Centro de Refinación de Paraguaná*), the El Palito Refinery (ELP), and the Puerto La Cruz Refinery (PLC) operate at minimum levels, which means that they are unable to supply the domestic hydrocarbon market (gasoline, diesel, LPG, lubricants, and others), forcing PDVSA to import hydrocarbon derivatives products. According to studies carried out by experts in the field, the range of operation ranges between 35% and 40%, for the years 2017 and 2018, with long periods of 30%. This means that the processed volumes of crude oil vary between 455 and 520 MBD.

475. Historically, Venezuela stood out as an exporter of refined petroleum products following the formal institutionalization of its oil industry in 1943. However, this structural condition changed dramatically by 2010, when the country began to record sustained net imports of refined products – marking a profound shift in its energy balance.

476. According to data from the EIA, Venezuela became increasingly reliant on fuel imports in the late 2010s, reaching a historical high in March 2018 with 5,290 thousand barrels of finished petroleum products imported from the United States. This unprecedented level of dependency reflected the severe deterioration of domestic refining operations and marked a turning point in the country's energy balance, transforming Venezuela from a traditional net exporter of refined products into a net importer – a reversal that has deepened further in subsequent years.[151]

477. Despite Venezuela's installed refining capacity being theoretically sufficient to meet domestic demand, the operational state of its refineries remains critical. According to the latest report from the US Energy Information Administration (EIA, 2024), the downstream sector of PDVSA remains severely impaired due to years of underinvestment, inadequate maintenance, and international sanctions. Since 2020, fuel imports from Iran have partially mitigated gasoline shortages, but refining throughput continues to fall significantly short of capacity. As of late 2022, PDVSA entered into a technical cooperation agreement with Iran to rehabilitate and maintain state-run refineries. Nevertheless, domestic fuel supply remains limited, forcing the country to import refined products during critical periods and severely undermining Venezuela's energy security. This persists despite the partial easing of

151. U.S. Energy Information Administration, *Petroleum & Other Liquids*, available at: https://www.eia.gov/dnav/pet/hist/LeafHandler.ashx?n=PET&s=MTXEX_NUS-NVE_1&f=M (last accessed 3 Apr. 2025).

US sanctions in 2023, which allowed the reactivation of joint ventures (JVs – *Empresas Mixtas*) with companies such as Chevron.

478. Figure 15[152] shows monthly US exports of petroleum products to Venezuela from January 2004 to January 2025. The graph illustrates the historical evolution of bilateral energy trade, marked by a steady increase in exports up to the peak period of 2012–2014, when US products supplied Venezuela amid a decline in its domestic refining capacity. A dramatic collapse is observed starting in 2019, coinciding with the imposition of US sanctions on PDVSA, which reduced shipments to near-zero levels between 2020 and 2022. A partial recovery began in late 2022 and extended through 2023 and 2024, as some sanctions were eased and US companies resumed limited operations in Venezuela. The monthly detail of the curve not only reveals the depth of the energy crisis but also underscores the high dependency on external supply during periods of domestic production collapse.

Figure 15 U.S. Exports to Venezuela of Total Petroleum Products

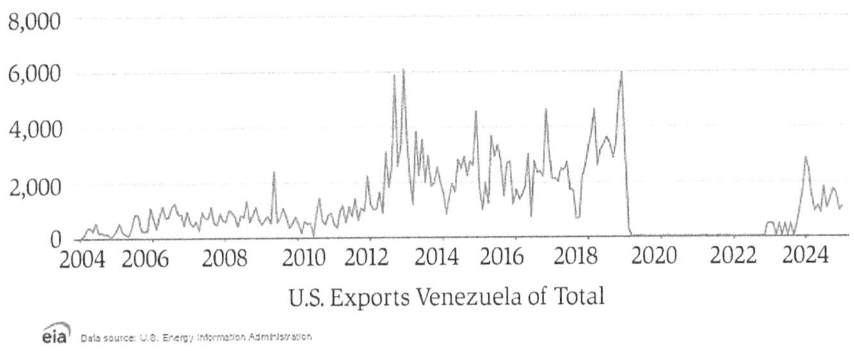

152. U.S. Energy Information Administration (EIA), *U.S. Exports to Venezuela of Total Petroleum Products (Monthly, January 2004–January 2025)*, last updated 31 Mar. 2025, available at: https://www.eia.gov/dnav/pet/hist/LeafHandler.ashx?n=PET&s=MTXEX_NUS-NVE_1&f=M (last accessed 3 Apr. 2025).

Chapter 3. Exploitation

479. On 2 November 2001, the LOH was issued to regulate all liquid hydrocarbon-related matters. This new Law somehow breaks the rule of a legal framework with origins in the 1943 LOH, which, with the subsequent amendments – including the nationalization of all hydrocarbons – remained partially in force until 1 January 2002. In fact, the superseded LOH represented a confusing system that generated contradictions and favoured legal insecurity and institutional instability in the sector, mainly due to the lack of general regulations that regulated hydrocarbon matters in a clear manner. Even today, as a reminiscence of such 1943 LOH, the estimates of the allocation of oil income calculated over the royalty amounts provided for therein are still in effect.

480. The complexity of this legal system is evident in the sole repealing provision of the LOH, where the diversity of provisions governing for nearly six decades is confirmed. Six laws are expressly superseded, and the sublegal framework is pending amendment and update, which would be in any case automatically superseded, if colliding with the new LOH.

§1. Activities Reserved to the State

481. The CRBV of 1999 and the LOH establish a new legal system of oil activity reserve. Specifically, Articles 1 (scope of the decree), 2 (reservoirs ownership), and 9 (primary activities) of the LOH, as well as Articles 302 (reserve over the oil activity) and 303 (granting constitutional status to PDVSA's shares) of the Constitution, set forth the scope of the reserve. In fact, the reserve covers activities of exploration to find hydrocarbon reservoirs, exploitation, gathering, transportation through special means, and primary storage. However, all matters related to existing refineries, as well as extensions and future improvements thereof, are also reserved to the State in order to guarantee the supply in the domestic market.

482. Now, what is the actual scope of the hydrocarbon industry reserve as of the last oil reform in Venezuela? Is the National Oil Industry more or less nationalized in relation to the 1975 LN? Or – to use an expression more appropriate to the current political debate – are we less or more sovereign in oil matters than we were before the last amendment? We will try to answer these questions based on the opinions of renowned personalities in the national political life. Therefore, we need to go back to the scope of the 1975 LN. As it may be recalled, its distinctive element was having every hydrocarbon-related activity exclusively reserved to the State; consequently, private entities could not participate unless it was by way of exception and in the cases expressly provided for in Article 5 – already broadly developed herein – whether through OAs or Strategic Associations, which required, in any case, approval by the Congress of the Republic. The essential condition inherent to these agreements was not to affect the activities reserved to the State, which remained under State control through the LN.

483. The enactment of the new LOH reduces the scope of the reserved activities without entailing liberalization or actual opening of primary activities. According to Álvaro Silva Calderón: 'The LOH is nothing but an action plan that upholds the premises of the Nationalization Law and assumes that investments are required though under the conditions of the State.' On the contrary, constitution expert Allan Brewer-Carías affirms that:

> Since 1999, however, the public intervention technique has changed, particularly in oil matters, by leaving the reserve to the State with regard to the industry (exclusion of financial freedom), denationalizing it and adopting intervention techniques based on the limitation of private financial freedom, with the consistent introduction of the authorization (licenses, permits) precept to enable execution thereof.

484. Brewer-Carías argued that:

> The first aspect of the industry denationalization process is the result of the reduction of the scope of the activities reserved to the State, which has remained focused on primary activities, the activities carried out in refineries existing when the Organic Law was issued, the domestic and foreign trade activities for natural hydrocarbons, and the domestic and foreign trade activities for by-products, the sale of which is reserved to the State by Decree.

485. It is worth adding that it is possible, through different ways, to stop primary activities from being State-exclusive; on the one hand, through the organization of JV, and, on the other, through the assignment of the Executive Branch's rights. In fact, as provided for by decree in Article 24 of the LOH, the Executive Branch may grant the operating companies the right to exercise primary activities, as well as the ownership or other rights over real or personal property owned by the Republic, required to efficiently exercise such activities. The Executive Branch may revoke such rights if the operating companies fail to meet their obligations, thus preventing accomplishment of the purpose for which such rights were assigned. This provision evidently offers a clear perspective on how fragile the scope of State-reserved and State-exclusive activities is. It is unavoidable to conclude that this new legal framework advances towards a clear reduction of the reserved activities under an apparent administrative control resulting from the majority of shares in the operating companies, which will not necessarily lead to better financial results; on the contrary, it may have a negative effect as such companies must assume the heavy load of a majority partner tangled in its own inefficiency.

§2. End of the Nationalization

486. It is worth mentioning that the denationalization of the oil industry referred to by Allan Brewer-Carías is reinforced by Article 303 of the CRBV, where PDVSA's shares were granted constitutional status. In this regard, Bernard Mommer made an interesting remark:

> Under the new Bolivarian Constitution, PDVSA, which is actually a holding company, cannot be denationalized, but such restriction does not apply to its upstream subsidiaries. PDVSA, unlike its subsidiaries, does not produce a single barrel of oil. Most Venezuelans are of the opinion that the Bolivarian Constitution has strengthened the nationalization. Nevertheless, what it has done, ironically, is to pave the way for the transformation of PDVSA – the holding company – into a liberal bidding agency at the service of the privatized industry.

487. Regarding this aspect of the granting of constitutional status to PDVSA's shares, Allan Brewer-Carías affirmed:

> Unfortunately, it was included in the law that the ownership of the shares 'of the subsidiaries, strategic associations, companies, and any other company organized or to be organized as a result of the business development of Petróleos de Venezuela, S.A. were excluded from that reserve'. That had the effect contrary to the one intended, since the reserve of the ownership of shares established in the Constitution referred only to the shares of Petróleos de Venezuela, S.A. (PDVSA), that is, the shares of the oil holding, but not to those of its subsidiaries (which are the ones that actually carry out all the operating activities in the oil industry), about which even the Constitution clarified that they may be sold. As a result, PDVSA's shares in JV established for primary hydrocarbon activities (currently reserved) could even be sold. In theory, PDVSA's shares in companies organized in previous years due to the Association Agreements could be sold too.

488. In this regard, Francisco Mieres said that 'the problem of having PDVSA divided into two is that now, more than ever, it is likely to be privatized'. That is why he considers that the immediate need to create subsidiaries in the East and the West must be provisional because under the CRBV, subsidiaries can be privatized. The Constitution guarantees the State ownership of PDVSA, though not the State ownership of the subsidiaries created afterwards. In contradiction, one of the accusations of different senior government spokespersons against the so-called old PDVSA is that about having wanted to privatize PDVSA. Today, precisely those in charge of running the euphemistic 'new' PDVSA are the ones who might privatize it.

489. In recent years, the Joint Venture model has become the primary mechanism for conducting primary oil activities, with PDVSA maintaining majority ownership. However, official data confirms that several subsidiaries have undergone restructuring or partial asset sales. In 2023, Venezuela resumed partnerships with foreign companies such as Chevron, under licences granted following the partial easing of US sanctions. This marks a shift toward a more flexible model of State control, allowing private participation under terms set by the Executive. These developments raise renewed concerns regarding transparency, accountability, and the true extent of Venezuela's oil sovereignty.

§3. CONTRACTUAL MODALITIES

490. As it may be recalled, the oil opening policy implemented in the 1990s was a strategy that allowed the participation of national and foreign private investment in the business of hydrocarbons in order to increase national production at a time when the international oil market claimed for better supply. In that atmosphere and with an oil basket of USD 14.79/barrel, the State, through PDVSA, reserved the most profitable and attractive fields and projects, assigning to national and foreign companies through bidding processes the more complex projects that required higher investment, new technologies, and entailed high risk, as they were matured reservoirs (marginal fields) or projects for the exploration and exploitation of hydrocarbons in the FPO.

491. This process gave rise to three contractual modalities supported by the legal framework in force, derived from the nationalization of 1976: the OAs, the Strategic Associations, and the Risk and Profit-Sharing Exploration Agreements. Then, since 2006 and 2007, a process to revert these agreements started with the enactment of the Law for the Regulation of Private Participation in Primary Activities (LRPPAP – *Ley de Regularización de la Participación Privada en las Actividades Primarias*), which declared the OAs incompatible with the new Full Oil Sovereignty Policy, complemented with the so-called Law of Migration that established that the activities carried out by Strategic Associations could be carried out by JV only, where the State should have a share of at least 60%. The following is an analysis of these contractual modalities to establish their basic characteristics and define their differences.

I. Operating Agreements

492. OAs were established as of 1992 as part of the Programa de Reactivación de Campos Petroleros, a programme to reactivate marginal, inactive, or low-production oil fields. The legal basis of these agreements is in Article 5 of the LN superseded, which provides for, verbatim:

> The State shall exercise the activities provided for in Article 1 of this Law (… 'exploration in the national territory to find oil, bitumen, and other hydrocarbons; exploitation of the reservoirs thereof; manufacturing or refining; transportation through special means and storage; domestic and foreign trade of exploited and refined substances, and works required for handling thereof', directly through the National Executive or through state entities, hence, being able to enter into the necessary operating agreements for best discharge of its duties, without these proceedings affecting the substance of the attributed activities'. This legal provision provided the constitutional and statutory foundation for the Operating Agreements, allowing the Venezuelan State, through PDVSA, to partner with private entities without relinquishing ownership or

control over hydrocarbon activities. The OAs thus emerged as a mechanism to enhance production efficiency while maintaining the principle of State sovereignty over natural resources.

493. These conditions also appear developed in the statement of reasons of the same law, which, regarding the aforementioned article, established the following:

> It does not exclude the execution of agreements or contracts with private companies for the execution of certain works or services for which these private companies shall receive the payment in cash or in kind, without the payment in kind affecting a fixed production percentage of a given field or the delivery of a substantial quantity of oil that changes the precept of the simple agreement or operation.

Thus, it was sufficiently clear that:

1. The OAs should not affect in any way whatsoever the reserve of the IPN in favour of the State.
2. The OAs would be aimed at works and services.
3. The private companies in charge of the OAs would receive a fee in cash or in kind that would not affect any percentage or any production quantity.

These conditions were itemized and broadened in the agreements entered into with the contractors, from which the following was extracted:

1. The contractor performed at its own risk and at PDVSA's account the commercial exploitation of the fields assigned.
2. The production obtained should be delivered to PDVSA.
3. The hydrocarbons were property of PDVSA.
4. The contractor would receive a fee that would recognize the value of the investments, the operating expenses, and the profit.
5. The contractor would pay a 34% income tax for industrial activity.
6. PDVSA, as oil owner, should pay the royalty, estimated at 1%, and the corresponding oil sale taxes, set at 67.67%.
7. The term would be twenty years.

494. With the above legal and contractual indications, thirty-two OAs were entered into by and between a total of fifty-three companies and fourteen countries in three rounds between 1992 and 1997, effective for twenty years, corresponding to: five to twelve local companies; three processed by prominent national universities, namely, Universidad Central de Venezuela, Universidad del Zulia, and Universidad de Oriente; and the remaining agreements to transnational companies from the US, Canada, Holland, England, Germany, China, Norway, Spain, Saudi Arabia, and Argentina.

495. During the first six years of the programme, the field production increased from an average of 2,000 barrels per day to approximately 403,000 barrels per day to reach a potential of 500,000 barrels per day. However, the OAs referred hereto have been object of harsh criticism by the current administration of the oil policy implemented in 1999, which is, in general, summarized as follows:

1. The OAs were never service contracts, since the operators were authorized to carry out exploration and production activities, that is, activities reserved to the Venezuelan State.
2. OAs did not pay royalties. In addition, their investments should be reimbursed in US dollars.
3. PDVSA paid the international companies USD 18 per barrel produced, while the barrel for Venezuela's State Oil Company has a cost of USD 4.
4. OAs paid taxes based on a non-oil rate of 34% instead of 50% for oil activities.
5. OAs were not authorized by the Congress of the Republic.

496. The objections about the OAs have generated confusion as to what would be more convenient for Venezuela. In this regard, we intend to conduct an objective analysis to contribute to any reflection on this matter.

497. It is worth mentioning that the first objection makes no sense because the activities carried out by the contractors on account of PDVSA referred, in fact, to State-reserved activities, which were carried out on behalf of the State and never on their own behalf or for different purposes. The companies received an agency, a delegation, as provided for in Article 5 of the LN referred hereto. This provision authorized the State to exercise the reserved activities either:

1. directly through the National Government;
2. through State entities; or
3. through OAs *for the best discharge of its duties* (emphasis added), without these proceedings affecting the substance of the attributed activities. Those duties were obviously reserved to the State under Article 1.

498. This explains that in the OAs, the contractors carried out their activities on account of PDVSA. The agreement itself provides as follows:

> The parties acknowledge that the development, exploitation, transportation, management, and exploration of hydrocarbons are reserved activities as provided for in the LN; consequently, the contractors shall carry out the Operating Services provided for hereunder, not on their own account, but on account of the subsidiary only. (Emphasis added.)

499. As to the second objection, it is absolutely logical that PDVSA had been the one in charge of assuming the payment of the royalty and all taxes derived from the subsequent sale of oil because, in addition, it never separated from the ownership of the crude oil. The product was delivered into its hands for sale thereof. The contrary is not legally admissible in this type of agreement. It would be like expecting workers extracting crude oil from a well under an employment contract to assume the taxes and royalties on behalf of the company that hired them. In addition, the nature of the royalty itself leaves no room for doubts as to who is to pay it. The company having the ownership of the extracted crude oil to be sold afterwards is bound to pay the royalty to the State, in our case, PDVSA. The same applies to the income obtained from the sale thereof. Once PDVSA sells the oil delivered by the contractor, the latter receives income on which it will have to pay the corresponding tax to the State. It is worth mentioning that in the First Round, the royalty was established at 1% and, in the Second and Third Rounds, at 16.67%.

500. As to the third objection, it is worth clarifying that it is impossible and illogical to compare PDVSA's production costs of USD 4 per barrel with the crude oil produced under the OAs in marginal, abandoned fields that demanded great economic input and highly expensive technologies.

501. The crude oil PDVSA produces at USD 4 is basically extracted from Maracaibo Lake, which flows by gravity or with minimum intervention. Other oils come from fields with a consolidated infrastructure. This was precisely one of the criteria applied in the oil opening: let PDVSA be in charge of the simplest operations and invite international companies to participate in far more complex operations that required large investment. This evidences why the costs under OAs were higher, particularly over the first years. Furthermore, it should be emphasized that total costs included operating costs, the amount of the investments, and the earnings.

502. As to point 4 mentioned above, regarding taxation of the OAs at a 34% rate pursuant to Article 53 of the LISLR in force upon signing the agreements, it is necessary to insist on what it has been already explained, that the contractors did not act on their own account but on account of PDVSA, which, as oil owner, had in turn the responsibility to pay income taxes on the sale of crude oil. The contractors declared their annual income based on the development of an industrial activity, in a service rendered to PDVSA.

503. The fifth objection mentions that the OAs had not been authorized by the former Congress of the Republic. This objection is illogical since that was not a requirement. The authorization of both Chambers in joint session referred to special cases, such as AA, provided for in Article 5(2) of the LN.

504. The criticism of the OAs surprised even the closest collaborators of the current administration of the Venezuelan oil policy. Such is the case of reputed professor Mazhar Al-Shereida, co-editor of the 2001 LOH – who wondered in shock about the decision of eliminating the OAs, and asked who had had the idea of turning them into JV – said: 'Some simple service contracts, where I pay you for your work, but you give me the oil because I am the absolute owner of that oil, and I decide on it' … 'the companies asking for it, we forced them to be our partners' … 'What is the gain for the country?'

505. In our opinion, it seems that the purpose of eliminating the OAs referred more to the idea of creating new associations with new rules. Putting forward their elimination based on the above legal arguments or patriotic or nationalistic reasons makes no sense at all. A logic action in that direction would have been renewing the OAs, the term of which would factually end during 2012, 2013, and 2017, and proceed with the operations with in-house staff, incorporating national companies. Instead, the current administration of the oil policy decided to benefit foreign companies by granting them 40% of the hydrocarbon exploitation rights in activities exclusively reserved to the State and dismiss over 20,000 highly qualified Venezuelan workers of PDVSA, with whom it would have been able to address the operations of the OAs by letting them expire on the corresponding dates established.

II. Association Agreements

A. Strategic Associations for Integrated Projects

506. The Strategic Associations for Integrated Projects (AEPI – *Asociaciones Estratégicas para Proyectos Integrados*) were agreements provided for in Article 5 of the LN, which allowed the State to associate with private entities to carry out activities exclusively reserved to the State in special cases, and where convenient for the public interest. These associations were designed for the exploitation of energetic resources of the Orinoco Belt, specifically for:

1. Production and conversion of extra-heavy crude oil.
2. Exploitation of natural bitumen and the construction of three bitumen production and emulsification modules for production of Orimulsion,® as well as for the development of offshore free natural gas reservoirs. Such agreements had to meet the following conditions:
   a. a limited-term;
   b. guarantee the control of the association by the State; and
   c. have authorization from the National Congress.

The term of the AEPI was established at a maximum of forty-five years as of the undersigning date thereof.

507. Control by the State was ensured through the creation of a company named 'Entidad de Gerencia' (Management Entity) (ME) in charge of managing, coordinating, and supervising the activities of the association. PDVSA owned privileged class A shares in that entity, which allowed it to have control over the decisions. However, PDVSA reserved the right to appoint and dismiss the president and deputy of the ME. This authority has special relevance, since for any decision made by the decision-making body to be valid, it required the presence of the president or his deputy.

508. As to the approval by the National Congress, it is worth mentioning that the first authorization by the Chambers in joint session was given on 10 August 1993, for the exploitation of free gas, under the name of 'Proyecto Cristobal Colon'. The respective agreement was established on 17 April 1994, under the name of

'Sucre-Gas, S.A.', with the participation of Lagoven (former PDVSA subsidiary) 33%; Shell 30%; Exxon 29%, and Mitsubishi 8%.

509. This project was suspended, though, as it was not financially profitable due to the conditions in the international market of liquefied natural gas (LNG – *Gas Natural Licuado*). However, it was resumed, and the execution thereof began in 2007, and it was reactivated with the name of Mariscal Sucre for an estimated term that ends in 2020.

510. Subsequently, four AEPIs for production, transportation, upgrading, and sale of extra-heavy crude oil from the FPO were subject to approval by the National Congress, as shown in Table 10.

Table 10 AEPIs Approved by the National Congress

Association	*Approval*	*Shares*	*Cost (MM USD)*
Petrozuata	1993 National Congress	PDVSA: 49.9% CONOCO: 50.1%	3,000
Sincor	1993 National Congress	PDVSA: 38% Totalfinaelf: 47% Statoil: 15%	4,200
Hamaca	1997 National Congress	PDVSA: 30% Philips: 40% Texaco: 30%	3,400
Cerro Negro	1997 National Congress	PDVSA: 41.67% Exxon-Mobil: 41.67% Veba Oel: 16.67%	2,000

511. Other important conditions of these AEPIs arising from the agreements are as follows:

- The AEPIs were exempted from the payment of municipal and State taxes.
- They paid a 34% tax rate under the general tax system for companies pursuant to Article 9 of the LISLR in force at that time.
- To ensure 10% profitability, the royalty was temporarily established at 1%. Once the initial investment was recovered, the royalty would go back to 16.67%.
- As to any resolution of conflicts or differences, it was established that the responsibilities that may arise from the execution of the agreement would affect the parties only, including PDVSA, but in no case would this impose any obligation whatsoever on the Republic. In the event of any controversy or claim, it should be processed by arbitration under the Rules of Conciliation and Arbitration of the International Chamber of Commerce (ICC), in New York City or any other place agreed by the Parties; however, the agreement shall be construed in accordance with and governed by the laws of the Republic of Venezuela.

– These agreements gave priority to the use of labour, capital assets, and services produced in the area where their activities were carried out, as well as technology transfer.

B. Agreements under the Profit-Sharing Scheme

512. On 15 September 1994, another Project of great dimensions was approved by the Board of PDVSA. This time it was the AA for the Exploration at Risk and the Production of Hydrocarbons under the Profit-Sharing Scheme (CAGc), maybe the most controversial of all, also based on Article 5 of the LN, which resulted in an appeal for annulment due to partial unconstitutionality filed before the CSJ in Plenary Session against the Agreement of the Congress of 7 April 1995, which authorized the signing of the AA for the Exploration at Risk of New Areas and the Production of Hydrocarbons under the Profit-Sharing Scheme, regarding Article 2(2) (4)(10)(17) of the agreement.

513. In this type of CAGc, the same conditions established for the AEPIs above explained had to be met, namely:

1. A limited-term agreement.
2. Guarantee the State control over the association.
3. The authorization by the National Congress.

The term of the agreement was established as follows:

a. three to five years for exploration, subject to a two to four-year extension;
b. twenty years of commercial operation as from the approval of the Development Plan; and
c. maximum term of thirty-nine years.

514. The State control over the CAGc was guaranteed through a control committee chaired by a representative of PDVSA or the subsidiary in charge with double voting right in the event of a decision-making tie.

515. In the execution of a CAGc, under which PDVSA would have had 35% of the capital stock and the investors 65%, the shares of the State oil company had a preferred value, that is, decision-making advantages in order to guarantee control thereof by the State.

516. The authorization by the National Congress was issued on 4 July 1995. Other conditions or requirements that may be extracted from the agreements are as follows:

– The activities of the association were exempted from the payment of municipal and State taxes.

- The income tax for these agreements was set at 67.7% under the Income Tax law in force.
- The royalty rate would be 1% for projects whose internal rate of return (IRR) was lower than 12%; 16.67% for projects whose IRR was higher than or equal to 20%; and it would range between 1% and 16.67% for projects whose IRR was between 12% and 20%.
- The State received an additional benefit, such as the State's Share in Profits (PEG) offered for each case by the contractor during the bidding process.
- Should the discovery of a reservoir be proved, Venezuela would have a share in the benefits ranging between 75% and 90% derived from the royalty, the income tax, and the right to participate as associate in the development.
- The sale of the production was made at market price by both the investors and PDVSA, in proportion to the share of the consortium. However, PDVSA received a share of the benefits after deducting the operating costs (financial costs excluded), the depreciation, and the production-related taxes from the gross income.
- The Agreement established conditions to maximize the use of Venezuelan labour and companies.
- The AAs have been governed by and construed in accordance with the laws of the Republic of Venezuela. The matters regulated by the Control Committee were not subject to arbitration. Any other controversy that could not be settled by an agreement reached by the parties would be resolved under the rules of proceeding of the ICC in force upon signing the Agreement.

517. Like the OAs, the AAs have also been subject to strong criticism, both legal and business-related, by the current administration of the oil policy in Venezuela. The main objection is that the AAs were companies where the State had a minority share, and the payment of royalties had decreased to the lowest level, 1%. These and other arguments have been discussed in point Arguments Against the Legal Sufficiency of Strategic Associations, which specifically refer to the AAs for the Exploration at Risk of New Areas and the Production of Hydrocarbons under the Profit-Sharing Scheme, which in this point are deemed valid and reproduced to explain the legal aspects discussed regarding the legality of the AAs.

III. Joint Ventures

A. Termination of Operating and AA

518. On 18 April 2006, by the LRPPAP, provided for in Decree No. 1510 of the Organic LOH, the early and unilateral termination of the existing OAs signed under the Law was declared. The Law referred hereto established the following main aspects:

1. Regularize the private participation in the primary activities provided for in Article 9 of the 2001 LOH (Article 1).
2. Unilateral early termination of the OAs (Article 2).

3. Possibility of creating JV with natural or legal private entities (Article 3) for primary activities as minority shareholders.

519. As with the OAs, a new regulatory framework was approved for the termination of the AAs. In fact, on 26 February 2007, the Law of Migration to Joint Ventures (LEEM – *Ley de Emigración a Empresas Mixtas*) was decreed for the termination of the AAs, which had to be transformed into JV under the terms and conditions provided for in Article 22 of the LOH. The relevant aspects of the LEEM are as follows:

1. Unilateral early termination of agreements.
2. Expropriation of contractual rights of contractors.
3. Retroactive application of Article 22 of the 2001 LOH.
4. Minimum 60% equity interest held by PDVSA in JV.
5. Assignment of the right to exercise primary activities to JV.
6. Need for prior authorization by the National Assembly.
7. Designation of the Venezuelan jurisdiction in the event of controversies.

520. From the analysis of both the LRPPAP applicable to OAs and the LEEM applicable to AAs, their main element, common to both instruments, is the legislator's intention to harmonize the legal framework for operating and AA legally in force with the provisions of the 2001 LOH, which included the precept of JV for State-reserved primary activities. Therefore, in order to achieve that purpose, the new contractual conditions were imposed through the above legal instruments with retroactive effect, thus resulting in a gross violation of the pre-existing legal framework. In conformity with such orders, on 1 May 2007, PDVSA took control of all the facilities related to the above-mentioned agreements.

521. The application of the LEEM meant, for the contractors that rejected the unilateral terms set by the State, the expropriation of their contractual rights, hence, their right to be compensated for damages caused by the Law under Article 115 of the Constitution:

> Article 115: The right of property is guaranteed. Every person has the right to the use, enjoyment, usufruct and disposal of his or her property. Property shall be subject to such contributions, restrictions and obligations as may be established by law in the service of the public or general interest. Only for reasons of public benefit or social interest by final judgment, with timely payment of fair compensation, the expropriation of any kind of property may be declared.

522. On the contrary, for the investor partner of an AA not objecting to the condition of minority partner provided for the new JV, it would be as if it was in effect accepted without the need of a bidding process under Article 6 of the LEEM, in agreement with Article 37 of the LOH.

523. As to the designation of the jurisdiction to settle differences arising from the decisions contained in the LEEM, it was sufficiently clarified that they would be subject to the Venezuelan jurisdiction. However, that does not mean annulment of the terms and conditions in the AAs regarding settlement of controversies in an arbitral jurisdiction, even abroad, that may arise from the execution, compliance, and breach of the AAs. Therefore, two out of the thirteen partners participating in the FPO – ConocoPhillips in Petrozuata and Exxon-Mobil in Cerro Negro – decided to reject the terms and conditions and claimed before the ICSID a compensation for the nationalization of their assets decreed by the Venezuelan government to establish the new structure of JV, where the Americans refused to participate.

524. However, other companies that also lost a few shares filed a claim before the ICSID, as in the case of the Opic company, which claimed having being expropriated from its shares in the West Gulf of Paria (6.5% of Corocoro project) and in the East Gulf of Paria (7.5%) after the approval and application of the LEEM. This is why there are many claims filed before ICSID against Venezuela. This event made the Venezuelan government to denounce the Convention on the Settlement of Investment Disputes between States and Nationals of other States, on 24 January 2012, before the World Bank In January 2012. Thus, Venezuela joined Ecuador and Bolivia as the only countries that have officially separated from the ICSID. Despite the decision of the Venezuelan government to abandon the jurisdiction of the ICSID, that arbitration body produced in April 2018 a favourable decision to ConocoPhillips and against PDVSA, by which it recognizes the right to more than USD 2 billion to compensate the expropriation of several oil projects in the country more than a decade ago.

B. JVs under the LOH

525. In accordance with Article 22 of the LOH in force, JV are companies where the State holds a share of over 50% of the capital stock and may be engaged in activities of exploration, extraction, gathering, and storage of hydrocarbons in their natural State, which are called primary activities under Article 9 of the LOH and State-reserved activities under Article 302 of the CRBV. These companies are considered under the LOH as operators.

526. The incorporation of JVs, as with the associations referred to in Article 5 of the LN, requires prior approval by the National Assembly, which will be informed by the Executive Branch about all the circumstances relevant to such incorporation, as well as regarding the conditions and requirements they must meet, including the special advantages provided for the benefit of the Republic. The National Assembly will have the authority to modify the framework of the conditions proposed and establish those it may deem convenient.

527. The conditions, requirements, and scope of activity referred to in the LOH are as follows:

1. Maximum twenty-five-year term for JVs, subject to being extended for a term mutually agreed by the parties but no exceeding fifteen years.

2. Indication of location, orientation, extension, and distribution of the area where the activities are to be carried out, and further specifications under the Regulation.
3. Holding of real and personal property acquired to carry out the company's activities, to be handed over to the Republic free of liens, and without any compensation whatsoever upon termination of the rights granted due to any cause, so that the possibility of continuing the activities is guaranteed, if applicable, or suspension thereof at the slightest financial and environmental damage.
4. Subject to the jurisdiction of the relevant Courts of the Republic for the resolution of any doubts and controversies of any nature that may arise, including arbitration in the cases allowed by the law, without them giving rise to any foreign claim.
5. Advantages for the Republic, which will be regarding the increase of the royalty, of the contributions or other considerations provided for in the LOH, for instance, payment for the granting of encumbrances on vacant lots; use and transfer of new and cutting-edge technologies; as well as the granting of scholarships, technical training opportunities or other human-factor development activities. These advantages will be optional for the State, which will decide whether to include them or not.

528. On 31 March 2006, the National Assembly, exercising the power granted in Article 33 of the LOH, approved the Terms and Conditions for the Creation and Operation of JV, which are generally based on the LOH with some variations explained below:

1. JVs may carry out primary activities under Article 9 of the LOH, as well as render services to other JV, State-owned companies, or other companies, without affecting the development of the main object.
2. JVs will have a twenty-year term.
3. The JV will be the operator in the Specified Area.
4. JVs will sell to PDVSA all the hydrocarbons they produce and do not use in the performance of their operations, except for the royalty in kind, if applicable, pursuant to Article 45 of the LOH, and the associated natural gas that PDVSA or its subsidiary does not accept to receive.
5. JVs are obliged to pay to the Republic the royalty and taxes set forth in the law.
6. JVs will be paid for the sale of hydrocarbons in US dollars, which JVs may have in bank accounts abroad and use to pay all the obligations required outside the territory of the Bolivarian Republic of Venezuela. The payment for the sale of methane gas set aside for the national market is excluded.
7. JVs will pay an additional royalty of 3.33% on the volumes of extracted hydrocarbons, to be allocated as follows:
   a. 2.22% for the municipalities of the Specified Area for a Special Fund for the People's Power (FOPO), which is directly managed by the Executive

Branch and will be dedicated to the endogenous development projects established within the framework of the guidelines of the National Development Plan.

b. 1.11% for the municipalities where the oil activities of the country are carried out, allotted as follows: 30% for the municipalities where the primary activities of the JV are carried out and 70% for the remaining municipalities of the country where oil activities are carried out, proportionally to the population and the human development index of each of such entities.

529. As mentioned on several occasions throughout this study, the debate surrounding contractual modalities has gained renewed relevance due to the partial easing of US sanctions since 2023 and the subsequent reactivation of JVs with select foreign companies. These partnerships, although limited in scope, have contributed to a modest recovery in crude output under stricter fiscal controls and increased state oversight. The government has reiterated its commitment to attracting foreign capital while maintaining state ownership of natural resources. However, the legacy of the 1990s contractual frameworks continues to shape current oil policy, raising ongoing concerns about transparency, accountability, and the strategic coherence of hybrid public-private schemes.

§4. Venezuela's Withdrawal from ICSID and Its Implications After Nationalizations

530. Venezuela's decision to denounce the Convention of the ICSID in 2012 marked a turning point in its foreign investment policy and its relationship with international dispute resolution mechanisms. The measure, adopted within the framework of a policy to reaffirm sovereignty over strategic sectors, was primarily motivated by the growing wave of claims filed by foreign companies whose assets had been nationalized. While the withdrawal was promoted as an act of economic independence, in practice, it did not prevent Venezuela from continuing to face litigation in international courts, resulting in multi-million-dollar rulings against the country.

531. Venezuela joined ICSID in 1993, during a period when its economic policy favoured foreign direct investment as part of a strategy of liberalization and market opening. However, with the rise of Hugo Chávez to power in 1999, the country took a radical turn towards a statist economic model, leading to the massive nationalization of strategic sectors such as hydrocarbons, telecommunications, mining, and banking. Under the argument of strengthening 'economic sovereignty', the government expropriated the assets of foreign companies without offering adequate compensation, triggering a wave of international lawsuits (International Institute for Sustainable Development) [IISD], (2012).[153]

153. International Institute for Sustainable Development, *Venezuela's Withdrawal from ICSID: What It Does and Does Not Achieve*, 13 Apr. 2012, available at: https://www.iisd.org/itn/2012/04/13/venezuelas-withdrawal-from-icsid-what-it-does-and-does-not-achieve/ (last accessed 3 Apr. 2025).

532. In response to this growing number of claims, in January 2012, Venezuela formally denounced the ICSID Convention. The government argued that the country's original accession to the treaty had been carried out by a 'weak and provisional government' without democratic consultation or popular legitimacy. Furthermore, it contended that the international arbitration system was designed to disproportionately benefit foreign corporations at the expense of states, citing skewed figures indicating that 99% of rulings favoured investors (IISD, 2012).[154] This stance aligned with a broader critique of the international economic order, in which ICSID was perceived as a neocolonial mechanism for protecting corporate interests.

533. Contrary to the Venezuelan government's intentions, the denunciation of ICSID did not resolve ongoing disputes or prevent new claims. According to Article 71 of the ICSID Convention, states that withdraw remain subject to its jurisdiction for an additional six months, allowing investors to file new claims during this period (Milbank LLP, 2012).[155] Moreover, Venezuela's existing Bilateral Investment Treaties (BITs) with various countries included 'survival clauses' that extended the jurisdiction of international arbitration mechanisms for decades after their termination (IISD, 2018).[156]

534. As a result, multiple cases proceeded in international courts, leading to adverse rulings for Venezuela:

ExxonMobil (2014): ICSID ordered Venezuela to pay USD 1.6 billion for the expropriation of the Cerro Negro oil project, significantly lower than the USD 10 billion initially claimed by the company.[157]

ConocoPhillips (2025): An ICSID tribunal rejected Venezuela's appeal against an award requiring it to pay USD 8.5 billion, with additional legal costs of USD 7.8 million (Venezuelanalysis, 2025).[158]

Crystallex (2016): The ICSID tribunal ruled in favour of the Canadian mining company, awarding it USD 1.386 billion in compensation for the expropriation of the Las Cristinas gold deposit (IISD, 2018).[159]

---

154. *Ibid.*
155. Milbank LLP, *Venezuela's Threatened Exit from ICSID*, 2012, available at: https://www.milbank.com/a/web/877/0507_Venezuela_Exit_From_ICSID.pdf (last accessed 3 Apr. 2025).
156. International Institute for Sustainable Development, *ICSID Tribunal Dismisses Expropriation Case Against Venezuela on Jurisdictional Grounds*, 24 Apr. 2018, available at: https://www.iisd.org/itn/2018/04/24/icsid-tribunal-dismisses-expropriation-case-against-venezuela-jurisdictional-grounds-bettina-muller/ (last accessed 3 Apr. 2025).
157. Reuters, *Venezuela Ordered to Pay Exxon $1.6 Billion for Nationalization*, 9 Oct. 2014, available at: https://www.reuters.com/article/business/venezuela-ordered-to-pay-exxon-16-billion-for-nationalization-idUSKCN0HY206/ (last accessed 3 Apr. 2025).
158. Venezuelanalysis, '*Venezuela Loses Multi-Billion Dollar ConocoPhillips ICSID Appeal*,' 27 Jan. 2025, available at: https://venezuelanalysis.com/news/venezuela-loses-multi-billion-dollar-conocophillips-icsid-appeal/ (last accessed 3 Apr. 2025).
159. International Institute for Sustainable Development, '*ICSID Tribunal Dismisses Expropriation Case Against Venezuela on Jurisdictional Grounds*,' 24 Apr. 2018, available at: https://

535. The Venezuelan government attempted to avoid the enforcement of these awards by transferring gold reserves and foreign currency to banks in China, Russia, and Brazil, countries considered less likely to enforce international embargoes (IISD, 2012). However, this strategy failed to prevent companies such as ConocoPhillips and Crystallex from seeking the seizure of PDVSA's foreign assets, including Citgo, its US-based subsidiary.

536. Beyond its withdrawal from ICSID, the Venezuelan government adopted an ideological stance against the international arbitration system, seeking legal alternatives to mitigate the effects of adverse rulings. However, the exit from ICSID presented significant legal and strategic limitations:

1. *Persistence of BITs*: Although Venezuela terminated some treaties, many remained in force, continuing to expose the country to international litigation (Fietta, 2017).
2. *Difficulties in Overturning Rulings*: As George Kahale III pointed out in the ConocoPhillips case, the system lacks effective checks and balances to challenge arbitral awards, even in cases of procedural irregularities (Venezuelanalysis, 2025).
3. *Use of Alternative Tribunals*: Companies such as ExxonMobil turned to the ICC, obtaining favourable rulings, including a 2012 decision that required PDVSA to pay USD 908 million (VOA, 2014).[160]

537. The accumulated adverse rulings exceed USD 10 billion, exacerbating Venezuela's economic crisis in a context of international sanctions and declining oil production. While the withdrawal from ICSID was presented as a measure to protect sovereignty, in practice, it did not shield Venezuela from claims based on BITs or from arbitrations in other international forums.

538. The Venezuelan case offers an important lesson for other developing states seeking to reshape their engagement with the global investment system: leaving ICSID without a comprehensive strategy for renegotiating treaties and managing liabilities is not a viable solution. Instead of simply abandoning the mechanism, countries should advocate for reforms in the investment arbitration regime to balance state sovereignty with the need for a stable and predictable investment environment.

539. Venezuela's withdrawal from ICSID represented a challenge to the international arbitration system and the influence of transnational corporations in dispute resolution. However, rather than mitigating the legal and economic issues arising from nationalizations, this decision exposed the country to greater financial

www.iisd.org/itn/2018/04/24/icsid-tribunal-dismisses-expropriation-case-against-venezuela-jurisdictional-grounds-bettina-muller/ (last accessed 3 Apr. 2025).

160. VOA, 2014. *A separate decision by the Paris-based ICC in 2012 ordered Venezuela state oil company PDVSA to pay Exxon $908 million.* Voice of America. https://www.voanews.com/a/icsid-venezuela-must-pay-exxon-16-billion-for-nationalizations/2478757.html.

risks and the loss of strategic assets. The Venezuelan experience underscores the need for a more sophisticated strategy to manage investor relations and reform the international investment protection framework.

§5. The Impact of Venezuela's ICSID Withdrawal on Its US Subsidiary, Citgo

540. Venezuela's withdrawal from the ICSID has placed its US subsidiary, Citgo Petroleum Corporation, in a precarious operational and financial position. As a direct consequence of multiple arbitration rulings stemming from expropriations and contractual disputes, Citgo faces the imminent risk of a share auction aimed at satisfying claims from at least eighteen nationalized companies and bondholders, collectively seeking approximately USD 21 billion in compensation.[161] Although initially scheduled for July 2024, this process has encountered legal obstacles and could extend throughout 2025 (Reuters, 2024).

541. The Citgo auction is a direct consequence of the Venezuelan government's refusal to honour its obligations arising from international arbitration rulings, making the company a primary target for creditors. In this context, the US Department of the Treasury, through the Office of Foreign Assets Control (OFAC), has imposed strict restrictions on Citgo's ability to repatriate dividends to Venezuela or process crude oil from Petróleos de Venezuela S.A. (PDVSA), effectively preventing any financial relief from Caracas (US Department of the Treasury, 2023).[162] Additionally, Citgo remains under the control of an ad hoc board of directors appointed by the Venezuelan opposition and backed by Washington, a situation that has consistently fuelled tensions with Nicolás Maduro's administration and obstructed any potential settlement with creditors.[163]

542. Despite these challenges, Citgo's current management has successfully implemented notable improvements in corporate governance and operational efficiency. In recent years, the company has reported sustained profitability, largely due to the optimization of its three refineries and the relative stability of the U.S. energy market. These measures have enabled Citgo to maintain its operations despite an environment of significant legal and financial uncertainty. However, there are no

161. Reuters, '*Gold Reserve Makes 'Stalking Horse' Bid for Shares in Citgo's Parent*,' 10 Mar. 2025, available at: https://www.reuters.com/markets/commodities/gold-reserve-makes-stalking-horse-bid-shares-citgos-parent-2025-03-10/ (last accessed 3 Apr. 2025).
162. U.S. Department of the Treasury, 2023. 'U.S. Sanctions and Restrictions Imposed on PDVSA and Its Subsidiaries, Including Citgo, by the Office of Foreign Assets Control (OFAC), Impacting Venezuela's Ability to Repatriate Dividends and Process Crude Oil.' *U.S. Department of the Treasury*. https://ofac.treasury.gov (accessed 22 Apr. 2025).
163. Reuters, '*Citgo Petroleum's Profit Plummeted to $305 Million in 2024*,' 6 Mar. 2025, available at: https://www.reuters.com/business/energy/citgo-petroleums-profit-plummeted-305-mln-2024-2025-03-06/ (last accessed 3 Apr. 2025).

guarantees that the company will be able to avoid the sale of its assets in the medium term (Citgo Petroleum Corporation, 2025).[164]

543. The future of Citgo remains highly uncertain. The ongoing auction could lead to the fragmentation of the company, fundamentally altering its operational structure and significantly reducing the Venezuelan state's influence over its foreign assets. Losing Citgo would constitute a major strategic setback for Venezuela, not only in financial terms but also in its ability to maintain a presence in the global energy market. Meanwhile, creditors continue to exert pressure to enforce pending arbitration awards, positioning Citgo at the centre of one of the most significant legal and financial disputes stemming from Venezuela's expropriation policies over the past two decades.

§6. Legislation for Non-traditional Players: A Military Oil Company

544. On 11 February 2016, the President of the Republic authorized the creation of the State Company, Anonymous Military Company of Mining, petroleum and gas (CAMIMPEG – *Compañía Anónima Militar de Industrias Mineras, Petrolíferas y de Gas*), attached to the Ministry of the People's Power for Defense (Decree No. 2231). This decision has raised all sorts of suspicions and doubts, particularly because this is an institution without experience and knowledge in the field of the exploitation of natural resources. However, the National Armed Force (FAN) is highly questioned by Venezuelans because of its direct participation in political activities in favour of the regime that governs under its protection and, second, because of its alleged participation in drug trafficking activities, smuggling of hydrocarbons and derivatives, gold and other minerals.

I. Object

545. According to the decree creating CAMIMPEG (Article 3), the company may engage in '… all lawful activities related to Oil, Gas and Mining Services in general, "without this implying any limitation whatsoever". The same article expands and clarifies what it is intended to mean by "without implying any limitation", by assigning to it the competence for the rehabilitation and maintenance of oil wells, the repair, maintenance, and administration of drilling rigs, the manufacture, repair, and maintenance of flow, pumping stations, and compression plants in terrestrial or marine areas; pump repair services, import, export, distribution, marketing, purchase and sale of chemical products for the mining, petrochemical, oil and gas industry, civil, mechanical, oil and electrical construction, or on plans for

164. CITGO Petroleum Corporation, '*CITGO Reports Fourth Quarter and Full-Year 2024 Results*,' PR Newswire, 6 Mar. 2025, available at: https://www.prnewswire.com/news-releases/citgo-reports-fourth-quarter-and-full-year-2024-results-302394132.html (last accessed 3 Apr. 2025).

oil spills, construction to manage oil waste, transportation and handling of drilling waste … ' and countless other unlimited activities in the sectors of oil, gas, and mining.[165]

546. This company, therefore, has all the competencies not only of PDVSA but also of all its subsidiaries, and with it, the risk that the progressive depletion of the functions of these companies will possibly occur.

II. Justification

547. The entry of the military enterprise into the scheme is seen by critics of the regime as an attempt by President Nicolás Maduro to gain more support from the armed forces, at a time when it was losing popularity due to the acute recession (2016), the scarcity of food, medicine, and the uncontrolled growth of the world's highest inflation. Its creation seems to be inspired by the Cuban military company GAESA, which operates in virtually every profitable area of the economy, controlling hotel chains, car rental agencies and sales companies, banks, credit cards and remittance services, supermarkets, clothing stores, real estate development companies, service stations, import and export companies, shipping and construction companies, warehouses, and even an airline.

548. However, because PDVSA has lost several lawsuits in international courts against multinationals that left Venezuela after expropriation proceedings, CAMIMPEG could receive PDVSA's assets, property, and traditional activities to try to evade the legal actions affecting the oil industry.

549. This company also seeks to legitimize the military's exploitation of the resources of the Mining Arc (AM – *Arco Minero*), which had already been carried out illegally by members of the Bolivarian National Armed Force (FANB) for several years through the smuggling of gold and diamonds, the collection of the so-called vaccine from artisanal miners, and complicity with irregular forces such as the Colombian Liberation Army and criminal groups operating in southern Venezuela.

550. The AM is a vast expanse of territory of 111,846.86 sq km, or 12.2% of Venezuelan territory, twice the size of the FPO. It is located mainly in the north of Bolivar State and to a lesser extent in the northeast of the Amazonas State and part of the Delta Amacuro State. The AM has large reserves of coltan (a mineral coveted by the electronics industry), bauxite, diamonds and gold, which some estimates put at about USD 2 trillion. Under a scheme of strategic associations, the Venezuelan government has granted mining concessions to various Chinese, Russian, Canadian, South African, Australian companies, and companies from other countries.

165. *See*, Decree No. 2.231, 2 Oct. 2016, Official Gazette of the Bolivarian Republic of Venezuela.

One of the concessionary companies is precisely CAMIMPEG; in other words, the portion of the 'cake' that the military caste has been given, for being the regime's main support.

III. Illegalities in the Creation of CAMIMPEG

A. *In the Area of Competences*

551. The creation of the company, CAMIMPEG, violates Article 25 of the Organic Law of Public Administration in relation to the principle of institutional integrity, by failing to 'respect the legitimate performance of the respective competences', which would occur in two ways: by the Ministry of Defence's violation of its own competences and in turn, by (the Ministry of Defence) violating the competences, on account of the subject matter, of the Ministry of Petroleum and Mining: As an example, we have the case of Compañía Anónima Venezolana de Industrias Militares (CAVIM),[166] which is a state-owned company, a company attached to the Ministry of Defence that has a monopoly on the import, export, storage and manufacture of arms, ammunition, and other materials. It would be impossible to imagine that these competencies would be assigned to another ministry, such as the Ministry of Oil and Mining, which by the way ended up in this gambit like a Chinese Vase.

B. *Violation of the Principles and Values of Public Administration*

552. There are abundant reports that the FAN or sectors within it allegedly have links with organized crime,[167] thereby violating the principles, values, and norms that the public administration must comply with, as provided for in Article 10 of the Organic Law of Public Administration, in particular the principles of honesty, transparency, and good faith.

C. *Abuse of Dominant Position and Overlapping of Functions: Judge and Interested Party*

553. Because the FAN would have a dual role: first as an entrepreneur through CAMIMPEG, seeking the best opportunities in the business, and second as regards the responsibility to protect the gold mining areas and of other minerals established as Security Zones, which would create a kind of monopoly, with a clear position of

166. Compañía Anónima Venezolana de Industrias Militares (CAVIM), *Decreto-Ley No. 883 sobre la Ley Constitucional de Inversiones Productivas Extranjeras*, Official Gazette No. 6,346 Extraordinary, 29 Apr. 1975, available at: https://web.archive.org/web/20130122124735/http://www.cavim.com.ve/quienes_somos.php (last accessed 3 Apr. 2025).

167. Carlos Tablante & M. Tarre. 'El gran saqueo.' *Quiénes y cómo se robaron el dinero de los Venezolanos, Caracas, Ediciones Cyngular,* 259–279 (2015).

dominion, in violation of Article 113 of the Constitution. Because in the jurisdictional sphere, the FAN has been assigned administrative police and criminal investigation functions normally exercised by the National Guard, making it a judge and an interested party.

D. The Possibility of Tax Evasion

554. An extremely serious aspect of this new style of doing business on the part of the government is that CAMIMPEG has escaped the fiscal control exercised by the OCGR as a result of a decision of the Political Administrative Chamber of the CSJ dated 14 December 2016. Indeed, on the occasion of a recourse for interpretation filed by the Office of the Attorney General of the Republic, the Chamber unexpectedly excluded the company CAMIMPEG from the scope of fiscal control by the OCGR, on the grounds that it is a 'military company'. Among other considerations, it clearly stated: '4. The General Comptroller of the Bolivarian National Armed Force exercises a sui generis external fiscal control over the Internal Audit Units of the decentralized entities functionally attached to the Ministry of the People's Power for Defense'. The role of the OCGR was thus relegated to a secondary position with respect to the external control of the decentralized entities attached to the Ministry of Defence, even though they have nothing to do with the defence sector, and they are companies that operate in the industrial or energy sector, such as the CAMIMPEG.

E. Assessment and Analysis Since the Creation of CAMIMPEG

555. Since its establishment in 2016, CAMIMPEG has operated within a framework of concerning opacity and discretion, consolidating itself as a key instrument of Nicolás Maduro's government to militarize strategic sectors of the economy and secure the loyalty of the FANB. The company was created through a presidential decree and was granted extraordinary powers to operate in the extractive sector for a period of fifty years, including the ability to enter into partnerships with both national and foreign companies (Correo del Caroní, 2022).[168] However, the lack of transparency regarding its operations and the management of allocated resources has generated significant criticism.

556. Although its founding charter stipulates that the board of directors must inform citizens about the administration of assets and the expenditure of company resources, this obligation has never been fulfilled. The organization Control Ciudadano has denounced that, six years after its creation, CAMIMPEG continues to operate without accountability and without undergoing independent audits. This level of discretion was further reinforced in 2020 when its statutes were modified to

---

168. Correo del Caroní (2022, 14 de febrero). Control Ciudadano denuncia opacidad en el manejo de Camimpeg a seis años de su creación. *Correo del Caroní.* https://correodelcaroni.com/pais-politico/control-ciudadano-denuncia-opacidad-en-el-manejo-de-camimpeg-a-seis-anos-de-su-creacion/.

grant greater autonomy to the company's president in resource management and administration, effectively eliminating internal controls over its operations.[169]

557. Another concerning aspect is the absence of publicly available information regarding CAMIMPEG's contracts and partnerships, which prevents an accurate assessment of its true impact. Despite the company's expansion into the mining and petroleum sectors, there are no clear reports detailing its revenues, expenditures, or contributions to the Venezuelan state.[170] This lack of transparency has raised concerns regarding potential irregularities in resource management and the use of funds for political purposes or to consolidate power within the FANB.

558. In this context, there is increasing evidence of the military's growing involvement in strategic economic sectors, encroaching into areas that traditionally do not fall within its jurisdiction and deviating from its primary mission of national defence and security. The lack of transparency in CAMIMPEG not only impacts the energy and mining sectors but also reflects a broader pattern of expanding military influence within the state apparatus, granting it a predominant role in areas that should be managed under civilian and specialized technical oversight.

559. Additionally, CAMIMPEG plays a significant role in the Orinoco Mining Arc, a region marked by high levels of conflict and numerous reports of human rights violations, where the armed forces have been accused of facilitating illegal mining operations and enabling the activities of criminal groups engaged in the illicit trade of gold and coltan.[171] CAMIMPEG's control over part of this exploitation reinforces the hypothesis that its creation was more about securing economic benefits for the military elite than developing a sustainable model for the country.

560. Ultimately, the creation of CAMIMPEG has not only strengthened the FANB's control over the Venezuelan economy but has also institutionalized a corporate management model characterized by opacity and a lack of accountability. Its minimal oversight, increased administrative autonomy, and involvement in strategic economic activities make it a pillar of the Venezuelan government's governance model, where military loyalty is rewarded with power and resources. Rather than serving as a tool for economic recovery, CAMIMPEG has become emblematic of the militarization of the economy and the institutionalized corruption that defines the Venezuelan state under Maduro's administration.

---

169. *Ibid.* (last accessed 3 Apr. 2025).

170. Control Ciudadano, *Informe sobre la Opacidad en la Gestión de CAMIMPEG y su Impacto en la Economía Venezolana*, 2022, available at: https://correodelcaroni.com/pais-politico/control-ciudadano-denuncia-opacidad-en-el-manejo-de-camimpeg-a-seis-anos-de-su-creacion/ (last accessed 10 Jun. 2025).

171. Crisis Group, *El Peso del Oro: Violencia en el Sur de Venezuela*, 2019, available at: https://www.crisisgroup.org/es/latin-america-caribbean/andes/venezuela/073-gold-and-grief-venezuelas-violent-south (last accessed 3 Apr. 2025).

§7. Elimination of Legislative Control over JVs

561. How could it be possible to suppress the legislator's control over the incorporation of JVs, without a reform of the governing Organic Hydrocarbons Law? Unfortunately, since the establishment of an authoritarian regime in Venezuela that enjoys the unconditional support of the CSJ and in particular the Constitutional Chamber and the Armed Forces, everything has been possible, not without dismantling the rule of law and the fundamental rules of democracy.

562. As has been developed in this chapter, the incorporation of JV's, as happened with the associations referred to in Article 5 of the 1976 LOREICH Organic Law that Reserves the Industry and Commerce of Hydrocarbons for the State(LOREICH – *Ley que Rerseva al Estado la Industria y el Comercio de los Hidrocarburos*), requires the prior approval of the National Assembly, as clearly stated and interpreted from Article 33 of the LOH, which we quote verbatim:

> The incorporation of joint ventures and the conditions governing the performance of primary activities shall require the prior approval of the National Assembly, to which effect the National Executive, through the organ of the Ministry of Energy and Petroleum, shall inform it of all the circumstances pertinent to such incorporation and conditions, including the special advantages provided in favor of the Republic. The National Assembly may modify the proposed conditions or establish such conditions as it deems appropriate. Any subsequent modification of said conditions must also be passed by the National Assembly, subject to a favorable report from the Ministry of Energy and Petroleum and the Permanent Commission on Energy and Petroleum. Joint ventures shall be governed by this Law and, in each particular case, by the terms and conditions established in the Agreement issued by the National Assembly pursuant to the law, based on the report issued by the Permanent Commission on Energy and Petroleum, through which it approves the creation of the respective joint venture in special cases and when it is in the national interest to do so. In addition, the rules of the Code of Commerce and other applicable laws shall be applied.

563. Although the article cited above is extremely clear and has been applied previously without major difficulties, for the national assembly to authorize the existing JVs and partnerships, as already explained in Part II, Chapter 3 of this work, they do not have sense, or logical or legal explanation that now cannot be possible. In effect and as it could not be otherwise, the Constitutional Chamber, responding in an recourse of interpretation[172] of Article 33 of the Organic Law of Hydrocarbons, which was decided in a single day, considered that by virtue of the

172. Constitutional Chamber of the Supreme Court of Justice, *Sentence No. 156 of March 29, 2017*, interpreting Art. 33 of the Organic Hydrocarbons Law, available at: https://pandectasdigital.blogspot.com/2017/03/sentencia-n-156-de-fecha-29-de-marzo-de.html (last accessed 3 Apr. 2025).

fact that the National Assembly could not function because the majority of the deputies who compose it were in contempt of their prior judgments (the National Assembly is a majority opposed to the government), the Assembly could not then exercise de facto the powers provided for in the aforementioned Article 33 of LOH.

564. Consequently, the Constitutional Chamber, in its ruling, determined that 'as long as the situation of contempt and invalidity of the actions of the National Assembly persists', the same Chamber proceeded to assume 'as a matter of law' the totality of the powers of the National Assembly, and consequently, to directly exercise the corresponding parliamentary powers, thereby attributing to itself the power to 'delegate' the exercise of those powers to 'the body at its disposal'.

565. Now, what was being judged here was not the validity or clarity of the functions of the NA derived from Article 33 of the LOH. What the State Attorney's Office was looking for was a legal subterfuge for the mixed companies that the government unilaterally wanted to constitute, with its back to the most democratic popular representation that exists, such as Parliament.

566. In that sense, the purpose of the appeal was to evade or disregard the rule, in particular 'in the present context' and 'in the face of new parliamentary omissions arising' from the contempt and, in this case, for the Chamber to rule on the following aspects:

1. whether or not prior approval of the National Assembly was required for the establishment of JVs and that consequently;
2. what the Executive should do in such circumstances; and
3. whether or not the National Assembly could modify the proposed conditions or establish those it considered appropriate.

567. The Constitutional Chamber of the CSJ decided to resolve 'the interpretation requested' of Article 33 of the Organic Law of Hydrocarbons, providing the following with 'binding character and erga omnes value':

> First, that despite the text of said Law to the contrary, 'there is no impediment whatsoever for the National Executive to establish joint ventures in the spirit established in Article 33 of the Organic Law of Hydrocarbons,' but with the difference that the Executive reports not to the National Assembly, but to the Chamber through the Ministry of Energy and Petroleum, with respect to all the circumstances pertinent to said incorporation and conditions, including the special advantages provided in favor of the Republic.
>
> Second, the Constitutional Chamber prohibited the National Assembly, 'acting de facto', from making any modification to 'the proposed conditions or pretending to establish other conditions'.
>
> Third, the Constitutional Chamber went on to 'attribute' or delegate the power to legislate to the Executive Branch, on this occasion only in matters of the Hydrocarbons Law, providing that: 'on the basis of the state of exception, the Head of State may modify, by means of an amendment, the rule subject to

interpretation, in accordance with the jurisprudence of this Maximum Court (see Decision No. 155 dated March 28, 2017)'.

568. Thus, based on the decision of the Constitutional Chamber of the CSJ No. 158 of 1 April 2017 on 6 July 2017, the Permanent Secretary of the Council of Ministers appeared before said Chamber requesting 'the authorization and approval' of the incorporation of Empresa Mixta, Petrosur S.A. for the production, improvement, and marketing of heavy and extra-heavy crude oil in the area called Junín 10, Production, Improvement and Commercialization of Heavy and Extra Heavy Crude Oil in the area called Junín 10 of the FPO, between Corporación Venezolana de Petróleo, S.A (CVP) and Stichting Administratiekantoor Inversiones Petroleras Iberoamericanas, remitting the necessary documentation to the Chamber. Upon such request, the Chamber decided that: 'there is no impediment whatsoever for the National Executive to establish joint ventures in the spirit established in Article 33 of the Organic Hydrocarbons Law … .'

569. The removal of legislative oversight over JVs has not only strengthened the discretionary power of the Executive but has also served as a strategic response to the international litigation that has affected Venezuela in recent years. Since the expropriations in the oil sector carried out during Hugo Chávez's administration, the country has faced multiple lawsuits in international courts, resulting in costly financial compensations. In response to this scenario, Nicolás Maduro's government has opted to reduce transparency and eliminate legislative oversight mechanisms in the creation of new JVs, thereby minimizing exposure to sanctions or future legal disputes.

570. Since 2017, the Constitutional Chamber of the Supreme Court has enabled the Executive to establish strategic partnerships without requiring parliamentary approval, consolidating a governance model in which decision-making is exclusively concentrated within the central government. This framework was further reinforced through the implementation of new regulations that allow agreements to be signed under strict confidentiality conditions, restricting access to public information and further weakening institutional oversight mechanisms.

571. In this context, the removal of legislative control has served as a legal shield for the Executive's decisions, granting it unilateral authority over the management of the hydrocarbon sector while reducing the risk of future international disputes. However, this strategy has also exacerbated the lack of transparency and weakened accountability mechanisms, fostering an environment where economic and strategic decisions are made within a framework of absolute opacity and discretion.

§8. From the Nationalization of Related Activities to the Administrative Militarization of PDVSA

I. Participation of Private Companies in Related Activities

572. The participation of private companies in the reserved activities of the industry and trade of hydrocarbons was permitted in the country both by the 1975 LOREICH, through OAs and AA, and by the 2001 Organic Hydrocarbons Law (LOH), through JVs. Similarly, private companies were allowed to participate in activities not reserved to the industry and trade of hydrocarbons, particularly providing services or carrying out works through contracts with State companies.

573. However, on 7 May 2009, this possibility came to an end with the approval of the Organic Law Reserving Goods and Services Related to Primary Hydrocarbon Activities to the State (LREBSC – *Ley Orgánica que Reserva al Estado Bienes y Servicios Conexos a las Actividades Primarias de Hidrocarburos*). With its entry into force, the activities were carried out directly by PDVSA or the subsidiary designated for that purpose, or through JVs under the control of PDVSA or its subsidiaries.

574. In accordance with the provisions of the LREBSC, the goods and services related to the primary activities subject to the reserve are the following: (a) injection of water, steam, or gas, which increases the energy of the deposits and improves the recovery factor; (b) gas compression; and (c) those goods and services related to the activities in Lake Maracaibo: boats for the transport of personnel, divers, and maintenance; barges with cranes for the transport of materials, diesel, industrial water, and other inputs; tugboats; flat barges, floats, cranes, gravel, laying, or replacing underwater pipes and cables; maintenance of vessels in workshops, docks, and piers of any nature.

II. Taking Possession of the Assets and Operations

575. The LREBSC expressly authorized PDVSA or its subsidiaries to take possession of the assets and assume control over the operations related to the reserved activities. In accordance with this Law, it is the Ministry of People's Power with competence in petroleum matters (MPPP) to determine by means of a resolution which goods and services of companies or sectors are framed within what the Law describes as 'goods and services related to primary activities'.

576. The LREBSC also provides that those contracts that have been entered into in the areas covered by the reserve are recognized as 'administrative contracts' and that such contracts will terminate once the MPPP issues the resolutions indicated above. Likewise, in order for PDVSA to take control and acquire possession of those assets related to the affected primary activities, the law includes special provisions for the taking of control and expropriation of assets.

III. Expropriations

577. In order to ensure compliance with the purposes of the LREBSC, the National Executive was authorized to decree the total or partial expropriation of the shares or assets of the companies that perform the services referred to in the Law, on the understanding that the calculation of the appraisal of the assets shall not take into account what refers to lost profits or indirect damages. In this sense, goods will be appraised based on their book value, deducting labour and environmental liabilities determined by the competent authorities.

IV. Measures to Ensure Operations and Absorption of Workers

578. Lastly, the Law provides that in order to continue uninterrupted operations, the MPPP shall dictate the necessary measures to guarantee the continuity of the activities covered by the Law, with the persons linked to the matter having to collaborate in the peaceful and orderly delivery of operations, installations, documentation, property, and equipment. The MPPP must also determine the personnel of the companies affected by the reserve that will become part of the payroll of PDVSA or its affiliates, guaranteeing, in any case, such personnel's labour rights.

579. Executing the Law, the MPPP issued a Resolution published in Official Gazette No. 39174 dated 8 May 2009, by means of which it indicated the services of companies or sectors and goods included in the reserve of the Law, which include docks, boats and tugs, and maintenance activities, among others. The Resolution mentions each of the thirty-nine companies that carry out such activities affected by the measure that will be transferred to PDVSA. In addition to the companies mentioned in the Resolution, 39 terminals and docks, 5 shipyard docks, 300 boats, 30 tugs, 30 barges, and 61 divers' boats will pass into the hands of the State. PDVSA will also absorb into its payroll more than 8,000 workers who until now provided their services to contracting companies. This operation, according to the government, would allow Venezuela to reduce production costs by 20%, since, according to it, the private company absorbed profits equivalent to 50% of the production cost of a barrel.

V. Effects of the Nationalization

580. The disastrous consequences of the nationalization of the related services of the oil industry were devastating for the oil industry, as well as for the population and the regional economy. The companies were dismantled, and many of them were abandoned due to the bad management of the new operators of the nationalized companies. The loss of thousands of jobs pushed the workers and labourers to fight for their demands and the government, without the slightest shame, responded by militarizing the conflict zones to control the discontent. The 'Bolivarian' government repressed mercilessly, while many citizens proceeded to sew their lips together and chained their hands and feet to call the attention of President Chávez, without any success.

581. According to the Lagunillas Association of Merchants and Industrialists (ACIL), commercial activity in the area contracted between 30% and 70%, depending on the connection of the businesses with the lake operations.

The expropriation affected the region at three levels: contractors, their direct and indirect suppliers, and local merchants. It is estimated that more than 6,000 small and medium enterprises were impacted, creating more misery and poverty, notably in Zulia State.

582. Seven years later, when the consequences and damages could no longer be hidden, the then Minister of Petroleum and President of PDVSA, Eulogio Del Pino, said publicly in a meeting of the Venezuelan Petroleum Chamber (CPV) on July 2016, 'We must move towards a new model with a majority of the private sector and that goes through a recognition of errors: I believe that what was done in Lake Maracaibo had many errors, we must recognize it and we have moved to a model in which we will give back their activities to all those businessmen who still want to continue.'

§9. Taking Advantage of the Reversal of the Nationalization and Privatization of Related Activities, Through a New Decree, 2018

I. Back to the Privatization of Related Activities

583. Minister Delpino's statements (2016) regarding the catastrophic results of the LREBSC opened the debate to try to correct the perverse effects of its application. A responsible action should aim at the repeal of the LREBSC and the compensation of the companies for the damages caused and return to the situation before the nonsense committed by this law. Notwithstanding the Minister's conviction, the road travelled was not as expected. Indeed, in April 2018, a new regulatory framework was enacted, whereby the government opened the doors to the reprivatization of the related nationalized activities and returned them to the private sector, not without committing open violations of the Constitution and special laws.

584. Thus, on 12 April 2018, Decree No. 3368, issued by the President of the Republic and published in Official Gazette No. 41376, was passed, which in turn allowed the promulgation of 'Decree No. 44 in the Framework of the State of Exception and Economic Emergency that establishes a special transitory regime for the operational and administrative management of the National Petroleum Industry.'

II. Decree Violates Legal Framework on Hydrocarbons and Opens the Path to Eliminate PDVSA

585. By means of Decree 44, a 'special' public contracting scheme was imposed on PDVSA, its affiliated companies, and the national oil industry in general, whereby the constitutional and legal framework on hydrocarbon activity and PDVSA's operations was arbitrarily modified, given that it is not possible to regulate matters reserved to the law by means of a presidential decree and, of course, to the approval of Parliament.

Specifically, Article 156 of the Constitution states that the regime and administration of hydrocarbons is the competence of the National Public Power, and for that reason and in accordance with Article 187 of the same CRBV, corresponds to the National Assembly:

> 1. Legislate on matters of national competence and on the functioning of the different branches of the National Power. In this sense, the aforementioned decree usurped the functions of the National Assembly, which makes it ineffective according to Article 138 of the (Venezuelan) Constitution, which provides that all usurped authority is ineffective and its acts are null and void.

586. In the same way and by virtue of the fact that the Decree was not authorized by the National Assembly by means of an enabling law, in accordance with Articles 203, last part; and 236, numeral 8 and first part, it has also violated the principle of separation of powers regulated by Article 136 in accordance with Article 137, both of the Constitution, which indicate that 'Each of the branches of Public Power has its own functions', and only the 'Constitution and the law define the attributions of the organs that exercise Public Power, to which the activities they carry out must be subject.'

587. The decree also violates Article 303 of the Constitution, which states that 'for reasons of economic sovereignty, politics and national strategy, the State shall preserve all of PDVSA's actions'. In effect, the illegal decree would allow the Minister of the People's Power of Petroleum to eliminate PDVSA itself, according to Article 2 No. 1, which establishes that it may 'create, suppress or make modifications to companies in the public oil industrial sector, including Petróleos de Venezuela S.A., and its affiliated companies'.

III. Basis 'Legal' of Decree

588. The 'legal' basis of the unconstitutional decree is found in the 'Constitutional Law Against Economic War for Rationality and Uniformity in the Acquisition of Goods, Services and Public Works', dictated by the National Constituent Assembly on 11 January 2018, in open violation of the competences of the National Assembly, the only competent organ to dictate laws in Venezuela. The fraudulent

National Constituent Assembly, elected by the regime's supporters, had as its purpose the drafting of a Constitution, which it has not done even two years after being elected, since its task is to act as a parallel parliament.

IV. The Decree Eliminated Tenders and Repealed the LREBSC

589. The decree that has created a special framework eliminated the process of public tenders for the contracting of works and services by companies in the oil industry. With this measure, PDVSA and its subsidiaries can now contract any activity they require through direct adjudication. Therefore, as Brewer Carias states, it can be said that the privatization of the services and related goods of the primary activities of the oil industry that had been nationalized in 2009 took place, but without this Law having been repealed or modified, which is absolutely unconstitutional, since an organic law cannot be reformed by means of a decree.

590. That is how PDVSA and its subsidiaries, invoking Article 5 of Decree No. 3368, have proceeded to purchase, acquire, and execute works through the modality of direct contracting and adjudication, of the same type as those reserved when the LREBSC was enacted, without any type of control. Among those that can be mentioned are: '(1) Water, steam, or gas injection services that increase the energy of the deposits and improve the recovery factor; (2) Gas compression services; and (3) Services related to activities in Lake Maracaibo, such as boat services for transporting personnel, divers, and maintenance; barges with cranes for transporting materials, diesel, industrial water, and other inputs; tugs; flat barges, floats, cranes, gravel, laying, or replacing underwater pipes and cables; maintenance of vessels in workshops, docks, and piers of any nature.'

§10. Summarizing

591.

1. The national oil industry and in particularly PDVSA are under military control.
2. It is probable that we will witness the definitive death of a languishing PDVSA.
3. Everything indicates that by December 2018, oil production could drop to 1 million b/d, or perhaps less.
4. CAMIMPEG could replace PDVSA and become exclusively a military business superstructure.
5. The strategy of military power is understood when we contextualize CAMIMPEG along with Decree 44, which grants unlimited powers to the oil minister, a military man.

592. According to a study conducted by Venezuelan engineer and energy expert Víctor Poleo, the state of production of these corporations is detailed in his report titled 'Joint Ventures in the Twenty-First Century. A legal analysis of this framework of association will be made in Part II, Chapter 3, of this work. Prof. Poleo points out that in 2017, of the 2 million b/d of oil produced by Venezuela, 51%, a little more than 1 MBD, came from these mixed companies. So far in 2018, Venezuela is producing a total of just 1.4 MBD, which means that the production of the JVs has also fallen, to the level of about 760,000 b/d.' The following information is also extracted from the aforementioned report:

Of the total number of existing JVs:

- eight produce less than a thousand barrels a day, that is, including one managed by Cuba and another by Vietnam (already closed). In the last four years, the production of this group of companies has fallen by 65%;
- twelve companies produce between 1,000 and 10,000 b/d, but their production has fallen by 50% in the last four years;
- twenty companies produce less than 10,000 b/d;
- eleven JVs produce between 10000 and 50000 b/d and include companies managed by ENI, REPSOL and CHEVRON, which have maintained their production, although with a clear tendency to decline, and without any signs of development or new investments;
- seven companies produce over than 50000 b/d.

Chapter 4. Transport

§1. Oil Transport Activity Reserved to the State

593. According to the LOH, hydrocarbon transportation may be carried out in its natural State or once they are processed and transformed into by-products for industrial or residential use or for vehicle use. Transport activities for hydrocarbons in a natural State shall be regarded as primary activities reserved to the State (Article 6 LOH) but may also be performed by mixed companies (Article 22 LOH), provided that the State retains control of its decisions and a participation greater than 50% of the capital stock.

§2. Permission to Transport Activities

594. Transport activities of products derived from hydrocarbons (Article 60 LOH) represent a public service and may be performed by individuals different from the State (Article 61), as long as they obtain in advance permits issued by the Ministry of Energy and Oil. Such permits shall be subject to the provisions set forth in this Law, its Regulations and the respective Regulations, and they shall not be assigned or transferred without previous authorization of the Ministry of Energy and Oil.

595. Until the mid-2000s, PDVSA marketed hydrocarbon by-products through a vast and diversified infrastructure distributed throughout the country. This network included 1,764 service stations and eleven fluvial stations; seventeen fuel distribution plants; 1,144 kilometers (710.84 miles) of product pipelines; and 2,237 ground transportation units supported by thirty-four carriers. In addition, the company operated twenty-four jet fuel supply plants located at twenty-three airports and one heliport, as well as four fishing ports in the states of Anzoátegui and Sucre. Infrastructure for maritime fuel and lubricant distribution included pipelines, cisterns, and barges at the airports of Cumaná, Güiria, and Punta Meta. PDVSA also maintained a specialized mixing and bottling/canning plant for PDV® lubricants, serving the automotive, industrial, and electric sectors. Distribution operations were supported by four commercial channels, which provided products to a total of 4,198 users: 1,658 service stations, 1,474 industrial customers, 493 aviation clients, and 398 maritime clients. This extensive infrastructure not only demonstrated PDVSA's nationwide logistical capacity but also constituted a critical component of Venezuela's energy distribution system.

596. The previously detailed infrastructure of Petróleos de Venezuela, S.A. (PDVSA) has experienced significant deterioration over the past decade, primarily due to economic mismanagement, international sanctions, and a lack of essential maintenance and investment. This decline has severely impacted Venezuela's ability to efficiently transport and distribute hydrocarbons.

597. The nation's extensive network of pipelines, refineries, and distribution stations has suffered from chronic underinvestment, leading to operational inefficiencies and frequent disruptions in the supply chain. The imposition of stringent US sanctions, particularly those targeting PDVSA, has exacerbated these challenges by restricting access to international markets and financial resources, further hindering the procurement of necessary equipment and technology for infrastructure maintenance (US Energy Information Administration [EIA], 2024).[173]

598. As a direct consequence, Venezuela has faced acute shortages of gasoline and diesel, manifesting in prolonged queues at service stations and the proliferation of black-market fuel sales. Despite possessing substantial refining capacity, facilities such as the Paraguaná Refining Complex have operated significantly below their potential, with utilization rates plummeting to as low as 10% in recent years (EIA, 2024).[174] According to the US Energy Information Administration, Venezuela has increasingly relied on Iranian imports, with tankers regularly delivering refined products to offset domestic shortages. Additionally, reports from Reuters highlight that PDVSA has resumed light crude imports to sustain production, further underscoring its dependence on external supplies.

599. In an effort to revitalize the sector, the Venezuelan government has sought to attract foreign investment by offering more favourable terms to international oil companies. Notably, Chevron received authorization from the US Treasury Department in late 2022 to resume limited operations in Venezuela, leading to a modest uptick in oil production and exports. However, the recent revocation of Chevron's licence in March 2025, reportedly influenced by shifting US policy and geopolitical tensions, has reintroduced uncertainty into Venezuela's oil sector. The decision, seen as part of broader diplomatic recalibrations, could reduce production by approximately 150,000 barrels per day and prompt the government to seek alternative partnerships with nations such as China and Turkey.[175]

600. However, despite these renewed investment efforts, the legal framework governing Venezuela's oil industry continues to present obstacles to a full recovery. While companies like Chevron have sought to expand operations, restrictive regulations and state control over oil transportation continue to limit the extent to which private firms can contribute to the sector's revitalization. The 2001 Organic Hydrocarbons Law maintains state control over oil transportation, effectively restricting private sector participation. While recent reforms have aimed at increasing private

173. U.S. Energy Information Administration, *Venezuela: Country Analysis Brief*, U.S. Department of Energy, 2024, available at: https://www.eia.gov/international/content/analysis/countries_long/Venezuela/pdf/venezuela_2024.pdf (last accessed 3 Apr. 2025).

174. U.S. Energy Information Administration (2024), *Country analysis brief: Venezuela*. Retrieved 22 Apr. 2025, from https://www.eia.gov/international/content/analysis/countries_long/Venezuela/pdf/venezuela_2024.pdf.

175. Venezuelanalysis, '*Venezuela: US Shrinks Chevron Wind-Down Period to 30 Days Following 'Crazy Cubans' Pressure*,' 4 Mar. 2025, available at: https://venezuelanalysis.com/news/venezuela-us-shrinks-chevron-wind-down-period-to-30-days-following-crazy-cubans-pressure (last accessed 3 Apr. 2025).

involvement, persistent legal and regulatory uncertainties – combined with the Venezuelan government's discretionary decision-making – have deterred further investment. According to a 2024 analysis by Reuters, the lack of clear and stable policies has led many potential investors to remain hesitant about re-engaging with Venezuela's energy market.[176]

601. In summary, the future of hydrocarbon transportation in Venezuela hinges on several critical factors: political stability, the potential easing of international sanctions, the restoration of investor confidence, and the comprehensive rehabilitation of the nation's oil infrastructure. Without substantial progress in these areas, the distribution of petroleum products is likely to remain a significant constraint on Venezuela's energy sector, with far-reaching implications for the broader economy and the well-being of its population.

§3. Existing Infrastructure

602. PDVSA markets hydrocarbon by-products through a nationwide infrastructure currently undergoing modernization. As of 2024, it operates approximately 1,800 service stations, of which 176 have been equipped with 333 new-generation fuel dispensers as part of a pilot programme launched in June 2024, aiming to renew all fuel dispensing systems across the country (HispanoPost, 2024).[177] This replacement programme is part of a strategic alliance between the Ministry of Petroleum and Banco de Venezuela, aimed at modernizing the nation's fuel distribution system through technological upgrades at service stations. This initiative includes the implementation of digital payment systems, improvements in metering and safety equipment, and the gradual replacement of obsolete infrastructure. In addition, several fuel distribution plants remain operational and are undergoing renovation and expansion as part of the Plan de la Patria 2019–2025, which outlines goals such as 'ensuring energy sovereignty, expanding national refining capacity, and optimizing logistics for domestic fuel supply' (República Bolivariana de Venezuela, 2019)).[178] The plan also includes the modernization of the existing pipeline network to improve the transportation of refined products and support increased hydrocarbon production. Although updated figures are not available for other infrastructure—such as river stations, land transport units, jet fuel plants, fishing ports, or lubricant

176. Reuters, '*CERAWEEK Venezuela's Opposition Drafts Energy Reform to Raise Foreign Pressure*,' 12 Mar. 2025, available at: https://www.reuters.com/business/energy/ceraweek-venezuelas-opposition-drafts-energy-reform-raise-foreign-pressure-2025-03-12/ (last accessed 3 Apr. 2025).

177. HispanoPost, '*PDVSA Inició Plan Piloto de Nuevos Surtidores de Combustible: 'Tenemos Instalados 333 en 176 Estaciones de Servicios*,' 14 Jun. 2024, available at: https://hispanopost.com/pdvsa-inicio-plan-piloto-de-nuevos-surtidores-de-combustible-tenemos-instalados-333-en-176-estaciones-de-servicios/ (last accessed 4 Apr. 2025). *PDVSA inició plan piloto de nuevos surtidores de combustible: 'Tenemos instalados 333 en 176 estaciones de servicios*' (14 Jun. 2024), https://hispanopost.com/pdvsa-inicio-plan-piloto-de-nuevos-surtidores-de-combustible-tenemos-instalados-333-en-176-estaciones-de-servicios/ (last visited 4 Apr. 2025).

178. República Bolivariana de Venezuela, *Plan de la Patria 2019–2025*, 2019, available at: https://residuoselectronicosal.org/wp-content/uploads/2020/04/Plan-Patria-2019-2025.pdf (last accessed 4 Apr. 2025).

processing plants—the official strategy envisions a phased recovery process aligned with national development priorities and the goal of securing reliable and sovereign fuel supply across the country (República Bolivariana de Venezuela, Plan de la Patria 2019–2025, Objective 5.2.1.2).[179]

179. República Bolivariana de Venezuela, Plan de la Patria 2019–2025: Segundo Plan Socialista de Desarrollo Económico y Social de la Nación 2019–2025, Objetivo 5.2.1.2, https://madretierraenlared.org/wp-content/uploads/2020/04/Plan-Patria-2019-2025.pdf (last visited 10 Jun. 2025).

Chapter 5. Distribution

§1. State Control over the Domestic Market

603. The LOH passed in 2001 rendered ineffective the domestic market opening for hydrocarbon derivatives, which started in the second half of the 1990s, and was reasserted by passing the LOAMI in 1998. This law centralizes the domestic market regulations (nowadays, domestic trade) in the same legal text, thus ending, somehow, with a cycle of separate laws for the regulation of hydrocarbon activities in the domestic market.

604. The LOH has provided that any domestic market activity will be included under the concept of public utilities, which makes evident the degree of control and intervention intended by the Government on this matter, leaving hardly any space for private initiatives. Actually, Article 27 and Article 58 of the LOH reflect a tendency to a close and limited scheme. The law has provided that any trading activity of natural hydrocarbons, as well as any hydrocarbon derivative included in any decree or resolution passed by the National Government, shall be performed only by the Companies listed in Article 27, which reads:

> The National Government shall be empowered by means of any decree issued by the Cabinet Meeting to create companies of the Government's exclusive ownership to perform the activities foreseen in said Decree-Law and whose juridical organization may be adopted as appropriate, including that of a Public Limited Corporation with one sole partner.

605. In this manner, a sole decree or resolution will be enough to have any product from hydrocarbon derivatives (gasoline, oils, diesel, etc.) traded exclusively and solely by State-owned companies. Therefore, the small space for private participation established in Article 58 was left without effect. Under these conditions, national and foreign companies decided not to make further investments to improve the quality of the products and services rendered. Therefore, Article 58 has stated that the trading activities of any derivative product excluded in Article 57 of the LOH may be directly performed by the Government or by any state-owned company, or by any joint enterprise with public and private capital, in any percentage whatsoever, and by any private company. The lack of clarity and precision with regard to which products this regulation is referring to makes us presume that the regulation would be referring to those products not included within the scope of the decree or resolution issued by the Ministry of Petroleum (previously known as the Ministry of Energy and Petroleum, or MENPET) or by the Government, that is, a discretional instrument used by the Government for determining the kinds of products and the manner in which said products may be subject or not to trading in the domestic market by any joint or private company or exclusively by the Government. It is obvious that, under said conditions, it becomes very difficult for any national or foreign company to make investments in order to improve the quality of the products, as well as the quality of the public utilities.

606. In Article 107 of the regulation proposed for the LOH, it has been ratified that domestic trading refers to any derivative product from hydrocarbons listed in the corresponding resolution issued by the MENPET through the different entities participating in the marketing chain. However, Article 108 ejusdem provides uncertainty in regard to domestic market by stating that, with the exception of those products reserved to companies of the Government's exclusive ownership (emphasis added), domestic market trading of remaining hydrocarbon derivative products may be directly performed by the Government or by said companies, although trading may also be performed by joint companies with mixed capital stock of any public and private shareholder's ownership participation or by private companies. That is, in any instance, there is no reference made to which products are reserved for the Government, much less to the products that may be traded by joint companies or by private companies, as it was provided for in former laws on hydrocarbons, such as the Law for Domestic Market Reserve, in 1973, and the Law for Gasoline Market Opening and other Derivatives, in 1998.

607. The excessive state control over the domestic hydrocarbon market, imposed through the 2001 LOH, has resulted in many of the negative consequences that had already been anticipated following the elimination of the previous legal framework, which allowed for greater private sector participation. The progressive liberalization established by the 1998 LOAMI was completely reversed, discouraging investment and leaving the state as the sole entity responsible for fuel distribution.

608. One of the most evident effects of this market centralization has been the persistent supply crisis, characterized by shortages, rationing, and long queues at service stations. Since 2017, fuel scarcity has particularly affected the country's interior, while distribution infrastructure has continued to deteriorate without clear recovery plans. The state-controlled model, lacking competition and private investment, has proven incapable of ensuring a stable fuel supply.

609. In an attempt to mitigate the collapse, in 2020, the government introduced a dual-pricing system, which established: subsidized gasoline, available in limited quantities and subject to government-controlled distribution; dollarized gasoline, sold at international market prices.

610. Rather than resolving the crisis, this measure has exacerbated inequalities in fuel access and facilitated the expansion of black-market sales and smuggling, worsening the situation. Meanwhile, the absence of clear regulatory provisions for private sector participation in fuel distribution continues to generate legal uncertainty, discouraging any attempt at infrastructure investment.

611. The collapse of the supply system under state control confirms the warnings raised when LOAMI was repealed. What was justified as a 'recovery of energy sovereignty' has instead resulted in a dysfunctional domestic market, characterized by inefficiency, distorted pricing mechanisms, and a structural inability to meet national demand. Despite partial attempts at market liberalization – such as the authorization of private fuel imports under specific conditions – the model remains fundamentally dependent on centralized state control, which has proven unsustainable.

612. More than two decades after the enactment of the 2001 LOH, the negative consequences of market centralization in fuel distribution are undeniable: recurring shortages and long queues at service stations; deterioration of distribution infrastructure due to lack of investment; expansion of black-market fuel sales and smuggling; inequality in access due to partial market dollarization; and corruption and discretionary issuance of distribution permits.

613. The promises of energy sovereignty have instead resulted in inefficiency and structural market failure. Without a comprehensive regulatory reform that enables a transparent and competitive market with greater private sector participation, Venezuela will continue to face severe challenges in fuel distribution, with significant repercussions for mobility, industrial production, and the daily lives of its citizens.

§2. Facilities and Registry for Domestic Market Activities

614. Article 64, in agreement with Article 65 of the LOH, establishes that regarding the construction, remodeling, expansion, demolition, or dismantling of buildings, facilities, and equipment for the domestic market of hydrocarbon derivatives, or for any operation intended to be carried out on such premises, registrars and notaries must refrain from processing any document related to these domestic market activities, as they require authorization from the Ministry of People's Power for Petroleum (formerly MENPET). Once construction has been completed and the beneficiary has obtained the corresponding permit, a certified copy of the facility's construction must be submitted to the corresponding Registry Office, including the registry data of the premises where the facility was built.

615. This copy must be attached to the Book of Vouchers, and a marginal note must be recorded in the corresponding Book of Protocol, stating that any operation intended to be carried out on the premises must be authorized by said Office (emphasis added). The beneficiary, after fulfilling these requirements, must submit a certified copy of the document to the corresponding Office in order to start the business activity. There is no doubt that this regulation could be used to prevent any private negotiation concerning the goodwill of service stations (E/S), assuming that prior authorization from the Ministry of People's Power for Petroleum would be required.

616. This provision may be defined as a restriction on economic freedom in matters that are of private concern to individuals. Simultaneously, Article 5 of the LOAMI remains in force under the LOH, guaranteeing preferential rights for individuals engaged in business activities related to hydrocarbon derivatives, while also acknowledging the value of goodwill.

617. We believe that this new regulation represents a setback in relation to the achievements made under the LOAMI, whose consequences are expected to become evident soon. Economic freedom, as established in Article 113 of the CRBV (1999), is considered restrictive in this particular business sector.

618. Since the implementation of the Organic Law for Reorganizing the Domestic Liquid Fuels Market (LORMI – *Ley Orgánica para la Reorganización del Mercado Nacional de los Combustibles Líquidos*) in 2008 and the deepening of state control over PDVSA in 2017, private investments in the domestic market have nearly disappeared. Currently, the dual gasoline pricing system (subsidized and dollarized) has created challenges for service stations, affecting their financial viability and further reducing investment in the sector (Reuters, 2020).[180] The national and transnational companies that invested in the domestic market, attracted by the market opening of the 1990s and early 2000s, have halted new investments due to: (1) International sanctions affecting transactions with PDVSA. (2) Lack of a stable regulatory framework for private investment. (3) The economic crisis, which has significantly reduced fuel consumption in the country.

§3. Domestic Market Present Condition: Profit Margins

619. The crisis in the domestic hydrocarbon derivatives market is undeniable. As was the case in the 1970s, this situation is highly likely to result in service interruptions or the permanent closure of service stations (E/S). The circumstances remain fundamentally unchanged: there is an imminent risk of bankruptcy for business owners in this sector. Profit margins, which constitute the primary source of income for fuel retailers, transporters, and wholesale fuel distributors, pose a serious threat to the sustainability of existing service stations. As profitability declines, an increasing number of businesses are facing closure. In the past, the revenues of fuel retailers, transporters, and wholesale distributors were determined by regulated profit margins. However, the introduction of a dual gasoline pricing system – comprising subsidized and dollarized fuel – has exacerbated disparities within the sector. On one hand, dollarized service stations generate higher revenues; however, they continue to face profitability challenges due to elevated operational costs in US dollars, declining domestic demand, and competition from the illegal fuel market. On the other hand, subsidized service stations struggle with extremely low profit margins, rendering them economically unsustainable without government intervention. Consequently, over 700 requests for property title transfers have been filed for premises currently operating as service stations, with the intention of converting

180. Vivian Sequera, & Deisy Buitrago, '*Venezuela's New Gasoline System Fails to End Epic Lines*,' 8 Jun. 2020, available at: https://www.reuters.com/article/business/venezuelas-new-gasoline-system-fails-to-end-epic-lines-idUSKBN23F09I (last accessed 4 Apr. 2025).

them into alternative business ventures. Furthermore, transport cooperatives, business owners, and sector workers have jointly submitted claims regarding profit margin inadequacies. However, these efforts have yielded only partial and insufficient government responses, as the adjustments implemented have failed to meet the sector's financial needs.

620. As previously stated, the dual gasoline pricing system introduced in 2020 has further compounded the difficulties faced by service stations:

1. Subsidized gasoline: Offered at artificially low prices, leaving many service stations financially unsustainable.
2. Dollarized gasoline**:** Sold at international market rates, generating higher revenues but accompanied by substantial operational expenses in US dollars.

This system has led to a significant divide among service stations, where some have achieved profitability, while others remain on the verge of closure.

621. During the market liberalization period (1998-2001), profit margins were more balanced, facilitating investment in infrastructure and improvements in customer service. However, due to the fuel supply crisis since 2018 and partial dollarization since 2020, conditions have changed. Today, subsidized service stations face extreme financial difficulties, while dollarized stations have achieved greater stability, albeit with higher operating costs.

622. Adjustments to profit margins have proven insufficient to stabilize the sector. In 2021, the government eliminated several fuel transport subsidies, resulting in increased logistics costs and diminishing the profitability of wholesale distributors. Although incremental price adjustments have been made for dollarized gasoline, many operators contend that profit margins remain inadequate to cover operational expenses, leading to the closure of numerous stations.

623. The issue of profitability in the service station sector remains unresolved. Currently, revenue must be sourced from fuel tax income or PDVSA's profits, both of which are insufficient to sustain the industry. Although the fuel market has been partially opened to private investment in recent years, regulatory instability and declining domestic consumption continue to undermine the sector's long-term viability.

§4. Domestic Market Framework since 2008

624. On 28 August 2008, the National Government – in an attempt to clarify the doubts arising from the Organic Law of Hydrocarbons LOH of 2001 – decreed the LORMI and cancelled the opening to private sector participation. Hence, the reorganization is construed as the concentration of activities previously carried out by both private and public companies, by the Government, contrary to the LOAMI of

1998, which promoted free competition between the participating factors, thus having a vast combination of national and foreign companies.

625. Under the LORMI, the Government has the power to control fuel transportation, which was in the hands of intermediaries that constituted monopolies, that is, the scourge of capitalism and detrimental to the economy. Consequently, 'Monopolies will be dismantled, and PDVSA will guarantee the Venezuelan people the supply of liquid fuel in a more effective, efficient and safe manner, all of which is aimed at homeland security and for national defence reasons.' This is a statement of the Vice President of the Energy and Mines Commission of the National Assembly, Jesus Ernesto Graterol, who also stated that the registration of service stations and the control of transportation in the hands of private companies played 'the delay card, thus generating illegal gasoline extraction in our borders' with over 300,000 barrels smuggled on a daily basis.

626. More than ten years later, the LORMI was decreed and, far from improving, the supply service of gasoline and other refined products had worsened. With that Law, Venezuela has made a leap backwards into the void. The concentration or monopolization of domestic market activities by PDVSA (the state oil company) prevents investment in the sector and, as a result, hinders the improvement of products and services. For example, the GNV project launched in 1995 aimed to export gasoline and diesel, while gradually raising their domestic prices by replacing them with gas. A clear example is the project on GNV implemented in 1995, aimed at exporting gasoline and diesel and progressively increasing their prices in the domestic market by substituting them with gas. By 1998, this project, replaced by Auto-Gas, counted on 148 operative E/S to supply gas to converted vehicles. Since 1999, the new administration has postponed the project and then reactivated it, but has failed to meet the goals set. In fact, barely 118 new stations have been built since 1998, and today we count on 266.

627. The longstanding fuel price freeze facilitated and promoted gasoline and diesel smuggling, particularly to Colombia. However, with the implementation of the dual-pricing system in 2020, the situation has partially changed. Although smuggling still exists, it has decreased due to the partial dollarization of the market and the narrowing of price differentials between Venezuela and neighbouring countries. Nevertheless, according to data from Venezuela Adentro (2024), approximately 40,000 barrels per day continue to be illegally extracted, primarily through the borders of Táchira and Zulia, as well as through clandestine operations in the Caribbean.[181]

628. Although smuggling to Colombia has decreased compared to 2018 levels, the illegal trade of gasoline, diesel, and lubricants has evolved within Venezuela

181. Venezuela Investigative Unit, '*Gas Smugglers Busted as Colombia-Venezuela Contraband in Flux*,' 17 Aug. 2021, available at: https://insightcrime.org/news/brief/gasoline-smugglers-busted-as-colombia-venezuela-contraband-dynamic-evolves/ (last accessed 4 Apr. 2025).

itself. In 2023 and 2024, there has been a notable increase in the sale of fuel in dollars through informal markets, particularly in Bolívar, Anzoátegui, and Caracas. This black market has emerged due to:

1. Shortages of subsidized gasoline at service stations.
2. Corruption in fuel distribution, with redirection to clandestine networks.
3. The collapse of public transportation, forcing many drivers to resort to informal sellers.
4. As Pérez (2024) highlights, this situation has led to the formation of a parallel fuel economy, undermining the effectiveness of state price controls.[182]

In conclusion, although smuggling to Colombia has decreased compared to 2018 levels, the dynamics of illegal fuel trade within Venezuela have taken on new forms and dimensions. The proliferation of informal markets and the emergence of a parallel fuel economy not only reflect deep distortions in the distribution system, but also highlight the inability of state policies to effectively control the sector. This situation poses significant challenges for energy security and governance in the country, making it essential to implement structural reforms that restore transparency and efficiency in the management of energy resources.

629. The shortage of fuels and lubricants, exacerbated by the collapse of public transportation and the lack of spare parts, has fuelled speculation in the black market. Since 2021, so-called fuel bachaqueros (black market resellers) have proliferated in urban and rural areas, reselling gasoline and diesel at prices 300% to 800% above the regulated rate. A 50-litre tank, which should cost USD 1 under the subsidized system, is sold for up to USD 40 in informal markets. In regions with severe supply shortages, prices may exceed USD 100 per tank (Rodríguez, 2023). This phenomenon has been tolerated in some cases by the authorities, contributing to the growth of a parallel fuel economy within the country.[183]

630. The Venezuelan fuel market has undergone a structural shift due to the prolonged economic crisis. In 2015, domestic gasoline consumption was 260,000 barrels per day (bpd). By 2020, it had fallen to 110,000 bpd, due to the pandemic and the transportation crisis. In 2024, consumption stood at 97,000 bpd, with a continued downward trend due to mass migration, the decline of the vehicle fleet, and a lack of investment in the sector (TheGlobalEconomy, 2023).[184]

---

182. Banca y Negocios, '*Contrabando de Gasolina en Venezuela Persiste Pese al Aumento de su Precio, Según Expertos*,' 7 Feb. 2024, available at: https://www.bancaynegocios.com/contrabando-de-gasolina-en-venezuela-persiste-pese-al-aumento-de-su-precio-segun-expertos/ (last accessed 4 Apr. 2025).
183. Transparencia Venezuela. '*Economías Ilícitas Obtuvieron Rentas Estimadas de USD 9.402 Millones en 2022*,' available at: https://transparenciave.org (last accessed 4 Apr. 2025).
184. TheGlobalEconomy.com, '*Venezuela: Gasoline Consumption*,' 2023, available at: https://www.theglobaleconomy.com/Venezuela/gasoline_consumption/ (last accessed 4 Apr. 2025).

631. According to the latest PDVSA reports (2024), domestic fuel production failed to meet national demand. In 2015, Venezuelan refineries processed more than 1 million bpd. By 2020, production had dropped to 90,000 bpd. In 2024, it remained around 95,000 bpd, with major operational failures at the Amuay and El Palito refineries (Energy Analytics Institute, 2025). Given this situation, PDVSA has increased fuel imports. Since 2020, Iran has become Venezuela's main gasoline supplier, delivering around 1.5 million barrels per month (Andarcia, 2021).[185]

632. For PDVSA, the reduction in domestic fuel demand has alleviated foreign exchange pressure, as the company has reduced emergency imports. However, gasoline subsidies continue to represent a significant fiscal burden. Since 2020, the government has implemented a monthly subsidy quota system, allowing each driver to access 120 litres of subsidized gasoline per month, at a price of USD 0.02 per litre. Once this quota is exceeded, gasoline must be purchased at the international price of USD 0.50 per litre. This system has led to market segmentation, where:

1. Subsidized users still receive nearly free fuel.
2. Those requiring additional gasoline must pay in US dollars, impacting sectors like public transportation and commercial logistics.[186]

633. Venezuelan refineries, including the Amuay, Cardón, El Palito, and PLC complexes, continue to operate well below their installed capacity due to structural failures, lack of maintenance, and technological obsolescence. This situation has forced PDVSA to significantly rely on fuel and diluent imports, with an estimated annual expenditure of around USD 2.5 billion, according to averages derived from the total amount of USD 12.5 billion invested between 2021 and 2024 (La Razón, 2025).

Operational Details:

- *Amuay* (capacity: 645,000 bpd): Operating at ~10% of its capacity due to recurring failures in critical units such as vacuum furnaces. *El Palito* (187,000 bpd): Only reaches 34% capacity in specific units, with frequent technical shutdowns requiring foreign assistance.
- *Puerto La Cruz* (310,000 bpd): Maintains intermittent operations, with naphtha reformers out of service since 2020.

185. Andarcia, M.V., '*Irán Toma Oro de una Venezuela que Ya No Tiene Petróleo con Qué Pagar los Favores*,' Global Affairs, Universidad de Navarra, May 2021, available at: https://www.unav.edu/web/global-affairs/detalle/-/blogs/iran-toma-oro-de-una-venezuela-que-ya-no-tiene-petroleo-con-que-pagar-los-favores-2 (last accessed 4 Apr. 2025).
186. Tellechea, R., '*Anuncio de Sistema de Citas para Gasolina Subsidiada*,' Efecto Cocuyo, 2024, available at: https://efectococuyo.com/economia/ahora-la-gasolina-subsidiada-se-vendera-por-cita-y-a-traves-de-una-app/ (last accessed 4 Apr. 2025).

Economic Consequences:

The dependence on imports, mainly light crude oil from Iran and gasoline, represents an average annual expenditure of USD 3.125 billion (La Razón, 2025),[187] although conservative estimates place the figure at USD 2.5 billion when considering offset exchanges with trading partners. PDVSA has prioritized the import of diluents such as Iranian condensate to process extra-heavy crude from the Orinoco Belt, whose production requires costly blends due to its high viscosity.

634. For PDVSA, the decline in domestic fuel demand has generated mixed economic outcomes. On the one hand, it has eased pressure on foreign exchange reserves, as the company has been able to curtail emergency fuel imports at international prices. However, this reduction in consumption is not indicative of improved efficiency, but rather a consequence of economic deterioration and structural deficiencies in the fuel supply chain. As depicted in Figure 16, Venezuela's domestic fuel consumption has exhibited a sustained decline, reflecting the collapse of public transportation (90% inoperative) and a 50% reduction in private vehicle circulation, primarily due to persistent shortages of spare parts, tires, and lubricants. Simultaneously, domestic gasoline production has dropped significantly, compelling PDVSA to increasingly rely on fuel imports to mitigate the supply deficit. Despite recent supply agreements with Iran and other international partners, dependence on external sources has continued to escalate as Venezuelan refineries persistently operate well below capacity due to chronic technical failures and insufficient investment in maintenance. Figure 16 underscores this trend, illustrating how domestic fuel consumption is now primarily sustained through imports rather than local production, highlighting the country's growing reliance on foreign suppliers.

Figure 16 Venezuelass Domestic Fuel Supply: From Self-Sufficiency to Growing Import Dependence (1999-2023)

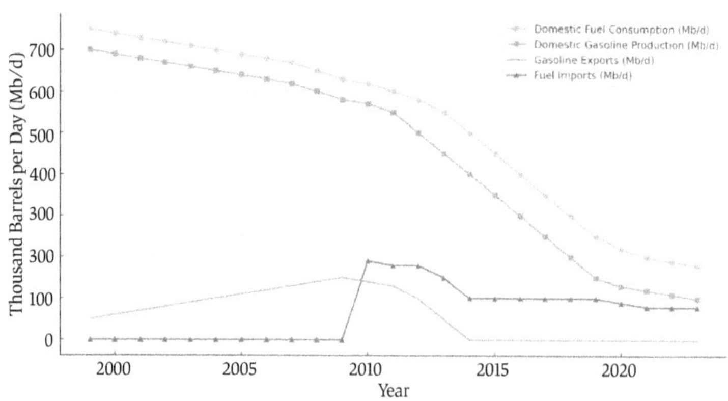

187. La Razón (2025).,'*De 2021 a 2024, el Gobierno gastó $us 12.500 millones en importación de combustibles*'. Disponible en: https://www.la-razon.com/economia/2025/03/09/de-2021-a-2024-el-gobierno-gasto-us-12-500-millones-en-importacion-de-combustibles/.

635. The current reference price of gasoline (RBOB) in the U.S. market (as of July 2018) is USD 2.16 per gallon (equivalent to USD 0.57 per litre). In Venezuela, 95-octane gasoline is sold at VEB 6.00 per litre, which equals approximately USD 0.0006 at the official exchange rate. This means that for every litre PDVSA purchases at USD 0.57 from the U.S., it could supply nineteen 50-litre vehicle tanks in Venezuela. At this pace of importing gasoline and other hydrocarbon products, PDVSA would spend USD 10 million per day, around USD 300 million per month. However, PDVSA sells gasoline below cost. The cost of producing 1 litre of gasoline is USD 0.02 and PDVSA is selling it at USD 0.0006. The experts assure that the amount of the subsidy granted only in 2011 for gasoline amounted to USD 13,170 million (taking into account the opportunity cost), equivalent to 4.4% of the GDP of that year.

636. The former minister and president of PDVSA, Rafael Ramirez, during the period 2002–2013, said repeatedly that Venezuela's gasoline subsidy loss amounts close to USD 12,500 million per year, which makes the Venezuelan fuel the cheapest worldwide. The percentage loss was only slightly reduced with the increase decreed in February 2016, after spending twenty years stalled, the increase in fuel prices was 1,328.5% for regular gasoline and 6,085% for super. Still, a litre of 91 octane gasoline costs only VES 1 and 95 worth VES 6. A beer costs, for example, VES 800,000 or a Coca-Cola 1,000.000. This distortion is associated with the economic crisis, inflation, and exchange controls prevailing in the country.

637. These disastrous results are the consequence of the wrong policies implemented since 2001. The system where the Government acted as a wholesaler through DELTAVEN, an affiliated company of PDVSA, transnational companies, and country-owned companies, was replaced. Thanks to the regulation promoting the opening, these companies ventured into the conquest of a market share with the expectation that fuel and lubricant prices would be increased, which was moderately met. However, multiple related businesses and convenience stores were developed, and the eco-friendly gasoline with additives was launched in the market in parallel, thus radically modernizing the infrastructure of E/S; consequently, the domestic market inherited the old monopolist form of the policy established in 1973 by passing the Law that Reserved the Domestic Market for Hydrocarbon Derivative products to the Government. From that period to the implementation of the opening policy, the domestic market was – as it is now – in a state of utter underdevelopment. That is why we have stated that we have leapt backwards into the void. The governance where users and market rules complemented the balance jointly with the companies was replaced by a system where the Government is the sole leading figure.

638. Although Venezuela has made adjustments to its fuel subsidy policy, the domestic fuel market remains distorted and financially unsustainable. Since 2020, the government has implemented a dual-pricing system, with subsidized gasoline at VES 0.10 per litre and an international price of USD 0.50 per litre at dollarized stations. However, PDVSA still relies on fuel imports, primarily from Iran, to meet domestic demand. Despite efforts to reactivate refineries, they continue to operate well below capacity due to a lack of investment, international sanctions, and corruption, exacerbating fuel shortages, long queues, and a black market. Although fuel subsidies have been reduced, financial losses persist, and state control restricts private sector involvement. In conclusion, structural issues within the fuel sector remain unresolved. Without significant investment and comprehensive reforms, Venezuela will continue to face fuel shortages, reliance on imports, and inefficiencies in its domestic fuel market.

§5. Distribution and Trading

639. Historically, Venezuela was a major global energy exporter, with crude oil and refined products being shipped primarily to Asia (40.4%), North America (35.5%), and the Caribbean (14.4%). In 2014, LNG exports were mainly directed to Brazil (64.9%) and the US (19.8%). However, due to operational difficulties and international sanctions, exports began to decline drastically.

640. By June 2018, PDVSA had already notified several international clients – including Lukoil, Nynas, Tipco, CHEVRON, CNPC, Reliance, CONOCO, and Valero – about its inability to meet oil supply obligations. At that time, PDVSA could only export 649,000 barrels per day out of the 1.495 million barrels committed. By May 2018, Venezuela's crude oil production had fallen to 1,392 mb/d.

641. In the following years, Venezuela's energy trade faced even greater restrictions. US-imposed sanctions since 2019, combined with declining production, have severely impacted the country's ability to export oil. Between 2011 and 2021, Venezuela's total energy production declined by an average of 8.2% annually, with oil and other liquids being the most affected sectors. Despite attempts at recovery, deteriorating infrastructure, lack of investment in refining capacity, and reduced operational capability at PDVSA have made Venezuela an increasingly irrelevant energy exporter in the global market.

Chapter 6. Consumption

642. Venezuela has historically been a country with high energy consumption, primarily based on oil, natural gas, and hydroelectric energy. However, in recent years, a combination of economic collapse, international sanctions, and lack of investment has led to a significant reduction in total primary energy consumption.

643. Figure 17 illustrates the evolution of primary energy consumption between 2013 and 2023 in various countries across the region. The thicker line represents Venezuela, clearly showing a downward trend, with a significant decline between 2013 and 2020. In 2013, Venezuela's per capita energy consumption was 125.1 GJ, which was considerably high compared to most Latin American countries. However, this consumption decreased to 66.7 GJ by 2020, followed by a slight rebound in 2023, reaching 87.8 GJ. This pattern indicates that, despite the previous years' decline, there was a modest recovery by 2023, although still below the levels recorded in 2013.[188]

Figure 17 Per Capita Primary Energy Consumption – Latin America

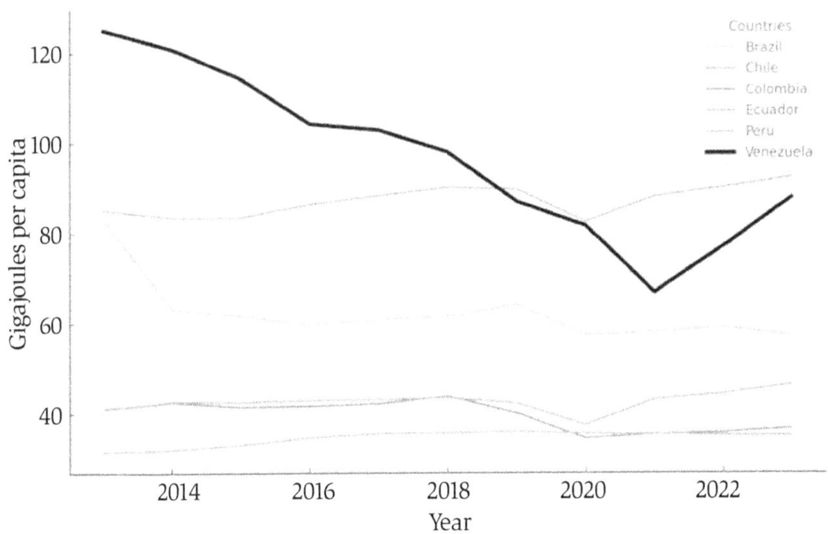

644. Figure 18 displays the refinery throughput in Venezuela, measured in thousands of barrels per day, from 2013 to 2023. Since 2015, throughput has experienced a drastic decline, dropping from over 900 thousand barrels per day to less

188. Energy Institute, *Statistical Review of World Energy 2024* (2024), accessible at https://www.bpb.de/system/files/dokument_pdf/Statistical_Review_of_World_Energy_2024.pdf.

than 150 thousand barrels per day.[189] This decrease reflects the collapse of the country's petroleum infrastructure, the lack of investment in the industry, and the ongoing economic crisis. Although there has been a slight recovery in recent years, the throughput remains extremely low, highlighting the persistent challenges within the refining sector. Additionally, as noted in the chapter on the electricity sector, hydroelectric generation, traditionally a key source of electricity supply in Venezuela, has been severely affected by infrastructure failures and maintenance issues. This has led to frequent power outages and nationwide energy rationing, which have also impacted the petroleum industry.

Figure 18 Refinery Throughout in Venezuela (Thousand Barrels Daily)

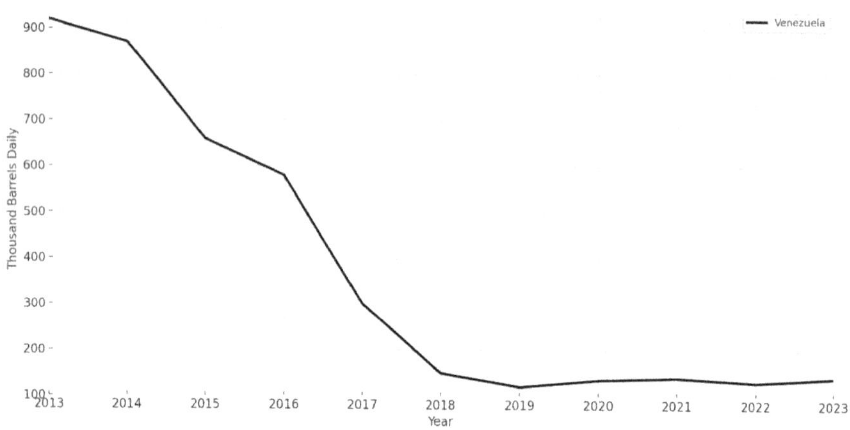

645. The collapse of the energy sector has impacted not only households but also the industrial and commercial sectors. The reduction in energy consumption is directly linked to the contraction of economic activity, with industrial facilities operating at minimal capacity and commercial sectors affected by recurring power outages and fuel shortages. The decline in hydrocarbon production and the shortage of refined fuels have imposed severe restrictions on transportation, significantly affecting mobility and logistics nationwide.

646. As energy consumption continues to decline, Venezuela faces a profound structural crisis that cannot be resolved without a fundamental transformation of the energy sector. The persistent lack of investment and maintenance has left the country's energy infrastructure obsolete, excessively reliant on a fragile hydroelectric system, and lacking adequate refining capacity to meet domestic fuel demand. Without comprehensive structural reforms and significant investments in energy generation, distribution, and refining, the energy collapse will continue to limit not only economic recovery but also the quality of life for millions of Venezuelans.

189. *Ibid.*

Part III. Regulatory Framework Concerning Gas

Chapter 1. General Introduction

647. The surge of the market opening in regard to natural gas, which started in the early 1990s, has endured significant political changes in Venezuela after the presidential elections in 1998. On 23 September 1999, a few months after the taking over of the new government, the Decree of the LOHG was enacted for opening the gaseous hydrocarbons market of non-associated gas to oil fields exploration, exploitation, transport, distribution, and trading stages to be directly executed by the State or by State-owned entities, as well as by other private national or foreign entities, including or not the participation of the State.

Chapter 2. Production

§1. Production of Non-associated Gas to Oil

648. This law promotes the development of gaseous areas of non-associated gas or free gas, whether inland or offshore developments, to take advantage of the potentiality and richness of the existing oil fields in those areas. For that reason, the above Law maintains the exploration of hydrocarbons-associated gas under legal reserve in favour of the Republic. The legal reserve gave rise to the LOH reform passed by the National Assembly on 16 May 2006. This law amended Article 2 to read as follows: 'Any activities related to gaseous hydrocarbons are governed by the Organic Law of Gaseous Hydrocarbons, with the exception of the oil-associated hydrocarbons extraction which shall be governed by this Law.'

649. Notwithstanding this reform, other activities subsequent to the associated gas extraction, such as the gathering, storage, processing, industrialization, transport, distribution, and domestic and foreign trading activities, remained open to the participation of public and private sectors under the terms established in the LOHG. In this sense, the LOHG has a legal framework to make feasible the gaseous hydrocarbons industrialization and building up of an integrated national market, for which it becomes imperative to count on the necessary gas and infrastructure. These conditions are required for developing the market opening up to competition, which is one of the main objectives of the LOHG, as well as limiting the creation of monopolies, whether public or private. In addition to the above, the LOHG promotes the economic balance among the parties involved in other activities of the gas industry as a primary concern in order to provide confidence to private investments and offer the customers the lowest cost possible for this service compatible with the guarantee of gas supply and also comply with any environmental, safety, and health regulation related to the activities inherent to the gas industry.

§2. General Objectives of the Current Gas Law

650. The LOHG lacks a regulation for the objectives intended. However, from the analysis of this legal instrument, it can be deduced that this Law is aimed at the promotion of:

1. Competition in gas industry-related activities.
2. Exploration and development of natural gas reservoirs.
3. Efficient use of associated gas in natural reservoirs.
4. National economic development through an intensive and efficient exploitation of gaseous hydrocarbons.
5. Creation of State-owned capital, assets, and services in order to participate under trustworthy and equitable conditions.
6. Efficiency, quality, and safety in the rendering of the services.

7. Economic equilibrium in regard to different activities of the gas industry and any parties involved, return on investment, and achieving the lowest cost possible for the consumers consistent with the guarantee of product supply.
8. Environmental protection and compliance with safety and health regulations related to the activities inherent to the gas industry.
9. Avoidance of the creation of monopolies in the gas industry-related activities.

651. The main objective of this Law, in agreement with the LOHG premises, is the development and promotion of competition among the parties involved. Notwithstanding the above, in order for this to become feasible, it is necessary to regulate public and private participation in the exploration, production, transport, and distribution activities, which require prior authorization through the proper concessions and/or licences.

§3. National Gas Company

652. PDVSA Gas, S.A., a subsidiary of PDVSA, organized in 1998, currently carries out activities of non-associated gas exploration and exploitation; gas compression; NGL extraction, fractionation, storage, sale, and dispatch; and methane gas transportation, distribution, and sale. These activities are carried out through the businesses that constitute the subsidiary, namely: Production, Compression, Processing, and Methane. In some cases, however, they are carried out by many subsidiaries, businesses, or organizations: exploration and production (PDVSA Petróleo, PDVSA Gas, many JV and Gas Offshore Licensing granted in 2001 and 2007); natural gas compression and processing (PDVSA Gas exclusively); Sale of natural gas by-products, such as methane, ethane, NGL, and LPG (PDVSA Gas and PDVSA Gas Comunal); and sale of NGL in the export market (PDVSA Petróleo, representing PDVSA Gas).[190]

§4. Natural Gas Reserves and Production

I. Gas Reserves

653. Venezuela has proved natural gas reserves that amount to 225 trillion cubic feet,[191] 85% of which corresponds to associated petroleum gas and only 15% corresponds to free gas. This difference is important to determine whether the associated gas is financially recoverable or not. The associated gas is dissolved in the

190. World Bank, *Venezuela, República Bolivariana de*, World Bank, available at: https://flaringventingregulations.worldbank.org/venezuela-republica-bolivariana-de (last accessed 4 Apr. 2025).
191. International Comparative Legal Guides (ICLG), *Oil & Gas Laws and Regulations Report 2025: Venezuela*, ICLG, marzo de 2025, disponible en: https://iclg.com/practice-areas/oil-and-gas-laws-and-regulations/venezuela (última visita: 4 de abril de 2025).

crude oil or as a 'plug' of free gas over the oil reservoir. Therefore, when the extraction is not possible, it is reinjected into the well and then burnt in a flare or released to the atmosphere. For instance, in 2014, 2,604 BSCF were injected in order to maintain the pressure of some reservoirs, i.e., 35.5% of the natural gas produced (7,422 BSCF).[192]

654. This unbalance between the amount of associated and non-associated gas in Venezuela, in addition to the amounts the oil industry requires to maintain the pressure of the reservoirs, has been a negative factor to develop the natural gas domestic market, since gas availability is dependent on oil production; whereas non-associated gas does not depend on the operations made for oil extraction. Hence, this type of gas has a special regulation to promote the exploitation thereof, which is further explained in Chapter 4.

655. Based on the progress of the exploitation, proved reserves are classified as developed and undeveloped. Reserves by 2014 in sedimentary basin are as follows in Table 11.[193]

Table 11 Natural Gas Reserves in MMBOE

Basin	*Proved*	*Proved/Developed*
Maracaibo-Falcon	7,543	1,352
Barinas-Apure	60	22
Oriental	23,782	5,394
Carupano	2,479	–
Total	**33,864**	**6,768**

656. In accordance with their production status, Venezuela's proved natural gas reserves are classified as developed and undeveloped. As of 2014, the total volume of proved reserves was 33,864 million barrels of oil equivalent (MMBOE), of which only 6,768 MMBOE were classified as developed. Table 11 shows the distribution of these reserves by sedimentary basin, highlighting the predominance of the Eastern Basin and the absence of development in the Carúpano Basin.[194]

192. U.S. Energy Information Administration (EIA), *Country Analysis Brief: Venezuela*, EIA, febrero de 2024, disponible en: https://www.eia.gov/international/content/analysis/countries_long/Venezuela/pdf/venezuela_2024.pdf (última visita: 4 de abril de 2025).
193. Petróleos de Venezuela, S.A. (PDVSA), *Informe de Gestión Anual 2016*, disponible en: https://elotrosaberypoder.wordpress.com/wp-content/uploads/2020/06/pdvsa-informe-de-gestic3b3n-anual-2016.pdf (última visita: 4 de abril de 2025).
194. *Ibid.*, at 246.

657. In the 2024 world ranking, Venezuela's natural gas reserves rank 9th globally and 2nd in the Americas, after the United States, as shown in Figure 19 and 20.[195]

Figure 19 Top Countries with Natural Gas Reserves in 2024

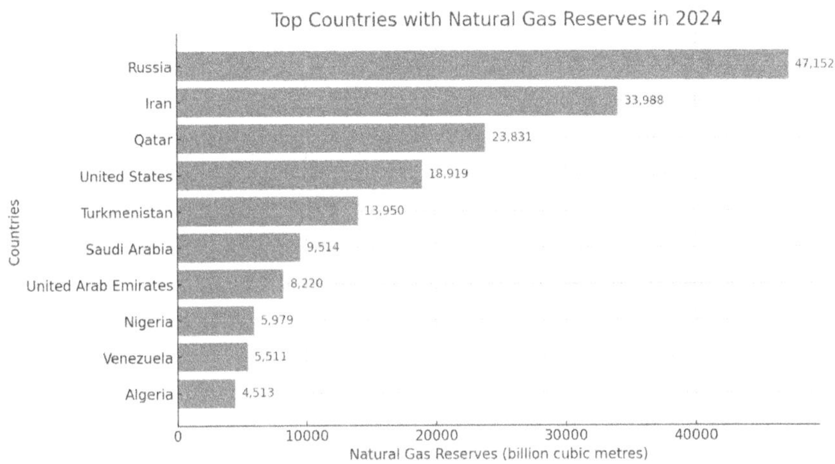

195. Eni. (2024). *World Energy Review 2024 – Natural Gas*. Eni S.p.A. [PDF document]. Retrieved from https://www.eni.com/content/dam/enicom/documents/eng/visione/wer/2_WER_2024_GAS.pdf (last accessed 4 Apr.2025).

Figure 20 Top Countries in the Americas by Proven Natural Gas Reserves in 2024

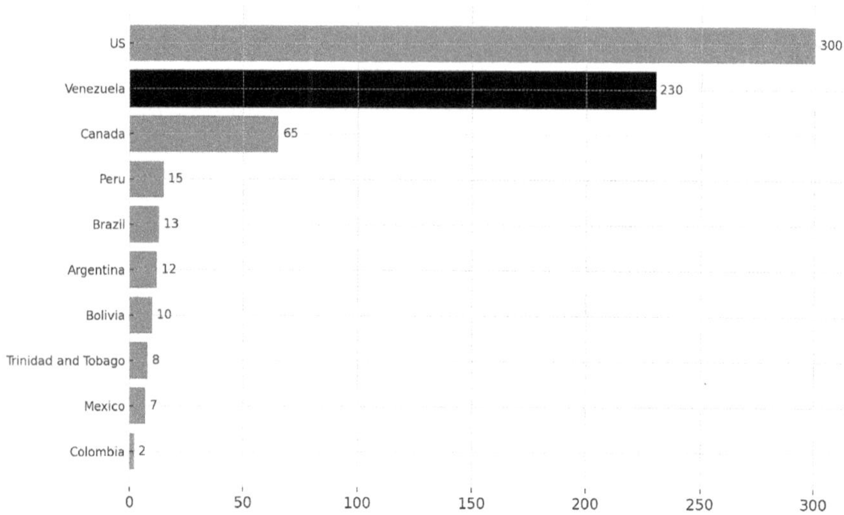

II. Gas Production

658. Natural gas production in Venezuela has historically been closely tied to oil extraction, as approximately 80% of the gas produced in the country is associated gas. This dependence implies that any decline in oil production directly impacts the availability of natural gas. For instance, in 2017, gas production declined by 300 million cubic feet per day (MCFD) compared to 2016, reaching 7,695 MCFD. Projections for 2018 anticipated a further decline to 5,700 MCFD.

659. Despite periods of growth in gas production, in 2017, non-associated gas production failed to offset the decline in associated gas production, resulting in a deficit of at least 4,525 million cubic feet per day (MPCD), an increase of 2,225 MPCD compared to 2016. This situation led to greater reliance on liquid fuels, particularly diesel, for electricity generation and necessitated natural gas imports from Colombia to meet domestic demand. In terms of production distribution, Petróleos de Venezuela S.A. (PDVSA) controlled 84% of gas extraction, while 11% was produced by JVs and 5% by private companies.

660. According to data from the Statistical Review of World Energy 2024, Venezuela's natural gas production has exhibited significant fluctuations over the past decade. In 2013, production stood at 30.6 billion cubic metres, increasing to 38.6 billion cubic metres in 2017. However, beginning in 2018, production entered a declining trend, falling to 25.6 billion cubic metres in 2019, with a critical drop in

2020 to 21.6 billion cubic metres (Figure 21). In 2021, production partially recovered to 28.1 billion cubic metres, remaining stable at 29.1 and 29.7 billion cubic metres in 2022 and 2023, respectively (Statistical Review of World Energy 2024).[196]

Figure 21 Natural Gas Production in Venezuela (2013-2023)

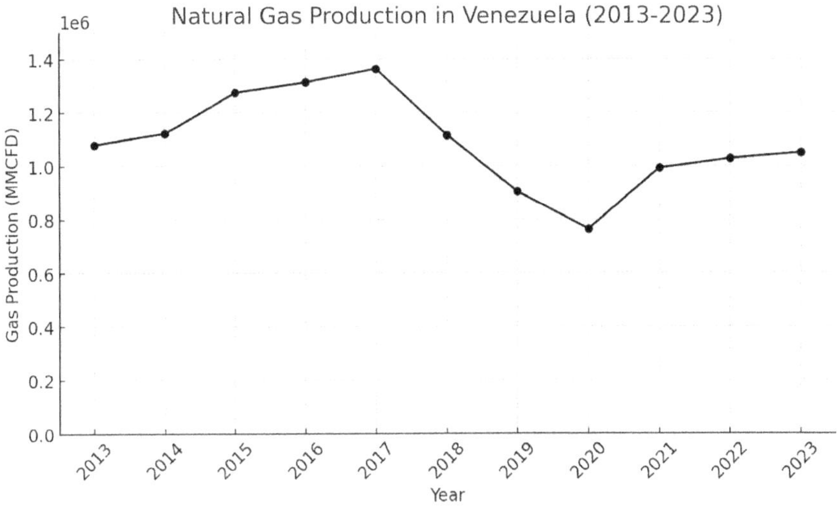

661. Despite recent efforts to revitalize production and export agreements with countries such as Trinidad and Tobago, the industry faces significant challenges, including deteriorating infrastructure, lack of investment, and regulatory constraints on the development of non-associated gas resources.

662. Although Venezuela holds one of the largest natural gas reserves in the Americas, its production has been characterized by fluctuations and an overall declining trend in recent years. The country remains heavily dependent on associated gas from oil production, which limits its availability for both domestic consumption and export markets. The recovery of Venezuela's natural gas sector will depend on infrastructure modernization, diversification of production sources, and investment in non-associated gas projects.

196. Energy Institute, *Statistical Review of World Energy 2024*, Energy Institute, disponible en: https://www.bpb.de/system/files/dokument_pdf/Statistical_Review_of_World_Energy_2024.pdf (última visita: 4 de abril de 2025).

Chapter 3. Exploitation

§1. Upstream: Licences

663. In agreement with Articles 24 and 25 of the LOHG and Articles 20 and 21 of its regulations (Regulation of the Organic Law on Gaseous Hydrocarbons (RLOHG – *Reglamento de la Ley Orgánica de Hidrocarburos Gaseosos*)), a licence issued by the MENPET granting the licensee the right of exclusivity in the specific geographical area to execute free gas exploration and exploitation activities is required. The authorization granted to the licensee shall be subject to the terms as follows:

1. The project description, whose aim is to contribute to the national development through the gaseous hydrocarbons exploitation, pursuant to Article 3 of the LOHG.
2. A maximum thirty-five-year term, subject to another thirty-year term extension.
3. A maximum five-year term for exploration and execution of other scheduled activities.
4. Indication of the area, shape, location, and technical boundaries of the area subject to this licence and other requisites set forth in the regulations.
5. Any special payments set forth in favour of the Republic.
6. Any directions set out for the lands preservation, and maintenance of the equipment, facilities, and other assets and real property included in the licence and the title of which shall be handed over to the Republic, free of any liens and waiving any compensation, as of the expiration date of the licence and for whichever reason this termination may be.
7. Participation in the bidding process.

664. However, according to the provisions set forth in Article 21 of the LOHG, a licence may be granted directly by the National Executive Branch without a bidding process, on the grounds of the public interest or for other special reasons in regard to said activities and is subject to the terms set forth in the Law. The MENPET may also cancel the bidding process in any instance whatsoever or declare it null and void without any compensation by the Republic.

665. According to this provision, it is the prerogative of the State to call for a bidding process or not. Additionally, it grants almost unlimited disposition rights to assign the gaseous hydrocarbons to anyone and anywhere at the Executive Branch's option. With regulations as above, any negotiations and concessions for the rights of exploitation lack transparency. Furthermore, there is a prolonged term of the first stage for thirty-five years, and the reservoirs would be almost finished by then, and this term is subject to a thirty-year additional extension, that is, sixty-five years in total.

666. The rights of exclusivity granted to the licensee are not subject to taxation, cannot be enforceable, shall be assigned with prior authorization by the MENPET, and may be revoked for the following reasons:

1. Non-compliance with the proposed exploration programmes.
2. Failure to start exploration within a five-year period according to the area specifications in the licence.
3. Non-compliance with the payments agreed upon.
4. Other reasons as specified in the licence.
5. On the grounds of the best interests of the Republic (Article 21 LOHG).

§2. Midstream and Downstream: Permissions

667. A permission issued by the MENPET shall be required to execute gathering, storage, processing, industrialization, transportation, distribution, and trading activities other than the exploration and production of fields in the search for free gas or other non-associated gas and which shall be subject to the terms as follows:

1. The project description, whose aim is the national development through the gaseous hydrocarbons exploitation, pursuant to Article 3 of the LOHG.
2. A maximum thirty-five-year term, subject to another thirty-year term extension. A request for extension should be submitted before the MENPET, after half of the term granted has elapsed, and five years before the expiration date (Article 97 LOHG).
3. Special payments set forth in favour of the Republic.
4. Directions set out for the preservation of the lands, and maintenance of the equipment, facilities and other assets and real property included in the licence and the title of which shall be handed over to the Republic, free of any liens and waiving any right to compensation as of the expiration date of the licence for whichever reason this termination may be.
5. Participation in the bidding process.

Chapter 4. Transport

§1. Licence for Transport

668. In agreement with Article 61 of the regulation of the LOHG, any person having permission to execute transportation activities shall have the exclusivity of this activity for five years and, in the event of distribution activity permissions, notwithstanding that the law and its regulation do not foresee a period of exclusiveness, it has been set forth that said period shall be determined according to each region and subject to the terms and conditions of each permission granted.

669. By establishing the exclusiveness of the terms and conditions for gas transportation and distribution, the legislator purports to guarantee gas supply in order to protect the consumers while the competitive market is developing, and it operates in this manner because it can be difficult to have free access to gas transportation, storage, and distribution systems in a market where the facilities are under the control of and operated by third-party owners. In the case of Venezuela, PDVSA is the owner of all existing gas pipelines in the country and, therefore, it has the major responsibility to promote or prevent competition.

670. Notwithstanding the existence of a monopolistic gas market in Venezuela, the LOHG and its regulations have strengthened the search for an open market by forbidding discriminatory, non-competitive, and monopolistic behaviours among the participants in the gas transportation, storage, and distribution activities (Article 37 RLOHG, No. 2). Additionally, it compels the companies designated for storage, transportation, and distribution of gaseous hydrocarbons and derivatives to give consent to other storage, transportation, and distribution companies for using their facilities provided that said facilities have the required capacity (Article 10 RLOHG). These activities are the sole liability of PDVSA and, therefore, are under the liability of the State, as previously stated.

§2. Requirements

671. Any company interested in obtaining permission for performing gaseous hydrocarbons transportation and distribution activities must submit an application to the MENPET with the information as follows:

1. Identification of the requesting party.
2. Operating technical capability assessment to be requested to the MENPET separately for its approval or denial after the corresponding analysis.
3. Commercial and financial capacity.
4. Project definition and description.
5. Domestic market participation proposals.

6. Participation in a bidding process, notwithstanding that the MENPET reserves its right to grant permissions without a bidding process on the grounds of public interest.
7. Other requisites as determined by the MENPET.

Chapter 5. Distribution

672. The first gas pipelines for residential, commercial, and industrial use in Venezuela date back to 1938, when Shell de Venezuela provided this service to the city of Maracaibo. By 1951, some neighbourhoods of Caracas (La Paz and Vista Alegre) began to enjoy direct natural gas. By 1961, the gas pipeline network was 657 km (408.24 mi) long, and in the late 1990s, an extraordinary development extended it to 4,200 km (2,609.75 mi).[197] However, since 2000, the expansion has stagnated, with only 835 km (518.84 mi) added in fourteen years, reaching a total of 5,031 km (3,126.11 mi). This sluggish growth contrasts sharply with the global natural gas boom, particularly in the US, Europe, and OPEC members such as Algeria (which expanded its network from 2,942 km to 4,168 km between 1999 and 2013), Libya (from 766 km to nearly 3,000 km), and Saudi Arabia, which had no gas pipelines in 1999 but developed a 3,000 km network by 2013.[198]

673. In the Venezuelan domestic market, gas is sold based on three methods: Direct natural gas, LPG, and LNG. Direct natural gas is distributed to industrial, commercial, and residential sectors through a gas distribution network.

674. By the end of 2014, nearly 400,000 users were integrated into the network, 91% in the cities of Caracas, Valencia, Barquisimeto, Guanta, Anaco, Cumaná, Barcelona, Barinas, Cagua, Maracaibo, Maturin, and La Vela de Coro. LPG is supplied to the domestic market by land, through the filling or sale of LPG cylinders. In 2012, it amounted to 42 MBD under the control of PDVSA Community Gas.[199]

675. NGL is sold both in the domestic and the export market. Sales in 2012 were at 141 MBD distributed as follows: Local Market 47 MBD (including domestic market, manufacturing companies, and petrochemical market), Inter-Subsidiary Sales 66 MBD (including Refining and Production and PDVSA Gas Comunal), and Exports 28 MBD, mainly to the US (49%) and Brazil (44%), and the remainder was sold to Morocco, Holland, Curacao, and Ecuador.[200]

676. Additionally, LPG supply logistics have deteriorated due to failures within the state-owned PDVSA Gas Comunal. Key issues include: a shortage of quality and functional LPG cylinders, deterioration of primary and secondary transport

---

197. Academia de Ingeniería y Hábitat de Venezuela, *La Industria del Gas Natural en Venezuela*, at 3, available at: https://acading.org.ve/wp-content/uploads/2023/02/LA_INDUSTRIA_DEL_GAS_NATURAL_EN_VENEZUELA.pdf (last accessed 4 Apr. 2025).
198. LibyaReview, '*Libya Has Second Longest Gas Network in Africa*,' available at: https://libyareview.com/30213/libya-has-second-longest-gas-network-in-africa/ (last accessed 4 Apr. 2025); Baker Institute, '*An Alternative Pipeline Strategy in the Persian Gulf*,' available at: https://www.bakerinstitute.org/sites/default/files/2013-08/import/TrendsinMiddleEast_AlternativePipelineStrategy.pdf (last accessed 4 Apr. 2025).
199. *Ibid.*, at 252.
200. Petróleos de Venezuela, S.A. (PDVSA), *Informe de Gestión Anual 2012*, disponible en: https://de.scribd.com/document/139607034/PDVSA-2012-INFORME-DE-GESTION-ANUAL-PARTE-1-DE-2-pdf (last accessed 10 Jun, 2025).

units, and administrative mismanagement in filling and distribution plants. However, the production of propylene (olefins from propane) for petrochemical input is reduced, causing failures and losses in the production of plastics and resins, which in turn negatively impact the production of containers, which are needed for the production of processed foods. It should be noted that Venezuela has not produced ethylene or other olefins derived from ethane (used for similar purposes as propylene) since 2008. Due to this, the limited domestic production of plastics and resins relies on imported ethane, propane, or their derivative olefins. The low domestic production of plastics and resins is done by importing ethane and propane or derived olefins.

Chapter 6. Consumption

677. Under normal operations and stability of operation of the oil industry in Venezuela, the consumption of natural gas is as follows: 67% is consumed in the operations of the oil industry, while 31% is directed towards the domestic market for residential, commercial, and industrial use, and the 2% difference is converted to LNG, as shown below.[201]

678. Despite possessing one of the world's largest natural gas reserves, Venezuela's gas distribution system has collapsed in recent years. This crisis is the result of a combination of deteriorating infrastructure, corruption, lack of investment, and poor operational management (González & Monaldi, 2021; Transparencia Venezuela, 2022).[202]

679. Since 2014, Venezuela's gas infrastructure has experienced progressive deterioration. The gas pipeline network, which in that year extended 5,031 km, has now shrunk to approximately 4,551 km due to operational failures, structural degradation, and the abandonment of certain pipeline sections. The lack of maintenance and insufficient investment in expansion projects have prevented the recovery of the country's gas transportation system (PDVSA Annual Report, 2015).[203]

680. Currently, gas transportation capacity has dropped to 3,700 million cubic feet per day (MMcfd), with efficiency declining due to technical and operational failures. The most severely affected regions are the country's inland states, where access to direct gas pipelines is limited, and reliance on bottled LPG remains high (Transparencia Venezuela, 2022).[204]

681. PDVSA Gas Comunal, established in 2007 to ensure access to household gas, has failed to fulfil its mission due to structural and administrative deficiencies. Currently, it faces severe logistical deficiencies in LPG distribution, including: (1) Shortage of LPG cylinders: There is a critical deficit of gas cylinders, as many have become unusable due to deterioration, theft, or diversion into the black market. In several regions, consumers must wait weeks or even months to receive a state-regulated gas cylinder (BBC News Mundo, 2021). (2) Deterioration of filling and distribution infrastructure: Filling plants are operating at reduced capacity, leading to delays in the delivery of LPG cylinders to the population. (3) Corruption and black-market activities: The illegal resale of LPG has increased in recent years, disrupting equitable distribution and inflating prices in the informal market. According

201. *Ibid.,* at 255.

202. Francisco Monaldi, Igor Hernández y José La Rosa Reyes, *The Collapse of the Venezuelan Oil Industry: The Role of Above-Ground Risks Limiting Foreign Investment*, 72 Resources Policy 102116 (2021), disponible en https://www.sciencedirect.com/science/article/abs/pii/S0301420721001306 (last accessed 4 Apr. 2025).

203. Petróleos de Venezuela, S.A. (PDVSA), *Informe de Gestión 2015*, https://fr.scribd.com/document/320466244/Informe-Gestion-Pdvsa-2015 (last accessed 4 Apr. 2025).

204. Transparencia Venezuela, '*Crisis Energética: El Colapso del Suministro Doméstico e Industrial,*' 2022, available at: https://transparencia.org.ve (last accessed 4 Apr. 2025).

to reports, this issue is part of the broader phenomenon known as 'bachaqueo', where state-subsidized products are resold at exorbitant prices by informal middlemen. In certain regions, LPG cylinders are sold in the black market for up to five times the official price (BBC News Mundo, 2021).[205]

682. Reports indicate that millions of households now rely on alternative cooking methods such as firewood and charcoal, exacerbating environmental degradation and worsening living conditions (Transparencia Venezuela, 2022). The decline in gas supply has severely impacted Venezuela's petrochemical sector, leading to a drastic reduction in propylene production (olefins derived from propane). This shortfall has disrupted key industries, including plastics, food packaging, and consumer goods manufacturing (IEA, 2023).[206]

683. Since 2008, Venezuela has not produced ethylene, another key petrochemical input derived from ethane. The lack of maintenance in processing plants, shortages of raw materials, and PDVSA's financial crisis have forced the country to rely on expensive imports to meet industrial demand (PDVSA Annual Report, 2015).[207]

684. The crisis in gas distribution affects not only residential consumers but also small businesses and local industries. The most significant consequences include: (1) Businesses and restaurants forced to shut down or reduce operations due to the unavailability of LPG (Monaldi, 2020).[208] (2) Increased use of firewood and alternative cooking methods, with negative health and environmental implications. In various regions, deforestation for firewood collection has intensified. (3) Increased strain on the electricity sector, as more households and businesses switch to electric stoves as an alternative to LPG, overloading an already unstable electrical grid and contributing to power outages in multiple regions (Outlook, 2023).[209]

685. To overcome Venezuela's gas crisis, urgent structural reforms and strategic measures must be implemented, including: (1) Investment in infrastructure: The rehabilitation of the gas pipeline network and the modernization of filling plants are essential to ensuring stable supply. (2) Restructuring of PDVSA Gas Comunal: Improving operational management and tackling corruption within the company is

---

205. BBC News Mundo. '*Por Qué Venezuela Tiene una Crisis con el Gas Doméstico Pese a Tener las Mayores Reservas Probadas del Mundo*,' 2021, available at: https://www.bbc.com/mundo (last accessed 4 Apr. 2025).
206. International Energy Agency (IEA), *Natural Gas Market Review: Venezuela*, 2023, available at: https://www.iea.org (last accessed 4 Apr. 2025).
207. PDVSA Informe Anual. *Reporte Anual sobre Producción e Infraestructura Energética.* Petróleos de Venezuela S.A. Recuperado directamente desde archivos internos citados por Transparencia Venezuela, 2015.
208. Monaldi, Francisco, Hernández, Isabel, & La Rosa Reyes, Juan, *The Collapse of the Venezuelan Oil Industry: The Role of Above-Ground Risks Limiting FDI*, Rice University's Baker Institute for Public Policy, 2020, available at: https://www.bakerinstitute.org/research/collapse-venezuelan-oil-industry-role-above-ground-risks-limiting-fdi/ (last accessed 4 Apr. 2025).
209. International Energy Agency (IEA). *Latin America Energy Outlook 2023*, IEA, 2023, available at: https://www.iea.org/reports/latin-america-energy-outlook-2023/executive-summary (last accessed 4 Apr. 2025).

imperative. (3) Transparency in distribution: More effective oversight systems are needed to prevent the diversion of LPG into the black market. (4) Revitalization of the petrochemical industry: Increasing domestic production of key inputs, such as propylene and ethylene, would reduce reliance on imports. (5) Diversification of energy sources: Exploring alternative energy options and improving gas-use efficiency could help reduce system vulnerability.

Part IV. Regulatory Framework Concerning Coal

Chapter 1. General Introduction

686. Oil and, in general, hydrocarbons were subject at first to the mining legislation and later on to the Regulatory Decrees on 'Coal, Oil, and Similar Substances' from 1917 to 1920, until 30 June 1920, when the first 'Law on Hydrocarbons and the Rest of the Fuel Minerals' was enacted, with which the oil legislation acquired a specific and autonomous character.

687. Once the separation of the regulation among the hydrocarbons, mines, and minerals took place, which included coal, each sector began creating its own dynamics. Contrary to the vertiginous juridical and economic development that oil reached as of the second decade of the twentieth century, coal did not follow the same path, which becomes evident in the scarce legislation and its meagre industrial and commercial development. This fact has generated important debates and considerations for the design of a new regulatory framework in the mining sector, where coal is included.

688. On that account, the current LM of 1999 proposed the review of some of the principles and rules contained in the former law, the LM of 1945, which had become obsolete during its validity, such as: the concept of the registration of a claim to a mine and the concession for exploitation by the optional granting of the National Executive Branch.

689. In this sense, the LM of 1999 proceeded to organize the legal system (Article 1) of the mines and minerals existing in the national territory, whatever their origin or presentation, including their exploration and exploitation, as well as the benefit, storage, tenancy, circulation, transport, and commercialization, whether internal or external, of the substances extracted, except for what is set forth in other laws.

690. With regard to the earth's crust, for example, the LM (Article 10) divides it in two (2) parts: the soil, which comprises the simple surface and the layer that reaches downwards up to the level of the works of the holder of the surface rights in activities not involved with mining; and the subsoil, which extends indefinitely in depth from the level where the soil ends. Mining activities performed in the subsoil do not generate compensation for the holder of the surface rights, unless they affect the soil or other properties. However, in no case, neither the owners of the soil nor the owners of the subsoil can claim ownership of the fields, which are at all times owned by the Republic.

§1. Coal Mines as Property of the Republic

691. The LM states (Article 2) that the mines and mineral fields of any class that exist in the national territory belong to the Republic, are State-owned property and, therefore, are inalienable and imprescriptible. This statement is confirmed in the legal system as of the Decree of the Liberator, passed in Quito on 24 October 1829, anticipating, far and away, the new theories and systems about the nationalization of the mines. Based on this principle, the State behaves as a true owner of the mining wealth and not as a simple administrator of such wealth. Therefore, it may exploit it on its own within a competition system with third parties through concessions, or it may reserve its exploitation, without giving up the ownership of the mines at any time.

§2. Domanial System and Role of the Ministry of Mines

692. The LM adopts the domanial system, which comprises the two systems previously mentioned, that is to say, the direct exploitation or exploitation through optional concessions; consequently, this generates the elimination of the regalian system, disappearing, therefore, the concepts of registering a claim to a mine, free exploration, exclusive exploration, and free use.

693. However, it ratifies public utility as a fundamental principle traditionally accepted in the Venezuelan mining system and incorporates for the first time the principle of sustainable development (Article 5), which implies the exercise of the mining activity in agreement with environmental aspects, territorial planning, economic stability, and social responsibility, coupled with the principles of rationality and optimal recovery of the resource.

694. The MEM shall have competence in all matters related to mining (Article 6), specifically in the exploration, planning, defence, and preservation plans, as well as the system for foreign investment.

Chapter 2. Production

§1. Commencement of the Production and the Reserves

695. Coal was first extracted in Venezuela in 1850 at the Naricual mines in the state of Anzoátegui. Subsequently, in 1915, the first concessions for its exploitation were granted in the state of Zulia. However, it gained significant importance only in 1952 when large-scale commercial extraction commenced.

696. Venezuela possesses approximately 731 million metric tons of proven coal reserves. In the Americas, the countries with significant coal reserves include the United States, Canada, Brazil, Colombia, Mexico, and Venezuela. Among these, Venezuela ranks 6th, as illustrated in Figure 22.

Figure 22 Top Countries in the Americas with Coal Reserves

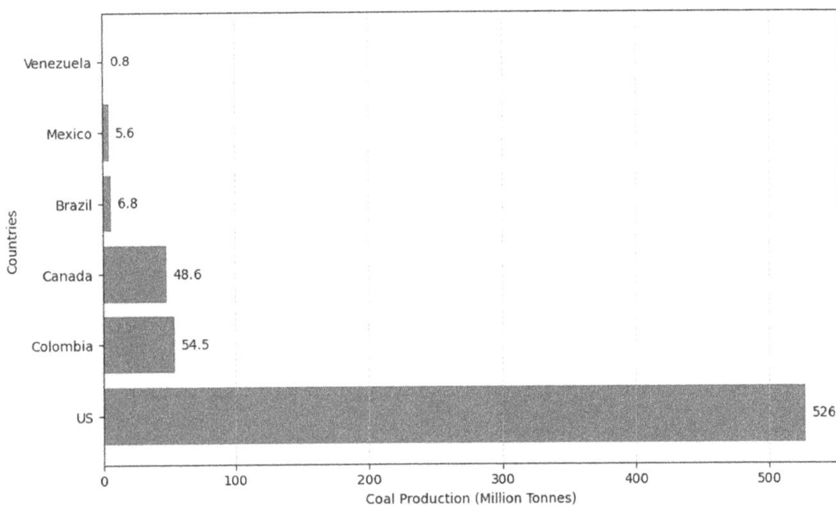

697. The Americas account for approximately 24.1% of the world's total coal reserves, with the United States being the dominant nation, holding around 249,537 million metric tons. Canada follows with 6,582 million metric tons, while Brazil and Colombia report reserves of 6,596 and 4,554 million metric tons, respectively. Mexico holds 1,211 million metric tons of reserves, with Venezuela contributing a relatively smaller share to the continent's total.

698. Approximately 95% of Venezuela's coal potential is concentrated in the Zulia Coal Basin, which represents about 0.5% of global coal reserves. The coal extracted from these fields, as well as that identified in other Venezuelan deposits, is predominantly bituminous, characterized by high energy efficiency and low concentrations of ash and sulfur. Presently, nearly all of Venezuela's coal production is designated as thermal coal.

§2. Production Trends

699. Historically, Venezuela's coal production has been modest. At its peak, production barely exceeded 8 million metric tons. However, rather than expanding, production has declined in recent years, as depicted in Figure 23.

Figure 23 Venezuela's Coal Production (2013-2023)

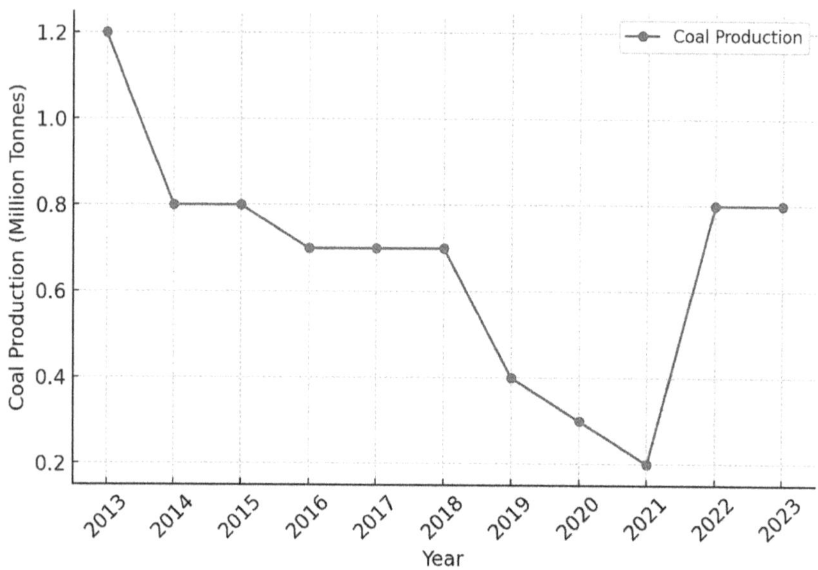

700. Overall, coal production in the Americas is largely dominated by the United States, which remains the leading producer in the region (Figure 24). The decline in Venezuelan production aligns with broader regional trends, where the transition toward renewable energy sources and environmental considerations has led to a reduction in coal extraction. Despite these trends, Venezuela's strategic coal reserves continue to offer potential opportunities for energy development and exportation, particularly within regional and global energy markets.

Figure 24 Coal Production by Country in 2023 (Million Tonnes)

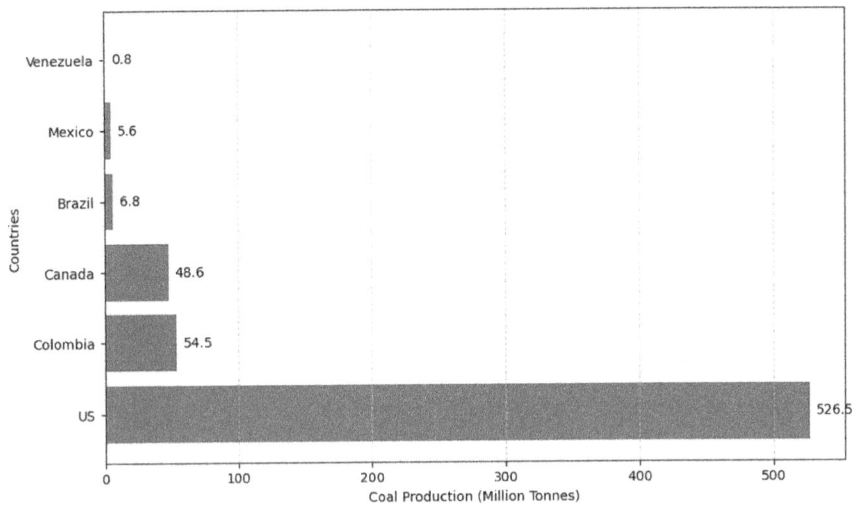

§3. Internal Market and Destination of the Production

701. Taking into account the little official updated information available, the contribution of coal in the national energy matrix is very low. In fact, the contribution of coal and firewood together in the production of energy in Venezuela roughly reaches 1.1%. From that cut, almost 99% is exported mainly to North America (52%), Europe (34%), and Latin America (14%).

Chapter 3. Exploitation

§1. Concession Regime

702. Title II of the LM regulates the exercise of the concessions, which may be executed under five modalities created for specific purposes to meet the requirements of the sector. Such modalities are the following:

1. Directly by the National Executive Branch.
2. Concessions for Exploration and subsequent Exploitation.
3. Authorizations for Exploitation to exercise the activity of Small-Scale Mining.
4. Mining Associations.
5. Artisanal Mining.

§2. Temporality

703. The LM establishes the principle of temporality of the concessions, according to which the exploitation of the mines has a limit in time and its exercise is circumscribed to determined geographical limits.

704. It is important to point out the setting of the sole concession system, which shall be for exploration and subsequent exploitation and whose duration shall not exceed twenty years and subject to extensions that, when added up, cannot exceed such period. Another characteristic of the designed concession consists in the elimination of the distinction based on the presentation of the mineral, regarding vein, nappe, and alluvium; that is, the licensee shall have the right to exploit the mineral, whatever its presentation.

§3. Right of the Licensees

705. To ease mining activities, the use of the surface and to allow the thorough development of such activities, the beneficiaries of mining rights shall enjoy, in addition to the possibility of creating easements, temporal occupancy and expropriation, as well as the right to use wastelands and the rational use and development of water in the public domain.

706. Within the scope of the concession, the National Executive Branch, by reason of collective benefit, may reserve the execution of mining activities on minerals not granted in the licence. The obligation of the licensee to notify the MEM about the finding of such mineral is established therein, given that, according to the new system, the concession does not cover all the minerals that may be found within the area granted, but rather those expressly referred to in the licence. The licensees have a preferential right before any other concession petitioner to receive the granting of any other mineral, and it will be sufficient to enter into agreements with the MEM to use such right.

§4. Mining Associations

707. The concept of the Mining Associations is also introduced in the LM (Article 77 and subsequent articles). Its essence derives from the Law on Mines of Spain and seeks to obtain a better development of the mining resources, ease technical operations of the fields, improve the efficiency of the exploitations, and protect the natural resources and the environment. The Association is oriented towards the improvement and organization of the mining activity, which would have a social repercussion in the areas where it is developed, allowing the holders of such associations the possibility to obtain a concession in the exploitation stage.

708. Another advantage of the Mining Associations from an economic standpoint is the concentration in one locality (region) of the activities resulting from them, reducing costs even if each company is small. Such concentration generates the possibility of having lower costs for related services and infrastructure and tends to produce more efficient suppliers, arising in turn the development of industrial complexes.

709. Likewise, Artisanal Mining is regulated (Article 88 and subsequent Articles), which shall be exercised by Venezuelan natural persons and is characterized by the personal and direct work of a mine, performed by means of manual, simple, and portable equipment and rudimentary extraction techniques and processing.

§5. Supervision and Surveillance

710. In Title VI, related to the Supervision and Surveillance of the Mining Activities, the National Mining Protection is created, as an auxiliary agency of the MEM, and shall be exercised by the Ministry of Defence through the Armed Forces of Cooperation (National Guard). This Mining Protection agency has, among others, the functions and competences of inspection, surveillance, and control, throughout the national territory, of the mining activities that may have directly or indirectly an effect on the regular development of such activities, the supervision for the compliance with all the legal provisions and the safeguarding of public order.

§6. Termination of Mining Rights

711. Title VIII establishes the grounds for the termination of mining rights, the existing causes on the lapsing of licensees' rights are broadened, and the grounds for the lapsing of exploitation authorizations are created. Likewise, the concept of reversion of assets acquired for the purpose of mining activities is kept and perfected, and such assets must be kept and preserved by the individual in good operation conditions throughout the entire term of the mining rights. By reason of this principle, such assets shall become a property of the Republic, free from encumbrances and taxes and without any compensation whatsoever, once the rights expire.

712. The possible closing of the mine from the very beginning of the term of the concession is foreseen, so that the corresponding measures are taken to have the slightest impact possible on the environmental interests of the State and the individuals.

§7. Term

713. The exploration term shall not exceed three years, in addition to a one-year extension. Conversely, the licensee is subject to the submittal of a feasibility study comprised of three aspects: technical, financial, and environmental. The submittal of the feasibility study and the corresponding plan represent the fundamental and compulsory requisites for continuing with the works and tasks of the concession. As a consequence of the submittal of both documents and upon compliance with the corresponding terms, the granting of the Certificate of Exploitation shall be performed, which is decreed by the MEM and grants the licensees, their heirs, and subrogees the exclusive right to extract mineral resources existing in the plots indicated. Likewise, the licensee shall have a maximum of seven years to place in a start-up stage of exploitation the plots under the concession.

Chapter 4. Transport

714. According to the LM (Article 86), the transport activities for coal and other minerals may be carried out by private companies, but such companies are subject to the supervision and inspection of the MEM, which may be absorbed or reserve them by a decree whenever it is deemed convenient in the public interest.

715. One of the weaknesses of the coal industry in Venezuela is precisely the lack of functional infrastructure for coal transport, and it becomes even worse because of the enormous distances that separate the extraction centres and ports, which do not have railways and have a limited port capacity for handling greater coal volumes at their facilities.

716. In the face of this situation, the National Executive Branch has set the goal of improving the infrastructure to strengthen the coal industry through the construction of a port at the exit of Maracaibo Lake, named Puerto America, which aims to become the main coal exit point in Venezuela. The construction of a railway from Sierra de Perijá to said port for the transport of the mineral is also projected. The new coal plan has caused problems with the indigenous communities, who are opposed to the exploitation of coal in Perijá. These projects have not been concretized yet, but they would give the sector the impulse needed to develop satisfactorily.

Chapter 5. Distribution

717. Venezuelan State-run company Carbones del Guasare, the greatest coal producer of the country, is committed to the exploration, production, transport, and commercialization of coal for the electricity industry and the use of steel mills within the world energy market. This company is in charge of the exploration of coalfields in the municipalities of Mara, Maracaibo, and Guajira, in the State of Zulia. Carbones del Guasare distributes and commercializes its products internationally through four commercial offices located in Maracaibo, Venezuela; two offices in London, England; and one office in St. Louis, Missouri, the US; and has its main office in Maracaibo, State of Zulia.

Chapter 6. Consumption

§1. Internal Consumption and Export Markets

718. Coal consumption in Venezuela remains *low (Figure 25)*, as the country primarily relies on *oil, natural gas, and hydroelectric power* for electricity generation. According to the *BP Statistical Review of World Energy 2024*, Venezuela's coal consumption barely reaches *0.24 million tons of oil equivalent (Mtoe)* – one of the lowest figures in the region.

Figure 25 Coal Consumption by Country in 2023

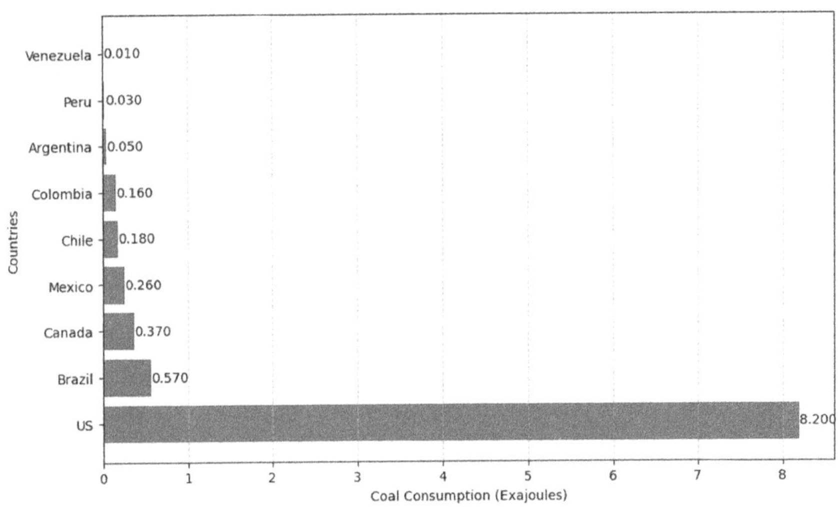

719. While domestic demand remains minimal, Venezuela is heavily dependent on coal exports, which account for nearly 99% of its total production. The primary export destinations include: 1. North America (52%). 2. Europe (34%). 3. Latin America (14%).

720. Between *2019 and 2020*, Venezuela's coal exports experienced moderate growth despite geopolitical challenges. In *2019*, PDVSA exported *310,000 metric tons of coal*, generating approximately *USD 40 million* in revenue. By *June 2020*, exports had risen to *365,000 metric tons*, with the *United Kingdom emerging as a key buyer*, despite international sanctions.[210]

210. Parraga, M., '*Exportaciones de Carbón Venezolano Aumentan Mientras EE. UU. Intensifica Sanciones*,' Reuters, 9 Oct. 2020, available at: https://www.reuters.com/article/world/americas/exportaciones-de-carbn-venezolano-aumentan-mientras-eeuu-intensifica-sanciones-idUSKBN26Y2GN/ (last accessed 4 Apr. 2025).

721. The vast majority of Venezuela's coal reserves are concentrated in the *Zulia Coal Basin*, which contains approximately *95% of the country's total reserves*, equivalent to *0.5% of global coal reserves*. The coal extracted from this region is *bituminous coal*, known for its *high energy efficiency and low levels of ash and sulfur*, making it valuable for international markets.[211]

§2. Environmental and Social Impact of Coal Mining

722. Coal exploitation in the Sierra de Perijá severely threatens the region's water resources. Maracaibo, the capital of Zulia state, relies on only two water sources: the Tulé and Manuelote reservoirs, fed by the Cachirí and Socuy rivers, respectively. Biologist Coribell Nava warns, 'Coal is located in the heart of the hydrological valley. The concessions being granted for coal exploitation in the Sierra de Perijá would deplete our water source.' Furthermore, coal mining has caused: (1) Destruction of vegetation and habitat fragmentation. (2) Water contamination by sediments and mercury. (3) Impact on local fauna. (4) Soil destruction

723. Impact on indigenous communities: Indigenous communities, including the Wayuu and Yukpa, have been particularly affected by coal mining. These groups have faced: (1) Displacement from their ancestral lands. (2) Health problems related to pollution. (3) Disruption of their traditional ways of life.

724. Some indigenous organizations, such as the Regional Organization of Indigenous Peoples of the Amazon and the Indigenous Organization of the Caura Basin (Kuyujani), have traditionally opposed mining. However, the situation is complex, as some indigenous leaders have defended their communities' right to practice mining.

725. Several environmental organizations and indigenous groups have opposed the expansion of coal mining in Zulia, arguing that it violates territorial rights and poses long-term risks to sustainable development.

§3. Challenges and Opportunities for the Coal Sector

726. Challenges: Insufficient infrastructure: One of the main barriers to the development of the coal sector in Venezuela is the lack of adequate infrastructure. The absence of railways connecting the mines to the ports limits transportation efficiency, increases logistical costs, and reduces the sector's competitiveness (Real

211. Fundación Andrés Bello, '*Carbón Venezolano: Una Puerta Fallida que Maduro le Abrió a China*,' 8 Apr. 2021, available at: https://fundacionandresbello.org/reportajes/carbon-venezolano-una-puerta-fallida-que-maduro-le-abrio-a-china/ (last accessed 4 Apr. 2025).

Instituto Elcano, 2024).[212] Furthermore, Venezuelan ports lack the capacity to handle large export volumes, restricting access to international markets and hindering the country's positioning as a relevant player in the global coal market.[213]

727. Decline in investment and economic instability: The lack of foreign investment and the deterioration of economic conditions have hindered the modernization of the coal sector. International sanctions, along with geopolitical risks, have significantly reduced the flow of foreign capital to Venezuela, affecting the implementation of long-term projects and the technological upgrades necessary to maintain competitiveness. In addition, political and economic uncertainty has made it difficult to plan and implement strategic projects in the energy sector as a whole (Farmonaut, 2023).[214] According to the World Economic Forum's Global Risks Report 2025, geopolitical and geoeconomic instability are key factors that exacerbate economic risks, which aligns with the challenges faced by Venezuela (World Economic Forum, 2025).[215]

728. Environmental regulations and global energy transition: International commitments to mitigate climate change have placed coal in an unfavourable position compared to cleaner energy sources. In this context, many countries have reduced their reliance on coal due to its negative environmental effects. In Venezuela, this trend is compounded by internal pressures from environmental groups, who have opposed mining projects in sensitive regions such as the Sierra de Perijá.[216] Additionally, adhering to international agreements such as the Paris Agreement requires the country to rethink its energy model towards more sustainable alternatives (Friedrich Ebert Stiftung, n.d.).[217]

729. Opportunities: Attracting strategic foreign investments: Despite the challenges, Venezuela has opportunities to attract foreign investments in the coal sector through strategic partnerships with countries interested in diversifying their energy sources. Strengthening trade relations with Asian and Middle Eastern markets could

---

212. Urbasos Arbeloa, I., '*El Retorno de la Venezuela Petrolera: Las Expectativas Frente a la Cruda Realidad*,' Real Instituto Elcano, 23 May 2024, available at: https://www.realinstitutoelcano.org/analisis/el-retorno-de-la-venezuela-petrolera-las-expectativas-frente-a-la-cruda-realidad/ (last accessed 4 Apr. 2025).
213. U.S. Energy Information Administration (EIA), *Country Analysis Brief: Venezuela*, EIA, February 2024, Available at: https://www.eia.gov/international/content/analysis/countries_long/Venezuela/pdf/venezuela_2024.pdf (last accessed 4 Apr. 2025).
214. Farmonaut, *Impact of Political Instability on the Agroindustry: Challenges for Agricultural Supply in Colombia and Venezuela 2023*, available at: https://farmonaut.com/south-america/impact-of-political-instability-on-the-agroindustry-challenges-for-agricultural-supply-in-colombia-and-venezuela-2023/ (last accessed 4 Apr. 2025).
215. World Economic Forum, *The Global Risks Report 2025: 20th Edition*, https://reports.weforum.org/docs/WEF_Global_Risks_Report_2025.pdf (last accessed 4 Apr. 2025).
216. Mongabay, *Venezuela's Environmental Crisis Is Getting Worse: Seven Key Issues* (2023), https://news.mongabay.com/2023/06/venezuelas-environmental-crisis-is-getting-worse-here-are-seven-things-to-know/ (last accessed 4 Apr. 2025).
217. Vázquez Heredia, O. *Crisis Climática y Derechos Humanos en Venezuela: Una Aproximación al Debate entre Justicia Climática y Seguridad*, Fundación Friedrich Ebert (2024), https://library.fes.de/pdf-files/bueros/caracas/21045.pdf (last accessed 4 Apr. 2025).

open new opportunities for Venezuelan coal exports and diversify trade destinations. However, ensuring political and economic stability will be key to consolidating these alliances (Dialogue Earth, n.d.).[218]

730. Development of strategic infrastructure: The construction and modernization of port and railway infrastructure represents a crucial opportunity to increase logistical efficiency in the coal sector. Projects like a railway system that connects the Sierra de Perijá mines to specialized ports could reduce operational costs and significantly increase the country's export capacity. These improvements would also facilitate greater integration with increasingly demanding international markets.

731. Diversification of coal production: Instead of relying solely on thermal coal, Venezuela can explore opportunities in derivatives such as metallurgical coke and synthetic fuels. These products are essential for industries such as steelmaking and petrochemicals, which maintain high global demand. Additionally, investing in technologies like carbon capture and storage (CCS) could position the country as an innovative player in the context of the global energy transition (U3 Explore, n.d.).[219]

§4. The Orinoco Mining Arc: Extractive Wealth, Regulatory Gaps, and Socio-Environmental Threats

732. In 2016, the Venezuelan government formally created the Arco Minero del Orinoco (AMO), a Strategic National Development Zone encompassing approximately 111,843 km^2 – about 12.2% of the national territory. Located in the country's south, the AMO spans significant portions of the Bolívar, Amazonas, and Delta Amacuro states. Its stated aim was to diversify the national economy through the extraction of gold, diamonds, coltan, and other strategic minerals. However, since its inception, the AMO has faced strong criticism for legal opacity, environmental degradation, and systematic violations of human and collective rights (Fundación Andrés Bello, 2021;[220] Human Rights Watch, 2020).[221]

---

218. Dialogue Earth. *Petróleo, Sanciones y Apagones: La Compleja Transición Energética de Venezuela* (2024). Retrieved from https://dialogue.earth/es/energia/petroleo-sanciones-apagones-transicion-energia-venezuela-compleja/ (last accessed 4 Apr. 2025).
219. Arminio, J. F. *Captura y Almacenamiento Geológico de Carbono: Oportunidades y Retos en la Transición Energética en Venezuela*, U3 Explore (10 Apr. 2023), https://www.u3explore.com/reports/captura-y-almacenamiento-geologico-de-carbono-oportunidades-y-retos-en-la-transicion-energetica-en-venezuela (last accessed 4 Apr. 2025).
220. Fundación Andrés Bello. *Carbón Venezolano: Una Puerta Fallida que Maduro le Abrió a China* (8 Apr. 2021), https://fundacionandresbello.org/reportajes/carbon-venezolano-una-puerta-fallida-que-maduro-le-abrio-a-china/ (last accessed 4 Apr. 2025).
221. Human Rights Watch. *Venezuela: Minería Ilegal Devastadora en el Arco Minero* (2020), https://www.hrw.org/es/news/2020/02/04/venezuela-violentos-abusos-en-minas-de-oro-ilegales (last accessed 4 Apr. 2025).

733. The Mining Arc was established by Presidential Decree No. 2.248, bypassing ordinary legislative procedures and without an environmental impact assessment, contrary to Article 129 of Venezuela's Constitution. That article mandates prior environmental and sociocultural studies for projects likely to cause environmental damage. Additionally, the state has failed to fulfil its international obligations concerning Indigenous rights, such as prior, free, and informed consultation as established in ILO Convention 169 (López Maya, 2017).[222]

734. Venezuela's fragmented mining regulations and weak institutional oversight have allowed a convergence of irregular actors, opaque JVs, and armed groups operating with impunity in the AMO. As a result, authorized and illegal mining coexist, contributing to a climate of lawlessness and exploitation (Transparency International Venezuela, 2020).[223]

735. The environmental impact of the AMO has been profound. Deforestation has escalated dramatically, especially in areas like the Caroní River basin, essential for Venezuela's hydroelectric energy supply. Reports from environmental organizations such as SOS Orinoco and Amazon Conservation highlight large-scale forest clearing, river sedimentation, and mercury contamination that affect aquatic ecosystems and community health (SOS Orinoco, 2022;[224] Amazon Conservation, 2021).[225]

736. Mercury, used to separate gold from sediments, is a toxic heavy metal that enters the food chain through fish, severely affecting Indigenous communities who depend on fishing. Studies have found elevated levels of mercury in women and children in communities along rivers like the Caura and Paragua (UN Human Rights Council, 2023).[226]

737. Socially, the Mining Arc has intensified territorial conflicts, fuelled illicit economies, and entrenched violent networks. Indigenous peoples have reported forced displacement, child labour, and the presence of non-state armed actors. The absence of meaningful consultation mechanisms has led to national and international legal challenges (Provea, 2021).[227]

---

222. López Maya, M. *El Arco Minero y la vulneración de derechos.* Revista SIC, 795, 2017, 25–30.
223. Transparency International Venezuela. *Corrupción, Opacidad y Minería Ilegal en el AMO* (2020), https://transparenciave.org/economias-ilicitas/economias-ilicitas-en-venezuela-una-renta-creciente-repartida-entre-aliados-el-arco-minero-del-orinoco-la-legalizacion-de-lo-ilicito/ (last accessed 4 Apr. 2025).
224. SOS Orinoco. *Reportes sobre el Impacto del Arco Minero* (2022), https://sosorinoco.org/es/informes/ (last accessed 4 Apr. 2025).
225. Amazon Conservation. *Amazon Mining Watch: Venezuela* (2021), https://amazonminingwatch.org/ (last accessed 4 Apr. 2025).
226. United Nations Human Rights Council. *Mercury Contamination in Indigenous Communities in Venezuela* (2023), https://www.ohchr.org (last accessed 4 Apr. 2025).
227. Provea. *Informe conjunto: Derechos humanos en el contexto del proyecto 'Arco Minero del Orinoco' en Venezuela* (2017), https://provea.org/publicaciones/investigaciones/informe-conjunto-derechos-humanos-en-el-contexto-del-proyecto-arco-minero-del-orinoco-en-venezuela/ (last accessed 4 Apr. 2025).

738. Organizations such as the Foro Penal and REDESCA have documented ongoing human rights abuses, including the criminalization of environmental defenders. These developments have drawn the attention of UN special rapporteurs and the Inter-American Commission on Human Rights (CIDH, 2021),[228] warning about deteriorating living conditions, weakened rule of law, and violations of Indigenous territorial rights.

739. The Orinoco Mining Arc exemplifies how unregulated resource extraction, lacking transparency and public participation, can trigger a large-scale socio-environmental crisis. Rather than solving Venezuela's economic challenges, the AMO has deepened structural problems, caused irreversible ecological harm, and violated the rights of Indigenous peoples.

740. A comprehensive review of the AMO, its alignment with environmental and human rights standards, and the adoption of a participatory and sustainable governance model are urgently needed. Protecting Venezuela's Amazon is not only a national responsibility but also a global obligation to future generations and the planet's biodiversity.

---

228. Comisión Interamericana de Derechos Humanos. *Situación de los derechos humanos en Venezuela* (2021), https://www.oas.org/es/cidh/docs/anual/2021/capitulos/ia2021cap4b.venezuela-es.pdf (last accessed 4 Apr. 2025).

Part V. Interaction Between Energy Law and Environmental Law

Chapter 1. Introduction

741. In view of their characteristics, the mining activities to obtain natural resources or raw materials, like oil, coal, and other minerals, may damage the environment and its community, i.e., the people. Hence, the need to develop a legal infrastructure to safeguard both sectors under the umbrella of human rights protection. That is why in the evolutionary process of human rights, the right to the environment has acquired special relevance, given the right inherent to the human person.

742. The evolution of human rights is in line with the Universal Declaration of Human Rights of 1948, issued by the United Nations General Assembly to foster and protect the human rights of Member States, together with the International Covenant on Civil and Political Rights and its Optional Protocol and the International Covenant on Economic, Social, and Cultural Rights.

743. At a regional level, the American Convention on Human Rights, the European Convention on Human Rights, and the African Charter on Human and Peoples' Rights stand out. The African Charter expressly includes the right to the environment as a solidarity right in terms of the human person's essential right to survival, which adds to the other human rights.

744. The United Nations Conference on the Human Environment (1972), held in Stockholm, Sweden, and the United Nations Conference on Environment and Development (1992), held in Brazil, are particularly important for the development of environmental rights. The Stockholm Declaration, approved in the United Nations Conference on Human Environment, provided for Principle 1:

> Man has the fundamental right to freedom, equality, and adequate conditions of life, in an environment of a quality that permits a life of dignity and well-being, and he bears a solemn responsibility to protect and improve the environment for present and future generations. In this respect, policies promoting or perpetuating apartheid, racial segregation, discrimination, colonial and other forms of oppression and foreign domination stand condemned and must be eliminated.

745. Furthermore, that conference led to the creation of the United Nations Environment Programme (UNEP), the main UN programme aimed at environmental matters.

746. In the conference held in Brazil, the Stockholm Declaration of 1972 was reaffirmed, and human beings and their individual and collective participation in the planning, conservation, and sustainable development processes were emphasized. It was established that 'Human beings are at the centre of concerns for sustainable development. They are entitled to a healthy and productive life in harmony with nature' (Principle 1). In order to achieve sustainable development, environmental protection shall constitute an integral part of the development process and cannot be considered in isolation from it (Principle 4).

747. The Conference was the opportunity the adopt an action plan for the twenty-first century, named Agenda 21, which lists some of the recommendations on the application of the principles of the Declaration. The plan takes into account matters related to health, housing, air contamination, sea, forest and mountain management, water resources management and sanitation, agriculture management, and waste management. Even today, Agenda 21 is the reference to apply the concept of sustainable development.

748. However, the Rio Summit emphasized the role of the different actors in the application of sustainable development: women, youth, and children, indigenous peoples, NGOs, local authorities, unions, companies, researchers, and farmers.

Chapter 2. Legislation Relating to Environment

§1. Legal Developments

749. Internally, Venezuela has deep historical roots in the search for a pollution-free environment, or free of any factor that affects the development of humankind activities and prevents the use of biological diversity and natural resources for the collective benefit of both present and future generations. In fact, the Laws of Indies (Leyes de Indias) and the Conservationist Decrees of the Liberator Simón Bolívar[229] are proof of such search.

750. In a subsequent development, the State issued the Forestry Law in 1910, the Hunting Law in 1944, the Forestry Law of Soils and Water, superseded in 1966 by the current Forestry Law of Soils and Water, and the Agrarian Reform Law of 1960, which superseded the Agrarian Statute, passed in 1949.

751. This multi-stakeholder approach is essential to fostering inclusive environmental governance and ensuring that energy and development policies are aligned with both ecological sustainability and human rights. Among these actors, Indigenous peoples and local communities play a particularly critical role, not only as rights-holders but also as guardians of biodiversity and traditional ecological knowledge (UNEP, 2021).[230] Their participation is indispensable for crafting energy transition strategies that respect cultural diversity, territorial integrity, and environmental justice.

752. In this context, the interaction between environmental law and energy law has become increasingly relevant. While energy law has historically focused on access, infrastructure, and supply security, environmental law contributes essential principles such as precaution, sustainability, intergenerational equity, and the right to a healthy environment (Sands et al., 2018).[231] The shift toward renewable energy offers a unique opportunity for both legal disciplines to converge in protecting environmental human rights (Boyle, 2012).[232]

753. Venezuela offers a compelling example of this needed convergence. Despite having constitutional provisions that recognize the right to a healthy environment (Constitución de la República Bolivariana de Venezuela, 1999, Articles 127–128), the country faces significant challenges in integrating environmental

---

229. Camacho, Carlos R, *La Educación Ambiental: Perspectiva Histórica de la Colonialidad del Conocimiento para Definir y Caracterizar la Identidad Nacional y la Cultura Latinoamericana*, 10 Educere 601 (2006), https://www.redalyc.org/pdf/356/35603505.pdf (last accessed 4 Apr. 2025).
230. United Nations Environment Programme (UNEP). *Unsung Heroes of Conservation: Indigenous People Fight for Forests* (2021), https://www.unep.org/championsofearth/news-and-stories/unsung-heroes-conservation-indigenous-people-fight-forests (last accessed 4 Apr. 2025).
231. Sands, Philippe, Peel, Jacqueline, Fabra, Adriana & MacKenzie, Ruth. *Principles of International Environmental Law* (4th ed. 2018), Cambridge University Press.
232. Boyle, Alan, *Human Rights and the Environment: Where Next?*, 23 Eur. J. Int'l L. 613 (2012), https://doi.org/10.1093/ejil/chs054 (last accessed 18 Jun. 2025).

standards into its energy and mining policies. The Orinoco Mining Arc project, covering over 12% of national territory, has raised concerns over deforestation, mercury pollution, and violations of Indigenous land rights (Human Rights Watch, 2020).[233] These impacts underscore the urgent need for institutional reforms that align national development strategies with international environmental and human rights norms.

754. As energy systems evolve to address climate change, States must ensure that the transition does not replicate past extractivist models but instead fosters new modes of governance based on transparency, participation, and sustainability. In Venezuela and other countries facing similar tensions, bridging energy and environmental law is not only a legal imperative but also a pathway to ensuring justice, equity, and ecological resilience.

§2. International Agreements

755. Venezuela has progressively reinforced its domestic legal framework through the ratification and implementation of a broad range of international treaties and agreements. These instruments have provided a robust legal foundation for the country's environmental, maritime, nuclear, and energy-related regulatory structures, reflecting Venezuela's commitment to international cooperation and alignment with global legal standards, particularly in the governance of natural resources and environmental protection. Among the most significant international instruments ratified or acceded to by Venezuela are: the Approving Law of the Convention for the Protection of Flora, Fauna and Scenic Beauties of American Countries (1940), one of the earliest regional initiatives aimed at the conservation of biodiversity and natural landscapes; the Approving Law of the Agreement for the Establishment on a Permanent Basis of a Latin American Forest Research and Training Institute under the Auspices of the FAO (1960), which underscores Venezuela's commitment to sustainable forestry management and regional scientific cooperation; tApproving Law of the Establishment of the International Union for the Protection of Nature (1955), evidencing Venezuela's early engagement in global environmental governance frameworks; the Ratification of the Statute of the International Atomic Energy Agency (1957), signifying Venezuela's adherence to international standards concerning the peaceful use of nuclear energy and nuclear safety; the Approving Laws of the Convention on the Territorial Sea and the Contiguous Zone (1961), the Convention on the High Seas (1961), and the Convention on Fishing and Conservation of the Living Resources of the High Seas (1961), which collectively demonstrate Venezuela's commitment to foundational principles of international maritime law and the sustainable management of marine resources.

756. In the contemporary environmental and climate governance context, Venezuela ratified the Paris Agreement on Climate Change – originally adopted in 2015

233. Human Rights Watch. *Venezuela: Violent Abuses in Illegal Gold Mines* (2020), https://www.hrw.org/news/2020/02/04/venezuela-violent-abuses-illegal-gold-mines (last accessed 4 Apr. 2025).

at COP21 – which entered into force in 2016. Venezuela formalized its ratification in the years that followed, thereby committing to global efforts to limit the rise in global average temperatures to well below 2°C above pre-industrial levels, and to pursue national policies on adaptation, mitigation, and resilience. Additionally, in 2017, Venezuela ratified the Stockholm Convention on Persistent Organic Pollutants, aiming to eliminate or restrict the production and use of hazardous chemicals posing long-term risks to health and the environment.

757. However, it is noteworthy that Venezuela has not ratified the Escazú Agreement – the Regional Agreement on Access to Information, Public Participation and Justice in Environmental Matters in Latin America and the Caribbean. This treaty, which entered into force in 2021, is considered a landmark instrument for strengthening environmental democracy and protecting environmental human rights defenders in the region. Venezuela's absence from this agreement represents a notable gap in its current international environmental law commitments.

758. From the perspective of energy law and policy, these instruments establish essential pillars for Venezuela's integration into international legal regimes that regulate access to, and the sustainable exploitation of, strategic natural resources. The country's involvement in multilateral institutions – such as the United Nations, the FAO, and the IAEA – demonstrates an active, albeit selective, engagement in the evolving architecture of global environmental and energy governance.

759. Looking ahead, Venezuela is expected to continue developing and expanding its international legal commitments, particularly through accession to emerging environmental, climate, and clean energy transition treaties, especially within the framework of the UNFCCC and regional cooperation mechanisms in Latin America and the Caribbean.

§3. Constitutional Provisions of 1961

760. The above first initiatives to protect the environment acquired constitutional status upon inclusion in the CN of 1961 (Article 106) of a rule whereby the State assumes responsibility for the defence and conservation of the Venezuelan territory's natural resources by aiming the exploitation thereof primarily for the collective benefit of the Venezuelan people. These regulations were complemented with the provisions in Article 50 of the CN, which provides for rights and guarantees that even though they are not included therein, they must not be deemed as rejected by the CN, but on the contrary, and even more if they are inherent to the human person, such as the environmental rights.

761. However, Article 76 of the Constitution provided for the right to health as a fundamental human right, which corresponds to the right to a healthy environment. This constitutional framework sufficed to formulate an environmental policy that translated into conservation, defence, and improvement of the environment and the renewable natural resources. As a result, the basis of the legal system development in environmental matters was established over the 1961–1999 period.

§4. Conference on the Human Environment

762. The Declaration of the United Nations Conference on the Human Environment held in Stockholm in 1972 set up the doctrinal basis for environment adopted by most countries, on the one hand, and, on the other, became the origin of the International Environmental Law that permeated the national laws and generated an overall conception of the environmental issues.

763. The existence of a legal framework based on the Venezuelan State's initiative to preserve natural resources and the environment, along with the influence of the Stockholm Conference, paved the way for the Legislative to issue in 1976 the Organic Law on the Environment (LOA – *Ley Orgánica del Ambiente*), which provided for an integrated approach between environmental conservation, natural resources, environmental planning, institutional competence, and socio-economic development of the country, in order to establish – within the comprehensive development strategy of the Nation – the environmental guiding principles.

764. The LOA of 1976 provided for in Article 1 the purpose of establishing within the integral policy of the country the guiding principles for the conservation, defence, and improvement of the environment to the benefit of the quality of life. However, neither the scope of such principles nor the definition of environment was included in the legal text or in any other sublegal text.

765. It is worth mentioning that the LOA became a progressive and advanced legal instrument upon establishing the guidelines for the State's action aimed at the legal protection of the goods considered by the entities of the public power and the society as environmental values essential to the existence and development of the population. However, it was still necessary to have criminal measures sufficiently efficient to penalize the facts and acts, both collective and individual, posing risks, dangers, and damages to the environment, which was partially achieved by the enactment of the Criminal Law of the Environment (LPA) in 1992.

§5. Constitutional Provisions of 1999

766. When referring to Environmental Rights, the CRBV puts emphasis on the protection of the environment and the conservation of the ecological balance as instruments to boost the country's sustainable development. Hence, the granting of constitutional status to the Environmental Law falls within the environmental law evolution process in the international field towards the human and social development of the population. In this context, the Constitution gives from its Preamble a significant importance to the environment as common and undeniable heritage of humankind. This dimension is reinforced with the provision that the State is responsible for developing an integral policy to preserve the environment (Article 15), the biological diversity, thc genetic resources, the ecological processes, the national parks and natural monuments, and further areas of special ccological significance (Article 127).

767. With the above guidelines, the authors of the Constitution of 1999 recognize the human right to the environment in the Democratic and Social State Subject to the Rule of Law and Justice, bearing in mind the values of social solidarity and equal opportunities as a theological action goal of the State. Therefore, the authors of the Constitution foresee the taking of financial, infrastructure, environmental education, and technology access and transfer measures that allow reverting the situation of environmental degradation in the country.

768. In short, the environmental rights are comparable to the fundamental human rights, like the right to life, health, education, among others. Thus, a chapter on Environmental Rights, where the main principles for the formulation and implementation of the country's environmental policy are identified, is granted constitutional status for the first time. These principles are expressly included in Articles 127, 128, and 129, complemented by the other articles of the CRBV.

769. The second paragraph of Article 127 of the CRBV, which provides that 'In contracts into which the Republic enters with natural or juridical persons of Venezuelan or foreign nationality, or in any permits granted which involve natural resources, the obligation to preserve the ecological balance, to permit access to, and the transfer of technology on mutually agreed terms and to restore the environment to its natural state if the latter is altered, shall be deemed included even if not expressed, on such terms as may be established by law', is especially relevant for this study.

§6. Organic Law on the Environment

770. Under the constitutional framework above indicated, a new LOA adjusted to the new trends of the international environmental development and the technological breakthrough and innovations was approved on 22 December 2006. The LOA adopts the guiding concepts and principles for the conservation of the environment under the premise of sustainable development and the global point of view of the environment.

771. The Law was intended to reinforce the role of the State with the active participation of the society to guarantee the right to an environment that is a guarantee for the survival of humankind and other living beings. Therefore, regulations, actions, and measures are established for the conservation of biological diversity, natural resources, environmental planning, environmental defence, information and research, environmental education and civic participation, environmental quality, incentives, and environmental fund.

772. The State's obligation to include the environmental dimension in plans, programmes, projects, and economic, technological, scientific, educational, and social development processes of the country is established, thus assuring due civic participation in decision-making. Likewise, the constitutional order to conduct environmental and sociocultural impact assessments, as control instruments in the execution of activities that may pose damage to the environment or to any environmental elements, is developed in general terms. However, the implementation of clean technologies as well as the setup of financial and tax incentives is promoted.

773. Even though the LOA has principles and substantive and adjective provisions, the application of which is preferable than other laws ruling the matter, there are other aspects that will continue being regulated by other rules, as in the case of criminal matters, which will be governed by the LPA, as well as the technical standards to be regulated by sublegal instruments.

774. Despite the LOA of 2006 setting out a comprehensive legal framework aligned with international environmental principles, its implementation has faced persistent challenges. As of 2024, no implementing regulations (sublegal instruments) have been issued to operationalize many of its provisions. This regulatory vacuum has weakened enforcement mechanisms, especially regarding environmental zoning, public participation, access to environmental information, and environmental impact assessments.

775. Although the LOA enshrines the promotion of clean technologies and fiscal incentives, these mechanisms have not been developed in practice. The National Environmental Fund remains largely inactive, and incentives for sustainable activities are rarely applied.

776. Additionally, Venezuela has not ratified the Escazú Agreement (2021), a regional treaty that reinforces many of the LOA's core principles – such as access to environmental information, public participation, and protection for environmental defenders. This omission reflects a disconnect between Venezuela's formal environmental commitments and its regional obligations.

777. The lack of institutional coordination, judicial oversight, and technical regulations has resulted in a fragmented and under-enforced environmental governance regime. As environmental degradation intensifies – particularly in sectors like illegal mining, deforestation, and water pollution – calls for reform and regulatory activation have become more urgent within academic, civic, and multilateral circles.

§7. Criminal Law of the Environment

778. The current Environmental Criminal Law (Ley Penal del Ambiente, LPA) was enacted on 2 May 2012, through Official Gazette Extraordinary No. 39.913, replacing the previous 1992 version. This comprehensive reform was driven by the mandates of the 1999 Constitution and the 2006 LOA, which required the modernization of environmental criminal legislation in line with contemporary legal principles, including sustainable development, precaution, prevention, and environmental justice.

779. The law grants the environment the status of an autonomously protected legal interest (bien jurídico), enabling the imposition of criminal sanctions on conduct that directly harms it, regardless of whether other rights such as health, life, or property are affected. As a result, environmental crimes are frequently complex and multi-layered, often impacting several legal interests simultaneously.

780. Although the LPA does not explicitly define the environment as a 'legal subject', its normative content supports such an interpretation. From Article 1 onward – by criminalizing conduct that directly harms environmental elements and providing for sanctions without requiring harm to individual rights – the law implicitly recognizes the environment as an autonomous legal interest, meriting direct protection under criminal law. This interpretation is reinforced by Article 3, which establishes an objective liability regime, allowing penalties to be imposed for the mere violation of environmental norms, without the need to prove intent or negligence. This evidences a clear legislative intent to prioritize the preservation of the natural environment itself. Furthermore, this reading aligns with Article 127 of the 1999 Constitution, which recognizes the environment as a collective right and duty, and imposes obligations on both the State and private parties to ensure its protection. Legal scholarship has interpreted this constitutional provision as recognizing the environment as a collective, cross-cutting, and public-interest right, thereby solidifying its status as a protected legal asset in its own right, beyond its instrumental value in safeguarding other rights such as health or property (Pérez Guerrero, 2015).[234]

I. Objectives

781. The LPA aims to criminalize conduct expressly identified as harmful to nature and the environment, while also providing for precautionary, reparative, and restorative measures. It introduces procedural rules specific to environmental offences and establishes mechanisms for institutional coordination.

II. Principle of Extraterritoriality

782. Article 2 of the LPA incorporates the principle of *extraterritorial jurisdiction*, allowing for prosecution of environmental crimes committed outside Venezuelan territory when the effects or risks manifest within the country. This is

234. J. Pérez Guerrero, *Derecho Constitucional Ambiental Venezolano,* Editorial Jurídica Venezolana, 2015.

conditional upon the alleged offender entering Venezuelan jurisdiction and not having been tried abroad, or having evaded prosecution.

III. Criminal Liability of Natural Persons

783. One of the most innovative elements of the LPA is the adoption of an *objective liability regime*. According to Article 3, the mere breach of an environmental norm is sufficient to establish criminal liability, without the need to demonstrate intent or negligence. This provision was upheld by the Constitutional Chamber of the Supreme Tribunal of Justice, which found that such a standard does not violate the principle of culpability, given the collective and preventive nature of the legal interest protected (TSJ, Constitutional Chamber, Judgment No. 1048/2015).

IV. Criminal Liability of Legal Entities

784. Legal entities may also be held criminally liable for acts or omissions that contravene environmental norms set forth in laws, decrees, resolutions, or other binding administrative instruments, without the need to identify specific individual perpetrators within the organization. This reinforces the principle of institutional co-responsibility, particularly in high-impact sectors such as mining, hydrocarbons, or large-scale infrastructure.

V. Penalty Classification

785. The law distinguishes between *principal* and *accessory penalties*:

1. *Principal sanctions*: imprisonment, detention, fines, the dissolution of the legal entity, and the confiscation of facilities or constructions involved in the offence.
2. *Accessory penalties*: permanent or temporary closure of establishments, permanent prohibition of polluting activities, land-use rezoning, suspension of corporate activities (up to six months), and disqualification from holding public office (up to two years). Public officials may also face professional disqualification.
3. A *notorious accessory penalty* is the compulsory publication of the judgment in a national and local newspaper, aiming at public deterrence and social awareness.

786. Although the LPA has not undergone formal amendment since its enactment in 2012, a number of recent developments have underscored both its operational limitations and the evolving nature of its legal interpretation:

787. The Organic Law on the Power System and Service:

1. *Judicial inertia*: Numerous environmental criminal cases have remained stalled in preliminary stages for over a decade, revealing structural shortcomings in prosecutorial effectiveness and a lack of judicial specialization in environmental matters (Pérez, 2020).[235]
2. *Constitutional validation of objective liability*: The Constitutional Chamber of the Supreme Tribunal of Justice has upheld the constitutionality of strict liability in environmental criminal law, a position that, while consolidating jurisprudential support for environmental protection, has generated academic debate regarding due process and the proportionality of criminal sanctions (TSJ, 2015).[236]
3. *Expansion of corporate criminal liability*: Both jurisprudence and legal scholarship have increasingly affirmed the applicability of criminal liability to legal entities, particularly in relation to high-impact sectors such as extractive industries and infrastructure development.
4. *Absence of codification within the General Penal Code*: Despite recent reforms to the General Penal Code and sectoral legislation, there has been no substantive integration or harmonization of environmental criminal provisions. The continued lack of a dedicated title for environmental crimes within the Penal Code remains a significant legislative omission.

235. L.A. Pérez, *El Derecho Penal Ambiental en Venezuela: Retos de la Judicialización*, 12(2) Rev. Derecho Ambient. Venezolano 45 (2020).
236. Tribunal Supremo de Justicia de Venezuela, Sala Constitucional (2015). *Sentencia No. 1048 del 10 de agosto de 2015*, available at: www.tsj.gob.ve.

Chapter 3. Electricity and Environment

788. The *Organic Law on the Power System and Service (LOSSE)* incorporates provisions aimed at ensuring environmental protection in the context of electricity supply. Pursuant to *Article 27(27)* of the LOSSE, the ministry with competence in electrical energy is responsible – together with the ministries in charge of environmental and public health matters – for ensuring the *prevention of environmental pollution* during the generation, transmission, and distribution activities carried out within the *SEN*. This provision reflects an approach of *shared and intersectoral responsibility*, consistent with the constitutional principles of *precaution, prevention, and sustainable development*, as well as with the provisions of the *LOA (2006)*.

789. With regard to power generation, *Article 44 of the LOSSE* mandates that the state entities responsible for the operation and delivery of electric service – particularly *CORPOELEC*, as the sole operator of the SEN – must *give priority to alternative and low-environmental-impact energy sources*, in accordance with the guidelines set forth in the *National Power System Development Plan (PDSEN)*. Although the legal text refers generically to 'operators and providers', such roles are in fact exercised *exclusively by public entities*, given the strategic nature of the electricity sector and the *State monopoly* established by law. The *PDSEN* functions as a *governing instrument of national energy policy*, outlining, in both programmatic and technical terms, the goals, priorities, and technologies that guide the expansion and sustainability of the electric system. In this regard, the legal obligation to prioritize low-impact energy sources is operationalized through centralized planning, which determines the specific renewable technologies to be promoted, the geographical regions to be addressed, and the timelines to be followed, all based on criteria of feasibility, energy efficiency, and environmental sustainability.

790. In relation to legal violations, *Article 93(3) of the LOSSE* expressly qualifies *damage to the environment as an aggravating circumstance* in the commission of offences. This provision integrates the sanctioning regime of the electricity sector with the environmental criminal framework set forth in the *Environmental Criminal Law (2012)*, thereby reinforcing the protection of the environment as an autonomous legal interest in the context of public service provision. Nonetheless, significant challenges remain in terms of effective oversight, the enforcement of sanctions, and the transparent implementation of environmental principles within the Venezuelan electricity sector.

Chapter 4. Hydrocarbon Sector and Environment

791. Hydrocarbon-related activities are governed by legal provisions aimed at environmental protection. Article 5 of the Organic Hydrocarbons Law stipulates that hydrocarbon activities should promote the comprehensive, organic, and sustainable development of the country, considering the rational use of resources and the preservation of the environment. In this context, the strengthening of the national productive sector and the local transformation of hydrocarbons will be encouraged, along with the incorporation of advanced technologies. This legal framework aligns with the constitutional principle set forth in Article 129 of the CRBV, which mandates that all activities potentially harmful to ecosystems must be preceded by environmental and sociocultural impact studies. Furthermore, it requires the State to ensure the conservation of ecological balance and the restoration of the environment if it is altered by such activities. This reinforces the responsibility of hydrocarbon activities not only to minimize their environmental impact but also to restore any damage caused. According to Article 3 of the Organic Law of Gaseous Hydrocarbons (LOHG), activities related to gaseous hydrocarbons must be carried out with consideration for the defence and rational use of resources, as well as the conservation, protection, and preservation of the environment. This provision also aligns with the stipulations in Article 129 of the Constitution, which emphasizes the need to assess the impact of these activities on the ecosystem before they are executed, and to ensure that contracts and permits granted implicitly include the obligation to respect ecological balance, provide access to technology, and facilitate its transfer under mutually agreed terms. The law must establish the conditions under which the environment is to be restored to its natural state in the event of alteration.

792. Despite the existence of a legal framework establishing mechanisms for environmental protection, as outlined in Article 5 of the Organic Hydrocarbons Law, Article 3 of the Organic Law of Gaseous Hydrocarbons, and Article 129 of the CN, hydrocarbon activities in the country continue to cause recurring environmental damage.

793. Over the last twenty years, a series of incidents have been recorded that highlight the disconnection between regulations and their effective implementation. One of the most emblematic cases is the gas leak and subsequent explosion at the Amuay Refinery (2012), which caused significant damage to infrastructure and nearby communities, releasing large quantities of toxic gases and impacting both the population's health and the ecological environment (COENER, 2013). This event, along with other oil spills in areas such as Lake Maracaibo, demonstrates the industry's inability to prevent and control leaks and spills that affect aquatic and terrestrial ecosystems (Provea, 2014).[237]

237. PROVEA (2014), *Análisis de la Situación Ambiental Petrolera Venezolana. Caso: Derrames Petroleros*, retrieved from, https://provea.org/publicaciones/investigaciones/analisis-de-la-situacion-ambiental-petrolera-venezolana-caso-estudio-estados-anzoategui-monagas-2012-2014/.

794. Additionally, deforestation linked to the expansion of extractive activities in the Amazon region and high levels of air pollution in oil-producing areas such as the Eastern Coast of Lake Maracaibo continue without an effective response to guarantee the restoration of ecosystems (Provea, 2014). While legislation requires the restoration of affected environments, in practice, corrective measures are insufficient and rarely implemented on the necessary scale.

795. The Organic Hydrocarbons Law and Article 129 of the CN aim for the sustainable management of natural resources, including the obligation to restore environmental damage. However, recurring events demonstrate the lack of compliance and effective execution of these regulations. The nature of the damages, combined with the absence of stringent sanctions, reflects the disconnect between the laws and their practical application, perpetuating environmental degradation in key areas of the country.

Chapter 5. Coal Sector and Environment

796. The mining activities regulated by the LM will be carried out considering the optimal recovery or extraction of the mining resource at all times, in accordance with the principle of sustainable development, the conservation of the environment, and the country planning (Article 5). For such purposes, the LM creates a Permanent Interministerial Commission, made up by the MEM, the Ministry for the Environment and Natural Resources, the Ministry of Finance, and the Ministry of Defence (Article 15) to coordinate mining-related matters, particularly the protection of the environment. As to matters related to the prevention of environmental damage, the MEM, jointly with the Ministry for the Environment and Natural Resources, will take the relevant actions to prevent the pollution of the environment resulting from mining activities (Article 36).

797. However, despite these regulations, the coal mining sector in Venezuela continues to generate significant environmental impacts. Issues such as air and water pollution, deforestation, and soil degradation persist in regions where coal is mined, particularly in Zulia and La Guajira, which host the country's largest coal reserves. The LM emphasizes sustainable practices, yet enforcement has been inconsistent, and these ongoing environmental challenges demonstrate the gap between regulatory intentions and practical outcomes.

798. Although coal is not one of the primary energy sources in Venezuela, its extraction has caused significant environmental impacts in the regions where it is mined. The LM establishes a regulatory framework that promotes sustainable mining practices, yet the coal sector continues to contribute substantially to environmental degradation, particularly in regions such as Zulia and La Guajira, which host the country's largest coal reserves.

799. Air Pollution: Mining activities associated with coal extraction have significantly contributed to atmospheric pollution, primarily through the emission of sulfur dioxide (SO_2) and nitrogen oxides (NOx), both of which adversely affect air quality. According to the Ministry of Environment (2018), areas near coal mines, particularly on the Eastern Coast of Lake Maracaibo and La Guajira, report airborne particulate levels that exceed those recommended by the World Health Organization (WHO). This pollution is directly linked to a higher incidence of respiratory diseases, particularly among populations living in proximity to mining operations.

800. Water and Soil Pollution: Coal mining has also led to significant water contamination in the surrounding areas. The Guasare River, located in Zulia, has been severely impacted by acid mine drainage, resulting in the degradation of aquatic ecosystems and the contamination of local water sources. According to a report by

PROVEA (2017),[238] the pollution of these water bodies has contributed to ecological imbalances, further reducing the availability of clean water for local communities. Moreover, open-pit mining has accelerated soil erosion, contributing to desertification and the loss of fertile land for agriculture.[239]

801. Deforestation and Ecosystem Disruption: The extraction of coal has caused massive deforestation in regions with rich biodiversity, particularly in areas such as Táchira and La Guajira. The process of coal mining requires the removal of large swaths of tropical forests, leading to the destruction of vital habitats. A study conducted by the Venezuelan Institute for Scientific Research (IVIC) (2016) estimates that more than 10,000 hectares of forest have been cleared in the past two decades due to mining activities. This disruption of ecosystems not only reduces biodiversity but also impairs essential ecosystem services such as climate regulation, air purification, and water cycle stabilization.

802. Health and Social ImpactsCommunities located near coal mines, particularly in La Guajira and the Eastern Coast of Lake Maracaibo, face serious health issues due to the environmental pollution resulting from mining activities. Reports indicate a significant increase in the prevalence of respiratory illnesses, such as asthma and chronic bronchitis, among these communities, attributable to exposure to harmful particulate matter.[240] Furthermore, indigenous communities have been forcibly displaced due to the expansion of mining operations and the contamination of their water sources. These displacements not only threaten their food security but also jeopardize their territorial and cultural rights.[241]

---

238. PROVEA, '*Mining and Its Environmental Impact in Venezuela: The Case of Coal*,' 2017, Available at: www.provea.org (last accessed 4 Apr. 2025).
239. O.J. Chávez González, *Impactos Socio Ambientales Ocasionados por la Actividad Extractiva de Carbón sobre el Pueblo Wayuu del Municipio Mara del Estado Zulia*, FLACSO Sede Ecuador, 2004.
240. R. Rojano, L. Angulo & G. Restrepo, '*Concentración y Relación de PST, PM10 y PM2.5 en Poblaciones Cercanas a Minería a Cielo Abierto: Caso Cerrejón, Colombia*,' *Revista de la Facultad de Ingeniería Universidad Central de Venezuela*, 30(3), 2015.
241. *Ibid.*

Part VI. Interaction Between Energy Law and Tax Law

Chapter 1. Hydrocarbons Taxes and Fees: Constitutional Basis

803. The constitutional basis of the royalty system is provided for in Article 113 of the Constitution of 1999. Its sole paragraph provides that 'when exploiting national natural resources or rendering public services, whether exclusively or not, the State may grant concessions for a fixed term, thus guaranteeing existence of considerations and offsets appropriate to the public interest at all times'. As to taxes, Article 156 of the CRBV, Res. 12, provides that the executive branch has exclusive authority to 'generate, classify, collect, manage, and control taxes … '. This constitutional framework is developed in special laws like the LOHG and the LOH and in the Income Tax Law (LISLR).

Chapter 2. Tax Regime for the Gaseous Hydrocarbons

§1. Royalties

804. The LOHG regulates the manner in which the State will have a share of the benefits arising from its status as owner of the natural gas reservoirs to be exploited pursuant to the LOHG and its regulation. Therefore, in accordance with Article 34 of the same law, the payment of a 20% royalty on the volumes of gaseous hydrocarbons extracted and not reinjected is required, that is, the result after deducting from the total production the volume reinjected in reservoirs in the area granted under the licence. At the MENPET's option, such payment may be in kind or in cash, totally or partially, with the specific clarification that, unless expressly required, it must be understood that the Government chooses to receive the total payment in cash. In this case, the company in charge of such payment will have to pay the price of the volumes of gaseous hydrocarbons at market value in the production field, under the procedure established in the regulation of the law (Article 38 of the RLOHG). If, on the contrary, the Government decides to receive the royalty in kind, that is, instead of cash, for the gas obtained from the exploitation, it will be entitled to agree with the corresponding company a price for the services of transportation to and storage in the location indicated by the MENPET (Article 34 of the LOHG).

805. For royalty calculation purposes for the exploitation of non-associated natural gas, the MENPET will set through resolutions the price of the respective production fields based on the following principles:

- Estimate of methane gas price by deducting gathering, compression, treatment, or processing costs from the price set by the MENPET for methane gas in the dispatch centres.
- Estimate of the market price of the heaviest hydrocarbon compounds in natural gas, based on the prices of these products both in the domestic market and the export market, as well as the costs of extraction, fractionation, and storage of natural gas liquids.

806. Notwithstanding the foregoing, the MENPET may establish (for royalty calculation purposes) methodologies based on other principles, provided that they do not affect the financial viability of the projects having licences acquired prior issue of the resolutions that modify the parameters to set new royalties (Article 48 of the Regulation of the LOHG).

§2. Taxes

807. Regarding taxes, the activities regulated by the LOHG are subject to the rates applicable under the LISLR of 2007. This Law gives special treatment to the activities regulated by the LOHG to motivate and facilitate their purposes. It is the granting of a special tax that exempts them from paying the 50% rate that persons engaged in the exploitation of hydrocarbons and related activities must pay.

808. In accordance with Article 11 of the LISLR, the companies carrying out activities, integrated or not, of exploitation of non-associated gas, processing or refining, transportation, distribution, storage, sale, and export of gas and its components shall be exempted from the payment of the 50% rate. Consequently, those companies shall pay a 34% rate in compliance with Articles 9 and 52 of the LISLR referred hereto.

Chapter 3. Tax Regime for the Liquid Hydrocarbons

809. The constitutional basis of royalties and taxes for hydrocarbons presented in the chapter on Gaseous Hydrocarbons applies the same way for Liquid Hydrocarbons. Having said that, the following is the explanation on how royalties are conceived in the LOH, as well as the treatment and classification of taxes in such Law and the special law on income tax.

§1. Royalties

810. As it was said, royalties are based on the right of the State to receive a compensation for the extraction of material from the subsoil, the ownership of which the State is inalienably and institutionally entitled to. The discussion about the effective period of the royalties, the setting of their amounts, and the possibility of increasing or reducing them based on the performance of the reservoirs has given rise to many debates. Its unequivocal implementation directly affects the economy, particularly in countries with large hydrocarbon reserves, such as Venezuela. Traditionally, oil income has been affected by the manner royalties and taxes have been applied to production and exploitation.

811. It is worth mentioning that, in the case of the Associations in the Orinoco Belt, the application of the legal provision contained in Article 41 of the 1943 LOH in force at that time was necessary. Under such article, the royalty was set at 16.67%, but the Executive Branch was empowered by resolution to reduce the royalty on a discretionary basis down to 1% through the current Ministry of Energy and Oil whenever deemed convenient to national interests.

812. The LOH in force establishes a different regulation and increases the amount to be received by the Republic as royalties from the 16.66% provided for in the 1943 LOH to 30% in the new legal framework. With the May 2006 amendment, that amount increased by 3.3% as a result of a new 'extraction tax', which is nothing but an increase of the royalty, currently estimated at 33.3%. This increase will be applied to PDVSA's production and the JV's production.

813. Regarding the possibility of reducing the royalties for certain projects, before the last amendment of 2006, the 2001 LOH established two scenarios up to 20% and the limit of 16.66%, in the following cases:

1. when a matured or an extra-heavy oil reservoir of the Orinoco Belt is not economically exploitable with the 30% royalty, it may be reduced down to 20% in order to achieve cost effectiveness, though being authorized to restore it, totally or partially, until reaching 30% again, upon proving that the cost effectiveness of the reservoir can be maintained with such restitution; or
2. when projects for bitumen mixtures from the FPO are not economically viable with the 30% royalty, it may be reduced down to 16 2/3%, in order to achieve the cost effectiveness of such projects, though being authorized to restore it,

totally or partially, until reaching 30% again, upon proving that the cost effectiveness of the reservoir can be maintained with such restitution.

814. After the above-mentioned May 2006 amendment and for eliminating the term bitumen from the law, Article 44 provides reductions for matured reservoirs or extra-heavy oil reservoirs only. Consequently, the second scenario was eliminated, and the first was maintained with the terms established.

815. Thus, there is a clear separation between the 1943 LOH and the 2006 LOH, inasmuch as the new regulations do not give the National Government any possibility for interpreting the limit of the reductions, which will be applicable up to 20%, provided that the non-viability of a project is sufficiently proved. The restitution, however, does not necessarily have to reach the original percentage at once. The regulation allows for a total or partial restitution until reaching 30% again.

816. This provision prevents the negotiation of the royalty percentage, which had been the practice to compensate for the activities carried out in low-production reservoirs. This clearly constitutes a loss of flexibility of the regulation. It also provides the possibility that the State has – at its choice – to receive the amount it is entitled to for royalty in cash, at market price, or in kind, as provided for by the 1943 LOH.

817. The reason that explains the increase of royalties and the reduction of the income tax – according to senior government officials – is the improvement of tax collection efficiency, given that royalty, which is based on volumes produced and on the mercantile price only, simplifies tax collection and compels greater efforts to reduce costs, where the owner and the investor share the risks resulting, for instance, from prices. Yet, under another analysis, according to Gonzalez Porras, the tax collection system must previously consider both the crude type and the reproduction costs, because the higher the quality of the crude oil, in terms of higher quotation prices and lower extraction costs, the higher the income reported to the treasury by the adopted taxation system. On the contrary, if the quotation prices are closer to the cost, that system would report the treasury a lower amount, from which it is inferred that the modification of the tax system constitutes an incentive for the exploitation of light crude oil, while it is a demotivating system for heavy crude oil.

§2. TAXES

I. Surface Tax

818. It entails the payment of 100 tax units per sq km or fraction thereof, which may be increased by 2% throughout the first five years and by 5% throughout the following years.

II. Tax on Fuel Consumption

819. This tax provides for the payment of 10% per cubic metre of by-products produced and used, calculated on the final sale price to the end consumer.

III. General Consumption Tax

820. In this case, the tax is on the sale of hydrocarbon by-products and establishes a tax ranging between 30% and 50% of the price paid per litre sold in the domestic market. This tax is paid by the end consumer; therefore, it is included as part of the sale price of the product, collected and paid to government agencies without affecting the company's consolidated statements of income.

IV. Value Added Tax

821. This tax is not collected because the sale of hydrocarbon by-product fuels, as well as inputs and additives aimed to improve gas quality and transportation service of hydrocarbon by-product fuels, is under tax exemption pursuant to Article 18(4) of the VAT Law.

V. Extraction Tax

822. This tax represents one-third of the value of all liquid hydrocarbons extracted from any reservoir. It must be paid on a monthly basis and is calculated on the same basis as the royalty payable in cash (the market value of the crude extracted in the oil field).

VI. Export Registration Tax

823. It is equal to 1% of the value of all hydrocarbons exported from any port in Venezuela, calculated on the sale price to the purchaser of such hydrocarbons. The tax base is the sale Price of the exported hydrocarbon. The Executive Branch may exonerate the General Consumption Tax, totally or partially, for the term established, in order to motivate certain activities of public or general interest. Likewise, it may restore it to its original level when the causes for exemption cease. The above-described taxes are deductible for income tax purposes.

VII. Income Tax

824. The Income Tax in Venezuela (ISR) applies to income from national or foreign sources obtained by natural residents or legal entities domiciled in the country and by permanent establishments of non-domiciled entities. Natural non-residents and non-domiciled legal entities are subject to ISR for Venezuelan-source income only.

825. In the field of hydrocarbons, it is worth mentioning that, in the Income Tax Code (LISR) of 1991, the income tax rate had decreased from 67.7% to 34% in the integrated projects for the transformation of extra-heavy crudes to prevent them from losing commercial value and being no longer attractive to investors in a low-price scenario. This criterion was upheld in the LISR of 2001, which excludes the payment of the 50% tax on exploitation, industrialization, emulsification, transportation, and sale of extra-heavy crude oil and natural bitumen.

826. In a new amendment to the LISR of 2001, the tax rate was reduced from 67.7% to 50% for companies engaged in exploitation and related activities, as refining and transportation, or in the purchase or acquisition of by-products for export, always referring to conventional hydrocarbons. This same law maintained the 34% rate for exploitation, refining, industrialization, emulsification, transportation, and sale of non-conventional hydrocarbons (extra-heavy crudes, natural bitumen), which were carried out through the so-called AA entered into under the LN or through agreements of national interest provided for in the Constitution. The same 34% tax applied to companies engaged in integrated activities of exploration and exploitation of non-associated gas, processing or refining, transportation, distribution, storage, sale, and export of gas and its components.

827. In the last amendment of the 2007 ISR Law, some criteria were modified after the migration of OAs and strategic associations to JV, which must now pay 50% under the LOH in force, applicable to oil companies with extraction businesses.

828. Taxpayers exclusively engaged in extra-heavy crude refining or improvement activities are subject to the regular rate of 34%, though, in practice, this preferential treatment has no application, since all the current projects in the extra-heavy crude area are implemented in a vertically integrated manner; therefore, refining or improvement activities will be carried out by a JV, which also carries out extra-heavy oil exploration and exploitation activities; hence, it is subject to the proportional fee of 50%.

VIII. Tax on Dividends

829. This precept provided for in the LISR is applicable to excess earnings paid to shareholders on the company's taxable income, and must be withheld at source at the time of the distribution; therefore, the 'tax on dividends' is designed to levy the earnings distributed to shareholders that are non-taxable to the company paying the dividend.

830. Under the statutes of PDVSA, the Shareholders' Meeting exercises absolute management and administration of PDVSA, having, among others, the powers to approve or disapprove the economic and financial results, as well as to decide on the allocation of the annual earnings of the company. By reason of this power, PDVSA orders the payment of dividends to the Republic, distributing a portion of its earnings to the Nation. These dividends are paid by PDVSA in the fiscal periods in which they are budgeted following instructions by the National Office of Treasury. When the taxable dividend is paid by a company engaged in exploration, exploitation, refining, and transportation of oil or oil by-products, it will be subject to a 50% tax.

§3. Contribution for Extraordinary Prices in the Oil Market

831. Due to the sustained increase in the price of a barrel of oil, the National Assembly approved, in April 2008, the first law intended to regulate the so-called Windfall Oil Price Tax, which levies high prices on hydrocarbon exports. This law has been amended three times, the last of which was made in February 2013 and was renamed as the Law Creating a Special Contribution on Extraordinary Prices and Exorbitant Prices in the International Hydrocarbons Market.[242]

832. Contribution on Extraordinary Prices: Due to the reform, Extraordinary Prices will be construed as those with a monthly average of international quotes of the Venezuelan liquid hydrocarbons basket that is greater than the price set out in the Annual Budget Law for the respective fiscal year, but equal to or lower than USD 80 per barrel, instead of the USD 70 per barrel provided in the partially derogated norm. The Windfall Oil Price Tax rate will be equivalent to 20% and will be applied on the difference between the prices.

833. Contribution on Exorbitant Prices: Exorbitant Prices will be construed as those with a monthly average of international quotes of the Venezuelan liquid hydrocarbons basket that is greater than USD 80 per barrel, instead of the USD 70 per barrel provided in the partially derogated norm.

834. Thus, when the monthly average price of international quotes of the Venezuelan liquid hydrocarbons basket is greater than the price set in the Annual Budget Law for the relevant fiscal year, but equal to or lower than USD 80 per barrel, a tax rate equal to 20% will be applied on the difference between such prices. For Exorbitant Prices, the special contribution rate may vary as follows:

- When Exorbitant Prices are greater than USD 80 per barrel, but lower than USD 100 per barrel, a rate equal to 80% of the total difference between such prices will be applied.

242. Official Gazette No. 40114 on 20 Feb. 2013.

- When Exorbitant Prices are greater than or equal to USD 100 per barrel, but lower than USD 110 per barrel, a rate equal to 90% of the total difference between such prices will be applied.
- When Exorbitant Prices are greater than or equal to USD 110 per barrel, a rate equal to 95% of the total difference between such prices will be applied.

835. The Law also provides a maximum cap of USD 80 per barrel for the calculation and payment of Royalties, Extraction Tax and Export Registration Tax, set out in the Master LH.

836. It is particularly important to analyse the reason why this new collection concept is created when a fiscal and tax regulation exists for regulating hydrocarbon activities. In fact, Articles 44 and 48 of the LOH and Articles 11 and 53 of the ISR Law set forth the methodology for collecting both the royalties and taxes per hydrocarbon volumes extracted from any field. After classifying the revenues derived from the extraordinary and exorbitant prices as 'Special Contributions', when they actually correspond to royalties and taxes, the result is that a way has been open so that what has been collected, exceeding the amount budgeted, may be used for other expenses, that is, extra-budgetary expenses, as specified by Article 34 of the Organic Law on the Financial Administration of the Public Sector.

837. In the case of royalties, for instance, once a cap is established, a deviation of the resources that should go to the national budget immediately takes place. Contrarily, such revenues are not subject to the control of the Budget Law and are then administered by the Executive Branch through the FONDEN as the beneficiary entity of said special contributions. Conversely, the Executive Branch becomes the sole beneficiary to the detriment of regional and local governments, which do not receive extra contributions because the extra gains are neither part of the national budget nor part of the regular distribution of financial resources established by the CRBV by means of the concept of Constitutional Revenue Sharing. On the contrary, said Law sets forth in Article 2 the destination that must be given to the resources, which should rather be used to guarantee the financing of the large missions created by the Executive Branch, as well as the projects for infrastructure, roads, health, education, communications, agriculture, food and, in general, for the development of the national productive sector, among others. This way, a very important part of the contributions to the Nation originating from oil is diverted to be managed and controlled in a centralized and discretional manner by the Executive Branch. This may have significant repercussions on the control, transparency, and rendering of accounts that must characterize the use of oil resources, and it also represents a violation of Article 34 of the Organic Law on the Financial Administration of the Public Sector mentioned *supra*. Furthermore, the contribution will be liquidated by the Ministry of the MENPET on a monthly basis and in foreign currency and must be paid to the FONDEN. The interaction between MENPET and FONDEN for liquidating and paying is not clear.

Chapter 4. Tax Regime for the Coal

§1. Surface and Exploitation Tax

838. The LM in Article 90, Letter c, establishes that holders of mining rights, particularly coal, shall pay the following taxes:

> Three percent (3%), calculated on its commercial value at the mine, for other minerals, which includes the costs incurred until the mineral extracted, whether crushed or not, is deposited in the vehicle that has transported it outside the limits of the area granted or to a processing or refining plant, regardless of the place where it is located, taking into account its richness and the price of the mineral in the buying market, among other relevant factors.

839. The LM also establishes the possibility of a reduction of the exploitation tax foreseen in Letter c, previously mentioned, to 1% whenever the economic conditions so require it. The National Executive Branch may reestablish, whenever it deems convenient, said tax to its original percentage, when the reasons motivating such reduction cease.

§2. Income Tax

840. The annual net earnings obtained by taxpayers involved in the exploitation of mines shall be taxed at the regular tax rate (maximum of 34%). Taxpayers, whether natural or artificial persons, who receive royalties or analogous participations from the exploitation of the mines are subject to a proportional rate of 60% for such earnings.

Part VII. Interaction Between Energy Law and Competition Law

Chapter 1. Introduction

841. As of the Constitution of the Republic of 1999, followed by the implementation of the three regulatory instruments that develop the liberalization of the energy market in Venezuela, namely, the LOHG of 1999, the LOH of 2001, and the LOSE of 2001, a new legal framework is created for the participation of the private sector and free competition with very particular characteristics that mark a new stage in the energy industry, which may be schematized in its evolution as follows: free competition-monopoly-opening. The first stage developed from the foundations of the IPN and until 1975, when the IP was nationalized. In the second stage, the monopoly extended until the beginning of the oil opening process as of 1989 and became real and was complemented by the Law for the Protection and Promotion of the Exercise of Free Competition of 1992 and the set of laws previously mentioned. Nevertheless, in a short period of time, as of 2002 and in a regressive process, a new stage is added, completing the scheme in the following manner: free competition-monopoly-opening-monopoly.

842. Throughout this work, these processes have been analysed, particularly highlighting the Internal Market and the electricity sector as two of the spheres where it may be affirmed that there was an increasing process towards a competitive market that was brought to a halt with the legal changes that have taken place over the last decade.

843. Only the gaseous hydrocarbon sector remains to this day without transcendental changes that may hinder, at least from the legal point of view, the development of a market with a certain degree of competition. For that reason, we affirm that the LOHG starts from a model of 'regulated competition', characterized by the encouragement of private initiative and free competition in the sector, without implying that the entrepreneurial and regulating conditions of the State are undermined. Undoubtedly, the LOHG combines both concepts: *free competition and regulation.*

844. Regarding free competition, this law offers a possibility of liberalization and opening when it does not consider certain core stages of the exploitation process of natural gas as public services. Hence, the legislator opens participation channels for the private sector (forbidden until now for over three decades of the State monopoly on the natural gas industry), trying to foster the development of the gas industry through the leverage of new investments originating from different sources of the public sector. In connection with the regulation, the law contrarily shows a State with unlimited powers of control and supervision under the constant threat that it may change the rules of the game at any time, resorting to that very wide notion of public service contained in Article 5 of the LOHG.

845. Therefore, it may be affirmed that the LOHG starts from a model of 'regulated competition', characterized by the encouragement of private initiative and free competition in the sector, without detriment to the intervention of the Public Powers as regulating entities of the activity, which, in accordance with Article 113 of the Constitutional Text, does not have the intent to establish a system of perfect competition in the sector, but rather effective competition.

846. Next, I plan to develop the elements that, within the LOHG, allow the implementation of a free market under the terms mentioned above.

Chapter 2. Competition Law in Gas Sector

§1. Vertical Integration Prohibition

847. The LOHG promotes prohibition of vertical economic integration, which facilitates the conditions for opening the gaseous hydrocarbons trading market to competition. Article 9 of the LOHG establishes this principle, as well as Articles 4 and 5 of the regulation thereof (RLOHG). However, it has been set forth by way of exception that the MENPET may authorize more than one activity once the producer, carrier, or distributor has demonstrated the feasibility of the project in the same region, and only if two or more activities of the same type are executed.

848. Otherwise, it is mandatory for the companies that have been granted this benefit to keep administrative control and record each account of the activity separately, without conditioning the fulfilment of one activity in regard to the other, and discount the rate for each service in the invoice, thus allowing the determination of the assets, liabilities, revenues, costs, and expenditures of each account. The intention of the above is to determine if the result of the traded products considered 'primary products' is the same as the result obtained from each activity physically executed separately.

849. The exception contemplated in Article 9 of the LOHG permits the concurrent authorization of multiple activities – such as production, transportation, distribution, or commercialization – within a single geographic region, provided that the applicant substantiates the technical and economic feasibility of the integrated operation. Notwithstanding, such exceptions may give rise to unequal market conditions and regulatory asymmetries, particularly where the terms of authorization diverge from those that would prevail under a competitive market structure. While the LOHG and its regulations delineate the procedural and substantive requirements for granting such authorizations, it should be noted that the supervisory function originally assigned to the defunct Superintendence for the Promotion and Protection of Free Competition under the LPPELC has been assumed by the Superintendence Antimonopolio. This body now exercises primary jurisdiction over competition-related matters in Venezuela. The Ministry of Petroleum (MENPET) remains the competent authority to initiate and evaluate requests pursuant to Article 9 of the LOHG; however, the Superintendence Antimonopolio may intervene to ensure that regulatory approvals do not result in market distortions, abuse of dominant position, or harm to consumer welfare (Superintendencia Antimonopolio).[243]

§2. Access to Gas Pipelines: Use and Guarantee of Supply

850. No doubt that access to gas pipelines has turned into one of the main elements to facilitate or prevent the opening of the natural gas market to competition.

243. Superintendencia Antimonopolio, *Órgano de Regulación y Supervisión de la Competencia en Venezuela*, Available at: https://antimonopolio.gob.ve/?page_id=1737 (last accessed 4 Apr. 2025).

So, in Comparative Law, the role that pipelines have for opening the market has been clarified. In order to make a domestic market fully operational – for instance, in the European Community environment – main obstacles are related to pipeline access, storage, and charging system. In this sense, there is full certainty that for competition to operate correctly, a non-discriminatory, transparent pipeline access at equitable prices should be required.

851. In effect, the LOHG and its regulations to facilitate access to new entities into the Venezuelan domestic market of gaseous hydrocarbons contemplate the obligation that producers, carriers, and distributors have to allow other users the use of their facilities under equal conditions. The above regulations are provided to take advantage of existing facilities, given that the high cost of these would delay the lapse of return on investment, thus minimizing the economic feasibility if each company entering into the market had to build its own pipeline system where there is an existing one.

852. Non-discriminatory access to gas pipelines foreseen in the above regulations includes, in principle, all gas systems from the starting point of the production facilities to the final consumer, as follows:

1. Existing gas pipelines from the production facilities to the final unloading or processing terminals and their ancillary facilities.
2. Processing and unloading terminals.
3. Terminals for LNG import and export operations.
4. High-pressure gas pipelines.
5. Natural gas storage facilities.
6. LPG storage facilities.
7. Gas pipelines for regional and local distribution.

853. The regulation for accessing gas pipelines additionally presents a four-system typology as follows:

1. Ex ante: Controlled access, profits control of the transportation and distribution companies as previously established and tariffs determination.
2. Ex post: The pipeline operator submits the tariffs before the regulatory body which is entitled to intervene.
3. Negotiations: Agreement between the parties.
4. Hybrid system: Consensual access but the regulatory body sets forth the procedures to be followed.

854. In Venezuela, the legislator has decided in favour of the consensual access by determining that the usage of the pipeline system shall be subject to the terms contractually agreed by the parties. Under the current circumstances, this regulation does not seem to make too much sense since the opening process has had little progress. However, there exists a legal ground to promote a national market of greater proportions in the future.

§3. Denial and Refusal to Gas Pipelines Usage

855. The LOHG and its regulation establish that access to gas pipelines is contingent upon availability of the pipeline capacity. In consequence, and with the possibility of access being denied, the requesting party may demand the intervention of the MENPET, which shall decide the manner for accessing the pipeline for the service required.

856. Access to gas pipelines in Venezuela has a very special connotation since the State owns 100% of the gas pipelines through the State-owned company PDVSA. In this respect, this Company is entitled to allow third parties to access pipelines in order to facilitate the opening process; therefore, Article 11 of the LOHG concedes the Executive Branch the responsibility of guaranteeing the operating conditions of the existing gaseous hydrocarbons transportation and distribution systems.

857. Article 14 of the Regulations to the LOHG sets forth the procedure applicable in cases where access to existing pipeline infrastructure is denied and no consensual arrangement is reached between the parties. In such instances, the applicant may petition the Ministry of Petroleum (MENPET) to impose access conditions or, alternatively, to authorize the construction of dedicated infrastructure to guarantee the provision of services.

858. Given the potential impact of such denials on market entry and competition, the Superintendence Antimonopolio – now the principal authority on antitrust oversight in Venezuela – may play an ancillary but significant role in ensuring that access-related decisions do not create de facto barriers to entry or confer unjustified competitive advantages to incumbents. This consideration is particularly relevant in the context of a vertically integrated market, where PDVSA retains full public ownership of pipeline infrastructure (Superintendencia Antimonopolio).[244]

§4. Conclusions

859. In this chapter, we will deal – by way of reflection – with some elements that, in our opinion, have had an adverse effect on both the legal framework governing the energy sector in Venezuela and in establishing a correct and sustainable energy policy. At the same time, we will refer in general to the ongoing conflict between two opposed models about the national energy industry and the risks and challenges the hydrocarbon sector and the power industry will have to face in the future.

860. The first reflection inevitably confirms the existence of a conflict between two models that have been competing to manage oil exploitation in Venezuela,

244. *Ibid.*

which are diametrically opposed. Under the first model, oil is conceived as a business and PDVSA as a company, while, under the other model, oil represents a matter of State and PDVSA is considered a government department.

861. In the hydrocarbon exploitation activity, these conflicting trends manifest themselves, in turn, in productivist and rentist models. Rentism has been translated into reducing the supply and the investment in the sector to generate high prices. Oil rentism fosters public affairs based on the State's oil income and to the detriment of private affairs and investment, leverages without which sustainable growth is impossible to attain. The climax in the political realm is determined by populism, as an expression of a 'distributive' mindset against a 'productivist' mindset. On the contrary, the productivist model is more representative of a strategy to expand production volumes, based on the high level of hydrocarbon reserves at a low-production cost and the strategic location of the country in the Western Hemisphere, which entails an aggressive sales policy to achieve a significant share increase in the world oil market, and naturally, a review of OPEC quota production system.

862. Both models have given rise to the development of a legal framework that has followed the lead of that who takes over the government, in a permanent zig-zagging, which explains to a large extent the successes and failures of the different energy policies, mainly since the 1970s of the twentieth century; hence, the inconsistency. The current framework generates distrust among investors due to its contradictions, to the point that, since 2007, at least seven transnational oil companies have abandoned or significantly reduced their projects in the FPO. Among the companies that have left Venezuela are ConocoPhillips, ExxonMobil, Petro-Canada, OPIC, Petronas, and even Lukoil. These companies did not transition to the mixed companies established by the Venezuelan government in 2007, reflecting the lack of stability and uncertainty in the relationship between the Venezuelan state and multinational corporations. This scenario has led to significant conflicts, resulting in multiple lawsuits against the Republic in international arbitration tribunals.

863. It is not just about adopting one model or the other, blindfolded, as if it were a recipe. In order to face up to this risk, it is necessary that the oil policy and, in general, the hydrocarbons policy involve all acting parties in its design and execution, as a matter pertaining to society as a whole. Therefore, it is necessary to make a retrospective evaluation that allows determining which aspects of either model could be adopted to develop a sound model that withstands the political turmoil. Hence, the preparation of an energy strategy must be carried out by general consent for such strategy to boost the sustainable growth of the economy, consequently generating well-being and improvement for each Venezuelan. The legal, social, and ethical base of this need comes from the concept that assigns the ownership of natural and energy resources to the Nation, that is, to any and all Venezuelans.

864. The oil paradigm, as a blessing or a curse, is a challenge to be faced by Venezuela in light of the adverse effects of abundance of this natural resource, with its quality and type of economy, the effect on poverty, and the delay of the political and institutional changes the country needs. Conversely, such abundance of resources that gave Venezuela some sort of supremacy shared in the West Hemisphere with the US and Mexico may be lost due to the diversification of energy sources and the debacle of the power and oil industry over the last decade.

865. On a national level, the main threat comes from the conditions of State-owned company PDVSA, which cannot guarantee continuity and stability of its operations. Alternatively, the political instability, legal insecurity, and collapse of institutionality prevent creating the conditions required for sustainable development of the hydrocarbons industry, hence, the country.

866. On a regional level, acting parties as Brazil, the national oil company of which, Petrobras, contrary to the situation in Venezuela and consolidated as a global corporation with operations and businesses in twenty-four countries, has changed the competitiveness paradigm in the region. Brazil counts on significant crude and gas reserves estimated at nearly 100 billion barrels and a stable legal and institutional framework aimed at the participation of national and foreign companies, which are undoubtedly facilitating Brazil's rise as a future oil-exporting country, possibly at the expense of the traditional markets of Venezuela.

867. On the international stage, Brazil has long been recognized as a leading oil producer in the Americas. However, the growth Brazil had achieved in recent years has stagnated, largely due to the political crisis and corruption cases that have affected *Petrobras*, the state-owned oil company. Corruption within Petrobras, exacerbated by the *Lava Jato* scandal, has significantly impacted the management and efficiency of the company, leading to a reduction in its investment capacity and the paralysis of key projects. Although Brazil's production decline has not been as drastic as that of Venezuela, it has experienced a significant slowdown, with stagnant production and ongoing operational challenges.

868. 'In contrast, Venezuela, far from improving, has suffered a total collapse of its oil industry, impacted not only by an economic crisis and international sanctions but also by corrupt management, which has further damaged its production capacity. While corruption has played a crucial role in both Petrobras and Venezuela's oil industry, its impact in Venezuela has been far more devastating, with production falling from over 3 million barrels per day in the 1990s to under 1 million barrels per day today. The Venezuelan government's inability to manage and reform the oil industry, compounded by a lack of investment in infrastructure and persistent internal corruption, has led the country to a state of near-collapse in its energy sector.

869. Alternatively, *Argentina*, with its vast reserves of non-traditional gas, particularly *shale gas* from the *Vaca Muerta* formation, is set to strengthen its position as a key energy player on the continent in the coming years. The country has significantly increased its production and is poised to become a major exporter of gas, reducing its dependency on imports and potentially even becoming a net exporter. Similarly, the *Colombian oil industry* has seen notable improvements in recent years, with the country focusing on increasing production from its mature fields and exploring new reserves. Moreover, *Peru* and *Bolivia*, with their significant gas reserves, are also enhancing their production capabilities, contributing to the diversification of energy supply in South America. These developments are reshaping the regional energy landscape, moving away from the dominance of a single country and towards a more *diversified and competitive energy market*.

870. At the international level, the United States has played a key role in the transformation of the hydrocarbon market, owing to the exploitation of vast reserves of oil and unconventional gas, particularly from shale formations such as the *Permian Basin*. This surge in production has allowed the United States, since 2015, to become the *world's leading oil producer*, slightly surpassing *Russia* and *Saudi Arabia*. Since 2018, the United States has also achieved the status of a *net oil exporter*, a significant shift that marks a new era for the country as an energy exporter. It is expected that *starting in 2025*, the United States will maintain its position as a global leader and remain a *net oil exporter* due to its unconventional production capacity. Moreover, the United States can rely on the vast *oil reserves of Canada*, its main ally, which places it in 3rd place globally, behind *Venezuela* and *Saudi Arabia*, with approximately *174.6 billion barrels of oil*. However, this scenario is contingent upon the preservation of the historical relationship between the two countries. The *diplomatic crisis* triggered by the *arrival of Donald Trump to the US presidency in 2025* has created uncertainty regarding the future of energy cooperation between the two nations. If the political tensions arising from this crisis do not destabilize this relationship, it is likely that the United States will continue to consolidate its position as a key player in the global oil trade.

871. However, *Iraq* and *Australia* have emerged as significant contributors to the global oil supply. In 2023, Iraq's oil production averaged approximately *4.4 million barrels per day (bpd)*. This positions Iraq as one of the world's largest oil producers, playing a key role in supplying energy to countries like *China*. Looking ahead, Iraq aims to increase its production capacity to *8 million bpd by 2027*, with plans to boost output from fields such as *Rumaila*, one of the largest oil fields globally.

872. In contrast, Australia has recently announced significant findings in the Arckaringa Basin, confirming the presence of approximately 233 billion barrels of oil. If these reserves are confirmed, Australia could potentially hold more 'black oil' than countries like Iraq, Iran, or Canada, placing it just behind Venezuela and Saudi Arabia in terms of oil reserves.

873. According to the most recent projections from the IEA, Venezuela does not appear among the countries expected to expand oil production in the coming years, despite having one of the largest hydrocarbon reserves in the world. This projection is neither final nor irreversible; however, it underscores the urgency of a profound change in the management of the energy sector. Even though Venezuela is currently facing a series of difficulties in undertaking the large-scale development of its hydrocarbon industry, it may reach that goal by using its full potential both in infrastructure and in knowledge, developed throughout nearly a hundred years. This process finds parallelism with the events of the 1970s, when transnational companies increased production to 3.7 million BD before the nationalization of 1975 and the foreseen reversion of 1983. As a result of the factual termination of their operations, they had stopped investing, thus affecting the security and the level of the reserves as well. The impairment of the infrastructure, comparable to the current infrastructure, required an unprecedented effort with spectacular results in less than ten years.

874. However, nothing will be possible without profound changes in energy policies. Throughout this work, it has been demonstrated that Venezuela's energy indicators must change in order to recover its economy and the quality of life of its inhabitants. Based on information provided by the World Bank, Venezuela consumed 2,658 kWh/per capita in 2014, 800 kWh less than before falling into recession. Although the economic crisis remains, *inflation* has begun to moderate in recent years, after reaching historic levels in the previous decade. Nevertheless, the *prolonged recession* and *lack of investment* continue to affect energy consumption, which remains on the decline. This pattern reflects not only the slowdown in economic activity but also the deterioration of energy infrastructure and limited access to basic services for the population, which has exacerbated the social and economic crisis in the country.

875. A similar scenario is emerging on the horizon. The transformation of the National Oil Industry (IPN) – and especially PDVSA – must include a paradigmatic shift: moving away from viewing Venezuela solely as an oil-exporting country and progressing toward national industrialization, in order to become a country with high energy consumption for productive purposes. Additionally, Venezuela must *diversify its energy industry* by embracing *renewable energy*, with the goal of reducing its dependence on oil and contributing to the *fight against climate change*. This change is not only crucial for environmental sustainability but also for the country's long-term economic stability, allowing it to diversify its energy mix and create new sources of employment and development in renewable sectors.

876. Venezuela must transform its economy by strengthening its internal energy consumption. This involves developing a *strong domestic market*, making it its main client through large-scale *industrialization*, *job creation*, and the *strengthening of service companies* for the oil industry. In the process of *energy transition* towards renewable sources, which must begin as soon as possible, Venezuela can leverage its *oil industry* as a catalyst to accelerate this change. Being a country with high energy consumption not only improves resource efficiency but also generates *capital flows*, *investment*, *technologies*, and a cycle of interdependence between oil activities, related industries, efficient energy consumption, and *sustainable economic and social development*. In this way, Venezuela can move towards a *diversified* and *resilient* economy, utilizing its current resources while driving the development of *renewable energy* and contributing to the *global fight against climate change*.

877. Regarding natural gas infrastructure, Venezuela has been unable to build even *5,000 km of pipelines* in *seventy years* to serve fewer than *500,000 users*, while *Germany* has developed a pipeline network of approximately *40,000 km*, covering a population of over *83 million people*. In comparison, *Spain*, which began using natural gas in *1969 – thirty years after Venezuela* – had a transportation network of *13,361 km* by *2022*, serving *over 47 million users*. This difference highlights the *lack of investment* and *deterioration* of Venezuela's energy infrastructure, reflecting the country's inability to modernize and expand its *natural gas systems* despite its abundance of resources.

878. In November 2011, *Germany* and *Russia* inaugurated a *1,200 km* underwater pipeline across the *Baltic Sea*, constructed in just *seventeen months*, which transports *55 billion cubic metres of gas* annually, enough to supply *26 million homes*. In contrast, the *Antonio Ricaurte Trans-Caribbean Gas Pipeline*, which connects *Colombia* to *Venezuela*, is *224.4 km* long and was built in *twenty-four months* at an estimated cost of *335 million dollars*. Despite the difference in the scale of the projects, both examples highlight the capacity of *energy infrastructure* to be developed efficiently and in relatively short periods, though the *magnitude* and *resources* employed are notably different.

879. Another challenge the IPN will have to face will definitely be establishing control mechanisms to ensure clear management by rendering accounts in a timely manner. In fact, these elements became the governing principles of the Norwegian oil industry, and its success has largely depended on how it has been managed, by making its reports available to the public each year. According to the latest Transparency International report, *Norway ranks 5th* among the least corrupt countries, with a score of *81 out of 100* on the *2024 Corruption Perception Index (CPI)*. In contrast, *Venezuela* ranks among the most corrupt countries, occupying *178th out of 180*, with a score of *10 out of 100*, reflecting a widespread perception of corruption in the public sector.

880. There is concern too about how the government has been managing at will the goods that PDVSA acquired from high-consuming countries, like Germany, in a carefree and unilateral manner. In fact, in 2010, PDVSA sold 50% of its shares in Ruhr Oel (Germany) to the Russian company Rosneft. The sale has been qualified as a 'gift' or a poor deal, which is evident just by looking at the current share value. According to experts, those refineries would not be built with less than USD 7,000 or USD 8,000 million, but the sale was closed at USD 1,600 million. The Russian company could not let that opportunity pass. The most incomprehensible matter of this deal is that the Government also announced its interest in building refineries in China, Malaysia, Vietnam, Syria, Iran, Jamaica, Brazil, or Argentina, while any other nation would rather have facilities in industrialized high-consuming countries. Changing the refining properties existing in industrialized countries for investments in developing countries or extremely distant countries in terms of geographic location, in addition to the high costs they represent, is a strategy that is to be thoroughly analysed.

881. The most recent case that is still affecting the credibility of the Venezuelan oil industry is the Abreu e Lima refinery located on the outskirts of the city of Recife in Brazil, the project of which was announced in 2005 by Brazilian president Luiz Inácio Lula da Silva and Venezuelan president Hugo Chávez. The refinery would process 230,000 barrels per day. However, PDVSA has not presented the guarantees required to obtain the financing that would grant the State-owned company a 40% share in the project. The costs got out of control, rocketing from USD 4,300 million to USD 17,100 million, based on the last calculations by Petrobras. Hence, Petrobras, which has already built more than 75% of the plant, would be likely to terminate the partnership with PDVSA due to breach of agreement by the latter; in any case, though, even if the partnership is not broken, the prestige of the Venezuelan State-owned company is already adversely affected.

882. Even though natural gas began to be used for street, public areas, and home lighting since the ninetieth century, it was not until after the World War II that the commercial exploitation of gas reached global dimensions, mainly for power generation and domestic use, especially due to technology breakthroughs that allowed building higher quality and longer gas lines.

883. Venezuela was a pioneer in the gas industry. Over seventy years ago, gas exploitation and use were not limited to the Oil Industry only, but at a residential level as well. By 1938, Maracaibo, one of the main cities of Venezuela, already had a direct natural gas network, though its further development seems to have disconnected from the first breakthroughs. That is mostly because it depends on the oil industry that uses over 70% of the national production for its own development plans, basically, for reinjection in oil wells. However, this percentage reflects the predominant energy policy over seven decades in the country, where oil has been the heart of the economic activity. In the legal scope, this statement is at its highest in the Law that creates the State monopoly over the gas industry of 1971, which expressly prohibited the exploitation of free gas by providing that only oil-associated gas could be liquefied, thus dooming major development projects for export of free gas to failure. That was happening almost simultaneously with the oil crisis (1973) that sent great economies reeling and made petroleum exporting countries, like Venezuela, rich.

884. The effects of the crisis, for instance in Europe, were the beginning of the search for alternative oil sources and the development of a single market. Some years later, natural gas had become a source of energy supply for the EU as soon as the North Sea fields began to produce, together with the development of the gas industry in Russia. This historic opportunity appeared before me, and I could not value the magnitude of the opportunities of those new markets. In Trinidad and Tobago, quite the opposite occurred, as their legislation allowed them to develop LNG projects and, nowadays, they are among the main LNG suppliers to the US.

885. As to Venezuela, the legal framework is focused on strengthening the State by granting it general control and supervision powers that allow it to modify the 'rules of the game' at any time, by resorting to the wide sense of public service provided for in Article 5 of the LOHG, constitutionalized as of 1999. The possibility for the private sector to participate can be shut down through this regulation by opportunistically arguing the Nation's ownership over energy resources, hence, giving a major leading role to the interventionist State.

886. It would not be a surprise if this policy is applied to the natural gas field. In fact, the Executive Branch has applied it to other areas. We just have to look at the takeover of some oil industry projects, the telecommunications company Cantv, the main cement companies, energy sector companies, food companies, LPG supply companies, and Banco de Venezuela, among many others.

887. For example, the LORSE tries to revert the main role of the municipal power in the provision of this service upon stating in Article 12 thereof that the importance of the power service exceeds the municipal and State scope, thus being a matter of the National Power due to its nature.

888. If that happens, and the government approves a new law on gas (there are proposals in this regard) that restricts even more the participation of the private sector, we would be going backwards and dooming to failure once again the development of a national gas market, which needs a substantial investment that the State cannot assume by itself. Just take a look at the experiences in Europe and in other countries, like Argentina, Canada, the US, Holland, Germany, and others.

889. Achieving national gasification for the business, trade, and residential sector requires the substitution of the complex network of existing regulations for a regulation that reintroduces the basic lines of the opening provided for in the LOHG; relaxes the conception of public service regarding gas supply by opening channels to the private participation in a competition-free system that guarantees gas supply at fair prices; turns the State into an actor with a different role that is more of a comptroller than an auditor, more to ensure and guarantee clear rules than destabilizing, more focused on generating trust than fear. Therefore, it would be necessary to create an independent regulatory body made up of the State, the companies, and the users in an equality system guided by cooperation principles and balance of interests. In addition, and as a basic problem, there is the methodology and the approach for developing correct policies that are not due to the ideological whim of the person governing the country, but the result of a wide national agreement.

890. The foregoing examples are just part of the countless cases evidencing the implementation of strategies with dubious success. Venezuela counts on its natural resources, energy resources, tradition, experience, and an industry built throughout hundred years that will survive the current crisis, but only through a sustainable energy policy approved and supported by all political, academic, and scientific forces, as a result of a major national agreement to benefit the entire Nation.

891. In the sphere of the electric sector, Venezuela faces an unprecedented supply crisis. The crystallization in 2001 of the Organic Law for the Electric Service was frustrated, and thus, the intention to modernize and introduce deep changes in the entire system. This law, approved by the consensus of all the political forces, including that which is now governing, promoted a model favouring decentralization, the introduction of competition in the generation and commercialization activities, and measures to hamper dominant positions within the market, for improving user service to guarantee the continuous and uninterrupted supply. This goal, far from being achieved, was replaced by a centralization and total concentration model through the creation of a Corporation that absorbed private companies. Now the State controls and renders the service, from the generation to the commercialization activities.

892. The enactment of the LORSE in 2007 and the LOSSE in 2010 represented the definite exclusion of the private sector, pioneer of the electric service in Venezuela and fundamental support during the twentieth century. The new legal framework means the construction of an unknown model for over a hundred years. It is important to point out that the electrification figure of the country was possible under a mixed scheme, where public and private companies performed the generation, transmission, distribution, and commercialization activities, even without a law, but rather with a sublegal framework that regulated the activities of the sector.

893. The consequences of this model are evident in the worsening of the service quality. By 1998, the electric service had reached greater than 97% national coverage and an operating reserve, which acted as backup for the system, meaning, that production exceeded consumption. Eighteen years later, this relationship has reversed, such that the available capacity to produce electricity presents a deficit vis-à-vis demand. Indeed, the country, with an installed capacity of over 34,000 MW, has only 17,220 MW available, or 50%, compared to a demand that exceeds 18,000 MW.

894. The current crisis of the Venezuelan electrical system is a consequence of a management model that has failed miserably. Getting to this point required a great deal of improvisation, ignorance, incompetence, lack of knowledge, faulty maintenance, lack of planning, bureaucratization, politicization, and corruption. Excuses of sabotage levelled against the political opposition, against harmless animals and now charged against the El Niño phenomenon, are not deemed credible by anyone.

Selected Bibliography

Books, Journals and Papers

Books

Alexander, Robert J. *Romulo Betancourt and the Transformation of Venezuela* (New Jersey, 1982).

Anaya, S. James. *Indigenous Peoples in International Law*, 2nd ed., Oxford University Press (Oxford, 2004).

Aponte García, Maribel & Amézquita Puntiel, Gaudencio (coords.). *El ALBA-TCP: origen y fruto del nuevo regionalismo latinoamericano y caribeño* (CLACSO, 2015).

Arnáiz Amigo, Aurora. *El Estado y sus fundamentos institucionales*, 36 (México, 1995).

Balestrini C., César. *La industria petrolera en América Latina* (Caracas, 1971).

Barroso, Lucas Abreu. *Propriedade dos recursos minerais e propriedade do solo e do subsolo no ordenamento jurídico brasileiro*, in *A Lei Agrária Nova*, vol. 2, pp. 299–309 (Juruá Editora 2006).

Bartlett Díaz, Manuel. *La disputa por el petróleo en México: Breve historia de los hidrocarburos*, en: Jaime Cárdenas Gracia (ed.). *En defensa del petróleo*, 12 (UNAM, Instituto de Investigaciones Jurídicas, México 2009).

Brewer-Carías, Allan R. *Aspectos organizativos de la industria petrolera nacionalizada* in *Archivo de Derecho Público y Ciencias de la Administración, UCV Vol. III* (Caracas, 1981).

Brewer-Carías, Allan R. *Dismantling Democracy: The Chávez Authoritarian Experiment* (Cambridge University Press, 2010).

Brewer-Carías, Allan R. *El Caso de la Apertura Petrolera* (Documentos del juicio de nulidad contra la autorización parlamentaria para los convenios de asociación petrolera 1996–1999) (Caracas, 2001).

Brewer-Carías, Allan R. La Constitución de 1999. Derecho Constitucional venezolano, vol. 2 (Caracas, 2004).

Brown, L. N. French Administrative Law, Oxford University Press (Oxford, 1998).

Dalloz, Edouard. *De la propriété des mines et de son organization legale en France et en Belgique*, vol. I, 28 (Paris, 1862).

Diego Bautista Urbaneja. *La política venezolana desde 1958 hasta nuestros días (Centro Gumilla, 2013).*

Espinaza Vendrell. El marco fiscal petrolero venezolano: evolución y propuestas 'Regímenes fiscales en economías petroleras', 271. (Revista Banco Central de Venezuela, Segundo Encuentro Internacional de Economía 1999).

Fritz, Thomas. *ALBA contra ALCA: La Alternativa Bolivariana para las Américas: una nueva vía para la integración regional en Latinoamérica*. Centro de Investigación y Documentación Chile–Latinoamérica (FDCL), pp. 10–12, (Berlín, 2007). Available at: https://thomas-fritz.org/file_download/32/ALBA-contra-ALCA-Thomas-Fritz-ES.pdf (last accessed 31 March 2025).

Galán y Gutiérrez, Eustaquio. *Los conceptos de Estado y Nación como categorías de la ciencia política y del derecho internacional*, 35 (Reus, Madrid, 1952).

García Montufar, Guillermo. *Apuntes de Derecho Minero Común*, 37 (Lima, 1989).

González Berti, Luis. *Compendio de Derecho Minero venezolano*, vol. 1 (Universidad de Los Andes, Mérida, 1960).

González Berti, Luis. *Compendio de Derecho Minero venezolano*, vol. 2 (Universidad de Los Andes, Mérida, 1970).

González Berti, Luis. *La Nacionalización de la Industria Petrolera Venezolana* (Colección Estudios Jurídicos no. 18, Caracas, 1982).

Jellinek, Georg. *Teoría General del Estado* (Buenos Aires, 1970).

Jiménez Guanipa, Henry. *Der venezolanische Energiemarkt: Liberalisierung oder Verstaatlichung?* Südwestdeutscher Verlag für Hochschulschriften AG Co. KG (Germany, 2011).

Lander, Luis E. *Globalización y mercado interno de los hidrocarburos en Venezuela* (Universidad Central de Venezuela, No. 2–3, Caracas 1998).

Lander, Luis E. *Globalización y mercado interno de los hidrocarburos en Venezuela* (Universidad Central de Venezuela, No. 2-3, Caracas, 1998).

López Maya, M. (2017). *El Arco Minero y la vulneración de derechos*. Revista SIC, 795, 25–30.

Martiré, Eduardo. *Historia del derecho minero argentino*, 59 (Buenos Aires, 1997).

Mayer, Alicia (Coord.). *México en tres momentos, 1810-1910-2010: hacia la conmemoración del bicentenario de la Independencia y del centenario de la Revolución Mexicana: retos y perspectivas*, Universidad Autónoma de México Volumen 1, 181 (México 2007).

McBeth, Brian S. *Juan Vicente Gómez and the Oil Companies in Venezuela, 1908–1935* (Cambridge University Press, 1983).

McBeth, Brian. *Juan Vicente Gomez and the Oil Companies in Venezuela*, 1908–1935, 37–39. (Cambridge U. Press 1983). (nuevo)

McBeth, Brian. *Juan Vicente Gomez and the Oil Companies in Venezuela, 1908–1935* (Cambridge: Cambridge University Press, 1983).

Mejía Alarcón, Pedro Esteban. *La industria del petróleo en Venezuela* (Caracas, 1972).

Mommer, Bernard. *Global Oil and the Nation State*, Oxford University Press (2002).

Puyuelo, Carlos. *Derecho minero* (Madrid, 1954).

Rodríguez, Pedro Luis, Rodríguez Luis Roberto. *El petróleo como instrumento de progreso: una nueva relación Ciudadano-Estado-Petróleo* (Ediciones IESA, Caracas, 2013).

Sands, Philippe, Peel, Jacqueline, Fabra, Adriana, & MacKenzie, Ruth. *Principles of International Environmental Law*, 4th ed. (Cambridge University Press, 2018).
Shelton, Dinah. *Advanced Introduction to International Environmental Law*, Edward Elgar Publishing, Cheltenham, 2022.
Tablante, Carlos, and M. Tarre. *'El gran saqueo.' Quiénes y cómo se robaron el dinero de los Venezolanos*, 259–279, (Caracas, Ediciones Cyngular, 259–279, 2015).
Tellería, Rodolfo. *Historia del Desarrollo del Servicio Eléctrico en Venezuela 1880–1998* (Caracas, 2014).
Vallenilla, Luis. *Petroleo venezolano, auge, declinación y porvenir* (Caracas, 1975).
Viñuales, Jorge E. (ed.). *The Rio Declaration on Environment and Development: A Commentary* (Oxford University Press, Oxford, 2022).
Vivacqua, Atilio. *A nova política do sub-solo e o Régimen legal de las minas* (Río de Janeiro, 1942).
Yergin, Daniel. *The Prize: The Epic Quest for Oil, Money, and Power* (Simon & Schuster, 1991).
Zenteno Barrios, F. Javier. *La Regulación de los Hidrocarburos en México* in *Regulación del Sector Energético* (Universidad Autónoma de México, 1997).

Papers and Journals:

Andarcia, M. V. '*Irán Toma Oro de una Venezuela que Ya No Tiene Petróleo con Qué Pagar los Favores*,' *Global Affairs*, Universidad de Navarra, May 2021, available at: https://www.unav.edu/web/global-affairs/detalle/-/blogs/iran-toma-oro-de-una-venezuela-que-ya-no-tiene-petroleo-con-que-pagar-los-favores-2 (last accessed 4 April 2025).
Barelli, Mauro. 'The Role of Soft Law in the International Legal System: The Case of the United Nations Declaration on the Rights of Indigenous Peoples,' Human Rights Law Review, vol. 12, no. 1, 2012, pp. 1–29.
BP (British Petroleum). Statistical Review of World Energy 2018, available at: BP (last accessed 13 November 2018).
Boyle, Alan. 'Human Rights and the Environment: Where Next?' Eur. J. Int'l L. 23, 613 (2012), https://doi.org/10.1093/ejil/chs054 (last accessed 18 June 2025).
Camacho, Carlos R. 'La Educación Ambiental: Perspectiva Histórica de la Colonialidad del Conocimiento para Definir y Caracterizar la Identidad Nacional y la Cultura Latinoamericana,' Educere 10(601) (2006), available at: https://www.redalyc.org/pdf/356/35603505.pdf (last accessed 4 April 2025).
Correo del Caroní. (2022, 14 de febrero). Control Ciudadano denuncia opacidad en el manejo de Camimpeg a seis años de su creación. *Correo del Caroní*. https://correodelcaroni.com/pais-politico/control-ciudadano-denuncia-opacidad-en-el-manejo-de-camimpeg-a-seis-anos-de-su-creacion/.
Crisis Group. *El Peso del Oro: Violencia en el Sur de Venezuela, 2019*, available at: Crisis Group (last accessed 3 April 2025).
Ellner, Steve. 'Venezuela's Crisis and Its Impact on the Global Oil Market,' Latin American Perspectives, vol. 47, no. 6 (2020): 45–62.
ECLAC (Economic Commission for Latin America and the Caribbean). *Panorama Social de América Latina 2017*, available at: ECLAC (last accessed 30 March 2025).

Selected Bibliography

ECLAC (Economic Commission for Latin America and the Caribbean). *The Transport of Natural Resources from Latin America and the Caribbean to Asia-Pacific, 2014*, available at: ECLAC (last accessed 4 April 2025).

Francesco Manetto. *The IMF Forecasts That Prices Will Increase in Venezuela by 1,800,000%*, El País (17 April 2018), https://elpais.com/economia/2018/04/17/actualidad/1523934621_077871.html (last accessed 30 March 2025).

Heffron, Raphael J., and Kim Talus. '*The development of energy law in the 21st century: a paradigm shift?' The Journal of World Energy Law & Business*, 9.3 (2016), available at: http://www.olade.org/sites/default/files/publicaciones/InformeSectorEnergetico-Z.PDF.

J. Briceño Ruiz, 'MERCOSUR: Crisis institucional y desafíos para la integración' (2013) 101 Revista CIDOB d'Afers Internacionals 137–160.

Kyoto Protocol to the United Nations Framework Convention on Climate Change, available at http://unfccc.int/resource/docs/convkp/kpeng.pdf (accessed 7 November 2013).

La Razón (2025). 'De 2021 a 2024, el Gobierno gastó $us 12.500 millones en importación de combustibles'. Disponible en: https://www.la-razon.com/economia/2025/03/09/de-2021-a-2024-el-gobierno-gasto-us-12-500-millones-en-importacion-de-combustibles/.

Maurer, Noel. The Empire Struck Back: The Mexican Oil Expropriation of 1938 Reconsidered, 71 J. Eco. Hist. 603–660 (2011).

Monaldi, Francisco, Hernández, Isabel, & La Rosa Reyes, Juan. The Collapse of the Venezuelan Oil Industry: The Role of Above-Ground Risks Limiting FDI, Rice University's Baker Institute for Public Policy, 2020, available at: https://www.bakerinstitute.org/research/collapse-venezuelan-oil-industry-role-above-ground-risks-limiting-fdi/ (last accessed 4 April 2025).

Maurer, Noel. The Empire Struck Back: Sanctions and Compensation in the Mexican Oil Expropriation of 1938 (The Journal of Economic History, Vol. 71, No. 3, 602, New York, September 2011).

Monaldi, Francisco. 'The Collapse of the Venezuelan Oil Industry: The Role of Mismanagement and Geopolitics,' Harvard Kennedy School Working Paper Series, 2018.

Monaldi, Francisco J., Rodríguez, Pedro L. & Morales, José R. *Direct Distribution of Oil Revenues in Venezuela: A Viable Alternative?* (C. for Global Development, Massachusetts, September 2012).

OECD, CAF & ECLAC, *Latin American Economic Outlook 2018: Rethinking Institutions for Development* (OECD Publishing 2018), available at http://dx.doi.org/10.1787/leo-2018-es (last accessed 30 March 2025).

Transparencia Venezuela. *Informe sobre la Crisis Energética: El Colapso del Suministro Doméstico e Industrial, 2022*, available at: Transparencia Venezuela (last accessed 4 April 2025).

PDVSA (Petróleos de Venezuela, S.A.). *Informe de Gestión Anual 2015*, available at: PDVSA Informe de Gestión 2015 (last accessed 4 April 2025).

PDVSA (Petróleos de Venezuela, S.A.). *Informe de Gestión 2016*, available at: PDVSA Informe de Gestión 2016 (last accessed 4 April 2025).

PDVSA (Petróleos de Venezuela, S.A.). *Informe de Gestión 2011*, available at: PDVSA Informe de Gestión 2011 (last accessed 4 April 2025).

Rojano, R., Angulo, L., & Restrepo, G. 'Concentración y Relación de PST, PM10 y PM2.5 en Poblaciones Cercanas a Minería a Cielo Abierto: Caso Cerrejón, Colombia,' Revista de la Facultad de Ingeniería Universidad Central de Venezuela, 30(3), 2015.

Sánchez, R., Castellanos, M., & Guaita, A. 'Angustia Creciente por los Apagones: La Crisis Eléctrica que Consume a Venezuela,' La Patilla, 7 April 2024, available at: https://www.lapatilla.com/2024/04/07/angustia-creciente-por-los-apagones/ (last accessed 2 April 2025).

Singh, Kelvin. 'Oil Politics in Venezuela During the López Contreras Administration (1936–1941),' Journal of Latin American Studies, vol. 21, no. 1 (1989), 89–104.

Savaresi, Annalisa. 'The Rise of Rights-Based Climate Litigation,' Journal of Human Rights and the Environment, vol. 14, no. 1 (2023), pp. 1–22.

U.S. Department of the Treasury, 2023. 'U.S. Sanctions and Restrictions Imposed on PDVSA and Its Subsidiaries, Including Citgo, by the Office of Foreign Assets Control (OFAC), Impacting Venezuela's Ability to Repatriate Dividends and Process Crude Oil.' *U.S. Department of the Treasury.* https://ofac.treasury.gov (accessed 22 April 2025).

VOA, 2014. 'A Separate Decision by the Paris-Based ICC in 2012 Ordered Venezuela State Oil Company PDVSA to Pay Exxon $908 Million.' *Voice of America.* https://www.voanews.com/a/icsid-venezuela-must-pay-exxon-16-billion-for-nationalizations/2478757.html.

Selected Bibliography

Index

The numbers here refer to paragraph numbers.

Index

Index